Quakers in Conflict

Quakers in Conflict

THE HICKSITE REFORMATION

H. Larry Ingle

THE UNIVERSITY OF TENNESSEE PRESS
KNOXVILLE

BX
7752
.I53
1986

Publication of this book has been aided by a grant
from the American Council of Learned Societies
from funds provided by the Andrew W. Mellon Foundation.

Copyright © 1986 by The University of Tennessee Press / Knoxville.
All Rights Reserved. Manufactured in the United States of America.
First Edition.

Frontispiece: Elias Hicks (1748–1830)
(Quaker Collection, Haverford College Library)

The paper used in this book meets the minimum requirements
of the American National Standard for Permanence of
Paper for Printed Library Materials, Z39.48-1984.
Binding materials have been chosen for durability.

Library of Congress Cataloging in Publication Data

Ingle, H. Larry (Homer Larry), 1936–
Quakers in Conflict

Bibliography: p.
Includes index.
1. Hicksites—United States—History—19th century.
2. United States—Church history—19th century.
I. Title.
BX7752.I.53. 1986   289.6'3   86-1528
ISBN 0-87049-501-1 (alk. paper)

for Becky

Contents

Acknowledgments — xi

Preface — xiii

PART I
The Background — to 1819

1 "No upstart thing," OR
   The Roots of Separation Go Deep — 3

2 "Sound as a bell, and firm as a rock," OR
   The Shapers of Evangelical Power — 16

3 "To curb these headdy high minded ones" OR
   What Makes a Reformer — 38

PART II
The Struggle for Reformation — to 1827

4 "The root of the defection," OR
   Evangelical Inroads — 65

5 "Antiquity ought not to sanctify error," OR
   Hicks's Quaker Theology — 81

6 "The tradition of the elders," OR
   Holding the Line — 96

viii   Quakers in Conflict

7	"No outward law," OR The Reformers React	122
8	"More for victory than truth," OR The Public Struggle	141
9	"Painful indeed the spectacle," OR Political Posturing	160

PART III
From Reformation to Separation:
Philadelphia, New York, Ohio, Indiana, Baltimore

10	"Let us separate!" OR The Prime Division	183
11	"A mistake if not a crime to be indifferent," OR Everyone Decides	201
12	"As soon have half their Teeth Pulled," OR From Four, Eight	225

EPILOGUE

"Cries down all, laws, both moral and Divine," OR The Seeds of the Future	247
Notes	251
Bibliographical Essay, OR Whence the Story	295
Index	303

Illustrations

Elias Hicks *frontispiece*

Arch Street Meetinghouse *and*
A Meeting for Worship
at Arch Street Meetinghouse *between pages* 79 *and* 80

Anna Braithwaite *and* Benjamin Ferris *between pages* 153 *and* 154

Map of Selected Monthly Meetings
of Philadelphia Yearly Meeting, 1827 170

Acknowledgments

UNTIL ONE MUST BEGIN TO ACKNOWLEDGE some of those whose help made possible a study like this, the task seems easy. After all, every other author has included such a page, so it is clear it can be done.

Institutions are the easiest, for theirs is the purpose of aiding scholarship. The University of Tennessee at Chattanooga, through a Faculty Research grant and a year's research leave, made possible two trips to the Philadelphia area for explorations of the rich archival resources there and also granted the time necessary for writing and thinking. Haverford and Swarthmore Colleges were extremely helpful—particularly the former, which furnishes guest rooms at rates a scholar on part-time pay can afford. The free shuttle service between these two campuses ought to be kept a secret, but its value and usefulness demand an expression of gratitude. Haverford's Quaker Collection and Swarthmore's Friends Historical Library were, of course, efficiently administered and literally crammed with the raw materials that make it possible for the historian to get the details of the story. Closer home, the Friends Historical Collection at Guilford College, though lacking the manuscript holdings of its sister Quaker institutions, possesses many of the basic printed sources. And for those who try to write Quaker history beyond Quaker country, the interlibrary loan service, operated for me at the UTC library, is indispensable.

Which brings me to people, and here the order of listing should not be permitted to distort the essential nature of each contribution: Neal Coulter, of the UTC library's reference department, is a resource that also should remain a secret lest someone entice him away from Chattanooga; if it exists, he can find it or where it is housed. Likewise Carole Treadway of Guilford's library and Albert Fowler at Swarthmore went beyond the call of duty to assist at critical points. David Smiley of Wake Forest College first awakened my interest in history as a way to understand the human predicament, and William Appleman Williams, then of the University of Wisconsin, taught me in one of his lecture classes and through his writings that one can demand rigor of oneself and others and still remain a caring human being; both men insisted on careful definition as a sure method for solving historical, which is to say human, problems. Elizabeth Addison and Chuck Fager, neither professional historians but both alert and aware Friends, each read the manuscript in one of its rawer stages and made important suggestions, all of which I took seriously; other invaluable suggestons came from two editors of the University of Tennessee Press, Cynthia Maude-Gembler and Lee Weiskopf. The unfeigned interest of Friends in Chattanooga Meeting encouraged me to explore some of the implications of the separations for present-day Quakers. Secretary Elke Lawson could turn out such beautiful copy so speedily that our department's lack of a word processor did not seem, to me at least, very much of an impediment. The names of some former students who decided to go on in history professionally and who demanded of their instructor more than he could sometimes give should also be mentioned: William B. Scott, Howard L. Preston, Charles Eagles, James P. Whittenberg, and Stuart McGehee.

As a continuing prod, who at times evinced more faith in me than I thought realistic, and as an alter ego, my colleague James A. Ward cannot avoid some major association with this study. Knowing me perhaps better than I knew myself, he first suggested I do some work on Quakers, then had to listen to nearly endless monologues about religious folk far removed from his Roman Catholicism, endure sometimes nightly telephonic updates on late-breaking discoveries, read the manuscript, and, after advising me to discard more versions of the "Preface" than I want to recall, put together a draft that forms the basis of its present incarnation. I even presumed to interpret his understandable grousing about these impositions as indirect encouragement. After undergoing a heart attack in the midst of my writing, I moved him with enough pity to extract a promise that he would finish the masterpiece in case I could not: "Greater love hath no man than this. . . ." I survived to write another day, leaving him only technically free of responsibility for what appears herein.

Finally my wife Becky, who saw me through graduate school and through the trials and tribulations of a young (and outspoken) assistant professor at two small southern colleges in the turbulent sixties, while we created a home for our two children, deserves, as she surely knows better than I, much more than the dedication.

Preface

THIS STORY IS A SAD ONE; it tells of schisms among five groups of Quakers in 1827 and 1828 that cleaved the Society of Friends for more than 125 years. Any time well-intentioned believers fall out over relatively trivial differences in belief and tear apart long-standing friendships and even family relations, tragedy can only result. The splitting Quakers created a real-life drama with a telling difference from a stage tragedy: the drama that opened in Philadelphia set in motion impulses that produced present-day Quakerism.

Indeed, the proposed shape of the future of the Society of Friends was one of the basic reasons for the splits. Like all people in the United States in the early nineteenth century the Quakers had to deal with a rapidly changing culture. Their options were few. Friends could either drop their pretense to peculiarity and join the mainstream Protestant denominations, or they could cling to the roots of their faith as they perceived them and dare the outside world to conquer them.

The group that I shall call traditional reformers, mostly residents of small-town and rural communities, sensed that the comforting world they had known was becoming unsettled and was slipping away. These folks championed traditional principles that Americans as a whole revere: individualism, diversity of belief, tolerance, and a nearly innate desire to preserve things as they had always been. Far from trying to create a new world, the reformers steadfastly upheld old standards that called into question the world they saw developing. Their prescription for the moral life was to return to the past. They sought to renew their ancient covenant to achieve an unfinished reformation, one blocked, so they thought, by powerful innovators.

Their opponents, the Orthodox or evangelicals, had adopted a new system of belief that allowed them to break with the past and live comfortably in the new urban, commercial, industrial age that was emerging; exhibiting much more doctrinal flexibility, they wanted to retain the husks of their old faith while enjoying the fruits of the New World. The complicating difference between the two factions was that the champions of the new order, the Orthodox, exercised power in the Society and savored the prestige it brought them. Feeling secure in their positions, they were indifferent about trying to hold the allegiance of a majority whose neutral or even apathetic feelings about the theological issues in the raging debate shifted only gradually after the agitation got underway. Much of the discussion—to use a polite term—revolved around doctrine, although at the most fundamental level the conflict was over who in the Society would decide the disputed questions: who would exercise power and moral authority. Much of the conflict's bitterness developed because the Orthodox promoters of the new order, from their lofty positions within the Society, often appeared contemptuous and high-handed toward people they seemed to regard as little more than rustic upstarts. In an age of the common man, needless to say, such attitudes did little to garner popular support for the evangelical theological and organizational position.

At this remove, it is probably an open secret that the champions of the common man ultimately triumphed in the Society of Friends. In defending their time-hallowed principles, these traditional Quakers emphasized the value of local autonomy in the face of the centralizing tendencies of their evangelical opponents, stressed the mystical and inward rather than the formal and outward, and insisted on the right of individual interpretation of doctrine. The ideas the reformers espoused encouraged an almost anarchic individualism that disdained practically all restrictions and left its partisans with no place to stand to exercise critical judgment. Their evangelical opponents, whose temperament and positions naturally caused them to fear disorder and unrest and led them to exaggerate the reformers' threat, took contrary positions. They had already torn down most of the barriers that made Quakers a peculiar people, and they eagerly embraced the newly emerging industrial world. Over the years their compromises left them with few marks to distinguish them from outsiders.

Hence our sad tale left a sadder, even tragic, legacy. Advocates of the reformation had set forces in motion that would turn Quakerism into a broad, inclusive faith. The evangelicals, accepting most of the givens of the secular world, could not use their outward standards to maintain Friends' peculiar ways, however much they were able to evoke orthodox statements of faith. So neither part of the Society of Friends could convincingly appeal to the mass of their contemporaries searching for meaning in a world that seemed out of control. Because it grew directly out of the historic experience that made Quakers a people, this failure partook of the classic nature of tragedy.

PART I

The Background — to 1819

CHAPTER I

"No upstart thing,"
OR
The Roots of Separation Go Deep

AS WITH ALL PROTESTANTS, Quakers confront a wrenching dilemma at the heart of their faith and practice—it is just that with Quakers the dilemma is more obvious and potentially more divisive than for all other Protestants, except possibly Baptists. The first Friend, the Englishman George Fox, a seventeenth-century wanderer from Drayton-in-the-Clay, best articulated the problem when he spoke in Ulverston parish church in 1652: "You will say, Christ saith this, and the apostles say this; but what canst thou say?"[1] If the first Friends did not immediately carry this Protestant and Enlightenment principle to its logical extreme, they certainly insisted that every person must make his or her own religious statement. On the other hand, they also created an ascending series of governing bodies or "meetings," resembling a presbyterian system, each endowed with power to exercise discipline over members, impose order, and hence hem in individual wills. Yet the first Friends still affirmed that ultimate spiritual understanding grew out of the individual's experience. Thanks to this contradiction between autonomy and community, the possibility of schism was built into the very structure of Quakerism.[2]

And divisions there were. Before Fox created formal meetings in the 1660s, various factions championed one charismatic leader or another. One antinomian group tried to prevent establishment of stated times and places for worship, preferring instead to await the leading of the Spirit in such mundane matters.[3] Another party, distrusting Fox's authority and fearing consolidated power, mounted a frontal assault on the leadership position but was beaten back by the late 1670s.[4] Later, a disputatious and brilliant

Scottish scholar, George Keith, attacked the mainstream position from the other direction when he charged that Friends had rejected the divinity of Christ. His little group of "Christian Quakers," hardly survived their leader's affiliation with the Anglican church in 1700.[5] Toward the end of the Revolution, a faction eschewing the Society's "peace testimony" emerged as "Free Quakers" and endured for half a century.[6]

Still, this tendency toward splitting was not the whole story. As Langdon Gilkey, a theologian at the University of Chicago, has shown, Christians' affirmations of their religious positions point inevitably to some historical tradition and to a community that embodies that tradition.[7] Early Quakers, in other words, knew themselves as Quakers because they were members of a local meeting: these groups gave meaning to their affirmations. With no professional and specially trained leaders, any member was theoretically free to give voice to the leadings of the Spirit. In practice those recognized as ministers by their monthly meetings were most likely to define Quaker beliefs. To minister usually meant to speak in general, even vague, ways that would threaten few auditors. Hence potential dissidents could get away with a great deal if they couched their disagreement in the right kind of language. Few Friends' sermons have survived from this era. Not only were there no texts, since preparation indicated that the speaker was not relying on the Spirit's leading at the moment, but the messages consisted mostly of admonitions to follow the Light, avoid the snares of the evil one, and remain wary of the attractions of the world's ways.

The world's ways had exercised an appeal to Friends even before the American Revolution, as some Quakers had permitted the counting house to usurp the traditional place of the meeting house.[8] The Revolution accelerated the decline of distinctiveness among some Friends. For younger Quakers especially, the patriotic appeal of freedom proved a more powerful magnet than the old peace testimony. Philadelphia Yearly Meeting disowned more than twelve hundred members for direct or indirect support of the war, while states like North Carolina made life difficult for Quakers by confiscating their land. The Quakers' refusal to pay war taxes led state governments to forcibly auction the property of Friends both as punishment and as a way to raise needed revenues.[9]

As some fell away—or were pushed out—those remaining endeavored to maintain the Society's adherence to traditional standards. For some Friends, the Revolution itself furnished a happy opportunity to push for a reformation that would insist on a stricter commitment to Quaker standards.[10] A Rhode Island minister complained about priests and chaplains coming among them "to preach up, and animate poor inexperienced youth, to war and fighting" but was relieved when the yearly meeting testified against paying war taxes.[11] Philadelphia Yearly Meeting, whose special history made it first among equals, warned against sending children to mixed schools and recommended a "Reformation" to foster separate training in "the Principles of Truth."[12] Progress in reform proceeded too slowly for some, anxious about the "plainness and simplicity and moderation of Truth." Hugh Judge, a minister living down river from Philadelphia, wrote in 1788 that extensive mixing with the people of the land held back the work of reformation, in both individuals and the community. Judge's grievance was specific: because parents wanted children to "have an education answerable to their expected fortunes," they sent them abroad to gain information and knowledge of the world. That the next entry in his journal inveighed against high rents and the spirit of covetousness among Philadelphia landlords indicates what Judge considered worldly evils.[13]

By the final decade of the eighteenth century, then, change was in the air. Specific demands for reform came from those who wanted, as Judge phrased it, "a warfare maintained against the spirit of this world in all its forms and shapes." The goal was to see that Friends remained a separate and distinct people; the means for achieving it was to combat the infiltrating and insidious spirit of riches and lusts.[14] All around them, Americans had witnessed change. The Revolution produced heady ideas of Liberty, equality, and freedom. The French Revolution added to the notion that common folk counted for something. In 1790, an American who reflected on the course of the country's government over the previous decade and a half could see reform in operation — the writing of not one, but two, federal constitutions, attacks on slavery and the slave trade in nearly every state, a broadening of the right to vote, and the modification of penal codes. Such salad days of hope encouraged people to believe that progress was indeed occurring.

Friends caught this reform spirit and sometimes repeated its langauge. In October 1783, 535 Quakers signed a petition to Congress appealing for an end to the slave trade and calling members' attention to the "solemn declarations often repeated in favor of universal liberty."[15] Shortly thereafter, Pennsylvania Quakers breathed life back into the short-lived Society for the Relief of Free Negroes Unlawfully Held in Bondage, the colonies' first anti-slavery society, which had expired soon after its birth, in

1775. The new organization, the "Pennsylvania Society for Promoting, the Abolition of Slavery, for the Relief of Free Negroes Unlawfully Held in Bondage, and for Improving the Condition of the African Race," soon spawned similar groups in New York, North Carolina, Rhode Island, and Connecticut. The Friends behind these groups read like a list of the wealthiest members of meetings in Philadelphia, New York, and Providence. The Pembertons, who had made their fortune from trade in such slave-produced commodities as rice, molasses, sugar, and tobacco, were matched by Waln, Coates, Cope, Hicks, Murry, Eddy, and Brown, whose money came variously from shipping, real estate, insurance, banking, and manufacturing; all added needed social prestige as well as a Quaker coloring to the struggle to abolish slavery. Such men were not the executive committee of the ruling class—because most Friends had forsworn on principle to participate in political affairs—but they made reform respectable and attracted other men of the world to the cause.[16]

Friends had done well—as the old saw had it—"done well while doing good," Too well and not too good, thought a group of Friends with a different set of ideals. Reformers, too, these critics went back to John Woolman, the Mount Holly, New Jersey, mystic who, in a mostly lonely crusade, galvanized Friends to clear themselves of owning slaves. Woolman sought a "reformation in our souls, manifested in a full reformation of our lives, wherein all things are new and all things are of God—in this the desire of gain is subjected."[17] He endorsed the testimony of an aged minister who spoke to the yearly meeting in 1764 "under a great exercise of spirit" about the barrenness that had settled on many meetings because ministers and elders had grown rich, wore fine, costly garments, and no longer exhibited the true humility characteristic of a "Plain, lowly-minded people."[18] In his widely circulated essay, "A Plea for the Poor," probably written in 1764, Woolman examined how little the pursuit of wealth could be reconciled to the best known Quaker teaching—peace. This essay spoke in clear judgment of well-to-do Friends busy creating abolition societies without looking too closely at their own motives and lives:

> Oh, that we who declare against wars and acknowledge our trust to be in God only, may walk in the Light and therein examine our foundations and motives in holding great estates! May we look upon our treasures and the furniture of our houses and the garments in which we array ourselves and try whether the seeds of war have any nourishment in these possessions or not. Holding treasures in the self-pleasing spirit is a strong plant, the fruit whereof

ripens fast. . . . Leave everything which our Lord Jesus Christ does not own. Think not his pattern too plain or too coarse for you. Think not a small portion in this life too little, but let us live in his spirit and walk as he walked, and he will preserve us in the greatest troubles.[19]

Woolman died in 1772 on a ministerial journey to England, but others elaborated his position. Hugh Judge's complaints about greedy landlords and Friends who fell short of high standards were echoed by the better-known, more creative, and hence more controversial Job Scott of Providence, Rhode Island. As a teen-ager—he was born in 1751—Scott was attracted to Baptists because their verbiage, he confessed, better "suited my itching ear" than the silence of Quaker meetings.[20] In his brief forty-two years, he traveled widely, going as far south as Georgia, and with the message of "the co-operation of our wills and endeavours with the divine will, in the work of reformation." He also encouraged southern Quakers to work for the emancipation of slaves.[21] Although often referred to as a "quietist"—one who depreciated spoken ministry and exalted silence for its own sake[22]—Scott's preaching on one journey to Philadelphia won him the title "son of thunder." On his feet for close to two hours, he pulled off his coat, unbuttoned his underjacket, tore off his neckpiece, and worked himself into such a state that "the Sweat Ran of him Like Watter." He declaimed that when he came into the "Awfull Silence" of a Quaker meeting, he had "to Unlern all I had Learned in My Own Will and Become a new Creature." Scott proved, concluded one semi-literate auditor, that a minister did not have to be "College Bread" to preach for people's edification.[23]

No doubt, Scott would have approved of that assessment. His theological position was that the *"Christ within* was ever the alone 'hope of glory' in all ages"; the gospel was "no upstart thing, of only about eighteen hundred years standing," but one "preached in every rational creature, the world over." This gospel, he believed, demanded obedience, "is ever connected with it, requires it, leads to it, and effects it." Salvation "is a real birth, arising from a *real union* of the seed of God, and man, spiritually," so that individuals became "a *son* of the living God, by real, and not by mere metaphorical regeneration." "God with man," he preached, represented the sum total of true religion.[24]

Scott's long essay, "Remarks upon the Nature of Salvation by Christ; Showing that It Is a Birth of Divine Life in Man," served almost as a handbook for the doctrines used by subsequent Quaker reformers of his kind.

He spiritualized traditional theology in a way that brought his brand of Quakerism to approach the ancient heresy known as Docetism. (Applied to the second century reformer Marcion, Docetism taught that, because the natural world embodied evil, Christ had only "appeared" — the Greek word *dokeo* meant "to appear" — to become man.) "The outward body of flesh and blood, which cannot inherit the kingdom of God, never came down from heaven," Scott explained; instead "the outward body was prepared for him who came to do the divine will." The divine word became "truly, and in the scripture sense, the *son of man*, as well as son of *God*. God alone is his Father. Every true believer is his mother." Speaking of Christ's sacrifice, Scott wrote words that would inflame a later generation of Friends, more interested in conformity to outward doctrine than mystical, spiritual experiences: "the sufferings of the *seed* in that one specially prepared body, could do no more toward reconciling a soul to God, than the blood of bulls and goats toward the washing away of sin."[25]

When regeneration took place, Scott believed that humans would have little need of outward law because the law of God would be written on their hearts and expressed in their lives. "The law, observed so far as respects outward actions, restrains only outward crimes, but the gospel lays the axe to the root of every corrupt, indeed every fruitless tree in the heart."[26] The plain truth was, though, that many among Friends did not evince the inward law. On a trip into the confines of Philadelphia Yearly Meeting in 1786, Scott had what he called an "opening" that led him to stress again and again how those who became rich neglected the things of the Spirit. On August 21, he informed a meeting that God would "as much reject us and our plain form, as any other people . . . where we depart from the life and the power." A week later at a large quarterly meeting, he felt it "no small cross" to appear among "several great and eminent ministers." Bearing his cross, he stood up and spoke "closely to the state of such as had not been faithful to divine manifestations:" some whose heads had been crowned as with crowns of gold would have the kingdom "rent from them, their crowns taken from their heads, and given to others that were better than they."[27]

Although Scott's *Journal* and sermons reverberated with such sentiments, he characteristically refused to be part of any effort to exclude anyone. After a trip into New England in 1784, he reflected on his experiences and decided that, while there were causes for mourning over the state of Friends, a promising remnant remained. This remnant, with which he identified himself, was bowed down under a sense of slackness, yet pulled by "the wild-fire zeal of divers." The "unsanctified zeal" of "cleansing the camp, cutting off rotten members" did more damage against a "real reformation" than even slackness. He catalogued the unnamed zealots' crimes: "extinguishing all the feelings of tenderness and charity in the minds of some, creating parties, disunity, schisms, and hard-thinking." To reach offenders' minds required laboring with them "in the spirit of meekness and love, with an earnest desire for their amendment, welfare, and restoration."[28]

Scott's approach was reminiscent of Woolman's with slave owners—refusing to compromise with the evil, speaking against it, but laboring with the offender until each saw the truth. True disciples did not impose their version of the truth legalistically on others; instead they appealed to the sense of justice in others and permitted the deity to work. Scott believed in the leadership of the Spirit, a kind of anarchy under God's lordship, a government that ruled not by outward laws but by the inward assent of each of the governed. Even if dissidents had to be disowned, they would, upon renewed visitation, come to see that they had been justly dealt with. "Oh!" Scott exclaimed, "how powerfully does this co-operate with the working of redeeming grace . . . and it helps to draw them back to their brethren."[29] The reformation Scott envisioned was a spritual one, nurtured by concerned and critical Friends, but expressing itself clearly in the way one lived, in a separation from the world and its ways. The plain people of God would remain plain in Scott's scheme of things.

By the time Scott died in 1793, like Woolman on a pastoral visit to the British Isles, other Friends stood ready to assume the mantle of reformer. The most notorious, if for no other reason than she was apparently one of the few Quakers ever to be disowned because of her opposition to war, was Hannah Jenkins Barnard. Three years younger than Scott, this eloquent and gifted member of New York Yearly Meeting received recognition as a minister and in 1798, endorsed by her meeting, left for Europe on a ministerial trip. Barnard's firm commitment to Friends' traditional peace testimony led her into what powerful Quakers regarded as heresy, for she challenged the Old Testament's assertions that God had commanded the Israelites to carry on bloody warfare against their enemies. At no time, she affirmed, had "the great and merciful Creator ever commissioned any nation or person to destroy another"; war occurred because of human passions, not divine authorization.

Although consistent with traditional Quaker views about free will, this position called into question the Bible's infallibility and drew the fire of Friends in both Ireland and England. In 1798 Ireland Yearly Meeting approved disowning any who questioned the authority of the Scriptures, a decision that an influential Philadelphia minister, William Savery, helped formulate.[30] So when Barnard arrived in London in May 1800 for yearly meeting, a critic charged her with "holding erroneous opinions concerning war." Following a trial before a select committee of ministers and elders from London, which, one contemporary observer charged, consisted of "feudal lords" determined to rule over the "poor commoners," Barnard was asked to stop preaching and return home. Upon her return, she faced another inquisition before the same meeting that had sent her off three years earlier but now she carried the added burden of a rebuke from London Yearly Meeting, the center of world Quakerism. Again, she lost and was disowned: Hannah Barnard, said her Friends, "not only imbibed . . . erroneous and dangerous sentiments, but is assiduous in disseminating them among others." A former traveling companion reversed his favorable opinion and now characterized her as "weak enough to be carried away by vain imaginations and carnal reasonings." The ousted Barnard joined the Unitarians.[31]

Scott's hope that Friends could avoid such bitter proceedings floundered because by the turn of the eighteenth century strong currents of evangelicalism had appeared among Quakers on both sides of the Atlantic. This movement was a complex one, at once a reaction to the kind of philosophical thought that sired the "natural religion" called Deism and, yet again, an attempt to simplify the gospel message of salvation. Evangelicalism had its roots in the intense fervor that marked the preaching of the founders of Methodism, the Anglicans John Wesley, his brother Charles, and their associate George Whitefield. These men attracted a large following by calling their hearers to repent of their sins and discover, at first hand, the Christ who offered salvation. One need not be a philsopher to make sense out of life, they proclaimed; all a person had to do was to accept forgiveness and cultivate a simple faith. The emphasis centered on the individual's lostness and the need to "feel" what being lost meant and to sense the assurance salvation brought.[32]

Then a curious, if natural, thing happened. This religion of feeling and emotional warmth, appealing across denominational lines to an ever-widening circle of believers, began itself to stress outward forms and modes of behavior. Wesley and his company of evangelical preachers taught that, once saved, an individual would become sanctified and move toward perfection. As an early exponent of this view phrased it, Christians "should be free of manifest offenses," and, more important "nobody who is afflicted with such failings should be allowed to remain in the church without fitting reproof and ultimately exclusion." A believer's behavior, in short, offered an opportunity for the church to judge the quality of that one's spiritual life.[33] Moreover, judgment was not limited to outward behavior, but came to apply to the things one believed. In reaction to the way Deists disparaged the Scriptures, evangelicals reverted to an older tradition of investing the Bible with absolute authority. The Bible should command acceptance without question, they maintained, for its doctrines represented what God expected a believer to affirm. Ironically, although they proclaimed their break with the rational approach to religion, evangelicals still insisted on the necessity of correct beliefs, thus, introducing a principle that could, and later did, reduce Christianity to a series of statements about faith. Such dogmas were much easier to assess and judge than the subtle qualities and individual differences that inevitably marked spiritual experiences.[34] A new orthodoxy thus emerged out of evangelicalism.[35]

Without the doctrine of original sin, evangelicalism could not have existed either as a theological system or a compelling analysis of the individual experience. It was not simply that all people had sinned — a proposition like that might be proved by a casual look at the state of human society — what mattered was that every person had been tainted by the fall of Adam and Eve and rightfully suffered alienation from God: humans deserved to die for the sins that grew out of their fatally flawed nature. What saved them was Christ's death that, in bearing the world's sins, satisfied fully God's offended sense of justice. An individual could appropriate Christ's Atonement through faith in the Saviour's sacrifice and God's love which that sacrifice revealed. Quaker evangelicals particularly stressed that faith represented more than intellectual acceptance or knowledge; as Joseph John Gurney, a noted Quaker theologian, insisted, "a saving faith in Jesus is not merely intellectual — it springs from the heart." Whatever problems this theology might possess, its appeal proved to be one of immense power.

Evangelicals considered that their position reflected the Biblical account of human history and of sinners' fate. Indeed, the Bible was for them the only source of knowledge about God's dealing with people. Unlike traditional Quakerism, which stressed the centrality of the inward leadings of

God's Spirit—the "Inner Light of Christ," George Fox called it—evangelicals came close to making the Bible all-sufficient for a saving knowledge of God's dealings with human beings.[36] Although he tried to reconcile traditional Quaker dependence on the leadings of the Spirit with his own evangelical view of the Bible, Gurney became more and more uncomfortable with the doctrine of the Inward Light and finally burst out with the assertion that it conflicted with "the ancient and acknowledged principle of our Society that the Holy Scriptures are the '*only fit outward test of doctrine.*' "[37]

Once adopted by leading Quakers, such a view had an important consequence. It took the determination of what was the correct faith out of the province of the individual and centered it instead in the hands of those in positions to weigh Scripture truth. If the Bible sometimes seemed unclear or contradictory, those in charge of meetings had the power to enforce their interpretations on believers. Thus in 1806, under evangelical influence, both Philadelphia and Baltimore Yearly Meetings made it a disownable offense to deny Christ's divinity and the "authenticity of the Scriptures."[38] For the Friends behind such proposals, this approach would avoid one of the ancient plagues of Quakerism—what the faithful called "ranterism." Contemporaries of George Fox and other early Friends, the ranters represented an extreme tendency, claiming they owed allegiance to no outward law or authority; they were free, under grace, to do whatever they felt called to do. Even one of the most accomplished of the first Friends, James Nayler, a plowman and revolutionary soldier, toyed with ranterism in permitting his followers in Bristol to proclaim him as the new Messiah, Christ returned. After being convicted by Parliament of blasphemy, whipped, having his tongue bored through with a hot poker and imprisoned, Nayler returned to the fold, but he stood out as a dire warning that leading Friends who rejected established authority could fall victim to ranterism.[39]

The Society's determined reaction to Barnard illustrated how questions about a relatively minor matter—whether God had authorized ancient Israelite wars—could feed fears about ranterism. David Sands, like Barnard a minister of New York Yearly Meeting but quite unlike her theologically, charged that her position threatened Friend's testimonies "of the doctrine of the Godhead of Christ and his propitiatory sacrifice; and of the Divine authority and inspiration of the Scriptures of truth."[40] The evangelical element in charge of the Society worried that any compromise with heresy would lead straight to rampant ranterism and a loss of the true faith. On the other hand, traditional Friends of a reforming tendency like Woolman and Scott never seemed to worry about such matters.

Evangelicalism, a movement with broad social implications, had one other characteristic that brought it into conflict with reformers of the Woolman-Scott school. In the first part of the nineteenth century, as the evangelical impulse waxed in popularity and become more conventional, it helped instill the moral discipline required to convert traditional people with traditional values into contributing members of the new industrial order. Appealing to well-to-do urban dwellers, themselves beneficiaries of the rapid changes produced by an unfolding industrial age, evangelical theology stood for a morality that sought to impose rigid rules—temperance, education by rote, Bible reading, sexual restraint—across the social order. Traditional Quaker morality had stressed that right living could only grow out of a right experience with the Divine Spirit, quite a different matter from imposing rules, however moral they might be, on people who had had no such experience. Hence traditional Quaker reformers distrusted those who talked about creating a new world using new rules rather than new people.[41]

Evangelical Friends, heavy of pocket book and social conscience, took the lead in forming anti-slavery groups, temperance organizations, and Bible, tract, and missionary societies. While some denominational associations were already devoted to such missionary activities, the more notable benevolent organizations drew the faithful to holy labor from across churchly lines. The American Bible Society, founded in 1816, and the American Sunday School Union, with roots reaching back to 1790, both tried to keep a broad representation on their boards of directors. Wealthy Friends took an active role in establishing the First Day Society, whose Sunday schools in Philadelphia aimed at promoting orderly habits and literacy among the urban poor.[42] In the first flush of activity, these groups expressed their hope that, for example, the simple expedient of putting a Bible in the home of every American family would hearld the coming Kingdom and Christ's thousand-year rule. A Presbyterian, who had been praying fervently for the millennium, inquired in 1814, "who until a few years ago, apprehended that an high way for our God was to be prepared among the heathen, simply by *multiplying the Bible*, or that this great event was to be ushered in by awakening a *missionary spirit* and the *erection of theological schools?"*⁴³ Progress, in this view, might be catalogued by counting the number of Bibles placed, missionaries commissioned, and theological schools opened.

Traditional-minded Friends, less given to such optimism, distrustful of outward means, and opposed to cooperation with other denominations, were not natural recruits to the evangelical cause. Their religion reflected a mystical experience that maintained ties to rationalism without falling into the deists' trap of intellectualizing faith.⁴⁴ For them, the Bible was not *the* word of God to be followed literally but *a* word of God to be considered among other testimonies to the Spirit's workings. The sacrifice of Jesus did not save a person; that work was accomplished by opening oneself completely to the divine Spirit, as Jesus had done. Religion was more a way of life than a series of statements about dogma. Traditional Friends did not see how "God's people" could associate themselves with the "world's people," especially when some of the latter were "hireling priests," pursuing good ends for worldly recognition, honor, and money.⁴⁵

As the case of Hannah Barnard revealed, however, evangelical doctrines and methods were making inroads among some powerful Friends by the beginning of the nineteenth century. This development, like the evangelical movement itself, was a complex one. Although some of the key evangelical doctrines did not appeal to Quakers, others did. Friends had always insisted on the need for an inward experience of Christ, just as they united with evangelicals in looking for outward manifestations of that inner experience. Urban Quakers, especially, found it easy to cooperate in benevolent associations, even teaching in evangelical Sunday Schools.⁴⁶ Practically all Friends shared with evangelicals the view that the world was evil and in need of redemption: both believed in the need for reformation.⁴⁷ The question was what kind of reformation, and in this, too, evangelicals and Friends agreed—each foresaw a new order that could only originate with the individual. Both groups might fulminate against the evils surrounding them, but their prescriptions amounted to patching up a wound here and there on the body politic.⁴⁸

Questions of religious doctrine, however, did not occupy the attention of Friends to any great degree as the nineteenth century began. The evangelical direction in which some Quakers were moving caused little alarm, particularly when much of their language remained the common property of all. Those reponsible for Hannah Barnard's fate, as their minute of disownment suggested, wanted to make sure that views like hers did not divert the Society from the course they were setting for it. For the same reason, New England Yearly Meeting refused about the same time to print Job Scott's journal.[49]

Such foreshadowings of future restraints suggested that even as the century began some influential Friends wanted to use evangelical doctrines to guide Quakers into more orthodox positions. To test their success, one need only observe the emphasis that came to be placed on correct doctrine, instead of on plain and distinctive style of life, or to ask the question: "Are Friends best known for their beliefs or for their way of life?" Those Quakers who had made their individual compromises with the world more avidly accepted evangelical doctrines. For them, whose way of life differed less and less from their non-Quaker neighbors, the matter of correct belief became all-important. Occupying influential positions, these Orthodox and evangelical Quakers could enforce their conclusions.

CHAPTER 2

"Sound as a bell, and firm as a rock,"
OR
The Shapers of Evangelical Power

THE EVANGELICAL ELDERS exercised power. Consequently, they were accustomed to having their way in Friends' meetings at every level because they usually defined the issues that Friends would consider. Most of them lived in Philadelphia, sat on the Meeting for Sufferings, a Quaker version of the Vatican curia, and kept in close touch with developments across the yearly meeting. Encountering each other almost daily as they pursued their secular and religious affairs, they built a close community of interest among themselves. As insiders, these men looked askance at those who were not like them or who were their social inferiors. In short, they had every reason to prefer the status quo, at least as far as their own power was concerned.

These Friends, however, did not necessarily oppose change—they simply wanted to be in charge of it. Their actions suggested that these elders saw their goal as moving the Society of Friends to a more evangelical theological position without setting off demands that they themselves share power. Most of them were urban Quakers, who had made numerous compromises with the world and its people already, so adopting an evangelical position would simply mark one more step toward breaking down the peculiar distinctions that separated Friends from other Christians. They evinced no little embarrassment when more traditional Quakers took to the public press to stress the errors inherent, say, in Presbyterianism.[1] Like most of those at the top, the elders preferred that things remain quiet, stable, and untroubled by controversy. Thus they said little. They already wielded power so they did not need to defend their position; they assumed things would go on as always.[5]

As a group, the Quaker evangelicals possessed wealth and the influence that almost always accompanies it. Primarily merchants, importers, or traders, they had enough wealth so that the periodic downturns in the economy did not seriously threaten them; indeed, when they extended credit to their less fortunate fellow believers they could even profit from economic distress. Successful older people for the most part, their advanced years gave them a comfortable attitude toward the world their efforts had created; it was theirs, predictable, controllable, and good.[3] Like others of their class in Philadelphia, they assumed, without ever being forced to examine their assumption, that social and political rule ought to proceed from those blessed with material success.[4] They were the natural rulers of the Society of Friends.

Their rule was not burdensome, nor was their yoke heavy. As a matter of fact, before the 1820s, few even recognized that there was a yoke, because the united community seemed to accept the same general values. Although the yoke was unseen, it was still in place. Elias Hicks, admittedly a partisan witness, was not far off the mark when he wrote four Philadelphia Friends in 1825 and described the "Strange Creatures," the Orthodox evangelicals, who continued "their struggle for power." They resembled some of his "no' horned cattle" that carried no outward weapons but had a "hard bunch of bone on their heads, which they cover with a soft bush of hair." They were "so Stubborn, and Stomachful, that they will not give up when fairly beaten," but wait for an opening "to fall upon their opposers in some indirect way." They looked innocent, true enough, but then they fell upon honest cattle unable to hide their horns. Hicks concluded that "these ought to be carefully watched for there is no confidence to be placed in them, after all their great shew of innocency."[5]

The man at the center of Orthodox power was Jonathan Evans, whose Welsh-planted family tree had roots in the early days of Pennsylvania. As a young man, he constructed houses, made wooden buttons, and operated a wood yard; with his carefully saved money, he commenced speculating in farm land in Delaware County, just outside Philadelphia, while he also bought houses and lots in the city. During the Revolution, his strong commitment to Friends' peace testimony led him to refuse militia service and resulted in a brief term in jail. By 1817, when he was fifty-eight, he retired from the lumber business and devoted all of his time to affairs of the yearly meeting. Long before this, at the age of thirty-one, without first being named to the post of elder, he joined Meeting for Sufferings, the most influential body in the yearly meeting, and then four years later his Pine Street Meeting appointed him to the post of elder. Evans rose rapidly, and in the following year, 1795, he began the first of sixteen years as clerk of the yearly meeting, the most visible office in American Quakerdom. In 1809, still clerk of the yearly meeting, he became clerk of Meeting for Sufferings, which appointment put under him the two most significant posts in the yearly meeting; he retained his position on Sufferings until his death thirty years later. By the 1820s Evans also chaired the yearly meeting's select meeting of ministers and elders, yet another powerful position.[6]

Evans epitomized nineteenth-century Quaker plainness and rectitude — "sound as a bell, and firm as a rock," wrote one contemporary.[7] Unassuming, quiet and retiring, he was a familiar, if slightly forbidding, figure when he left his home in Union Street to go for a walk; his knee breeches, long stockings, buckled shoes, and broad-brimmed hat, its back customarily turned up, lent him an out-of-date air. He avoided the limelight; his preferred arena was a committee of like-minded Friends who shared his values and deferred to his views. His usual seat on the top row of the gallery in the Arch Street meetinghouse during the yearly meeting reflected the influence he had gained by careful hoarding rather than by pushing himself forward. He was as regular as the sunset, retiring promptly at nine o'clock when his Irish maid brought him water to drink and a flickering candle to light his way to bed. When he died in the first month of 1839 at the age of eighty, his careful habits had resulted in an accumulated estate valued at over forty-three thousand dollars, a princely sum for an eminent Friend.[8]

Evans was too rigid and disdainful of the mass of Friends to enable him to gain much support from those who did not share his views, rather he derived his power from his long experience with Quaker practices. One hostile witness recalled an incident in 1823 when the evangelical leader succeeded in ensconcing his supporters in significant positions of power. At a Pine Street meeting to appoint a nominating committee for overseers, Evans named one person and then, contrary to usual practice, ventured that there was another name on his mind he would mention if Friends did not object. A short, awkward pause followed, and someone observed, "The friend had better mention it." The man nominated had never before held a significant position, but out of deference to Evans the meeting approved him for service on the eight-man committee. Later when the committee met, one member, supported by four others, proposed Henry M. Zollickoffer, a reformer, as one of the overseers. Evans expressed amazement that a person with unsound principles could be so advanced, which provoked even one of his evangelical cohorts to wonder at such a slanderous indictment. Evans's nominee toed the line with his mentor. After some debate, one person said, "we could not consent to omit Henry's name," but Evans impatiently retorted, *"Then we must sit here,"* implying that he would sit the others out, all night if necessary. Zollickoffer was dropped.[9]

Unlike many Friends of comparable stature, Evans published no journal of his religious labors, nor did he leave behind many letters or publications under his own name. Although his wife Hannah was recorded as a minister by their meeting, Evans never was, so he seldom spoke during worship, and he almost never traveled to other meetings. Hence he had few opportunities to make known his theological position. Evans did distrust any attempt to modify a strictly literal interpretation of the Bible. Once, in an animated family debate, he deplored the tendency to infer from biblical evidence something that was not explicitly there.[10] He feared that questioning received doctrines would lead to Friends falling away to deism and atheism; he once lamented that an "insidious spirit" had taken some Friends unaware and made the "doctrines of the gospel" and "the propitious sacrifice of the Lord Jesus" repugnant to them.[11]

Evans probably never consciously adopted evangelical views, and he never carried them as far as Joseph John Gurney, their foremost English Quaker champion. Instead Evans's temperament, more comfortable with continuing things as they were, led him to ground his faith on the stability of the written Scriptures. In the 1825 yearly meeting, he suggested that the time was past when meetings might use people "who denied the propitiatory sacrifice, mediation and intercession of our Lord," and he publicly rebuked a young man who referred to these doctrines as "notions."[12]

Evans signed, if he did not compile, the controversial "Extracts from the Writings of Primitive Friends" that Meeting for Sufferings approved in early 1823. In a highly selective fashion, this document marshalled quotations from early Friends to demonstrate that they accepted evangelical doctrines about the Bible, the Trinity, and the person and work of Jesus — practically the same tenets, in short, that a Baptist or Methodist might hold.[13] The "Extracts" aimed at stressing the similiarities between Friends and other Christians instead of emphasizing the differences, as traditional Friends were wont to do. Evans probably did not view the "Extracts" as a creed but only as a restatement of the faith he believed the Society had always affirmed. As an elder, he was determined to judge the ministry of other Friends, a prerogative of his office and of Meeting for Sufferings. He acted from the same motives when he rebutted Elias Hicks to his face in December 1826 at Pine Street Meeting. On this occasion, Hicks preached on one of his favorite topics: that Jesus was the Messiah only for the outward sins of the Jews. To a meetinghouse crowded to the doors with youthful supporters of Hicks, Evans rose, awaited the end of derisive hoots, and declared, "I believe it my duty to say, that our religious Society has always believed in the atonement, the mediation, and the intercession of our Lord and Saviour Jesus Christ. . . . Any doctrines that go to invalidate these fundamental truths of the Christian religion, we can not receive, nor have any unity with."[14]

In the same gathering, Hicks admonished the younger Friends present not to follow their parents' course and "settle in the traditions of their fathers," else they be led into error.[15] Committed to maintaining the status quo, Evans took umbrage at sentiments likely to encourage youthful unrest. Evans had already remonstrated with the visiting minister for advising the youth to disregard their elders, particularly as regarded using products made with slave labor.[16] On this point, indeed, Evans was especially sensitive, for he had previously eschewed all goods produced by slaves, but having decided that the line between free and slave products was too difficult to draw, he had stopped making the attempt.[17] On another occasion at Pine Street, immediately after a young follower of Hicks delivered a message warning Friends not to taint themselves with slave-produced commodities, Evans abruptly closed the meeting with the observation that the "covering of solemnity" had been removed and it was time to proceed to business. He frankly distrusted such "professions of universal benevolence."[18]

Evans valued the status quo even more than evangelical theology. When he was a relatively young forty-one, he shuddered at "Notions, ideas and new fangled doctrines" that might entangle his feet in the Devil's snare.[19] If he ever left his position on Meeting for Sufferings, he informed another Friend, *"The Society would be overrun with spurious books."*[20] And five months before his death in 1839, he regretted the acclaim that Joseph John Gurney was winning among Quakers in the city where Evans had held sway for so long. Gurney's nicely composed prayers might win popular approbation but they did not merit Evans's support.[21] Stung by this rejection from a fellow evangelical, Gurney described Evans as "pretty much king of the Society in the Philadelphia Yearly Meeting."[22]

If Jonathan Evans was king of the realm in Philadelphia, his sons were its princes. The second, Thomas, only twenty-nine at the time of the split, played a relatively minor role in developments that preceded it, but as the likely author of a batch of anonymous Orthodox pamphlets in 1827 and 1828, he drew the grudging admiration of his opponents.[23] After the divisions and a visit to New England, he came to doubt the efficacy of investigations into the doctrines Quakers professed, even as he remained a firm supporter of Orthodox practices in Philadelphia.[24] The elder brother, William, born in 1787, served as a minister and on Meeting for Sufferings. A druggist by profession, his business remained small, a fact that gave him a good bit of pride, and left him free to travel in the services of truth and its evangelical expression.[25] He kept a firm rein on his passions, judging from a newsy letter he dispatched to his betrothed only nineteen days before their wedding in December 1824. His recent visit with Elizabeth Barton and a letter from her convinced William "that we may expect to find in each other all the enjoyments that are derived from the marriage union."[26]

In the theological controversy of the day, William saw himself as standing in the middle between the Hicksites, who he alleged denied Christ's divinity, and those who insisted on a literal interpretation of the Scripture. The Bible, he wrote, pointed to the things followers of Christ had believed, but "it is God alone who can give true and saving faith in his beloved Son and in the truths of the Gospel."[27] Unlike his father and brother, he was willing to draw inferences from Biblical events and apply them to contemporary situations, even as he condemned the followers of Hicks when, as he phrased it, they glossed over their real sentiments to "deceive if possible the very elect" Friends at Arch Street Meeting.[28] Despite his strenuous effort in behalf of evangelicalism in rural areas, he complained about the inroads made by "unsound doctrines" and grieved over "the woeful consequences" of persisting in rejecting the outward Cross.[29]

The three Evanses won the nearly unanimous disapprobation of their opponents. One vicious attack, illustrated with cartoons festooned with obscure symbols, was entitled *Hole in the Wall*. Referring to the many positions that the older Evans had occupied — "from that of dog whipper . . . to that stupendous height of power and pre-eminence, for which thou art at present distinguished" — the anonymous author discovered no one more qualified to administer discipline, "to govern and guide the Society, both spiritually and temporarily through the intricate labyrinths of doubt and danger, shoals and quicksands, Orthodoxy and Heterodoxy." Worldly interests, the author asserted, had blinded the elders so they could not distinguish between the precious and the vile and led them to unleash a creed, "a paper Juggernant," upon a peaceful Society of humble believers.[30] A scurrilous "New Confession of Faith" that circulated in New York in 1825 used the "Apostles Creed" as a model for an assault on "everlasting orthodoxy:"

> I believe in Jonathan Evans, father of the faithful, maker of creeds and doctrines; — and in Billy Evans, his eldest son, who was conceived in the spirit of opposition — born of religious persecution and suffered under Elias Hicks, is reviled, insulted and laughed at. He ascended into the Gallery and sitteth upon the right hand of Jonathan his father — From thence he continued to judge ministers & elders, creeds & doctrines.[31]

Certainly the Evanses, father and sons, were near the center of the evangelical movement, for together they commanded immense power where it mattered in the yearly meeting. Needless to say, they were not alone. Samuel Bettle, for example, rivaled Jonathan Evans in importance. Bettle ran a clothing business and was one of the first prominent Friends to take off his knee breeches and appear in trousers. In 1811, at the age of thirty-six, he became assistant clerk and occupied the clerk's chair itself in 1817 for the next fourteen years. He was short but not plump, and he darted quickly when he moved.[32] Possessed of one of the sharpest minds among the evangelicals, he was once asked by the opposing attorney in a lawsuit to distinguish between "also" and "likewise," two words that dotted his testimony. "I think I can," Bettle came back with hardly a second thought. "Our counsel here is a lawyer; thou are also, but not likewise."[33] Still, he often spoke ungrammatically, as well as pronounced his "Vs" like "Ws" so that "vinegar" came out as "winegar." He liked to tie himself to the past, boasting that his ancestors accompanied William Penn to Philadelphia; as a boy when he saw George Washington walking the city street, he thought the President "the most dignified looking man I ever saw" — an appropriate enough assessment from a future haberdasher.[34] His theology was more evangelical than the "Apostles Creed" because he held that the Bible was the standard by which to test one's belief. Friends, Bettle believed, differed from other Christians only as regarded "war, oaths, and in relation to ministry," and unspecified "other things." His job as clerk was to summmarize the discussion and express the sense of the meeting in a statement called a "Minute"; by his own testimony, he customarily deferred to the views of those Friends who held the "weightier" positions—in other words, the Evanses and their kind.[35] The assumption that the respectable part of the community inevitably shared sound views came naturally to Bettle.[36]

By the 1820s, what had come to identify a Friend's relative weight was whether he served on Meeting for Sufferings. Normally, a member had to be either an elder or a minister, and because rural meetings customarily appointed Friends from the city to represent them, the body amounted to a closed corporation of prominent urban men. No woman had ever served on this powerful body. Not surprisingly, evangelical strength centered in Meeting for Sufferings. Its members distrusted democracy—despite the Quaker principles that guaranteed everyone the right to participate and required universal assent to proceed. The members acted as though they feared that if the business of the yearly meeting were turned over to the mass of Friends, anything might result. "Remember," warned one evangelical, "truth does not go by *bulk*, but by *weight*."[37] One of the staunchest of the stalwarts, Ellis Yarnall, who was given to weeping when he preached, once had a civil suit for twenty thousand dollars filed against him and three other future leaders of the anti-Hicks group. He wrote his brother to complain about the judge, "who resides in one of the Back counties of the State . . . with perhaps too little to recommend him but his Democratic principles; . . . to say the least," he continued, "he was not prejudiced in favor of our Society."[38] The evangelicals constantly stressed the youth of the reformers, their unfamiliarity with accepted practice—Bettle was aghast when a member of the Hicks party stooped to quoting Sir Isaac Newton in a yearly meeting session[39]—and the disrespect they showed their elders.

The Evanses and Bettle offered leadership to the evangelicals on Meeting for Sufferings and in the yearly meeting, and the troops that supported them were some of the most powerful Quakers in the city. In fact, the evangelicals were an amazingly uniform group, forming, as one of their number phrased it, a tight "little circle."[40] One list of twenty-one of the most important evangelicals classified all but four as some kind of merchant or gentleman. Their estates ranged from a low of three thousand dollars to a million and a half; for those whose wealth was known, the average was a bit more than forty-five thousand dollars. Practically all were over fifty years of age, the average being sixty-two. Given the similiarities of age, occupation, and wealth, it was hardly surprising that they united in opposition to the Hicksites. Thus, for example, of the fifty-two members of Meeting for Sufferings at the time of the split, only ten followed the Hicksites, while not quite 60 percent of the elders across the yearly meeting remained with the evangelicals.[41] The leaders demonstrated their commitment to the institution, the course, after all, to be expected of any leadership worthy of the name.

As an example, the two elders from Green Street Meeting, the center of reform sentiment in Philadelphia, could hardly be expected to throw in their lot with those trying to purge them from their positions. When the city's male elders wanted to present a united front against Hicks on his 1822 visit to Philadelphia, Joseph Scattergood and Leonard Snowden, both elderly merchants, naturally went along, risking their positions but expecting support from the top. The case against the two—Scattergood died before the matter petered out—dragged on for four years, poisoned relations between the two factions, and ended only when the Hicksites separated and left Snowden behind with his friends.[42]

Then there were evangelicals like Thomas Cope and Thomas Stewardson, whose combined wealth dwarfed that of all the major Hicksites together. These two held large quantities of stocks and bonds—so many that one reformer referred to them as "6 per cent men"[43]—had extensive land holdings, and were involved in railroad, turnpike, and canal construction. They exemplified the kind of go-getter, speculative spirit that Elias Hicks so often inveighed against.[44] Cope despised people who stooped to engage in what he called "low company electioneering" and had fundamental doubts about juries made up of common people. Such scruples may have made him decide to stand for the legislature in 1807, in violation of the expressed advice of his meeting's overseers.[45] Richard Humphreys, who made and sold silverware and had been disowned for serving as an officer in the Revolutionary War, represented the same tendency to compromise with the prevailing secular order, although he maintained a sound theological position.[46]

The sterling example of a prominent evangelical was a Philadelphian, Thomas Eddy, who lived most of his adult life in New York. Born in 1758, Eddy made a fortune selling cheap goods dearly to the English during the Revolution. He then went into the insurance business and later became senior partner in a commission brokerage. Eddy epitomized an active involvement with worldly concerns: A founder of the American Bible Society, his philanthropic good works included prison reform, anti-slavery, Indian welfare, homeless boys, and the colonization of freed slaves outside the United States. Not only did he promote construction of the Erie Canal, he served on its board. Eddy had every reason, not even considering theological ones, to win the appellation of "one of the warmest orthodox advocates."[47] So when he sounded his tocsin in an essay about the dangers of Hicks's brand of Quakerism to the Evans family in 1822, evangelicals listened.[48]

His essay enumerated Hicks's errors rather than explaining Eddy's own views. In this, he typified the evangelical approach. These men of affairs had little time for theological and other speculation, and since they never expected to be displaced at the top of the Society, they spent little time articulating a defense. (It was not until after the separation that they began publication of a regular periodical, but once it got under way, it had a tone, appearance, and character quite a bit higher than earlier Quaker papers, which were nearly all reformation-oriented.) Thus they left behind no systematic, pre-separation statement of their thought. Once the split occurred, they moved to justify their course to the world. The yearly meeting following the split authorized publication of a "Declaration" that explained the evangelicals' position. This invaluable thirty-two-page pamphlet, signed by Bettle as clerk, mixed theological and political arguments in a fascinating way. So intertwined were these two aspects that it is impossible to disentangle them and determine which was the more important as a motivating force. As one instance, the author proposed "to trace the subtle workings of that spirit of unbelief and insubordination which has been the primary cause of " the schism.[49]

Throughout the "Declaration," this equal emphasis on both doctrine and a "restless aspiring disposition . . . to throw off those salutary restraints, indispensible to the existence of every well regulated society" recurred. According to the "Declaration," Friends had become "lukewarm," they had eagerly pursued the world's riches, fashions and pleasures, they had failed to curb transgressors against the Discipline while admitting persons not grounded sufficiently in the doctrines of Christianity, and they had neglected to teach their children so they might avoid "the cavils and sophistry of designing men." Enter Elias Hicks, at first covertly, then openly. He undermined the "subordination and respect due from youth, to age and experience, which true religion ever enforces." He criticized observance of the first day of the week and compared "those who did not join him in rejecting the produce of slave labour . . . with the most abandoned and wicked characters." Then, exalting the light within, he lessened the authority of the Bible, asserverated that Jesus was only an example, and denied that his death was an offering for the sins of all. Infidelity and insubordination had marched hand in hand into the Society of Friends in the person of Hicks, wreaking havoc among the unsuspecting faithful.[50]

The basis of the Orthodox statement, like the heart of evangelicalism, was the authority of the Scriptures—in the words of the "Declaration," "The Society of Friends have always fully believed in the authenticity and divine authority of the Holy Scriptures, and acknowledge them to be the only fit outward test of doctrine, having been dictated by the Holy Spirit of God, which cannot err." The evangelical Friends did affirm "the light of Christ as the immediate means of salvation" but denied that this belief would result in undervaluing the Bible; indeed, "the more we become obedient to the manifestations of the light of Christ in the heart, the more precious and valuable are those inestimable writings to us."[51] The statement then moved on to profess its author's belief that Jesus was born of a virgin, that "all the fullness of the Godhead dwelt in him bodily," that he suffered for the sins of all people and bore them on his person, and that he arose from the dead.[52] Long sections contrasted these beliefs (and those of early Friends) with the alleged heresies of Hicks and the reformers.

The "Declaration" concluded on the same note with which it began, charging the Hicksites with unbelief and insubordination: "We believe it to be a religious duty thus to stand forth in the defense of the gospel of Christ, against the Spirit and principles of libertinism and infidelity."[53] The statement revealed as much about the social values of the Orthodox as it did about their theological presuppositions. Although the Orthodox evangelicals always proclaimed that the issues underlying the split were doctrinal in nature, their own oft-expressed concern that young and old remain subordinate to the elders suggested that something more was involved, namely, a question of authority.

After the separation, one evangelical champion made this issue clear. To climax a lengthy published debate with three Hicksites, this anonymous author warned his opponents that they would rue the day they challenged authority. Still insisting that "the original cause of the separation [was] the new doctrines," he warned that without authority "every wild enthusiast must be received as the inspiration of Heaven," and continued, "the moment you check the least of the flock, no matter who nor how, you come back to human authority." Any other position was "so wild and visionary, that it scarcely deserves a serious answer."[54]

In the years immediately prior to the split, all published studies but one focused in part on the matter of authority. The exception was the work of Elisha Bates, an erratic Ohio newspaper editor and the most accomplished theologian Orthodox Friends produced in the United States. He focused instead on applying evangelical insights to traditional Quakerism. Unfortunately for Bates's historical reputation, his 1837 disownment cast a long shadow over his creative contributions to the cause.[55] Bates need not have been an embarrassment, for his 1825 work, *The Doctrines of Friends*, involved a major effort to meld evangelical doctrines to those of the reformers.

Originally from Virginia, where he was born in 1781, Bates, who was largely self-educated, ran a Friends school in York County. About the same time that he published a pamphlet opposing slavery in 1817, he, his wife, and their six children moved to Mount Pleasant, Ohio; probably the two events were related, for eastern Virginia was not the best of places for abolitionist activity. Editing an antislavery newspaper called the *Philanthropist*, Bates used his characteristically strong language to attack the peculiar institution, but he resisted a "root-and-branch" approach likely to alienate those he tried to convince of slavery's immorality. Despite his appointment as clerk of Ohio Yearly Meeting in 1818 — a post he held in 1825 and 1826 and again from 1828 to 1831 — Bates was not sectarian in his position and aimed his arguments at a large audience. His respect for the owners equally enthralled in slavery and his attempt to appeal to concerned Christians of every persuasion underscored his basic commitment to received institutions, even as he tried to correct one blatant abuse.[56]

The same approach — strong, even vituperative language, coupled with a profound respect for accepted institutions and doctrines — also marked Bates's theological writings. In an article in another journal he published, he excoriated those "stimulated by the thirst for popular applause, or by some other corrupt passion" and who "leaving the frequented paths have struck out into the devious wilds of fancy." But never fear, he warned: "however infidelity may shift its ground, however it may assume the grossness of a Paine, or the refinements of ancient and modern unbelievers — we need not apprehend that it will ever be able to triumph over those important truths, which were spoken by the Lord."[57] Evidently some evangelicals complained about Bates's willingness to excite controversy, forcing him to admit that his was a "painful business" but absolutely necessary "in all cases where falsehood and error are set up in opposition to what is right." And he went on to identify himself with the controversialists who led the Reformation; significantly, however, he did not see his efforts as extending the Reformation in the present.[58]

Instead Bates defended evangelical orthodoxy in his 1825 book, *The Doctrines of Friends*, in a fashion unique among his fellow believers. Rather than beginning with the Scriptures, he took the more traditional Quaker approach and stressed the centrality of the "Word of God," or Christ. Indeed, he got nearly halfway through his book, all the way to chapter seven, before considering the Bible at all; and, once there, he denied it the appellation of the "Word of God," reserving that term for Christ. The Scriptures, he continued, were not "superior to that Spirit from which they were given forth, and by which they must still be unfolded to the human mind." Neither reading the Scriptures nor hearing them preached was necessary for salvation, otherwise slaves who could not read or were taught by "unqualified persons" had no chance of experiencing the word of God.[59]

Bates's most creative contribution to Quaker theology, his central focus, concerned the role of Jesus in the process of redemption. Every other evangelical among Friends echoed the belief of other orthodox Christian groups that Christ's sacrifice was necessary for salvation. Bates gave the doctrine a unique Quaker slant. Redemption, he explained, stressing an insight of the seventeenth century apologist Robert Barclay, had two aspects: "The first is the redemption performed and accomplished by Christ for us, in his crucified body, without us; the other is the redemption wrought by Christ *in us*." That the second followed the first and depended on it did not lessen the impact of Bates's point; indeed, his identification of God's grace with one's inner experience led him to conclude that no one could "partake of the *first* [the outward work of redemption], or secure to himself the true benefits of it, but as he witnesseth the last [the inward experience]."[60]

At another time, when the Society was not exercised by so much controversy, Bates might have enjoyed a better reputation. His gloss on the doctrines of redemption and the Bible suggested a way that Friends could conceivably have accepted some insights from evangelicals without jettisoning traditional Quaker insistence on the internal workings of the divine light. But Bates lived in a contentious time and, being more than a little pugnacious himself, thrived on it. Within a bit over a decade his book sold fifteen thousand copies—or so he claimed[61]—and each sale propelled him even further into the center of controversy. The *Berean*, a Wilmington, Delaware, paper published by the reforming element among Friends, carried on a running journalistic battle with him, and an Ohio lawyer took matters further in a polemic entitled *Orthodoxy Unmasked; or All Is Not Gold that Glitters* that concluded of Bates: "a phiz that seems to scowl at sin,/oft veils hypocrisy within."[62] Bates found himself pushed by the pressure of the conflict to a more extreme evangelical position; this pressure finally led him to espouse baptism and to submit personally to that rite.

Bates unveiled a new journal in 1827, the year of the separation in Philadelphia. His *Miscellaneous Repository* served as a vehicle to attack the Hicksites for their objectionable doctrines and, more important, for their refusal to submit to those in authority in the yearly meetings. Bates complained that the separatists held Deistic tenets: that was bad enough, but worse yet was their approval of "rules and regulations unknown to the discipline of *our* Society," and their withdrawal "both from the *Society* of *Friends*, and from the *exercise of its salutary discipline*" that defined the correct doctrines.[63]

Before Bates found himself caught up in the controversy, he made a valiant effort to find a ground on which both contending factions could stand. But, swept along by events, he abandoned his conciliatory position and joined those in Philadelphia who had firmly anchored themselves on their authority to exercise discipline and define acceptable doctrines. Jonathan Evans, Samuel Bettle, Thomas Stewardson, and Thomas Eddy were fortunate to have a man as accomplished as Elisha Bates defend the interests of the Society of Friends, as they perceived them. He served as clerk of a committee of evangelical Friends from across the continent that convened in Philadelphia in August 1829, and he probably wrote the lengthy "Testimony" or statement of faith that emerged from the conclave; at least it reflected his *Doctrines* of four years earlier.[64]

Still, Bates's doctrinal discussions remained essentially a side issue to the matter of authority—who had it, who used it, and to what purpose. A published story involving John Fothergill—no doubt apocryphal, for it seems almost too good to be true—will illustrate the point about authority. Fothergill, a prominent English Friend of the previous century, supposedly rose in meeting one First Day and said, "My friends, I have been thinking of one word with three syllables and that word is *orthodox*." After a timely pause, the speaker continued, "And I have been thinking of another word with three syllables and that explains it, and that word is *uppermost*." Whereupon Fothergill took his seat, and the meeting proceeded.[65]

Abetting Orthodox efforts, in fact giving the major impetus to the struggle against the reformers associated with Hicks, was a covey of English Friends who flocked in ministerial visits to the United States in the 1820s. Without the presence of this foreign group, American Quakers might well have muddled through their disagreements, casting over them their characteristic mantle of understatement and broad assertions of good will that had usually softened conflicts of doctrine and power in the past. Once the outsiders appeared on the scene, however, all hope for conciliation vanished. Strongly Orthodox, traveling with letters of endorsement from London Yearly Meeting, premier center of world Quakerism, and eager to bolster American evangelicals as they struggled against infidelity and insubordination, the visitors fueled a warfare of pamphlets that spread the word much farther afield than mere sermons could have done. With no direct stake in the issues, they could appear as impartial observers anxious only to speak the truth. Thus they helped isolate the reformers and made them appear to be heretics, operating without the sanction of those who guarded the legacy of George Fox and early Friends.

The English evangelicals' intention was summed up in a letter of instruction that one of them, Isaac Braithwaite, wrote an American Friend. Braithwaite suggested that it was time to move against Hicks for violating the Discipline, even if the charge of detraction should be leveled by Hicks against them. "In my view," the English evangelical said, "any charge of Detraction should in this Instance be considered a minor point, & the exercise of fnds should be directed to the far more important part, namely that of unsoundness of doctrine." This champion of good order and friendly charity went on to warn, though he had never met Hicks, "you have to deal with a Man who is no stranger to strokes of generalship & who will not scruple to avail himself of any thing in which he can foil friends in their proceedings." Braithwaite insisted that "it is high time that EH's horribly blasphemous preaching should cease, or in other words that he should no longer be allowed to move as a minister sanctioned by our Society . . . it will not do to be lulled into supineness under the idea that if we will only be quiet things will all work right." Closing with a reminder that some of the brethren "are too timid in a case of this importance," Braithwaite endorsed "judicious manly firmness & brotherly unanimity."[66] Such emissaries of evangelicalism sprang from the same social class as their American counterparts and shared many of the same views. They seemed also to have become more accepting of the secular culture than had American Friends. Even visiting American evangelicals commented on the differences between English Quakers' rich style of living—clothing and household furnishings—and the more scrupulous standards followed by their New World cousins.[67] They differed also in that they came from the country where evangelicalism had begun and where close ties between Friends and other Christians had become more accepted than in the United States. Even the early evangelical firebrand David Sands reported that British elders had once warned him to say nothing against the English clergy, "as it only tended to cause the Society to be considered *disloyal*." American Friends now found themselves confronted with calls to adopt doctrinal positions, particularly on the Bible and the life and work of Jesus, that they had previously associated only with other denominations.[68] A sharpening of theological issues thus resulted from the English evangelical onslaught.[69]

The most influential foreign evangelical, Joseph John Gurney of Norwich, did not travel in the United States prior to the split, but his books and intimate associates circulated widely. Gurney came from a long line of Friends into which the influence of wealth had become intertwined. His father, who died in 1809, left his twenty-one-year-old son the responsibility of heading the Norwich bank and managing the elegant and gay family estate at Earlham Hall. Gurney had already spent two productive years at Oxford, exploring the classics as well as delving into such subjects as optics and mineralogy, acquiting himself well in all. His bank responsibilities did not prevent him from pursuing Biblical studies, which resulted in an ever-growing stream of theological works after 1824. A perfectionist, he drove himself nearly unmercifully, not only in his studies but also by supporting a wide range of benevolent activities. Despite his association with Methodist clergymen and Anglican bishops, he made a conscious decision in 1812 to make the "humbling sacrifice" of appearing as a plain Friend, dressed in slightly archaic garb, speaking an out-of-date language, and adhering to the ancient Quaker testimonies against war, tithes, and oaths.[70]

Gurney always retained his loyalty to the unique Friends' form of worship, but his theological opinions were at sharp variance with traditional Quakerism, especially in his stress on the outward, historical events of the gospel story. His scholarly defense of the truth of orthodox, evangelical Christianity won him a wide readership, not only among fellow believers but also from members of other churches. He absolutely refused to accept any suggestion that the Bible and the stories it contained were untrue: "the *authorized* record" of the doctrines of Christianity, "the true and only true religion," were "the genuine compositions of the inspired men"—the Holy Scriptures. At the very heart of this record was the sacrifice that Jesus made on the cross for the sins of all, a sacrifice that men and women might appropriate for themselves by the simple expedient of believing in it.[71] By the time he finally came to the United States in 1837, he had all but rejected the distinctive Quaker doctrine of the "Inward Light of Christ" because he had decided it lacked Biblical support.[72]

None of the English visitors spoke expressly against the doctrine of the Inward Light during their American tours, but their emphasis centered on the outward events of the New Testament and the necessity to test theology by the letter of Scripture. George Withy, noted for loud and vigorous preaching during his five-thousand-mile travels across the continent, recognized that his repeated calls to forsake "airy" speculations for the test of Scripture did not go down well. In his 1822 final address, he denied that he wanted Quakers to "become ministers of the letter" by relying on the Bible; instead, a close adherence to "the plain truths of the gospel" would prevent "devinations of our own" and take away any chance "enemies of the truth" would have of accusing the Society of infidelity. That way Friends could "maintain the ancient doctrines of our religious society."[73] Withy, whose visit ended before the controversy between the evangelicals and the reformers fully jelled, stood as a kind of transition figure, stressing that "religion is an inward work" yet insisting also on the necessity of belief in the divinity of Christ.[74]

The influx of the remaining evangelicals coincided with the start of Gurney's career as an active minister, one of the most influential in London Yearly Meeting. As such, he maintained close ties with those other ministers who ventured over to the New World bringing the new gospel. One of them, William Forster, four years Gurney's senior, married into a family connected with the banker's family and joined the wealthy and patrician Quaker circle in Norwich. Unlike Gurney, Forster was a mediocre preacher who had difficulty holding his audiences' attention, but observers nevertheless noted that his doctrine was "sound, searching, and very pertinent."[75] He arrived in Philadelphia in 1820, his visit destined to drag on for five years—so long, in fact, that one opponent estimated at his departure in May 1825 that "the generality of friends do not regret" his leaving.[76] Gravitating immediately to the side of the elders, Forster saw infidelity just about everywhere he looked, except in the well-appointed homes of well-to-do Friends like Thomas Stewardson. During worship preceeding meetings for discipline, he would warn those present to defer to the weight and experience of the leaders and advise clerks to look to them for guidance.[77] He saw himself as a missionary to promote use of the Bible among Friends and promised Gurney before he went to the United States, "I shall be glad to be helpful in furthering the object in other parts."[78] He was especially close to William Evans—they were near the same age—and encouraged him not to lose heart because of the lack of faith around him.[79]

Forster did not grate on the sensibilities of the reforming element nearly as much as two other close friends of Gurney's, Anna Braithwaite and her husband Isaac.[80] Anna, born in 1788, was the most controversial because she seemed to delight in singling out the reformers' errors in her sermons. She made three trips to the United States, 1823, 1825, and 1827, the first without her husband and six children, thus provoking the suggestion that she should not have left her family to fend for itself.[81] The typical Quaker cap she wore covered a head shaved so that a wound on it could be opened every two or three days to allow the accumulated blood to drain away. She had a sharp mind and a caustic way of expressing her disagreements and spoke forcefully in practically every meeting she attended. One report sneered that she once took the floor seventeen times in a three-hour meeting, a "sufficient opportunity of displaying her eloquence." Her usual tack was to deny that she had been aware of any theological controversy in the American meetings before arriving and then express shock at the divergence from Christian doctrine that she had uncovered. She rode grandly in her fine carriage, leading one of her admirers, more honest than most, to remark that "however she may *walk*, she does not *ride humbly*, although she may do justly and love mercy."[82] She was not without defenders. One woman rhapodized, "I am entirely captivitated by her special smile, her eloquent eye, harmonious voice, majestic air, sound reasoning, deep humility, heartfelt piety."[83] Braithwaite's published interview with Hicks in 1825 initiated a pamphlet warfare between the two Quaker factions that did not subside until long after the separation.

Anna's husband Isaac was more retiring and said little, but the two stood together in their support of the evangelical cause. The direction in which the Braithwaites were moving in the 1820s became even clearer in the 1830s when they both united with the small group of English Friends who broke with London Yearly Meeting because it was not Orthodox enough for them. Like Gurney and numerous other evangelicals, they came to the position that the doctrine of the "Inward Light of Christ" lacked Biblical support and should be given up by Friends.[84]

Perhaps even more than Anna Braithwaite, Ann and George Jones most irritated the reformers associated with Hicks. Born in 1774 in Leicester, Ann had a spinal injury from which she never fully recovered, but it did not inhibit her labors in behalf of the evangelicals. Her husband, nine years her senior, was a draper by profession. George's marriage to Ann in 1815 was his third. When they came to the United States in 1826, he seemed a retiring figure willing to indulge his wife as she took a leading role. Observers commented on George's habit of waiting for his wife to give him a nod when his turn had come to minister, and they customarily followed the same procedure when he closed meeting by initiating a round of handshakes, sometimes so quickly after his wife was finished that no one else had a chance to offer a message.[85] The husband did act alone on some occasions. At Green Street Meeting in early 1827, he announced that his certificate made him a member of that meeting, and he asked it to condemn Hicks for his "sentiments subversive of the Christian religion."[86]

The reform press trumpeted the news that Ann Jones preached against Hicks's "*diabolical* and *luciferian* and *damnable*" sermons, allegations that encouraged the reformers to lie in wait for the Joneses' arrival in their particular locality.[87] At Concord Quarter in Wilmington, Delaware, in February 1826, in a revealing display of her temper, Ann blazed when the men's meeting refused to hear her promptly: she would not embark on "so solemn an engagement, at the command of man," since she sensed that the "right time" for the performance of her duty had passed by.[88] So when she got to Darby, Pennsylvania, on the occasion of its quarterly meeting in May, four of the quarter's elders sent her a letter rebuking her for aspersing ministers with words such as "diabolical" and "luciferian." Her efforts, the elders solemnly warned, were "calculated to sow discord among Brethren & produce discord in the Church." No such sentiments as the ones she had attacked were present among them, they asserted.[89] Heedless of this warning, the very next First Day, Ann, George, and an entourage of supporters appeared at Darby meetinghouse once again to renew the battle. Ann charged her opponents with undervaluing the Scriptures, acting in a manner so unruly it would cause sailors to blush, and general infidelity. A day or so later, two elders waited on the English traveler at her sumptuous lodgings at Thomas Wistar's, but a one-hour conversation got nothing more from her than her statement that she spoke only what arose in her mind.[90] After the separation began, reformers welcomed her appearance, for her overbearing mien inevitably won them converts among rural holdouts.[91]

Elizabeth Robson, a Yorkshire woman, was five years in the United States, from 1824 to 1829. The wife of a linen manufacturer, she was an inveterate traveler, reputedly having visited every Friends meeting save one in the world. When she arrived from England at age fifty-three, she was following in the wake of her elder brother, Isaac Stephenson, who showed up the year before. Her ministrations were quite catholic, leading her to pay calls on statesmen such as President John Q. Adams, as well as inmates in workhouses, prisons, and asylums.[92] Presumably, such encounters gave her the ability to diagnose Hicks as "that poor deluded old man."[93] Typically, her messages stressed the necessity to believe in outward, historical events, citing verses to prove that God required people to accept Christ's blood atonement for their sins. But she could also use the language of the reformers to further the evangelical message: "for I cannot conceive that anyone can get into a state of unbelief, but through disobedience to the simple pointing of the spirit of truth in the heart, and by letting in their own reasoning—carnal reasoning. . . ."[94] Taken as a whole, however, such moderate-sounding words could not convince rural Friends or ardent reformers. At London Grove, Pennsylvania, at a quarterly meeting in November 1826, only three of the twelve hundred Friends present openly approved her efforts. And when eight days later she got the endorsement of a local Presbyterian divine, the reformers chortled, "thus we see Quakerism & Presbyterianism amalgating and mixing together."[95]

Of all the English, the most troublesome for the Hicksites was Thomas Shillitoe, more self-effacing and mystical than any contemporary Friend, Hicks included. Shillitoe was a native Londoner, who, though born an

Anglican, became a Friend at the age of twenty four in 1778; fourteen years later, his meeting recognized his gift in the ministry.[96] His reputation as a traveling evangelist for Friends and his unwillingness to move until he felt a firm call from the Spirit had spread his fame through the Society.[97] He prayed to be like "a cork on the ocean, wafted hither and thither as the spirit of God should blow."[98] Unlike the other English ministers, he was unpretentious and could not be sneered at for high living. In fact when Hicks first saw him, he wrote another reformer that Shillitoe was "plain almost to a fault."[99] However deep his traditional Quaker life style, Shillitoe adopted an evangelical position on doctrine, probably influenced by his early years as an Anglican. His theology reflected less the mystical experiences by which he guided his day-to-day activities than a thoroughly Biblical belief in the divinity of Christ and his sacrifice. Near his life's end, he wrote his credo, "I feel I have nothing to depend upon, but the mercies of God in Christ Jesus. . . . I trust my past sins are all forgiven me—that they have been washed away by the blood of Christ, who died for my sins."[100] Methodist founder John Wesley could hardly have put it better.

Shillitoe did not arrive from Britain until September 1826, which was rather late in the game, but he went quickly to work. Having circulated reports that he had come to help them, the reformers were acutely and abruptly disappointed when he allied himself with the evangelicals. "If he should turn out like his predecessors," worried Edward Hicks before he formed a clear picture of the new arrival's views, "I shall be really sorry."[101] Shillitoe immediately threw himself into the fray, exhibiting a political shrewdness that most other evangelicals could not approach. After refusing to be drawn by Hicks into a public display that might be interpreted as an endorsement—though Shillitoe had to pass Hicks's house on the way to meeting in Jericho, he firmly resisted attempts to get him to enter—he took the lead of the Orthodox forces in quarterly meetings. To reveal the true state of New York Quakers, he proposed that superior meetings dispatch committees to visit local meetings of ministers and elders and determine how faithful they were; this procedure, he insisted, would allow the queries to be answered without glossing over infidelity. At Flushing, the meeting went on for seven hours until the exhausted gathering breathed its approval of this plan. Shillitoe knew quite well that he was dividing Friends but he decided "to move quietly forward and mind my great Master's business."[102] To protests that he was an outsider, he responded that his certificate from England "constitutes me as much a member of this Yearly Meeting as any other member of it."[103]

By his own admission Shillitoe was not above using meetings for worship for partisan purposes. On November 2, during the worship preceeding Purchase Quarterly Meeting, he was reflecting on the unsoundness he had found, when a man he had never seen rose and spoke a few words "fully comporting with the opening of my mind." Shillitoe hesitated, not out of fear of detracting from the first expression of truth, but "lest the individual who had broken the silence of the meeting should be in league with that disaffected part of the body, which had been gaining ground in this quarterly meeting." After a period of time, the English evangelical did add his message; he learned later that the first minister was on the sound side. Perhaps Shillitoe was more candid about his motives than others, but this incident revealed that he saw his mission in America as lending his reputation to the evangelical side.[104] It was also revealing that the warning words he heard whispered to his heart's ear in London—"Do not go from house to house"—only moved him when he approached towns that were hotbeds of reform sentiment, such as Jericho, New York, and Wilmington, Delaware.[105]

Instead the houses he went to, like Thomas Stewardson's in Philadelphia, were the well-appointed homes of wealthy and influential evangelicals.[106] He chose to travel with companions—in fact, he fought to get evangelical escorts—whose opposition to the reform cause repelled the majority of Friends.[107] Thus despite his reputation for wise discernment and his plain appearance, Shillitoe lined up on the side of the evangelicals, lending them his prestige and endorsing their theology and authority. Like the other English visitors, Shillitoe plunged into the whirlpool of controversy, agitated it vigorously, and then watched as the Society of Friends floundered hopelessly in the current. The legacy of the missionaries from the East was a divided Society.

CHAPTER 3

"To curb these headdy high minded ones"
OR
What Makes a Reformer

DURING NEW YORK YEARLY MEETING in 1812, debate arose over the question of enforcing the discipline about plainness—the requirement that Friends wear the traditional dark clothing with a distinctive broad-brimmed hat or bonnet. In Baltimore, Hugh Judge heard reports that some wanted to alter the testimony on plainness. "So then lower the standards as the People Degenerate; to sute them and their Disfractions, instead of living them up to the Standard; have we a single instance," he asked his close friend Elias Hicks, the Long Island minister,

> Of the law of Moses in any part thereof; being changed to sute the revolting & rebellious Israellights; did not the almighty; use way & means to humble them & who is humbled by the Chastisements of Deep Sufferings they were awakened to see they had sinned; . . Its a Day of great liberty & indulgence in our society in all ranks more or less; the Doctrine of Self denial & the daly cross; seems all most to have taken its departure; & what can we say to the lower orders among the People. . . . Some of our younger Preachers . . . have brought with them some things & continue in the indulgence thereof; which has strengthened a libertine spirit; & by which the testimony respecting plainness; has been weakened & wounded. There is a spirit & disposition among us which seeks Popularity.[1]

Later, alluding to "some in high rank," Judge noted that in the city "they don't keep from mingling & mixing with the adultered spirit of the times." "The Church," he thought, "must arrive to a greater Degree of clearness

& strength, which will give her Power & authority; to curb these heaqdy high minded ones."²

Judge was a reformer. His complaint bespoke of a man out of tune with the times and determined to champion old ways in the face of those who had made their peace with the contemporary world. Earlier reformers, such as John Woolman and Anthony Benezet had also inveighed against this same tendency, but their pleas had not stopped the Quakers' rush toward modernity. Indeed, according to Judge, the "headdy high minded ones" were becoming more worldly all the time, fueling fears that the Society of Friends would gradually discard its peculiar and ancient testimonies and become indistinguishable from the world's people.

Judge and Hicks represented one of the three kinds of Friends upholding the traditional position. By the second decade of the nineteenth century, they were both getting on in years—Judge was born in 1749 or 1750 of Irish Catholic parents, Hicks in 1748 on Long Island. Both lived most of their lives close to the land—Judge was a miller, Hicks a farmer—and both feared the urban and modern turn the new century was bringing. They had seen cities; Judge, for instance, at one time or another lived in Baltimore, New York, and just outside Philadelphia. But at sixty-five he moved to a rural and isolated area near Barnesville, Ohio, where despite a weak heart, a bad back, shortness of breath, and deafness, he put in a crop every year, and could record despite his infirmities, "We live here very happy."³ Both treasured the kind of autonomy and control that the modern world threatened to destroy. Both had traveled extensively in the ministry, leaving behind everywhere they stopped a coterie of acquaintances able to carry on in the faith.

Hicks, of course, was the most noted of the reformers, widely hearlded and acclaimed as the leading minister in the Society of Friends.⁴ Tall, with the dark complexion that marked his family, he had long hair parted in the middle and hanging straight below the top of his collarless coat. His dark eyes had a piercing quality that seemed to cut through solid matter. Friends valued in their leaders a kind of psychic "sixth sense" that enabled them to intuitively discern the needs of those with whom they came in contact. Hicks apparently possessed an extra measure of this mysterious quality, for it was often remarked on. One person noted, "the more I am with him the more I am edified by him re his extensive knowledge of divine things and appears to have a sense of other peoples states and very much a master of his own."⁵ Walt Whitman, the people's poet who, as a young man, heard the eighty-year-old Hicks preach, sensed this same quality, an "unnameable something beyond oratory" that emanated from Hicks's heart to his audience. Whitman thought it a "powerful human magnetism"[6] (later generations called it charisma), the quality that drew crowds to hear the old gray Quaker as he rose from the stillness of the meeting room's gallery to gather up his audience and mold it into a unit, intent on following the truth as propounded there. One entranced observer explained it as "presence," which Hicks had more than any man who could be named.[7]

On his next-to-the-last trip to Philadelphia and environs, in 1826, Hicks traveled with a young city supporter and members of a prominent family, William Wharton. At thirty-six, Wharton, less than half the old man's age, was clearly impressed. The two visited isolated small meetings in Delaware and New Jersey, staying with country Friends; they shared the same room, often waking before dawn and conversing until time to rise. Wharton thought Hicks "a prodigy, . . . in every situation unusually edifying, and perfectly at home everywhere, never at a loss in any company upon any subject, as familiar with the literate upon astronomy, navigation, &c as with the *unlearned* upon the most simple subjects of shooting birds or catching fish." Wharton asked his wife, "is it not most extraordinary for a man almost 79 years of age to preach 2 such sermons in a day as we hear no one else deliver, eat apples without paining, nay even crack shellbarks with his teeth a great part of which he still retains." If there were any changes in him, "it consists in an increase of bodily health & strength, and an additional vigour of mind." No wonder that the small meetinghouses they visited attracted crowds of admiring Quakers, old and young, male and female, black and white.[8]

Adding to his appeal was the fact that Hicks lived a life consistent with his principles. When he spoke against enchaining blacks in slavery, his listeners were aware that Hicks refused to eat sugar or wear cotton cloth. On his death bed, in the damp cold of a Long Island February, a cotton cover was spread across his bed to hold in his slowly dissipating body heat. The hand not paralyzed by his final stroke fumbled to remove it, to push it aside, until one perceptive well-wisher suggested that a blanket of wool, not contaminated by slave labor, be substituted. That done, Hicks's fingers felt the stiffer wool, he nodded and then drifted off into a calmed sleep.[9] One observer explained how, both at home and abroad, Hicks's life and conversation corresponded with his doctrines.[10] When he wanted to beard his opponents, he could be dogmatic, assertive, and bold; but at other times, as in meetings where discipline for wrongdoers was discussed, he showed a "tender" and "condescending" side, never pushing things too far.[11] The very complexity of his character made him appealing.

The meetings he attended were almost always filled, and often people were turned away or had to stand around waiting for a chance to glimpse Hicks as he left. Reading his extemporaneous sermons now—after his ideas became controversial, stenographers often came to take down his words and publish them for partisan purposes[12]—they seem hardly above the ordinary, devoid of humor, the only illustrations rather abstract ones. He always started slowly, gesturing gracefully and with dignity, his voice deep and melodious. Before long, his natural fervor captured him, and he would snatch his broad-brimmed hat from his head, dash it to the seat behind him, and continue his earnest, pleading sermon. With a natural and unlearned eloquence, he often touched his audience so deeply that many began to weep softly. Only occasionally did he become argumentative, and he never mentioned the name of a critic, leaving his listeners to guess to whom he might be referring. The only book he ever cited was the Bible, and that he quoted from memory, indicating his respect and longtime acquaintance with the Scriptures.[13]

Hicks was no theologian. His formal schooling had been elementary and limited, but he early became an avid reader, particularly of books on Quakers.[14] His use of language was undisciplined, and he seldom defiined his terms very precisely. This characteristic gave his opponents an opening to charge that he denied the Scripture, rejected the divinity of the Christ, and slighted the atoning work done on the cross.[15] Hicks did not seem overly worried by such charges, for he spoke from his personal experiences of the divine. "All that these outward helps can do," he once said of the Bible, "is to direct to the light, and fountain of power, or the law of God written upon the table of our hearts. . . . So none can read the law of God, but by the light of God in their own souls."[16] He once asked Hannah Evans straight out, "hast *Thou* ever been sensible of any advantage that thou hast derived from the Crucifixion of Jesus Christ by the Jews?"[17]

Hicks might not have been a theologian, but he could articulate a theology. Despite its age, it was a theology that spoke to a rising generation of Friends uncomfortable with the widening gap, as they saw it, between their faith and the kind of life that the leaders of the Society enjoyed.

Hicks took traditional Quakerism and, having honed it to a sharp edge, used it to slice away at the evangelical doctrines that had invaded the society and weakened the distinction between the world's people and Friends. To him, these evangelical doctrines were diametrically opposed to the Quaker critiques that George Fox and Job Scott had championed. He called for a reformation, beginning first with Friends and spreading from them into the larger society. He pictured nineteenth-century Quakers as standing in and carrying on the reformation begun, but not completed, by Martin Luther, John Calvin, and George Fox.

The evangelical doctrines that many urban Friends had adopted represented for Hicks the kinds of notions against which the earlier reformers had rebelled. Hicks and his fellow Quaker reformers insisted that religion—vital religion, true religion—must eschew mere tradition and reflect a living experience with the Spirit of God. But he warned that attempts to codify the experience itself could create a deadening tradition. At Pine Street Meeting in December 1826, with the elite of Philadelphia's Quaker community listening on, Hicks attacked hollow tradition as comparable to an outward law, not binding on the individual believer. "I conceive that the law written in the heart, if we attend to it and do not turn to it to build up traditions . . . is the easiest thing to be understood that can be. . . . Here now we see what tradition is. It is a departure from this law. . . . Be serious, my dear Friends, it is an awful thing. . . . Here we see that we could have no possible tradition—no such thing."[18]

In implying that those who had accepted evangelical notions had forsaken the truth for empty and vain traditions, Hicks was grouping them with those who had fallen short and needed a spiritual reformation. Speaking in rural Montgomery County the same month, he preached his most explicit sermon on what he meant by reform, and in the process he detailed the ills that had befallen the Religious Society of Friends, which once had been so open to the promptings of the divine Spirit. With Adam's sin, he explained, humans had fallen into sin, a state of darkness and death that left them no hope. "Here then we may see, my friends, what reformation means; it is to gather back, and come out of this fallen state and to renew the convenant in our part with Almighty goodness." Instead of reforming their hearts, people concentrated on improving their lot in the world, thus violating the Lord's commandments: "Cease to do evil; learn to do well; seek judgement; relieve the oppressed; judge the fatherless;

plead for the widow." What God desired was for people to respond to others' needs. "In relation to our Creator we can never hurt him, we can neither take from nor add to God. It is only our fellow creatures that we can take from, or add to." People knew this because the word was written on their hearts; books and outward instructors were useless, led to darkness, even obscured the light. "No book is light—no man is light, as it regards us. God only is light, and he is in us and not without us." About all men and books could do, he decided, was "to rally you to the standard of light in your own souls," to witness to the truth that each individual had to find within; "there never can be a true and thorough reformation among the children of men through any other medium," he concluded.[19]

Hicks's long experience led him to doubt that older Friends would ever forswear their worldly possessions and live, in the Quaker phrase, "plainly" or simply. He preached to all, both young and old of course, but among the older his words fell on too many ears stoppered, as it were, with wealth, power, and worldly influence. Some older Friends like Hugh Judge, whose experience with greedy landlords had opened his ears, did respond, but their influence in the halls of power was minimal. To these older, more worldly Friends, Hicks spoke—again a Quaker word—"closely," or quite specifically. "What hard work it was to convince the aged" of the pervasiveness of slavery, he lamented on a trip to Philadelphia in 1824. Those "glutting upon" its fruits might speak of justice but they defined it as "that which comports with their own selfishnesss; their own gratification; their own sensuality. Here they make justice like a nose of wax to satisfy their desires." The only hope lay with "the dearly beloved young people of the day."[20] It was no wonder that on this visit, William Evans, one of Hicks's most relentless critics, confided to his betrothed, "I should be quite satisfied if it should approve his last visit to our City."[21]

When he reminded his young listeners that no former generation had arrived at perfection, he was recommending that they should avoid their elders' example "because in the same proportion as we advance in reformation, the way is open for greater advancement."[22] Again and again, at every stop, he warned against tradition—not the tradition he promoted, the one calling people to respond to the inward promptings of God's spirit, but the empty tradition of men that encouraged would-be disciples to embrace outward testimonies, outward laws, outward words, in place of inward conviction and experience. Become passive, he advised, like the meal in which the housewife hid her leaven; let God's spirit work like the yeast. "So they who presume to build up a structure with their own materials, they shall die to God; because by so doing, they turn away from the divine law and command." Hicks held each individual responsible for everything big or little that he or she chose to do. "Here it is, that evil originates. Here it is, that men and women create all the sin in the world; by following foolish fashions, and turning away from simplicity and truth, for fear of man — for fear of the world's broad laugh, and the finger of reproach."[23] War, and slavery, and the oppression of one's fellow humans he saw as the direct result of individual choices not governed by the Spirit.[24]

The central question was how to determine the right choice. The evangelicals insisted that after all other methods were tried and had failed or did not satisfy, then one should rely on the Bible. Hicks spoke instead of reason: "one should not believe what one can not understand" was the principle that guaranteed a debate wherever Friends gathered. But reason, for Hicks, was tempered by revelation. In December 1826, at a meeting marked by clamorous and rowdy interruptions, not to mention hoots and hisses, Hicks explained that "right reason and revelation go hand in hand." "Now there are the two witnesses," he said. "The witness for God which he has placed in every mind — the revelation of his spirit in the irrational and immortal soul of man; and the reason which he has a capacity of exercising in conformity to what the spirit makes manifest." Human reason, Hicks held, was activated by revelation and lies dormant until awakened by the light of heaven; reason was lower than revelation and dependent upon it.[25]

For Hicks and his followers, both the Bible and the historic Jesus revealed divine power and wisdom, but neither alone was sufficient to show God's full nature and will; when humans waited and received the Spirit, then the truth that outward aids testified to was confirmed or not as the case might be. Were a person to come to an incorrect conclusion, the internal witness would produce an uneasy restlessness, "like an epistle written in the heart."[26] Or as Paul Tillich, the German emigrant theologian who made this same point in 1963, said "the divine Spirit witnesses to the content of the Bible, and in this way the Bible can become an authority. Only through the witness of the Spirit can the Bible cease to be a merely external authority."[27] Hicks was merely reaffirming the truth that Fox had insisted upon when the latter realized that the only one who could speak to his seventeenth century condition was "Christ Jesus." Although he never used the word "intuition," Hicks was describing an intuitive process for understanding reality and one's place in it.

Hicks's critique and message undercut the elders' position and in a powerful way exposed the dark side of the emerging world that the evangelicals were eager to embrace. Education and the tradition it furthered were reserved for an elite, while the spirit of God could speak to each and every individual. Outward words and creeds reduced the individual's autonomy and control over the life that God had given, while the inward guide would furnish the direction necessary to lead each person; the same spirit could unify and govern a meeting of believers. Hicks saw the tragic result of people trying to create a world by their efforts alone: results like war, slavery, empty fashions, a social order—now, in truth, a religious order!—that dominated and subordinated individuals. Even the Bible, which he saw as a liberating force, had become a tool for subjecting people to an elite's control. Hicks's traditional Quakerism was a radical Protestantism that cut through human pretensions and insisted that each person listen to the voice of God.

An astute Quaker, destined himself to side with Hicks's opponents, recorded in his diary the most penetrating description of Hicks and the basis of his conflict with the Philadelphia elders of any contemporary. William Brobson, a lawyer from Wilmington, Delaware, whose move away from traditional Quakerism led him to accept a lieutenancy in the Delaware militia during the War of 1812, was not favorably impressed with Hicks even after hearing him several times. The Long Island itinerant was a good man, Brobson granted, one who had seen Friends succumb to worldliness—"the love of fine garments, . . . the luxuries of the table, good eating and drinking, omitting the alcohol, splendid houses and furniture, costly equipages, an assuming and pharisaical demeanor, contentions, rivallry, and all uncharitableness," a more extensive list than Hicks's own; if any group ever needed the services of a reformer, the Society of Friends in the 1820s did. For the Delawarean, however, Hicks undermined Christianity. Indicating how far along the evangelical trail he himself had come, Brobson wrote that Hicks "takes too much from revelation, and refers too much to the faculty of reason. The Spirit is his teacher, and not the Bible—the precepts of which, he only regards as valuable, so far as human reason will approve them."[28] If that last clause was a bit overstated, Brobson still caught the essence of his subject.

Brobson also underscored another aspect of Hicks's ideas that roused the ire of his opponents. Hicks was so alienated from the emerging urban and industrial world that he saw little good in the kind of economic development others praised and promoted. He flat-out opposed the Erie Canal, observing that if God had wanted internal waterways, "he would have placed them there, and there would be a river flowing through central New York." He thought constructing railroads a "business that principally belongs to men of this world, but not the children of light, whose kingdom is not of this world."[29] One of his harshest critics, Thomas Eddy, himself a director of the Erie Canal Company, castigated Hicks for venting himself against "Banks, East India trade, civil government, agricultural societies, chemistry (which he called the 'Black Art,') [and] the Grand Canal."[30] And Brobson condemned Hicks for making war on "almost all the institutions of society; and among them the Sabbath, which I heard him speak of as useless and unnecessary! To the fine arts, painting, sculpture etc. he gives no quarter."[31]

As a lifelong tiller of the soil who cared little for city life, Hicks saw the nineteenth-century world as weaning people away from the true religion. Hicks told audiences in New York during the yearly meeting week in 1825 that learning the world's sciences was "as trivial as the ribbons on the dear young women's heads." Prosperity might bring "great comfort and plenty for the body, but not for the soul." The prerequisite for encountering the Father was to "surrender our earthly delights, and if we do not, it is equivalent to attempting to take away his prerogative." Such a worldly spirit, he thundered, led to the rich "grinding the faces of the poor."[32] While these views might anger urban boosters of internal improvements, bankers, and merchants, they struck a sympathetic cord among traditional rural Quakers already jealous, even fearful, of the strangely enticing city life.[33]

These rural Friends composed a second segment of the reformation cause. A pervasive distrust of the city and the wealthy people who congregated there—and not coincidentally exercised power in the yearly meeting—ran through the experience of small-town and rural Quakers, among whom Hicks found his largest following. Such sentiment was compounded of a number of factors. Every yearly meeting reinforced country Friends' awareness that life in Philadelphia was different and probably more attractive and comfortable than their own. A poem about the 1813 sessions contrasted the "luscious pies and puddings . . . Sparkling wine or beer . . . cranberry pie or tart . . . coffee—amber clear . . . beds of softest down," and the "thrice-fill'd plate" of the city with "homely fare . . . skim'd milk or homely beer . . . bread not wroth a rush . . . milking with the light . . . beds of straw," and "our fingers raw" that "brother clods" had to endure once they got back home.[34] Such tales made country Friends ever more aware of the distance separating them from their city cousins.

This distance increased for those who found themselves indebted to city bankers and merchants. Edward Hicks, Elias's younger cousin who dabbled with paintings later destined to sell for thousands, had a tendency to live from pillar to post, so when he borrowed money in 1811 to buy a small farm in Newtown, Pennsylvania, he fell victim to a "usurer" and had to declare bankruptcy.[35] The experience was so traumatic that he even took to dreaming about a bank—an "anti-christian nursery of usury"—that suffered the fate of bankruptcy.[36] And when Edward had to borrow to travel in the ministry, he groused about "squandering other people's money, and idling away that time, that, in one sense, properly belonged to my creditors."[37]

Given such experiences, Edward Hicks naturally channeled his antagonism toward those in the Society of Friends who possessed power and wealth. Throughout his memoirs, he referred to the elders as "Royal Americans," shorthand for Philadelphia aristocrats who lorded it over other people as good as they. The young Hicks almost gloated after he screwed up his courage and publicly rebuked a "rich pompous merchant," who had told him during a visit to a wealthy Philadelphia meeting, "Young man sit down, thy words have not the savor of divine truth." It was something for a bankrupt farmer to crow about.[38] His attitude made him nearly universally detested among the Orthodox, even more so than Elias. One Friend damned him as "worse than the Devil wanted him to be." [39]

Halliday Jackson, born in 1771 and nine years older than Edward, was another small-town birthright Quaker intensely disliked by the evangelicals. In his younger years he taught agriculture to Indians in northwest Pennsylvania, but after his 1801 marriage in Pine Street Meeting he and his wife settled down in Darby, raising crops and twelve children. As an elder who had held nearly every office among Friends, he knew practically everyone in the yearly meeting and seemed able to dredge up from his memory endless tales of how Philadelphia's elders had sought to control the Society from the beginning. He customarily exhibited such a polished tone that his opponents griped about his "oily manner." The strongly reform-inclined Southern Quarterly Meeting named Jackson one of its representatives to Meeting for Sufferings in 1826, a move that raised major questions about the right of quarterly meetings to change their representatives at will. With extensive contacts in Ohio, he helped spread reform doctrines there. And he once told William Evans, who was visiting Byberry Meeting at the same time he was, that the evangelical "had come to that meeting with a lie in his mouth—that the divine spirit had never authorized him to preach such doctrines" as he had delivered.[40]

Jackson wrote an uncompleted history of the separation sometime after 1832. He took the usual Hicksite position that the split occurred, not because of doctrine, but because of the rise of a party spirit among men of great wealth who had acquired "considerable influence over their fellow members and become actively engag'd in the management of the more weighty concerns of the church." Determined to rule the society, they sought to "compel all to submit to their views and Ideas of religion and discipline." This spirit, concluded farmer Jackson, "was more conspicuous in the city of Philadelphia than elsewhere."[41] To overcome this influence, Jackson came up with the idea, just prior to the 1827 separation, that the out-of-town quarters should send additional representatives to the yearly meeting and thus swamp the evangelicals in a tide of farmers. Given this record, it was no wonder that the Orthodox considered Jackson one of the main fomenters of the separation and tried to sully his reputation in the west to hold the line against reform.[42]

The mild-mannered and cultured John Comly, two years Jackson's junior, seemed an unlikely candidate for principal architect of the split. A teacher and schoolmaster who lived on a farm in Byberry, Comly had saved enough to give him financial security. He watched helplessly as his friend Edward Hicks's fortunes unraveled and, worried lest Hicks be disowned, lashed out at the way "worldly concerns" and "making *haste* to be rich" had infiltrated the Society. Speculation caused many to fall into snares and trapped young men into becoming the prey of unscrupulous leaders. "Alas! alas! Public confidence in Quakers is much lost. Where are our overseers?" he wanted to know.[43]

Comly seldom spoke of such things in public and pointed ways, but his memoirs clearly indicated his concern with city Friends who mingled with the world's people, adopted their "corrupt customs," and invested in the cotton mills and banks that developed in the northeast after the War of 1812. When Comly visited Rhode Island, in 1818, he asked some of the Friends he met if covetousness was not the leading principle of banking. The answers he received seemed specious and self-serving and suggested that the light of salvation had dimmed in their minds. He concluded from such encounters that it was almost useless to preach the gospel to urban folk. "Oh!" he expostulated, "when will Zion arise and shake herself from the *dust* of the *earth*!"[44]

Comly's comments were doubly significant because they came from one who exercised power and enjoyed a reputation of cautious sagacity. A minister since 1813, he served on Meeting for Sufferings and sat beside the firmly evangelical Samuel Bettle as assistant clerk of Philadelphia Yearly Meeting.[45] His accustomed approach to problems was to advise patience and quietness. Part of this attitude, it was true, flowed from his commitment to free choice, especially in religious matters, but it also mirrored a balance in Comly's personal make-up that was less evident in other reformers. Hence upon visiting the Erie Canal in 1828, he conceded that critics like Hicks were right to worry that it would likely woo people into worldliness, yet he granted grudgingly that "Christian humility and meekness" could, even if rarely, continue to exist under the new order.[46] His innate love of good order and harmony surfaced most evidently during the crisis of April 1827 when events thrust him into the center of the separation vortex. Wanting to avoid an "abrupt explosion," he simply advised those opposed to the elders' dominion "quietly to withdraw from communion and break off all connection in religious society with our opposing brethren."[47] Comly clearly epitomized the cautious reformers among the Hicksites.

Jesse Kersey, whose 1815 treatise on Quakerism went through numerous editions and made him one of the best known Friends of the early nineteenth century, shared Comly's ideas and approach. His influence, however, was compromised by an unfortunate addiction to opium and brandy. Although slow to join the reformers, when he finally did the impact shook the evangelicals.[48] His home was Downingtown, nearly forty miles west of Philadelphia, and he, too, shared a rural distrust of city life. His experiences in London in 1804, when he was thirty-six, provoked him to an outburst that "if the pure principle of Divine wisdom had been followed, it would never have crowded so many human beings together, as are in that place." Before moving from the country to a city, he suggested, people "would do well seriously and deliberately to consider their motives." The worldly spirit of cities caused meetings to wither and flattered Quakers into associating with hireling priests, luring them to forget that they had been called to remain a separate people. Although Kersey evinced no open anger when his addiction led to his removal as a minister and he considered leaving the Society, Friends' traditional teaching on the need to remain separate from the world kept him from resigning his membership. During the process of separation, he became one of the most open speakers for the reform cause.[49]

Another future Hicksite, a Chester County schoolmaster suffered disownment for economic reversals and in the process learned a lesson about urban power. Emmor Kimber, a member of Uwchlan Meeting, was forty-six in 1820 when the postwar depression caught up with him. He requested a committee of his meeting to confer with him and his city-based creditors to work out some mutually agreeable arrangement about his debts. When two of his creditors, both Friends from Philadelphia, refused to follow this unusual if creative procedure and demanded satisfaction, the broken Kimber was embittered. Friends who had sent their children to his school withdrew them, while others advised him to "sink out of sight like other people who have failed." Faced with a united front from his creditors, Kimber went to a local court to prevent the forced sale of his school's farm and succeeded, but then his monthly meeting disowned him for "having extended my trade and business beyond my ability to manage." An appeal to the yearly meeting, whose examining committee included two associates of his hungry creditors, brought only confirmation of the monthly meeting's judgment. Kimber resolutely resisted the "arbitrary power" he saw among the city's elders—a power strong enough to "Draw the third part of the stars of heaven, cast them to the earth, and make them subservient to its purposes"—but he came away determined to expose this arrogant class of men who violated gospel order. They never forgave him, and two decades later Thomas Cope was still gloating about the fall of those like Kimber who had risen "from the dregs of Society to a giddy eminence."[50]

Priscilla Coffin Hunt Cadwallader found herself facing the same attitudes. Born in piedmont North Carolina in 1786, she got a meager education but claimed to have the read the Bible through at the age of six. She had two disastrous marriages: the first ended in the death of her husband, the son of Nathan Hunt, Tar Heel Quaker patriarch, after two years and one daughter; the second, an 1827 union to a widower, turned out to be unhappy. After her first husband's death, she moved to frontier

Indiana and developed a preachig style that mesmerized her rural audiences but did not go over very well among classy Philadelphians.[51] She visited Arch Street Meeting in February 1823 to relate a vision she had of a city's spacious buildings being undermined to the point of collapse by men who toiled all day seeking empty forms and showy garments rather than eternal substance. "I have seen the Gospel trumpet laid down in this city. False alarms have been sounded here and believed. True alarms have been sounded and not believed." Only a remnant, she believed, remained to hear her truth.[52] Hunt won no applause from well-to-do Quakers for what all considered her "close" words.

For some few Philadelphians, Hunt's words had the ring of truth. Centered at Green Street Meeting, located in a rapidly growing area then on the fringes of Philadelphia, these future Hicksites made up a part of a third and urban segment of the reform movement. Many had only recently moved to the city, and they tended to exist closer to the margins of prosperity than their more affluent brethren. They possessed neither social prestige, political power, nor economic sinews.[53] One of five city meetings, the only one to side with the reformers, Green Street attracted members who were acutely conscious of their lack of status when compared with those belonging to other meetings; this reality easily translated itself into a questioning of power and authority. The travail of Green Street to select its own leaders in the mid-1820s offered an immediate and concrete demonstration of why a reformation was needed; the struggle served to galvanize hesitant, distant, and doubtful Friends in the cause. In the larger reform movement, Hicks's Philadelphia supporters represented a decidedly weak minority, but, near to the center of power in the yearly meeting and able to watch at close hand, they experienced directly and often personally the sometimes heavy hand of the elders.

Philadelphia's most visible reformer was the combative Abraham Lower, a self-styled illiterate cabinetmaker and a power in Green Street Meeting. Fifty years old in 1826, Lower did not enjoy birthright membership, having joined Friends when he was past twenty, but about 1821 he became a member of Meeting for Sufferings, the center of power in the yearly meeting. Apparently he did not side immediately with the reformers, for in 1822, the evangelicals who were casting about for ways to control Hicks included Lower in one of their conclaves. It did not take him long, however, to sour on these powerful Friends who treated him as a johnny-upstart when he did not take the usual passive role expected of a junior member, especially one with his limited social attainments. Roberts Vaux, perhaps Philadelphia's most socially prominent Quaker, once advised a gathering not to "lower its dignity, by listening to the flimsy sophistry of Abraham Lower." He bristled at the presumptuousness with which Jonathan Evans and other elders approached such matters, for example, as making appointments to important posts.[54] He informed a well-fixed Arch Street Friend that he paid "no more attention to a man with a long purse, than one with a short one."[55]

A strong believer in the autonomy of local meetings, he became a natural recruit for the reform effort and was cultivated by Hicks.[56] He soon had no rivals in his vigorous promotion of the cause.[57] Lower was actively involved in publishing the reams of pamphlets that the reformers got out to defend Hicks and attack the evangelicals in the mid-1820s.[58] He was undoubtedly the main strategist in the long struggle to unseat Leonard Snowden as an elder of Green Street. He once confessed that when speaking of strong cases he customarily used "language conformable with my apprehension of the nature of those cases"—words like "dark designs," "unrighteous proceedings," and "abominable combinations to overturn the rights of conscience."[59] To defend the rights of conscience, he risked a contempt of court charge for refusing to answer questions dealing with spiritual matters during testimony in a New Jersey civil action after the separation. "I deny the authority or right of a temporal court to interfere with things purely spiritual," he proclaimed.[60] His wife, Susan, likewise took a prominent role in resisting the introduction of evangelical ideas into their meeting.[61]

With Lower as their leader, Friends at Green Street retained a near unity of sentiment absent from the four other city meetings.[62] The reform phalanx there, with second-line leadership from relatively obscure men such as shoemaker Samuel Noble, grocer Edward Edwards, and lumber dealer John Lancaster, paralyzed the handful of evangelicals in their meeting after moving to unseat their well-to-do elders.[63] The struggle with Philadelphia Quarter on this issue helped forge the besieged meeting's unity under its Hicksite majority. Elias Hicks never failed to receive a warm and cordial reception at Green Street, and other visiting reformers got similar welcomes. In fact, on at least one occasion, Green Street Friends scheduled a meeting to hear a guest one half hour before another gathering at Arch Street for one of the English female evangelicals; this ploy, complained an Orthodox critic in an example of classic Quaker understatement, "looked like a design to supercede hers."[64]

Of course, what unified Green Street's Friends was the successful effort of Lower and his comrades to silence or purge vocal critics of Hicks. One revealing glimpse of this strategy was the way a group of women dealt with a young woman, Mary Randolph, of the well-to-do merchant family, who expressed her doubts about whether unity could exist where ministers preached sermons with little reference to Christ's sacrificial atonement. Demanded one reform-minded overseer, "How dare thee, how dare thee, a young woman like thee, to undertake to bring charge against a Meet^g?"[65] That other meetings in the city did not evince such unity suggested that the evangelical leaders could not easily keep their vocal and active Hicksites in check. Or to put it another way, the power that the elders exercised at the yearly meeting level was not automatically transferred down to lower levels. Thus reformers remained active in every city meeting, even though they did not occupy official positions outside Green Street.

The most resourceful and talented of all the Philadelphia reformers was a drugstore owner, Thomas McClintock, a member of Pine Street and later the Northern District meeting. McClintock kept in frequent contact with Hicks, maintained a careful watch over developments in the city, and took a leading role in preparing answers to evangelical attacks on Hicks and the cause of the reformation. Despite his active involvement in the cause, his letters revealed an exact, thoughtful, and tolerant man of balance and insight, one satisfied to work behind the scenes. He was always careful about speaking the truth, holding that any exaggeration on the reformers' part would only serve their opponents' interest in the long run. So retiring was he that an occasional rumor would pop up that he desired to make "his peace with the rich and influential." On one such occasion, he referred a questioner to "our *orthodox brethren* of the firm of Jon^a Evans, & Co. They no doubt can inform thee whether they consider me as *leaning* toward them, or in any degree disposed to truckle or temporize!!!"[66] McClintock's cautious nature caused him to have some doubts about Hicks's stronger statements, but did not prevent him from contributing his considerable energies to the reformation.[67]

If McClintock was a reformer out of conviction, another Pine Street Hicksite, William Wharton, associated himself with the cause because of the personal magnetism of Hicks. One of the youngest of the group—he was born in 1790—Wharton grew up as a member of one of Philadelphia's most prominent families. Unlike the other reformers, he never worked for a living, and he had plenty of time to pursue his concerns, one of which was promoting the reformation.[68] Because he did not have to be as chary as some reformers, Wharton's public support of Hicks and opposition to evangelical "bigotry" and "intolerance" must have cut deeply among the elders. He could be bold and forthright. When his meeting approved dispatching a minute to Jericho opposing Hicks, Wharton was quite explicit about his view: "I know Elias Hicks, I have been much with him, at home, and abroad, in sickness, and in health, and I am not afraid or ashamed, to declare in this meetg, nor before any body of people, here, or anywhere, that I am greatly attached to this dear friend."[69] For support from a prominent man like Wharton, Hicks could overlook a certain lack of theological depth.[70]

The struggles of these urban reformers, particularly Green Street's attempts to unseat their elders, showed other Friends what would take place if the evangelicals ever imposed their theology and policies across Quakerdom. Lower, McClintock, and others less active helped maintain a reform presence in Penn's City, but they were simply too few to do much more than serve as irritants to the elders and examples to others. They lacked any real power—except, of course, at Green Street—they were younger and less experienced, and their social and economic positions were rather tenuous, subject to outside economic conditions over which they had little direct control. Even a man as prudent as McClintock had to uproot himself, his family, and his store in the summer of 1825 and move to a new location, always an unsettling experience.[71] To succeed, the reformation cause needed even more than the renowned Elias Hicks, more than country Friends who could be dismissed as bumpkins and ignored because of their distance from the city and their lack of time to devote to yearly meeting affairs.

The Quaker reformers had in Hicks a man with a popular theology, a captivating personality, and a secure reputation. Hicks had few problems keeping the mass of rural Quakers on his side because he articulated traditional and appealing ideas. But Hicks was not much of a tactician. Indeed, he often dashed off letters to unknown correspondents that, once circulated or published, proved embarrassing to the cause and occasionally brought rebukes from more politically astute reformers like McClintock.[72] Seldom considering such political ramifications Hicks could offer advice and serve as a visable leader for the reformers, but his interests simply did not run to making decisions involved in the public promotion of the reformation.

This vital task fell to another segment of the urban reformers, a self-appointed group of Friends in Wilmington, Delaware, about thirty miles down the Delaware River from Penn's city. This group of three or four lived in a community that in the early nineteenth century vibrated with the hopes of urban boosters who envisioned their city growing to rival Philadelphia as a commercial and manufacturing center. Though older than its neighbor, Wilmington developed slowly, too slowly to keep abreast of dynamic Philadelphia, which by 1820 was more than ten times as large. By the beginning of the century, it was true, Wilmington had become a kind of central place to which farmers in adjacent Pennsylvania counties shipped their grain for forwarding out to the larger world, but the War of 1812 and the subsequent frenzy for improvements in internal transportation quickly left Wilmington floundering in the wake of its up-stream neighbor.[73] Wilmington might resemble Philadelphia under like Quaker influence—neat red-brick homes, well-swept door steps, shaded streets, and verdant rear gardens[74]—but economically it lagged far, far behind.

If the Delaware town was not Philadelphia, neither was it an integral part of the Diamond state. Geographically, Delaware simply did not help meet Wilmington's aspirations. Downstate, the farmers grew their grain with slave labor and then shipped it eastward on numerous small streams to the Delaware River and bay; they did not need the port at Wilmington.[75] Nor did they need the antislave influence that Friends encouraged there. As early as 1801, Wilmington boasted a Quaker-promoted abolition society, and in 1820 a large gathering in the town hall shouted its opposition to slave expansion into Missouri. Delaware's rural population, with few economic ties to the state's major city, became even more hostile toward what they considered its baleful influence.[76]

In this anomaly of a town, Friends exercised considerable influence. In 1814, Quakers were presidents of two of the city's three banks, and there were numerous "merchant-millers" who were Friends, as well as schoolmasters, dry goods dealers, a druggist or two, a doctor, and a manufacturer from among them. The 580 members of Wilmington Meeting represented better than 10 percent of the population and were prosperous enough to raise the necessary money—nearly $13,000—and erect a new, large meetinghouse in less than two years.[77] Various Friends, even some of those most closely involved in the Hicksite reformation, played active roles in community and political affairs.[78] Hence the Wilmington Quakers' criticism of their upstream evangelical neighbors may have been influenced by a kind of civic yearning and a devotion to traditional Quakerism.

William Poole stood at the center of this Wilmington group. Without him, his contacts, and his political acumen, the reformation cause would never have gotten off the ground; coupled with Hicks's preaching, Poole's efforts brought the party that finally bore the name "Hicksite" into existence. After the separation had begun, he rightfully played down his own personal public activity in the "great and glorious Revolution," rather seeing to it he said, "that more suitable agents have been employed."[79] The Wilmingtonian, born in 1764, was sixteen years Hicks's junior, but their friendship was deep and abiding. They shared the same theological concerns and sharpened their positions by long, philosophical letters, but Poole was much more a man of the world than Hicks. He served five terms on Wilmington's borough council and ran successfully for the Delaware legislature. A silversmith by training, he became a miller after his marriage in 1791, a prosperous occupation that permitted him time to pursue such differing interests as directing a bank, promoting road building, raising money for Greek relief, and working to abolish slavery.[80]

Poole looked to Hicks for guidance on theological matters, but he also expressed his own opinions forthrightly, and the letters that went back and forth from Wilmington to Long Island reflected the interplay of two minds struggling with difficult doctrines. As early as 1820, Poole began to circulate Hicks's letters among Wilmington Friends and importuned him to allow his views to be published in a Philadelphia journal called the *Reformer*.[81] After some consideration, Hicks demurred and expressed doubts about whether Friends were ready for his views. Poole agreed that some were not but came back firmly: "On the other hand, I believe that many are, and some I know are, and would be glad to see them." Poole felt that since many people refused to think about such subjects, "the Sound of the Gospel should be propagated in their Ears with a noise of Thunder or by the publication of some ideas of a different nature from those that have been entertained."[82] Unless they acted, he told Hicks in January 1821, Friends would endure what they had "long suffered from opinions embraced and propagated by individuals that are founded in degree in error." "The *radical cause of disbelief*" in such persons centered in their unwillingness to surrender something they insisted on retaining—" 'the love of the flesh'—'the love of the world.' "[83] Before long, Poole attributed such erroneous views to "a scheme that originated in England some years ago to remove some of the 'peculiar doctrines' that stand in the way of a participation in the *honours and emoluments of the* 'Established Church.' "[84]

It was not difficult for Poole to find other Friends in Wilmington who assented to the need for reformation. The area practically seethed with Enlightenment enthusiasts bent on reforming the world. One of those who gravitated to the cause, William Gibbons, studied medicine under the famous Philadelphia physician and revolutionary leader Benjamin Rush and was well known for his benevolent activities. Committed to black education, temperance, and peace promotion, Gibbons naturally identified Quakerism as much with its social testimonies as with its doctrinal questions. His most important contribution involved editing his journal, the *Berean*, the reformers' house organ during its truncated life of four years in the mid-1820s. In 1827, at age forty-six, he founded and presided over the Delaware Acadmey of Natural Sciences, viewing it as a way to demonstrate that "man displays an almost inexhaustable fund of resources" once enlightened by science and rational thought.[85] One detractor cited him as the "founder of the [Hicksite] heresy in Wilmington."[86]

Gibbons's familiarity with contemporary philosophical and theological currents was characteristic of the Wilmington wing of the reformers. The *Berean* trumpeted the biblical description of the people from Berea from its masthead—"These were more noble than those of Thessalonica, in that they received the Word with all readiness of mind and searched the Scriptures daily, whether those things were so"—but its tone reflected a much more rational approach to religious truth. In editorials like the one he ran on January 10, 1826, for example, Gibbons clearly tried to reinterpret "natural religion," the slogan of Unitarians, and give it a gloss acceptable to Friends. After denying any human authority in religion, including the Bible, he explained that what theologians described as "*natural* religion, or that light which men have independent of books, or of men," was required to illuminate "revealed religion, or the scriptures. . . . Thus this natural religion, turns out to be, at last the very foundation of Christianity. It is, in fact, the only religion that is *revealed*." He then quoted an unnamed writer who held that "the religion of Christ must be understood, before it can, or ought to be believed; and that it must be proved to be a consistent and rational religion, before they can be under any obligation to receive it."[87]

Evan Lewis, another future Hicksite editor associated with the Wilmington group, was born in 1782. Trained as a tanner, he had taught at a girls' school in New York, but lived in Wilmington when he linked up with the reform movement in 1821.[88] The work of the reformation required "digging through the rubbish of traditional religion," he informed Hicks, something most Friends "do not seem prepared to be for."[89] To get them ready, he edited *The Friend; or, Advocate of Truth*, a Philadelphia Hicksite effort begun after the separation; it proved a veritable bulldog of reform sentiment until Lewis's early death in 1834.

Such men had come to expect opposition from those with entrenched power. In fact, they all but viewed opposition as a necessary endorsement of their activities. As the editor of the *Berean* noted in early 1828, "no reformation was ever effected on the ground of Christian principle, without opposition." These who opposed the reformation, he went on, best exemplified the principle governing human beings, "the *love* of power," and used bigotry and superstitution to enlist unsuspecting souls in their selfish cause.[90]

Although both Lewis and Gibbons were prominent figures among Wilmington Friends, they did not shine as brightly as Poole's most important contact, his nephew by marriage, Benjamin Ferris, who became the most articulate and accomplished leader of the reform movement excepting Hicks himself. Born in 1780, he was mostly self-taught, but he served as an apprentice to a clockmaker in Philadelphia, where he lived from the age of fourteen until 1813. While in the Quaker City, he developed cosmopolitan interests, learned French, read widely, and moved easily in sophisticated circles. He wrote incisive letters and, with a healthy fund of interesting stories, proved an appealing conversationalist. His two unpublished histories of the separation were marked by pleas for tolerance, even if he did not always act on his own advice. As clerk of the Hicksite separatists, he signed, and probably wrote, the epistle explaining what had happened. His wide contacts and sharp mind, revealed especially in the letters he wrote under the name of "Amicus" in the *Christian Repository* from 1821 to 1823, made him a formidable antagonist for the evangelicals.[91]

Ferris's fundamental concern was not simply theological, although he certainly held his own when called upon to elucidate Friends' doctrinal positions. From the first time he wrote Hicks, in July 1821, until 1847 when he finished his "Historical Review of the Rise and progress of the Separation of the Friends of Philadelphia Yearly Meeting," Ferris insisted that the tap root of the problem was the effort of the "enemies of Truth" to exercise their control over the Society. As he told Hicks, the false brethren who were attacking him were "instruments in the hand of the adversary to close thy way and oppose the progress of truth." He spoke often of "sound doctrine," but he wanted its clarity tested against the leading of the divine Spirit within each individual. Quoting William Penn, he explained the "blessed principle" of the inwardly revealed *"Light and Life of Christ:"* It was "the only foundation of the saint's faith, the root and spring of the true Gospel ministry"; it gathered Friends "out of the world to be a 'peculiar people' "; it "drew them from all outward dependence, into an inward silence and waiting upon God to know his will"; and it "quickened and made alive" the people unto God.[92]

Few, if any, of the reformers around Hicks would have disagreed with these formulations, but Ferris's strong emphasis on them gave the reformation cause an individualistic twist. His research into the Quaker past uncovered a collection of leaders who differed with each other on numerous points—some Trinitarians, some Socinians, others a mixture—yet were still able to live peacefully together in the same religious community. "Uniformity of opinion," said Ferris explicitly, "was never by them considered as the basis or ground of religious union. It is unity of purpose, unity of feeling, unity of spirit, that constitutes the bond of Christian fellowship.'[93] This view suggested that a Friend was free to believe pretty much as he or she pleased, as long as a unity of purpose, feeling, and Spirit was maintained; Ferris, of course, asserted that doctrines had nothing to do with this unity, which could exist despite wide theological chasms that divided Quakers.

None of Ferris's contemporaries realized what he had done in adding this new rung to the ancient Reformation stile. This stile rested on the Bible; its first step defended personal interpretation; its second affirmed the primacy of the Inner Light; and now Ferris added a third step that brought the believer down in a place where practically any tenet was possible. Even in his most provocative and far-reaching statement, a letter to his neighbor Phebe Willis in 1818, Hicks had not gone this far. Every step of reformation, he wrote, had been carried on "when the reformers, kept close to the leading, and inspiration, of the spirit of truth" and permitted nothing, neither books nor people, to turn them aside. Every man and woman was bound to have the same understanding of truth, for God "must, and no Doubt has, given to every Man and Women, a complete and sufficient rule of faith and practice, without the aid of books or men."[94]

This difference between Hicks and Ferris was a subtle but vital one. The older man held that God's spirit would work to bring unity among believers, who would then come to share the same theological understandings. Individuals would seek the truth for themselves; then they would be brought into unity with one another. Ferris, on the other hand, played down the Spirit's work in forging a unified body of believers, and laid his stress on individual responsibility. A new era was dawning, he affirmed, when "friends of 'pure and undefiled Religion' . . . *will judge* for themselves of the doctrines held out to their acceptance." This reformation age, marked by "a spirit of free inquiry," would see the tottering of "gross errors and grievous impositions" that came from outside.[95] As a Friend, especially one who had enlisted in the reformation cause, Ferris could not overlook the Internal Light — indeed the passage just mentioned introduced an essay on the subject. He cast this key concept, however, in purely individual terms: the Inner Light illumined each separate person but played little role in bringing them into doctrinal unity. Ferris exulted that he lived in a time when "many are not only disposed to seek the truth for themselves, but, under the blessings of civil and religious liberty, have grown up into a capacity for reflection, and maturity of judgment."[96]

Hicks preached traditional Quaker doctrine, but as his ideas passed through Ferris's more cosmopolitan and sophisticated mind the reformation movement acquired a new and more modern tone. At the time, no one realized what had happened. The reformers were pleased to have such an accomplished individual on their side, and in the far from precise world of Quaker theology, Ferris's words had the right ring, if a new substance, to them. Moreover, his vigorous activities on behalf of the cause, especially his lengthy debate in the *Christian Repository*, helped obscure some of the minutiae of his thought. The Ferris emphasis expanded and, like a runnel fed by heavy upstream rains, inundated the reform movement and ultimately became synonymous with the Hicksites.[97]

The flood did not sweep all before it, however. One Wilmingtonian, also a budding journalist, wanted the reformation to be more thoroughgoing. Benjamin Webb, well enough off to match the hundred dollars Ferris and the city's postmaster each contributed to the meetinghouse fund, served as general agent for the *Berean* and, by his own testimony, was a latecomer to the reformation cause of liberty of conscience. But he discovered that reform in this instance had a way of feeding on reformers. After the separation, Webb wanted to carry the principles announced by the others to their logical extreme and so defended the idea that "belief was no merit, nor unbelief a crime." Whereupon Wilmington Meeting, with Ferris as clerk, disowned Webb for publishing a newspaper, the truculent *Delaware Free Press*, that espoused the principles of free-thinkers like Frances Wright and Robert Dale Owen. Appeals to Concord Quarter and the yearly meeting brought no satisfaction, so Webb turned the *Free Press* into a vigorous anit-Hicksite journal. Week in and week out, he asked such questions as, "If the Hicksites are ready to amalgamate with other professors to put down heresy, what is their between them and there orthodox brethren?" And he alleged that even unbelievers like Tom Paine and Voltaire had never advanced principles more opposed to Christianity than had Ferris and Gibbons.[98]

The Wilmington wing of the reformation party, its members more attuned to intellectual currents of the day than older and small-town elements in the group and also more free of the limiting influence of Philadelphia's elders, lent a new emphasis to the cause. At the time, because the main targets were rigid evangelicals, the reformers' more individualistic and rationalistic stance was not as evident, but it would later come to define Quakers generally. This nascent distinction, of course, had roots deep in the Protestant past, for it involved the question of authority. Hicks and the more traditional Friends held that God's law and light, revealed inwardly, would create and maintain a covenant of unity among serious and sincere seekers. Ferris and the Wilmington element built on this perception, but they went on to insist that unity was less important than individual liberty of conscience, which allowed Friends to believe whatever seemed rational. Seldom describing these differences but sensing accurately where Hicks's ideas were leading, the evangelical elders solved the problem of authority in the way those with power usually do—they sought to impose their own understanding on the Society of Friends.

PART II

The Struggle for Reformation — to 1827

Evangelicals
(In order of prominence and power within Philadelphia Yearly Meeting)

Jonathan Evans,
Samuel Bettle,
William Evans,

Thomas Stewardson,
Thoms Wistar,
Stephen Grellet

The British expeditionary force

William Forster,
Anna and Isaac Braithwaite,
Ann and George Jones,

Elizabeth Robson,
George Withy,
Thomas Shillitoe

Reformers
(In order of influence in the cause prior to 1827)

Elias Hicks,
William Poole,
Benjamin Ferris,
William Gibbons,
Thomas McClintock,
Abraham Lower,
Edward Hicks,

Priscilla Hunt,
Halliday Jackson,
John Comly,
William Wharton,
Samuel Noble,
Jesse Kersey,
Thomas Wetherald

CHAPTER 4

"The root of the defection,"
OR
Evangelical Inroads

AT THE BEGINNING OF THE nineteenth century, the small world of American Quakerdom was a stable and quiet one. Most Friends liked things that way. The approximately seventy thousand members seemed content to lead their separate, peculiar ways. Scattered along the eastern coast, in Rhode Island and Massachusetts, in New York east of the Hudson River, in the middle states, and in North Carolina and Virginia, Friends were hard-working, prosperous people, mostly farmers except for the grandees in commerce, banking, and real estate in Philadelphia, New York, and Providence. All wore the distinctive garb that, with minor changes, had marked a member of the Religious Society of Friends for more than a hundred years—the dark, lapelless coat, underjacket, collarless shirt, and broad-brimmed hat for men and the equally dark dress and bonnet for women. Quakers and the "world's people" differed even in their use of language: Friends clung to seventeenth-century habits, using "thee," "thou," and "thy," and stubbornly refusing to invest anyone, no matter the official status, with a title. Their religious services, called simply "meetings," convened without agenda, music, or clergy.[1]

Those meetings formed the base of Quaker distinctiveness, and the leaders worked hard to keep them that way. At the center of Quakerism abided the conviction that the divine Spirit, whom Friends identified with Christ, guided the waiting worshippers in the right paths, gave them words to utter, and strengthened them for their tasks. Any person attending the meeting might sense a call to speak the word of God, but most messages came from designated ministers, who sat in the raised gallery on a "facing bench" at the head of the body. Both women and men were recognized as ministers, for Friends drew no formal sexual restrictions. Sharing the facing benches, elders were charged with looking after members' spiritual well-being and conducting the ministry. Overseers were responsible for discipline in the meeting community—which might include punishing offenses ranging from dealing with jugglers to keeping one's hat on during prayer. Above these "monthly meetings," so designated because they met monthly to conduct business, rose a series of assemblies that offered oversight and advice, as well as guidance to the subordinate groups below. Quarterly meetings included monthly meetings from adjacent areas, while the yearly meetings were general assemblies—there were six in 1800—that met annually to consider business, hear reports from the bodies below, communicate with other yearly meetings, and occasionally decide appeals. For the average attender, the yearly meeting presented an opportunity for Friends from distant areas to get together, renew acquaintances, discuss church politics, and perhaps even find a husband or a wife. Separate women's meetings functioned at the various levels, but their power was much more limited than the main meetings, which the men tended to control.

Meeting for Sufferings best exemplified the dominant male influence, for no women served on this assembly. In Philadelphia Yearly Meeting, the most prestigious of American Quaker bodies—though not the most venerable, for New England Yearly Meeting, founded in 1661, antedated Philadelphia by two decades—Meeting for Sufferings dated back to 1756 and consisted of twelve Friends appointed by the yearly meeting with four additional representatives from each quarter. The *Rules of Discipline* provided that the twelve yearly meeting appointees had to reside "in or near Philadelphia" and that twelve would compose a quorum. The Meeting for Sufferings acted as a kind of executive committee between annual gatherings, a function assuring its members a familiarity with the intricacies of Quaker policies, not to mention giving them immense weight in the Society's affairs. The *Rules of Discipline* did warn that the Meeting for Sufferings "is not to meddle with any matter of faith or discipline" not given them by the yearly meeting.[2]

Quakerism was a religious faith based on experience, on each individual's unique encounter with the Spirit of God. Systematic theology played as small a role in Friends' affairs as formal theological training did, and that was none at all. Quakers often kept journals to record their temptations, insights, and experiences, usually expressed in very general terms. Elias Hicks's *Journal*, for only one example, abounded with sentences like this one describing a small meeting he visited in 1816: "Many hearts were much broken and contrited by the prevalence of divine love and power that accompanied the testimony borne, and spread generally over the meeting, to the praise of His grace who is calling us to glory and virtue."[3] Likewise, messages in meeting, although quite meaningful to participants at the time, were couched in such commonplace language that often it required an experienced observer to know what was going on. An alert but unaware Unitarian once visited a meeting and came away bewildered. Quaker preachers, he decided, avoided "everything like explicit statement, or logical deduction." To one unfamiliar with their methods, a sermon appeared like "refined mysticism," in which everything "is hinted and vaguely shadowed forth"; upon coming away, the uninitiated would be astonished to discover "that the speaker has been carrying on a controversy, or administering a sharp rebuke in a discourse, which seems to him scarcely intelligible. . . ."[4]

For average Friends the monthly meeting represented the most important religious institution with which they came into contact. There were at least two "meetings for worship" on Sundays — "First Days," as Friends said — and one on Thursday. Often a meeting sponsored a school to assure children would receive "a guarded education." Since 1755, at least in Philadelphia Yearly Meeting, monthly meetings had been required to answer a list of queries for review by the quarterly and yearly meetings. Dealing with such things as sleeping in meeting, reading "pernicious literature," frequenting taverns, and testifying against oaths and military service, the queries offered a way for individuals to evaluate themselves and, just as important, for quarterly and yearly "meetings for discipline" to exercise oversight of the meetings below them. Examining answers to queries offered a way for observers to assess the "state of the Society."[5] Friends concerned about weakening standards often used responses to the queries to justify their complaints, as Joseph Scattergood, a future Orthodox supporter, did in 1815 during the yearly meeting. He confided that answers showed "that many deficiencies exist among us," and "excited" a travail "under which their causes and effects were in a feeling manner traced."[6]

In his typically vague statement, Scattergood failed to mention what conclusions the meeting arrived at. If they did more than trace the matter, they no doubt sent leaders of the yearly meeting to visit subordinate meetings to stir up a concern for a stricter submission to the Discipline, a solution used since the last major reform impulse in 1755.[7] This practice of visiting meetings, staying for a period of time, and perhaps holding family visits was a common one. Individual Friends who wished to travel in the ministry received a certificate from their home meeting indicating that the person bearing the document enjoyed the favor of the local group and had its approval for visiting beyond its limits. Such traveling permitted ministers to spread their ideas far and wide, create groups of close associates, and exert broader influence, both on points of doctrine and matters of Discipline; the result was a more uniform practice. Leading Friends, such as Job Scott, Elias Hicks, Henry Hull, William Evans, John Comly, and Priscilla Hunt, criss-crossed the eastern United States in their travels and labored to promote the cause of truth as they saw it. Moreover, English Friends sailed back and forth across the Atlantic to bring their evangelical messages. One count revealed that between 1790 and 1827 twenty English ministers visited the New World, some treks lasting as long as four years and covering as much as eleven thousand miles on this side of the water.[8] These close ties and enduring contacts thus succeeded in molding a trans-Atlantic community that informally bound Quakers together.[9]

By 1805, some were seeking to replace these informal ties with a tighter structure that would produce more uniformity among Friends. Philadelphia Meeting for Sufferings first broached the matter of a uniform Discipline that would combine the world's disparate Quakers into one unified body. In New York Yearly Meeting this idea garnered little support, but Baltimore Yearly Meeting judged that it would be a way to produce among American Quakers lives "more fully consistent with our religious profession." When little progress occurred, Philadelphia Yearly Meeting the following year rewrote its own Discipline and introduced among the grounds for disownment a new offense—denying "the divinity of our Lord and Saviour Jesus Christ, the immediate revelation of the Holy Spirit or the authenticity of the Scriptures."[10] This new standard reflected the rise of evangelical sentiment in the yearly meeting and was an attempt to set a doctrinal standard for Quakers. Until this time, yearly meetings had not found it necessary to prescribe a certain doctrinal position: Few Quakers had ever denied these beliefs, they simply had never thought it necessary to require members to affirm them.

Another, less direct, way of promoting uniform beliefs had a long history among Friends. Under this method, a Quaker body—in Philadelphia, the Meeting for Sufferings—could withhold approval for publication of works that might tarnish the "reputation of Truth." In Fox's time in England, the Second Day Morning Meeting of London ministers had evolved into a kind of publication committee to review Friends' literary efforts; at one point in 1676, Fox himself was refused the meeting's imprimatur for one of his essays.[11] In the United States at the turn of the eighteenth century, a major concern was Job Scott's unpublished writings. The three most prestigious yearly meetings on the American continent, New York, New England, and Philadelphia, were entertaining serious reservations about him. New England's Meeting for Sufferings had undertaken to publish all of Scott's works, a task on which they had already expended two decades of effort, when doubts emerged about his views. "Some may call me a heretic," he had written, because "I expect no final benefit from the death of Jesus, in any other way than through fellowship with him in his sufferings."[12] They did not designate him a heretic, but the three yearly meetings could not see their way clear to approve publication of such views; New York Friends found that his doctrinal points were "of a nature so delicate as to admit of varied applications and . . . curious criticism."[13]

Such new concerns with doctrine, in and of themselves, were not the main points of subsequent controversy. The primary question was one of authority. Few Friends would question another's statement of faith if it were based on an immediate experience with the divine leadings of the Spirit. For traditional Quakers, that experience remained central; those few who deviated from the Society's norms evoked general concern and might be labored with, but as long as they refrained from divisive action and abided charitably with others, there would be no problem. In its revised Discipline, as well as in subsequent attempts to define and assert what Quakers believed—or by implication, should believe—Philadelphia Yearly Meeting created an outward standard, which might not entirely reflect the inward individual experience. The evangelicals now in control of the yearly meeting sincerely believed that Quakerism shared the historic and orthodox Christian faith—all they wanted to do was to find ways, such as disownment standards and firm statements of Discipline, to measure right belief.[14] They would see to it that succeeding generations of Friends would grow up naturally in the faith as now defined. This desire also explained the Orthodox interest in education. Years later, after the split, an Orthodox spokesman, Richard Mott, looked back and uncovered the "root of the defection"—"the want of religious education of the youth," not just "*school* education" but "*home* education."¹⁵ This concern recurred again and again and represented an attempt "to stir up the members to more faithfulness."¹⁶

Traditional Friends did not deprecate education when it was useful, but they certainly regarded what one learned by cultivating the mind as less important then, as Job Scott phrased it, "know[ing] the son of God *begotten*, formed, and brought forth in himself, wherein alone the union with God, or the Immanuel state, consisteth." Scott explained that a person "may try devotion, prayers, sermons, psalms, ceremonies, forms and performances of religion. . . . He may hear and tell a great deal of Christ, of faith, of imputation, and of being complete in Jesus," but all these would never "centre him in God."¹⁷ Yet it remained for Elias Hicks to sum it all up: "mankind are generally creatures of habit and lovers of same[;] their knowledge of things is more generally founded in tradition and education than on that right experience, that is the laborous fruit of free inquiry and impartial investigation." People so trained, he concluded, "feel a certain aversion to everything that calls any part of those principles into question, or that leads to reformation, and it is very obvious that from this force all persecution, and opposition to free investigation and reformation arises."¹⁸

Though written in 1810, these words foreshadowed coming events and help explain the heart of the differences between the Orthodox and their opponents. Hicks and other traditional Friends sought a reformation, which seemed blocked by those in power. Never very specific about what they intended, they used the term "reformation" as a kind of catch-word to describe their mission. Previously, Job Scott had warned that Friends would fall victim to their prosperity and become proud, vain, and indulgent unless a reformation occurred; let Christ's people, he counseled, forsake "improper desires and imaginary wants" or they would "make themselves slaves." He predicted that "thousands and tens of thousands . . . who are growing weary of lifeless forms" would flock to Friends if "we [refuse to] give way to that flatness and lethargy which has too mournfully overspread some among us."¹⁹ On his preaching trips, such as the one into the confines of Philadelphia Yearly Meeting in 1813, Hicks explained that apostasy had entered the church when "Christian professors" had allowed themselves to be "too closely attached to the several particular leaders" rather than the "perfect righteousness of the gospel," so that reformation had been retarded.²⁰ Five years later, Hicks told a New York audience quite bluntly that outward ordinances, such as water baptism and the Lord's Supper, were contrary to the truth of essential Christianity and served only to obstruct the "progress of reformation."[21] To rely on outward forms, both Scott and Hicks averred, was to put one's faith in the shadow rather than in the "true light that lighteth every man who comes into the world." Another reformer, after reviewing the Protestant Reformation, concluded that it changed popular thinking about the externals of religion, "without producing the desirable effects of the Divine spirit, charity, love and affectionate regard for one another." Reformation signified a willingness of individuals to be guided only by the Spirit, neither by others' interpretations nor by the express letter of the Scriptures.[22]

As long as sentiments like these were expressed in general terms, they elicited little or no disagreement—indeed even some who would later cast their lots with the Orthodox assented to calls for reformation. In 1800, for example, Jonathan Evans warned that "horrid" sentiments and opinions were espoused by those "whose eminent stations made them more dangerous." "Notions, Ideas and new fangled Doctrines are here and there creeping into view," leading Evans to fear "the artful and powerful assaults of the grand Adversary" that Hicks had warned about on a 1798 visit to Philadelphia.[23] Four years later, Evans looked at the state of Friends and decided that "we need to be shaken from inferior dependencies and more certainly know our feet established upon the Sure foundation."[24]

These were, it is true, general responses to generalized complaints about a general falling away from traditional standards. The rise of evangelical sentiment among Friends sharpened the perceptions of some to the dangers inherent in the stress on inward experience; they feared all the talk of inwardness would cause resistance to the new orthodoxy. In 1808, New York Yearly Meeting reviewed its subordinate meetings' responses to the queries and found numerous deficiencies, particularly regarding how young Friends spent their First Day afternoons. Hence the meeting dispatched a committee, including Elias Hicks, on what turned out to be a rugged ten-week visit to local meetings to stir up parents and children to more faithfulness. As it happened, the rough terrain over which they rode turned out to be the minor problem.[25]

One of Hicks's companions was Stephen Grellet, the thirty-five-year-old son of French nobles, monarchists to the core. Although styling himself "a complete disciple of Voltaire," Etienne de Grellet du Mabillier hurriedly left France in 1791 to escape the Revolution, joined the royalist forces organized by Prussia and Austria, and marched back into his homeland in a vain attempt to unseat its new government. Having experienced the evils of political upheaval, the noble scion had reason aplenty to distrust anything likely to promote disorder. He joined Friends in 1796 in Philadelphia and, rising rapidly, became a recorded minister eighteen months later. In 1799 he removed to New York and went into the mercantile business with his brother, a Friend destined to be disowned by his meeting.[26] Throughout his career as a Friends minister, Grellet never wavered from what he called "the first rudiments of the Christian religion, the fall of man, my own fallen and sinful condition, [and] redemption and salvation by Christ alone"—taken along with his devotion to the Bible, a concise statement of the evangelical creed.[27]

Not far into their trip, Grellet began to express reservations about Hicks's theological soundness. Perhaps these concerns grew out of differing ideas about their mission. Hicks thought the committee's goal was "to promote a reformation" by reminding members of monthly and quarterly meetings of their deficiencies.[28] Grellet, on the other hand, fretted that young people were not properly supervised by their parents on First Day afternoons, a situation permitting them to spend their time visiting rather than reading the Scriptures and other worthwhile literature. This refugee from the French Revolution felt greater disquiet about "the threatening affliction that I see coming upon us" than any he had experienced in his native land, for Hicks's sentiments were "repugnant" to Christianity. His subtle assertions tended "to lessen the doctrines of the Holy Scriptures, to undervalue . . . our holy and blessed Redeemer, and to promote a disregard for the right observance of the first day of the week." Laboring with his elderly associate, Grellet extracted a promise that Hicks would desist, but the old man neglected to keep his commitment and boldly continued, according to Grellet.[29] As for Hicks, he considered the trip a success because the faithful had been "strengthened."[30] The next March, Grellet left New York on another ministerial trip to the South and Philadelphia, worrying privately and publicly about infidelity, even as he insistently preached evangelical doctrines of salvation through Christ's death on the cross.[31]

Less than two years after this mission, the Spirit moved Grellet to return for his second trip to Europe, his first to England. With his French accent, swarthy complexion, and sharp facial features, Grellet captivated English Friends and became acquainted with the evangelical wing of London Yearly Meeting. He traveled with Ann Burgess, whose ministry with her husband, George Jones, a decade and a half later would sharpen the divisions between the followers of Hicks and the Orthodox evangelicals; Burgess and Grellet had time to talk and found themselves united in "Gospel fellowship." In York, he met members of the Tuke family, father William, son Henry, and grandson Samuel, all leading evangelicals, especially Henry, whose book defending his brand of Quakerism would be a standard for most of the century. He toured with Joseph John Gurney, a staunch evangelical friend of bishops and merchant princes, and a leading banker; Grellet approved his companion's "watchful spirit."[32] His many "occasions" — the quaint Quaker word signifying periods of joint spiritual and theological exploration — with Friends of this stripe and his journeys through the areas that George Fox had frequented confirmed his view that the Bible was the final authority for the Society: "if any man, pretending to be under the influence of the Divine Spirit, asserts any thing contrary to the plain testimony of the Scriptures, he is under a delusion." The reality was, he grieved, that many of Fox's descendents in American "now trample under foot, or set at naught these principles that were so dear to their ancestors."[33]

Grellet's new acquaintances were making ideas such as these the accepted ones among British Friends. Henry Tuke's 1805 *Principles of Religion, as Professed by the Society of Christians, usually called Quakers*, as well as a shorter compilation of early Friends' writings a few years earlier, grafted evangelical doctrines onto Fox's unsystematic "openings." It elevated the Bible, its Old and New Testaments, its divine commands to the Israelites to go to war and Jesus' commands to love one's enemies, to a level of authority never before propounded by Friends. From such grounding, other evangelical views easily took root — original sin, transmitted by birth from the original parents to all succeeding generations; Christ's "godhead"; and the Redeemer's propitiatory sacrifice, without which no one could be saved. Tuke's *Principles*, broadcast widely in numerous editions on both sides of the Atlantic, could be found in nearly every Quaker home of the nineteenth century.[34]

As evangelical sentiments began to spread among Friends, the distinctiveness that had characterized Quakers started to disappear. This development was hardly surprising, for people tend to act from their perceptions of themselves; when Friends came to share the same doctrinal positions as other churches, they saw little need any longer to be different, to maintain their testimony of plainness that marked them a "Peculiar People."

Benjamin Ferris reported that an Episcopal clergyman had invited British Quakers to scrape the dirt from Fox's grave, bury their peculiarities with him, and unite with their fellow believers in the established church.[35] Differences in church organization and ways of life became less important than whether believers shared the same theology. Evangelical Quakers came presently to consider themselves as close to other evangelicals as to Friends.[36]

One mark of this change was Quaker involvement in Bible, tract, and missionary socieities. Friends had never opposed efforts to convince others to turn to the Light of Christ within, nor obviously did they reject the necessity of living a godly life. But they insisted that cooperation with the world's people, particularly if led by those they deemed "hireling priests" meant that Friends inevitably accepted someone else's commitment and fatally compromised their own.[37] One Quaker opponent of Bible societies suggested that evangelical doctrines had infiltrated London Yearly Meeting when its members began to amalgamate with English clergymen. Traditional Friends had the same problem with efforts to enforce stricter Sunday observance. Elias Hicks complained that Quakers who pushed such laws had "quieted their consciences so as to get along easy in the Mixture with the multitude"; the end result, he averred, would be to obstruct the reformation and lessen "our usefulness as a peculiar people called to hold forth to the world of mankind pure and peculiar testimonies."[38]

Grellet, however, saw no problems with such endeavors. Already he had remonstrated with Hicks for slighting Sabbath observance, and he found every reason to applaud wealthy Englishmen, both Quaker and non-Quaker, for their self-denial in contributing to poor relief. When he arrived in Russia in 1819, he waxed enthusiastic about a Bible society he happened upon in Odessa, organized as it was by schoolboys.[39] Traditional Quakers sharply rebuked such ecumenical efforts. A Friend writing in a Philadelphia monthly thundered, "Alas how fulsome," and declared that even prisons would be better than the "oppression and tyranny that the mass of labourers and poor in England, now lie under, from the overbearing hand of their lordly oppressors, the great landlords . . . and the dignified clergy, that our Quaker calls his friends."[40]

Quaker reformers sometimes approached viciousness in their attacks on missionary activity. Elias Hicks, who seemed constitutionally unable to call a spade anything but a spade, particularly when he could thereby embarrass his opponents, took the lead in this vituperation. Someone sent him a copy of a Presbyterian missionary's report about laboring in Hick's area of Long Island. Money to educate ministers, it appeared, was collected at Sabbath schools, prayer meetings, and monthly musical concerts. Hicks examined his soul and announced that he was sickened at the way this missioner extracted money from the poor. Like death, "the hireling clergy and their greedy missionaries" never seemed satisfied—"*covetousness hath no bowels.*" The missionary in question had gone on to malign Hicks himself for his "pernicious heresies" and charged that the Quaker had classed Bible and tract societies with gambling and horse racing. Hicks refused to plead immediately on that one, but he parried his opponent's thrust by reminding his readers that gambling and racing were recognized as notoriously vulgar and depraved amusements, while Bible societies masqueraded under "the specious pretext of doing much good." Any man, he went on, "so sottishly ignorant" as to think that the good God would call together "men of licentious morals, slave-holders, warriors of the highest grade" to preach the gospel, was beyond hope. Convened in fancy halls, such men uttered formal prayers, gave each other flattering titles, voted thanks to one another—"*verily,*" quoth Hicks from Jesus, "*they have their reward.*" Hicks knew that such strong language might be misconstrued, so he took care to reaffirm his oft-stated position that he regarded the Bible as the best of books.[41]

These disagreements between traditional Friends and those espousing evangelical doctrines, first manifested in the disownment of Hannah Barnard and in the yearly meetings' refusal to publish the writing of Job Scott, had not yet, by about 1815, led to open conflict. Indeed, large and significant areas of agreement remained between those holding the two points of view. Both groups held that the inward experience of Christ within each individual produced a saving faith. And both looked to the appearance of the divine Spirit within the silent meeting to lead and guide the seeker. Traditional Friends had never called these beliefs into question, for they represented positions handed down from the days of George Fox. Neither did evangelical Friends, despite the strong emphasis the latter gave to outward manifestation of the Spirit. William Evans related how, as a young man, he searched the Bible in what turned out to be a vain attempt to regain his lost faith in Christ. The truth was hidden from him for a long time until, walking one evening, he sensed the presence of the Holy Spirit reviving his faith. He saw that salvation "is not founded merely on what is read, but is really of the operation of God in the heart." Of course Evans, writing after the separation, had no use for the Hicksites and what he considered their Unitarian-like denial of the divinity and atonement of Jesus, but he carefully distinguished himself, too, from those who made the Bible "the origin and foundation of true faith." "God alone," he exulted, "can give true and saving faith in his beloved Son and in the truths of the Gospel."[42] Evans did not always write so carefully, and as time went on he tended to elevate the Scriptures to a much higher level of authority, thus helping sharpen the nuances of difference between the two sides.

Such differences had always existed and could be expected to continue among Friends without leading to a division. Good humor and mutual respect could go a long way in preventing disagreements over abstract doctrines from becoming so all-consuming that proponents of differing views could not live with each other. For instance, one of Hicks's more active supporters, Abraham Lower, had a close friend, Joseph Scattergood, whose own theological position led him to align himself with the Orthodox. In 1814, before the participants realized they were on different sides, the two men bantered back and forth with each other about how the other would be ashamed of his theology before he died. They traveled together in the ministry, and Scattergood, at least, depicted Lower's messages as "sound searching testimony."[43]

For conflict to surface among chums like these, the lines had to be drawn. By the middle of the century's second decade a theological debate over the role of the Bible and the nature and work of Christ had emerged. Peripheral questions like Sunday observance, missionary societies, and the personal use of products made with slave labor added color to the discussion but never assumed a major role. Moreover, this discussion fed another debate about what group, what body, what authority, should decide the correct answers, both to the major and minor questions. And even if everyone finally agreed that the Bible should be authoritative, the question of who was to settle disputes about variant interpretations still had to be tackled.

To complicate things even more, personalities also played an important role in the conflict. The followers of Hicks nearly always seemed more combative, doubtless taking their cue from their leader. As early as 1785, when he was in his thirties, Hicks received a letter from a Presbyterian complaining about his "railing invectives" and alleging that he had been "uncivil" in a public meeting.[44] Another correspondent, this one a Friend, warned Hicks that tossing off phrases like "dupes of others" and "lacking of common sense" tended to shut people's minds rather than convincing them.[45] Hicks seemed to enjoy using language that was inflammatory. Once during a message in Philadelphia, he echoed Job Scott in declaiming that "the actual blood of Christ in itself was no more effectual than the blood of bulls and goats," a sentiment hardly calculated to win support for his point that believers should experience Christ's sacrifice inwardly.[46] Such attitudes ran in the family, or at least cousin Edward Hicks thought so. In relating how he had written a harsh letter to yet another Presbyterian critic of Friends, Edward described himself as "feeling a degree of that warmth peculiar to a *Hicks*."[47] Other reformers were only a bit more circumspect: Abraham Lower and Halliday Jackson responded testily when asked questions at a post-separation hearing over property in New Jersey in 1830.[48]

Of course, the strategy of the evangelicals was enough to infuriate their opponents. Because they had their hands on the instruments of power in the Meeting for Sufferings, leaders like Jonathan and William Evans, Samuel Bettle, and Thomas Stewardson did not have to stoop to answer their critics. Being able to define the issues, these men used their position and power to raise the questions they believed important, control the debate, and then implement the decisions once they were made. One reason that Elias Hicks became a symbol for those who supported traditional Quakerism was that he, as a member of New York Yearly Meeting, could remain relatively free from the control of the Philadelphia elders. As long as he could secure minutes of support from meetings in New York, he was free to travel wherever the Spirit might lead him, and increasingly after 1817, Hicks felt himself called to embark on extensive preaching missions within the confines of Philadelphia Yearly Meeting, there to make his contacts, rally his friends, and, like a sting nettle, irritate the elders.

The evangelicals now attempted to consolidate their position across the Quaker spectrum. In 1816, their leaders in Philadelphia Yearly Meeting organized an unofficial but influential Tract Association "to explain and enforce the doctrines of the Christian religion" by distributing reprints of ancient Quaker writings; New York and Baltimore evangelicals within the next two years created similar bodies.[49] About the same time, Hannah Evans, wife of Jonathan Evans and herself an evangelical minister, set out with another woman minister and her son William to confront some in New York Yearly Meeting who, it was reported, were undervaluing the Scriptures. At the 1816 sittings of the annual gathering the visitors were shocked to hear Elias Hicks affirm that the spread of the Bible "was a part of the system of priestcraft." When invited to stay at the Hicks's home, Hannah tried to bring her host to see the damage he was doing, but her efforts were unavailing, and Hicks continued to oppose Bible and tract societies.[50]

Philadelphia Yearly Meeting proceeded to reintroduce its proposal for a continental conference to discuss a uniform Discipline, a move heartily concurred in and strongly supported by the coterie of visiting English evangelicals.[51] Influential foreign Friends had sought to unify British and American yearly meetings since 1811, a move given added urgency by the continued appeal of Unitarianism to some Friends. In 1812, London Yearly Meeting had confirmed the disownment of one Thomas Foster, charged with belonging to the Unitarian Book Society and entertaining "low views of the person of Christ."[52] The proposal in Philadelphia set off an acrimonious debate. A committee of thirty-two, including a number of Hicks's close friends, considered the idea. Its report on April 24, 1817, recommended that the matter be endorsed and referred to other yearly meetings in the hope that it would produce a "more intimate feeling & knowledge of its [the Society's] state."[53] Such hopes failed to mollify those opposed to centralization. One young minister bluntly warned the gathering that "if the proposition to establish this head of aristocracy is united with by this meeting, it will ruin the Society of Friends." Proponents counterattacked with the kind of broad, orotund, and rolling phrases designed to warm the hearts of all those interested in the good of the Society. Did not Friends wish to establish "the authority of the church upon a firm and substantial foundation"? Had they not learned from wise "age and experience" what was necessary? An opponent replied that while supporters "*hoped* he *feared*, and whilst they *rejoiced* he *sorrowed*," but such expressions failed to derail the evangelical plan.[54]

Philadelphia Yearly Meeting's suggestion provoked reaction elsewhere. Reformers surveying developments later realized that this project flagged the most determined effort yet on the part of Philadelphia's evangelicals to standardize Quakerism under their guidance. While some found the idea relatively harmless, others suggested it might threaten the Society's internal harmony.[55] Their strategy was to lay the matter aside in the belief that time would kill it. Hicks was at first unclear about the intention behind the proposal, believing "it opened a wide field for the imagination to rove in," so New York Yearly Meeting in 1817 simply agreed to look at it some unspecified time later.[56] His friends, however, thought they saw more clearly what was motivating the scheme. From Ohio, Hugh Judge reported his suspicion that Philadelphians seemed to want "whole & sole controle & government of all the Yearly Meet[gs]" on the continent. Judge catalogued the reasons his yearly meeting also decided to defer action: the congress would have no women; it would "take cognence" of all that was done; no new yearly meetings could be established without its approval; a college would train young men "to the knowledge of the tongues to make them wise for such a convention"; no one could travel in the ministry without the conference's approval; and the "old simple unlarned will be of no use whatever."[57] Although probably no one had conceived of so comprehensive a program, Judge's fears suggests how far-reaching reforming Quakers viewed the machinations of evangelicals.

Opposition to their proposal led the evangelicals to their first open attack on the reforming element. Richard Jordan, a leading Philadelphia minister who had traveled in England, went with a group of influential Friends to New York to lobby for their idea. Jordan was so irate at the yearly meeting's rejection of the conference notion that in visits to a number of local gatherings he attacked Hicks openly for leading the opposition.[58] When Hicks lined up against the proposal at Baltimore Yearly Meeting, explaining that "Christ was our head & we need no other," the evangelical wing had yet another reason to rue the reformers' growing influence.[59] But despite successes elsewhere, when they looked at Philadelphia where evangelical power was most deeply entrenched, the reformers saw they had had little success; as Edward Hicks wrote his cousin, the yearly meeting in Penn's City would not search out the "radical caus of the great defesincys and departures from primative purity and perfection."[60]

To view Philadelphia as the seat of "defesincys and departures" helps clarify the points at issue between the two groups of Quakers. Provincial, "unlarned"—by one admission, anyway—distrustful of centralized power (Benjamin Ferris, at home in Wilmington, wondered at the presumption of those who would control Friends scattered over 300,000 square miles from Maine to Carolina, from the Atlantic to the Mississippi[61]), opposed to the power of wealth, and rejecting evangelical doctrines to perserve traditional Quaker ones, the reformers knew the ultimate issue was a question of authority: who would determine what kind of people Quakers would

Arch Street Meetinghouse. Venue of Philadelphia Yearly Meeting activities and of the divisive 1827 sessions. For business meetings, women convened on the right side of the building, men on the left. (Friends Historical Library, Swarthmore College)

A Meeting for Worship at Arch Street Meetinghouse, Philadelphia. During a meeting for business the scene would be similar, save that the women would have withdrawn to their side of the house and the clerk and assistant clerk would be seated behind a table in center of the top row.

(Friends Historical Library, Swarthmore College)

be? Points of doctrine inevitably became intertwined with this question and much of the debate would focus on it, but the real issue always lurked just beneath the surface. When they rejected the plan for a national conference of Friends, the reformers were saying a loud "Nay" to those who wanted to define the faith in their terms.

Turning back the conference idea did not mean that the debate was over. Each side, in the decade after 1817, seized every opportunity to make its theological points and in the process to parry each successive thrust of its opponents. The feud at its essence, however, transcended the niceties of theology; it represented a struggle over power. In this fundamental sense, those who espoused evangelical doctrines had the advantage because they already wielded influence. To win, the reformers had to dislodge them, and as in all such battles those in fixed, established positions had the advantage. The dispute over the conference proposal foreshadowed the end of the calm and quiet that had heretofore marked the Society.

CHAPTER 5

"Antiquity ought not to sanctify error," OR Hicks's Quaker Theology

ELIAS HICKS HAD TO SNATCH time from a busy schedule to respond to the critical letter he received in the third week in May 1818. Yearly Meeting would convene in New York at the end of the week, so the farm had to be made ready for his and Jemima's departure. Entertaining a Friend from England had eaten into the time available, meaning that moments for writing letters had to be stolen from the usual farm tasks. Hicks preferred not to answer his correspondent's queries in such a hit-or-miss fashion, but extra minutes were few for the seventy-one year old patriarch. He composed his long reply on scraps of paper, piled on his cherry desk, as he hurried in from feeding the cows, quickly replacing a broken fence rail, and getting the bean seeds for the summer into the ground.[1]

His correspondent, if not the subject matter, was a bit surprising. Perhaps the tiny handful of evangelicals in Hicks' monthly meeting were using this method of letting him know of their concern about his views.[2] Phebe Willis and her husband Thomas, both elders in Jericho Meeting, had had good relations with Hicks until recently. They had reluctantly concluded that the potential harm of some of his statements outweighed the general confidence they had in him.[3] Consquently Phebe Willis wrote Hicks inquiring about his views on the Bible and its authority for Friends. She might have simply conferred with him some First Day after meeting or paid him a visit at home, as she and her husband had previously done. That she had not chosen these methods suggested that she viewed her effort as a semi-official way of conveying her misgivings about Hicks's recent course; a letter would also have the advantage of preventing him from monopolizing the conversation.[4] It was not an unfriendly missive, however, and Hicks reponded in a conciliatory tone.

His reply, however, was like a non-Quaker bombshell, at least to those with doubts about Hicks and his brand of Quakerism. Fundamentally, Hicks called for a continuing reformation based, as all previous efforts at successful refrom had been, on what he called the "leading and inspiration of the spirit of truth." Reformation, like Luther's, that began with the Bible inevitably produced dissention and a final recourse to the sword. George Fox had understood this, Hicks claimed, so he had relied on "the light and spirit of truth in the hearts and Consciences of Men and Women, as the only sure rule of faith and practice." For his stance, more literal Christians, devoted to the Bible or their own interpretations of it as "their chief Idol," condemned Fox as a heretic. Friends should, Hicks insisted, suffer "nothing, whether books or men, to turn them aside from their ever present, and ever blessed, sure guide."

Hicks's statement went to the very heart of the conflict developing among Friends. One can imagine an irritated Phebe Willis demanding to know as she read these lines, "then, what kind of assurance can we have that we have found the truth?" Hicks's reply was that the unchangeable God had "given to every Man and Women, a complete and sufficient rule of faith and practice, without the aid of books or men—this rule came from the inward guide who instructed, helped, and led those who never turned aside to the precepts and traditions of men."[5] That Hicks coupled the leadings of this guide to the need for a reformation gave his opponents their principal concern; his position undercut the new doctrines that had become popular among evangelical Friends and attacked the outward authority that endorsed these innovations.

Significantly, Hicks made special appeals to young Quakers. The Lord, he told a youthful audience in Philadelphia, was visiting the young and "will lead them off from all dependence on man . . . and they will have no need that any man teach them." This same God would "overturn all man's work in religion, And put an end to all man's forms, creeds, and professions, that stand in man's will and spirit, that *He only*, may come to reign in the heart of his children."[6] If people depended on the written word, Hicks prophesied, they will become "dry and formal." Already, some Quakers had turned from the inward teacher, "who teaches as never man taught, nothing but the truth," and had come to emphasize books and men, "teachings to suit their own ends."

Significantly, too, Hicks admitted to Phebe Willis that he had changed his views, a concession he later partially retracted. Perhaps, when he conceded that the language in her letter "would not many years since, have been on my own," he was merely trying to find common ground so as to move his correspondent along with him.[7] Whatever his motive, such an admission gave his opponents ammunition to charge that his was a new doctrine, and they could not paint him and his followers as deists, Unitarians, and disciples of Thomas Paine, the notorious skeptic. Unwilling to carry the principle of the inward guide to its logical extreme, as Hicks did, the evangelical Friends could not be brought to see his central message: If the inward guide revealed God's word, then Friends need rely on nothing else. No other authority was required.[8]

Yet there were Friends within each yearly meeting who embodied authority, who possessed and exercised power. These Friends believed they were responsibile for defining and determining what correct doctrines were. To a leader like Samuel Bettle, for example, the matter was simple: "The ground of the unhappy schism in the Society of Friends, is the difference of doctrine." True, he went on, the dissidents had proposed procedural changes to dilute the influence of those who occupied central positions in the yearly meeting, but their actual goal, Bettle held, was "to forward the views of the seceders in relation to the introduction of new faith and doctrine."[9] And Jonathan Evans, the leader of the evangelical wing, allowed as how innocent people had "been plunged into complete infidelity" by "the deleterious principles of the deceitful, subtle spirit, which worked under the specious garb of outside morality and great professions of universal benevolence."[10] Hicks and his followers might asseverate that Friends' only true guide was the inward one, but the way the Society had developed required some body to decide whether the leadings of this guide were legitimate or not. In their demands for a reformation, traditional Quakers might be following in early Friends' footsteps, but they were also running counter to historical developments that had brought Friends to their current position.

The progress of the separation between the two groups occurred little by little and step by step, sometimes over what now appear to have been trivialities. When Hicks and his associates convinced New York Yearly Meeting in 1818 to refrain from reading an official letter from London, the evangelicals were horrified.[11] In August 1819, Hicks, Samuel Bettle, and William Evans attended Ohio Yearly Meeting at Mount Pleasant. Hicks and Bettle sat together in the commodious meetinghouse and participated in the deliberations. Bettle recalled later that Hicks had had every opportunity to introduce any "peculiar" views, but that "he came out in the ancient ground and foundation," thus causing no alarm to anyone.[12] Evans, on the other hand, did not approve of Hicks's testimony during one meeting. According to the Philadelphian, Hicks preached that when a person was born anew, the Father, the Son, and the Holy Spirit lived in him or her. For an evangelical like Evans, statements like this verged on denying the Trinity, "the Three that bear record in heaven." He therefore suggested to Hicks, as they walked from the meetinghouse, that his ideas ran contrary to Biblical statements about Jesus being glorified at the Father's right hand. Hicks evinced some irritation and shot back, "the Apostles were often misunderstood."[13] After the two Pennsylvanians returned home, a rumor spread that Hicks had treated the young Evans with some "disrespect."[14]

On the way back to Long Island, Hicks took the opportunity to visit friends and hold meetings across a wide area. He progressed through northern Virginia and Maryland, occasionally speaking against slavery, and arrived in Philadelphia for a week's stay in late October.[15] The old minister, lively and plain-spoken, attracted large and curious audiences, perhaps because he seemed to be more specifiic than usual in his communications. Warning that relying on the traditions of their elders retarded reformation, he advised young Friends to follow the leadings of the inward Spirit.[16] To another meeting, where those who sat in the gallery were noted for their wealth, he preached against usury and the "sin of living in luxury and idleness on the labour of others." To those with "uncertain riches," he counseled humility. And he bluntly told one well-known elder that he admired his ignorance.[17]

The events of Wednesday morning, October 27, at the "meeting for discipline" at Pine Street, where the Evanses held their membership, became almost legendary among Hicks's followers and seemed made to order for those who saw evangelical influence blocking the reformation. Here he broached the question of the use of products made with slave labor, subject of a pamphlet he had written nearly a decade earlier. Hicks interpreted the traditional Quaker prohibition against buying or selling goods taken by pirates as applying to the use of sugar, cotton, rice, and molasses, since these items represented the labor of Africans, wrenched by force from their homeland. Pointedly he said that some Friends, who had previously avoided the use of these products, had changed and were now little better than thieves and murderers; "there were some who had gone retrograde." Jonathan Evans shifted restlessly in his seat and twisted his face into a grimace at these cutting references.[18]

His testimony over, Hicks asked the meeting's permission to attend the women's business session at the other end of the building. Evans, from his seat in the raised gallery at the front, indicated that he could not unite with Hicks's request, but nearly all the rest acceded and designated an elder, Isaac Lloyd, to escort their guest. Not long after the two men had departed, Evans, still agitated by Hicks's aspersions, proposed the meeting adjourn and finish its business at another time, a move amounting to a rebuke of the New York minister. Despite opposition, including some from a visitor from rural Darby, the meeting arose, some of its members staying behind at the door of the now empty room awaiting Hicks's and Lloyd's return. As they listened, they heard the minister's full, deep voice coming from the women's area.

Hicks's ministry among the women lasted an extended period. Upon returning and finding the men's meeting already closed, he expressed surprise at this unexpected turn of events, picked up his coat, remarking that it was kind of them to have left it for him, and returned to his lodging. That night a number of his supporters dined with him and reviewed the day's episode. Hicks, of course, was hurt at the snub and wondered to his friends if this was the way Jonathan Evans and his cohorts treated visiting strangers. As word of the slight spread through the Quaker community, the feeling grew among Hicks's followers that the day's happenings had ripped the cover off the hostility that older, wealthy, and powerful evangelical ministers and elders bore their leader. That Hicks's characteristically strong language had played a role in provoking Evans's rudeness was overlooked.[19]

Evans did try to make amends for his affront. Sometime later, perhaps that very evening, he appeared at the door of Samuel Fisher's, the Friend at whose home Hicks lodged. The two discussed what had occurred, Evans objecting to Hicks's appeal to the youth to disregard their elders' authority. Hicks reminded his caller that the elders had opposed John Woolman's attempt to end slavery. Perhaps so, Evans countered, but Woolman "bore his testimony in simplicity" and "never called his friends thieves and murderers." They then wandered off into a discussion of whether Hicks had misquoted the Bible, and the wearied Long Islander said the conversation should cease until Evans apologized for adjourning the meeting without waiting for his return. Seeing no reason for an apology, Evans left. The two proud men never carried on a civil conversation again.[20]

Many Friends and others asserted that one of the separation's main causes was Hicks's close testimony against using products made with slave labor. It seemed more to the point that Hicks's vehemence against the use of such products, as well as his attacks on usury and wealth, called into question the kind of life urban Quakers had come to accept as a matter of course. Thus his altogether traditional views appeared to be the epitome of radicalism, sowing distrust between young and old, rich and poor.[21]

Hicks left for home the middle of the following week, but his supporters carried on. An anonymous pamphlet presently appeared containing one of his letters attacking the practice of setting Sunday aside as a holy day. According to one of Hicks's correspondents, the pamphlet successfully combatted superstition and won over some who had entertained contrary views. The same writer had himself been galvanized by Hicks's visit; Friends, he concluded, had become too timid "to shake the ears of the auditory with the whole mind of truth," and he asked Hicks for a letter describing his version of Quakerism. Hicks's friends seemed heartened by the large and favorable response they sensed he had evoked and by the bad light Evans's affront had cast on the evangelicals.[22]

Early in the new year, Hicksites in the Philadelphia area found a new monthly journal, *The Reformer*, a convenient vehicle for restoring Christianity to "its primitive simplicity and native innocence."[23] The editor was Theophilus R. Gates, something of a spiritual stray who had preached Methodism in the South but now proposed "To expose the clerical schemes and pompous undertakings of the present day, [which were launched] under pretense of promoting religion, and to show that they were irreconcilible with the spirit and principles of the Gospel."[24] Special targets were priests, missionaries, Bible and benevolent societies, and creeds—anything that represented a threat to the spiritual quality that traditional Quakers wanted to preserve. Running through every issue was a tone of distrust for those with wealth and power, as well as recurrent suggestions that the common folk were likely to be bilked out of their worldly goods by fast-talking individuals with noble-sounding aims.[25] Though not ostensibly Quaker—*The Reformer* carried items about Baptists, Episcopalians,

Presbyterians, and Catholics, as well as Friends—the monthly gave special attention to the apostasy that its supporters saw overtaking the Society. It amounted to a virtual house organ for the proponents of Hicks's traditional views, representing an open declaration against the evangelicals and their position.

The Reformer's pieces struck home. In April 1821, a person who signed himself "A Friend to the Reformer," attacked an address that had been made by William Allen, one of the most influential Quaker philanthropists in history, to an interdenominational English society to aid juvenile delinquents. Allen was quoted as saying to these Christians of diverse connections that he anticipated from them "the melioration of the mass of mankind," a declaration that drew shouts of "hear, hear" from an audience he described as consisting of "distinguished clergymen" and other social reformers. In a note the magazine's editor included his view that if Allen's speech exemplified general attitudes in his Society, then British Friends "have indeed deviated very materially from the integrity of the testimony borne by their primitive members."[26]

The Reformer's publisher, Joseph Rakestraw, related how a delegation of leading Friends visited him to protest the attack on Allen. Stephen Grellet, one of the three critics and one who had traveled with Allen in Europe, described the piece as "very *bitter, bitter*" and expressed his opinion that Allen had been misquoted. But then he judged that men of the cloth concerned with youthful criminals might be accurately called "*'dignified clergy'* on account of the principle they acted upon." William Forster, the visiting British minister, took exception to Rakestraw's defense that Allen's statements were hardly proper for a Friend to use in referring to clergymen. Forster commented that, of course, Rakestraw would not wish to receive gain from publishing such material.

More significant than this incident itself was what it revealed about the workings of the reforming party. Abraham Lower had previously recommended publication of the article critical of Allen, so he received some of the censure for its circulation. All those involved in the initial decision to publish knew what they were doing and understood the implications of their actions—one of which was to increase *The Reformer's* subscription list and spread the sentiment for reformation.[27] As the editors explained in a front-page statement in the June issue, the article on Allen "may be unpleasant to some who highly esteem" the English leader, but it might also help "in checking a disposition, now too prevalent, to take a part and be distinguished in some of the specious institutions . . . which seem more calculated to efface the simplicity of the christian religion than promote the salvation of men."[28] Such incidents pulled Hicks's party together and broadcast his views.

From early 1820 until July 1822, except for two brief trips within New York Yearly Meeting, Hicks remained most of the time at home. He wrote an article or two—one in *The Reformer* responded to an attack from a Presbyterian who had complained in print about Hicks's baleful influence on Long Island[20]—but mostly he kept up his farm work, read, and carried on the correspondence that had made his Jericho home the center for traditional Quakers working toward the reformation. As he went through his day-to-day activities, the septuagenarian minister sharpened his theological position, honing it against the critical letters that came in, and then tested its keenness by sharing his ideas with interested friends. Hicks's thought did not change much, but this time of reflection made it more sytematic and defensible; the theology identified with Hicks received its final gloss in this period. By the time the Spirit moved him to go once more to Penn's City in 1822, Hicks would be ready—and, as it happened, because his supporters had been so active, his antagonists would be prepared to take action against the threat he represented to them.

Like the positions of George Fox and other early Friends, Hicks's theology was a theology of experience, personal and mystical, tempered and to some extent hampered by the necessity of putting it in words. Inevitably, therefore, it lost some of its living quality and became more intellectual and rational as the Hicksites wrote back and forth to defend their conclusions. There was a certain irony in this development for the reformers had serious reservations about imprisoning spiritual truth in schoolbook logic. Education, after all, tended to perpetuate tradition and custom. They applauded natural reason, so long as it remained unhampered by education and the dead hand of the past. To a critical inquirer, Hicks applauded "that which has begun a good work on thy vision . . . and shewn thee . . . how mightily tradition and custom tyrannize over the human mind and bind it down as with fetters of iron too strong for reason alone to rend asunder and set the captive soul free."[30] Fortunately, he concluded, many Friends were no longer satisfied with the "old moldly crums of tradition and education."[31]

Hicks and his followers talked a great deal about God and the divine work in the world, but theirs was not so much theology—the word about

God—as it was anthropology—the word about human beings. Hicks told a friend, in the proverbial way he often spoke, "They talk of the devil—I tell thee, Walter, there is no worse devil than man."³² Because Quakerism grew out of the Puritan Revolutionary era,³³ it upheld the belief with its Congregational, Presbyterian, and Baptist cousins that human beings were tainted by sin and could not redeem themselves. There existed two wills in the world—God's will and each individual's will. The divine will represented the wishes of the "invisible God, who is an eternal, self existing, undivided, unchangeable spirit, who is the alone Creator and first cause of all things"; and the human will insisted on its way. It was impossible, said Hicks, for two wills to govern, for "there is always a want of right harmony" in such a case. As in a family, "God graciously ordained, that the Woman should be subject to her husband, and he should rule over her, and this subjection, ought to continue, untill both surrender their wills again to God . . . and then man's sovereignty over the woman, is entirely done away with, and God's will becomes all in all."³⁴

John Comly said the same thing in a different way. He argued that humans had two sharply distinct natures, the one, a lower animal disposition that was tied to the earth and lower passions, the other, a spiritual quality or soul, that was governed by the law of God, to quote the gospel of John, "the true light, that lighteth every man that cometh into the world." For followers of Hicks, every person was endowed with the right to choose whether to be ruled by the lower or higher nature. Evil occurred when one chose to be controlled by the lower animal nature.³⁵ Happiness, the state every human longed for and which constituted heaven, resulted when people subordinated their independent wills to the divine law written on their heart. Electing to be ruled by this law, they no longer possessed wills that conflicted with God's intentions.³⁶

Neither Hicks nor his adherents had much use for history, at least the kind that evangelicals insisted supported their interpretations of Christianity. Hicks asked one critic, "why shouldest thou strive so earnestly to establish thy faith on mere history, and tradition?" Still, the Hicksites relied on their own reading of history to support their demands for reformation. Hicks reminded the same elder that if reformers like Luther, Calvin, Fox, Woolman, and Anthony Benezet, the Quaker abolitionist of the Revolutionary Era, had followed traditions and history, then the church and the people would have continued under Rome's control. Reformations, he concluded from his historical study, started with one individual, and he intended to do his part.³⁷ Let the traditional professors charge us with heresy and schism, he asserted, we shall answer them: "So Worship we the God of our fathers;" our generation "has the work of their day assigned to them, by the great head of the Church, in a way to promote continually, a reformation on the earth."³⁸

The Hicksites used history, in addition, in a way that related more fundamentally to the theological issues behind the looming split. For them, the history of Israel was the history of God's dealings with the outward human circumstances. Because they were not ready to be ruled inwardly, the Jews had established an outward religion, one of ceremonies, laws, circumcision, even an outward God. Adherence and submission to these outward forms would assure that there would be the necessary union of the human and divine wills, and thus happiness. Thanks to their bondage in Egypt, the Israelites "were reduced to such a state of sensuality and ignorance . . . that the height of their desires, generally as a body of people in regard to happiness, were comprehended, in a deliverance from their outward Captivity, and being placed in full enjoyment of temporal blessings."³⁹

The man Jesus was the "God and Savior of this outward Covenant," for with the exception of the prophets, the Jews had never wanted to "be instructed any other way, than through the medium of their external senses." He was "the top stone of that Shadowy dispensation, given only to the people of Israel."⁴⁰ Jesus demonstrated to his fellow Jews what they might become if they were as faithful to the outward covenant as he was. Based on his own episodes with the divine Spirit and his reasoning from them, as well as the biblical record, Hicks had become an "adoptionist," holding that at Jesus' baptism and when the Holy Spirit descended upon him, Jesus became God's spiritual son. Hence the last ritual of the old covenant was Jesus' water baptism, which prepared him "for entering the Gospel State, by reception, or more full defusion of the Holy Spirit which descended upon him." Thus clothed with power, Jesus preached his gospel of peace and salvation, but, because of the carnality of the Jews, he found few disciples. His example, now under the new covenant, as previously under the old, showed what others might be if they were faithful to the divine will. After Jesus was crucified, "his immortal spirit rose superior to all their Malice," with the spirit of the penitent thief, to paradise. The outward body was raised three days later, Hicks affirmed, to typify how God could deal with fallen men and women despite their corruption.⁴¹

More than any other aspect of the Hicksite position, this interpretation of the significance of the Crucifixion infuriated the evangelicals, for it denied standard Christian dogma. To accept such notions, as the evangelical Friends understood it, would be to call into question not only the doctrine of the Atonement but the divinity of Christ as well. The Hicksites protested that they never had any doubts about Christ's divinity—and they did not—nor his miraculous birth, nor, for that matter, most of the other accepted doctrines about the Messiah. Hicks and his disciples simply gave such theological ideas a spiritualized twist, based on their own experiences. As Comly phrased it in a discussion with an evangelical Friend, quoting the gospel of John, " 'He is the propitation for our sins,' which I fully believe in; but this does not allude to the body, the manhood that dies on the outward cross. It was the Spirit of Truth operating in us, to produce, by our uniting with it, a state of acceptance or reconciliation with God."[42]

One anonymous reformer, in a pamphlet answering an evangelical attack, put it as well as anyone else. Those literalists who insisted on an outward saviour would have a would-be disciple go to Jerusalem and await there for the coming of God's Spirit. "Will nothing satisfy this reviewer," asked the pamphleteer, "short of our going with him on a pilgrimage to the outward Jerusalem?—Could he be prevailed upon to turn inward, he might there see who has been wounded by his transgressions, and bruised by his iniquities, who it is, that oppressed and afflicted, openeth not his mouth! Let him sink down and liberate the suffering seed! permit it to grow, and become a plant of renown."[43] Hicks's reformers wanted people to experience in their own persons the truth—and reality—of the gospel, not to cite it, or impose it, but to know it personally.

Under this gospel, the law and covenant became "spiritual, and universal, written in the heart of every rational being under Heaven," just as the true Messiah was spiritual and known spiritually. The Hicksites held that believers should experience themselves the reality of the things that happened in Jerusalem. Outward dogmas and creeds were simply no substitutes for one's own personal experience. These traditional Quakers insisted that the Messiah was only "spiritually and internally known and manifested . . . for everyone that has pierced him shall see him and as every man and woman has pierced him with their sins, so every eye shall see him, inwardly, but not outwardly, for only one man pierced the outward Mesiah, but all have pierced the spiritual Mesiah."

If no worse devil ever existed than human beings, how then did one experience salvation? Hicks responded that when in an act of divine grace, the Holy Spirit, the Comforter promised by Christ, visited the passive and willing soul of a person, then a new being, a child of God, came into existence, was nursed by the soul as a mother, with the aid of the heavenly husband, and grew to full man or womanhood to overcome the wicked one. "Hence is fulfilled Spiritually, all what Jesus passed through, outwardly and externally," Moreover, as Jesus was divine, partaking of the divine nature, so likewise were "any other of his children, born anew by his spirit, and they become partakers of his divine nature, [and] they are likewise divine." Hicks tied this heterodox interpretation to the Bible, quoting Paul — Christians are heirs of God and joint heris with Christ Jesus. But he realized how evangelicals would view his theological excursions: "I have several times thought," he told a correspondent, "in the course of writing this long letter, that if our friends generally had the perusal of our Correspondence, many of them I apprehend would tax us of heresy." But he ended his letter averring that he still followed the law and the prophets and worshipped the "God of our Fathers."[44]

And fundamentally Hicks was correct. He and those who stood with him against the introduction of evangelical doctrines into the Society were closer to the mainstream of Quaker history and theology than were their opponents. He was unlearned, he was not systematic in his theological musings, especially when he spoke in meeting, and, as a rustic thinker, he often went to extremes. But his theology did not differ in any substantial way from that of Job Scott, John Woolman, or, for that matter, the notoriously unsystematic George Fox. Had he published a book of theology, his reputation would have been made more secure; without such a work, he still remains near the top of Quaker thinkers.[45]

Hicks and his group were not unitarians, as their opponents liked to charge, primarily because the basis of their religious faith did not rest on reason but on their personal mystical experiences. (Indeed, the evangelicals, like the Unitarians, were more influenced by the eighteenth century's stress on reason than were the followers of Hicks.) Most reformers were rather unfamiliar with Unitarian sentiments and agreed with Hicks when he called himself a "stranger to their general tenets." Hicks did firmly reject the doctrine of the Trinity as unscriptural and fostering the notion of three gods. Moreover, with his usual twist, he opined that all sects, such as Unitarians, Nestorians, and Arians, resulted from the kind of apostasy that enabled scheming leaders to seek their own gain with little concern for the "genuine spirit of Christianity." Friends had best wait, he advised, until the Spirit of Truth came upon them with power and knowledge and united them "with all those of our fellow Creatures, whose lives, and conduct are directed, and regulated by it."[46]

Hicks deeply believed that such an eventuality was possible and that all should work for the coming of that day, but he and his cohorts had to spend an enormous amount of time and effort to undo the misunderstanding his iconoclastic words produced.[47] In fact, they never succeeded. No matter how much he wrote privately — "I have ever believed that the divinity of God, and of Christ are one"[48] — nor affirmed publicly — "I apprehend no minister in the Society of Friends has more often in his public communications, asserted the divinity of Jesus Christ the Son of God"[49] — he and his supporters could not shake the charge that they denied Christ's divinity.

But because this doctrine, as such, was less important than whether individuals permitted the Spirit of God to overwhelm and control their wills, Hicks did not seem unduly concerned. He wrote a Jericho minister, Thomas Willis, in a letter that produced an "unpleasant sensation" in the mind of this staunch evangelical, that to smoke tobacco grown with slave labor would be a "much greater sin" than believing one way or another about the story of Jesus' birth.[50]

Also serving to tar the Hicksites with the brush of unitarianism was the conflict between New and Old Lights in New England. In contrast to Hicks's group, the New Lights were primarily urban Friends who had come into close contact with the world's people during the prosperous years after the War of 1812; some had even joined Bible and tract societies. The New Lights chafed under the power of rural elders to dictate lifestyles and theology, and by 1822 Friends' meetings, particularly in New Bedford and Lynn, Massachusetts, faced such bizarre behavior as a New Light woman appearing in meeting clad in a sheer white gown to twit the elders' notion that Friends should obey external rules. Strongly influenced by rationalism, the New Lights' central belief was captured by Mary Newhall, one of their leaders, when she announced, "we are not bound to believe what we cannot understand." To powerful governors of the society, such sentiments smacked of ranterism, the ancient fear of Friends.[51]

Hicks's friends expressed interest in these developments but knew little about them at the time, although on one of his ministerial tours, John

Comly had met and grown to admire Micah Ruggles, one of the New Light champions.⁵² Hicks also knew of Ruggles, a recently convinced Friend of some local prominence, and divined that his opposition toward the less progressive elders had played a major part in provoking the New Light agitation.⁵³ By 1824, the discontented minority had either been silenced or disowned, most ending up as members of the Unitarian Church.

One New England legacy would continue to haunt the Hicksites. A former Presbyterian who had studied for the ministry at Brown University, David B. Slack, published in 1820 and 1821 a series of five pamphlets with the overall title of *The Celestial Magnet*. Although Slack did not join Friends, his pamphlets came close to echoing the position of the Quakers associated with Hicks.⁵⁴ Slack emphasized the Holy Spirit—the "Celestial Magnet"—and stressed, too, that people can know only the truth they themselves experienced at first hand, regardless of what holy books said. With an audience of his former Calvinist fellow-believers in mind, he wrote that God did not intend that the Bible should "be the chief rule of man's conduct." Using primarily literary evidence, Slack reasoned that God would not have spoken in only one language if he wanted people of other tongues to know his will, nor would he have allowed the Bible to be canonized for the partisan reasons it was.

"All that is required of man," said Slack, "is to acquaint himself with, and to believe what does actually exist; and to obey no other power, than that which actually torments him if he disobeys, and rewards his obedience with felicity." Nor did he have any use for the gods whose existence only reasoning could prove: they seemed "such brittle and delicate creatures as to require the vigilance of an empire of Priests to keep them in any tolerable shape and consistency." The true God's "throne is the heart of man." Slack concluded his third pamphlet with an explicit endorsement of the Society of Friends for upholding the abolition of creeds and outward laws and their replacement with the law written on the individual heart.⁵⁵

Slack's pamphlets caused division among New England Friends, just as they unsettled the none too placid waters in Philadelphia and New York Quakerdom. Hicks circulated copies of the pamphlets among Friends in Jericho and broadcast them ever farther afield in Pennsylvania and Ohio. One Friend convened a number of discussion sessions to read and consider the pamphlets; they decided that nothing in them could harm anyone. To Thomas Willis, however, Hicks's approbation of *The Celestial*

Magnet confirmed that elder's misgivings about the old man's doctrinal unsoundness. Others concluded that Slack was a deist and connected Hicks with his sentiments. Some whispered that Hicks had coached Slack. At one point Jonathan Evans even urged that Hicks's having purchased the pamphlets and mailed them to Ohio were indications that he had spread "unsound doctrines."[56] But such stir did not worry—nor deter—the Jericho patriarch. He curtly informed one critic that early Friends had also been called deists; he considered it "full and clear evidence of the weakness and futility of a cause, when it requires defamation and detraction to support it."[57] The "luke warm and Lethargic Society" needed its weighty members shaken up, a process that might just "remove these quite out of the way, by opening their unsoundness and inconsistency to the right minded and honest seekers in Society." The reformation, in short, must go on.[58]

Others reached the same conclusion. Hicks's supporters seemed less inclined than previously to sit back and let the Society be run by the evangelicals. They had become more aware of the need for reformation and the necessity to extend their influence to encourage reform. One, William Poole, suggested that it was time to stop answering affirmatively the query about ministers' doctrinal soundness when "there are few evidences of a sound ministry among us." He complained about the reluctance of Friends to seek conversions.[59] Poole also passed Hicks's doctrinal letters around among Friends in his meeting, and he pressed his older Friend to permit him to send the letters to Philadelphia for publication.[60]

Poole also recruited for the cause. One contact, his nephew by marriage, Benjamin Ferris, was bothered by what he referred to as the "snare" of human learning that had trapped many Friends into "setting it in place of better things." Friends, Ferris judged, had remained too much in the background of late and ought to become more aggressive in publicizing their views.[61]

Poole, of course, agreed. The small band of Hicks's followers were persuaded, as Poole phrased it, that "the Society is now suffering, and has long been suffering, from opinions embraced and propagated by individuals that are founded in degree in error." "I feel sure," he added, "that antiquity ought not to sanctify error."[62] Within months of penning these words in January 1821, he and his nephew would become involved in a controversy that would shake the foundations of those who exercised power and represented authority in the Society of Friends.

CHAPTER 6

"The tradition of the elders,"
OR
Holding The Line

THE REFORMING COTERIE AMONG FRIENDS concluded they had to find some way of forcing the hand of their opponents, the evangelicals who controlled Meeting for Sufferings in Philadelphia. The almost gleeful pleasure with which they circulated news of Jonathan Evans's affront to Elias Hicks at Pine Street Meeting in 1819 indicated that they were looking for an incident that would convince neutrals to side with them. But Evans's action might be discounted either as a quirk of his personality or his unwillingness, after a decade as clerk of Meeting for Sufferings, to brook opposition. Viewed in this way, the incident revealed nothing of what the reformers saw as the evangelical determination to slip the Society into a new direction.

As if to reassure cautious Quakers, some of the evangelicals did seem to be more politic than Evans and a bit less heavy handed in dealing with the opposition. William Forster, a prominent visitor from England, wisely did not renew the proposal for a large congress of Friends when he attended Philadelphia Yearly Meeting in April 1821; the idea, after all, had not won the approbation of eastern Friends in earlier years. But he did bring up the matter in the fall at Ohio Yearly Meeting in Mount Pleasant. Under a good bit of pressure from their visitor, the men's meeting appointed a committee to report back the following year, but the women's meeting resolutely rejected the whole idea. Still not satisfied, Forster saved some face by getting a commitment from the meeting to consider the proposal in 1822.[1] The lesson was that the evangelicals could not gain approval for one of their pet projects even in a young yearly meeting out on the periphery of American Quakerdom.

They were, in fact, appearing increasingly vulnerable, as a dispute in 1821 between Jonathan Evans and Isaac T. Hopper demonstrated. Hopper, who exhibited the combativeness for which he was noted throughout his life—he would later be disowned by New York Hicksites for defending abolitionists critical of Friends' weak stand against slavery—told Evans to his face that the Society might as well be ruled by a pope if it countenanced the kind of domination he exercised. The incident itself involved a minor matter of whether a committee of the Meeting for Sufferings had informed the full body that it had altered a memorial statement sent up from a lower meeting for departed a Friend. Having spread the story that the committee, on which Evans served, had not been entirely candid, Hopper was waited upon at home by an angry Evans one August evening. Accompanying the offended elder were overseers from Hopper's own meeting, brought along to extract an apology from the rumormonger. The neutral overseers rejected Evans's complaint; then, Hopper turned the tables and charged Evans with uttering some unspecified but harsh words against him in a recent business meeting. The overseers confirmed Hopper's side of the story, the same thing as proving Evans to be lying. Hopper concluded his tale of the affair by exulting that the powerful elder "has found out something he never knew before."

Incidents like this one not only buoyed the spirits of the reformers, they also suggested that the elders, if not floundering, did not automatically enjoy the support of rank-and-file Friends. Indeed, what amazed Hopper more than anything else about the confrontation was that the overseers were swayed neither by Evans's obvious rank—clerk of Meeting for Sufferings—nor his eloquence. And Evans, if Hopper be a fair judge, realized the same startling truth.[2] Evans had already concluded that the degeneracy among Friends approximated that of the Jews but believed that the faithful should stand their ground and declaim against the age's corruption.[3]

Evidence of corruption, enough to worry the least saintly elder, seemed to pop up everywhere. The New Light agitation in New England had opened the door to ranterism. A respected minister from Trenton, New Jersey, had forcefully preached against Bible and missionary societies because they were dominated by hireling priests—"shall I say thieves?" he asked from the Wilmington meetinghouse gallery. Meeting for Sufferings had rejected a request from a leading minister to publish his manuscript because it tended to "bind friends to certain doctrines not consistent with the light of the present day," that is, evangelical doctrines. And, it was bruited about, young ministers within Philadelphia Yearly Meeting were eagerly adopting and just as eagerly preaching the sentiments of Elias Hicks.[4] It was little wonder that a committee of Meeting for Sufferings, surveying the state of monthly and quarterly meetings for the yearly meeting in 1822, complained that "the love and unity which characterizes the followers of Christ, is in many, but little felt, and in some places, is almost entirely laid waste."[5]

The most serious threat to the elders emerged about thirty miles down the Delaware River in the town of Wilmington, home of William Poole and his versatile nephew, the scholarly Benjamin Ferris, young and vigorous at forty-one. The controversy surrounding this at first little-noted series of events was so far-reaching it would later cause even the instigators to have serious second thoughts about whether or not they should ever have begun.[6]

It started in December 1820. Robert Porter, printer, publisher, and Presbyterian layman, announced the beginning of a religious periodical, the *Christian Repository* to herald weekly the glad tidings of Zion. In Porter's magazine, these tidings would include news of Bible, missionary, and tract societies, as well as word of revivals and conversions. When the audience for such intelligence proved disappointing, Porter, who would be neither the first nor last publisher to try such tactics, decided to introduce a bit of the yeast of controversy into his columns. A new Presbyterian minister in town, a recent student at Princeton Seminary, the Reverend Eliphalet W. Gilbert, now twenty-eight years old, was a man with a sharp, logical mind and a master debater. Gilbert agreed to write a piece about Quakers, of whom there were many, both in town and just up the river.[7]

It is always easy to make a long story short, and this one needed shortening, for Gilbert's letters, signed with the pseudonym "Paul," ran for twenty-one months and came to concentrate on theological minutiae and the kind of arcane points that could drive even committed participants to doubt their worth. Gilbert was a "New School" Presbyterian, one who championed both interdenominational Bible and missionary societies as well as modifications of strict Calvinism to make Christianity more acceptable to frontier Americans. But he was still much too orthodox for most Quakers, as he demonstrated on May 12, 1821, when he took the ground—whether high or low remained a matter of debate—from which he never retreated:

The Society of Friends held doctrines, he charged, "inimical to the principles of the Gospel." He carefully addressed each essay "To the Society of Friends," as though each Quaker embodied the infidelity he intended to expose. From Friends' style of dress and desire to be a peculiar people to their view of Biblical authority and the Trinity, Gilbert's pieces ran the gamut of anti-Quaker attacks, stretching back to the beginning of the Society.[8]

Philadelphia's evangelical Friends would have preferred to let Gilbert have his say and then let matters rest. They seldom deigned to engage in controversy because they did not need to—their power and influence within seemed secure from outsiders' assaults. But in Wilmington among the followers of Elias Hicks, another sentiment prevailed, particularly because "Paul" attacked Hicks by name. It was also felt that engaging Gilbert would be a way to promote the reformation, loosen the hold of hireling ministers over the people, and allow readers to see that "it is not in consequence of *mind notion* that Friends hold the doctrines that they profess." Poole hurried off news of the first articles to Jericho and hinted that Hicks might like to respond. As a former member of Meeting for Sufferings, Poole realized an unauthorized response to "Paul" ran counter to the authority that the central body in Philadelphia liked to exercise over doctrinal statements. Misgivings aside, Hicks's followers in Wilmington decided to go ahead and answer their Presbyterian challenger.[9]

Benjamin Ferris took the primary responsibility for the "Amicus" letters, but he had the assistance of William Gibbons and Evan Lewis, with advice from Poole and Hicks.[10] Ferris's background and interests were as broad as almost any contemporary Quaker's. At age ten he bought and read *Pilgrim's Progress*, a rather un-Quakerly act given author John Bunyan's opposition to Friends; he worked at one time or another as a surveyor, draftsman, writer of legal documents, and historian, in 1846 writing an account of early settlements along the Delaware.[11] His learning and ability certainly impressed his college-educated opponent.[12] Ferris saw himself as like the primitive Quakers who had "pressed though the crowd of oppressors" to advance to reformation. Despite his own learning—he had more than eighty books in his library by professors of other denominations—he agreed with Hicks that "*human learning*, however valuable when under the government of the pure principle, may become a snare and has become a snare that has caught many in our favoured Society." The result was that many, "from timidity, or a false

Charity, or a disposition to stand well with the enemies of Truth," opposed dealing plainly with "the falsehoods and calumny of this Clergyman." Ferris did not succumb to such temptations and saw "Amicus' " endeavors as a *"temperate exposition of our* principles and *their* gross errors." He asked Hicks for advice and assistance.[13]

The targets of Gilbert's attack were "the characteristic notions and conduct of your society" — in short, the very things that made Friends Friends and not Presbyterians. "Paul" charged that Friends neglected religious newspapers, opposed Bible and missionary societies, and unsocially separated themselves from other denominations.[14] He also wrote as though "Amicus" had been officially delegated to defend the Society. Inflammatory labels like "Atheist," "Deist," and "Infidel" flowed from his pens.[15] "Paul" quite rightly perceived that the premise that distinguished Quakers from other Christians involved the basic question of authority. Thus he attacked the "internal Light" as a "radical error," which, once loosened, would "sap the whole building" of Quakerism, and if permitted to stand, would "leave every man at the mercy of his own worst enemy," his sinful, evil, and deceitful nature. We Christians, "Paul" crowed, have the "letter of scripture," the only way to "know whether a way which *seems right*, is right!"[16] From that point he excoriated his foes for their views on baptism, holy communion, the Trinity, Christ's divinity, atonement, and justification. He rejected all their positions as biblically unsound.

At first "Amicus" followed an almost pedantic course, writing so many abstruse essays about baptism and the Lord's Supper that both the editor and Gilbert tried to shake him from his single-minded pursuit of every trival point.[17] On November 17, six months into the discussion, "Paul" opened the question of the Trinity, on which he considered Friends especially vulnerable, but Ferris plodded on and refused to be diverted until a month later when he addressed the matter of the authority of the Inner Light. From then on, the discussion became more pointed.[18] "Amicus" usually refrained from direct attacks on "Paul" as a believer. Despite his belief that the leadings of the Spirit were more authoritative than the Bible, he based almost all of his arguments on the written Scripture, but "Paul" never noticed that his opponent had accepted the ground of his argument as the basis for their debate. The two threw biblical citations at each other, tried to explain away contradictory references, and allegorized inconvenient passages.

Occasionally, "Amicus" showed what he might have achieved had he not bound himself to struggle on scriptural grounds alone. In January 1822, he commented that deism — the position each labored personally to avoid while tagging his opposite with the label — rejected divine revelation. Since "Paul" claimed God spoke only through the Bible, he denied knowledge of the Divinity to three-fourths of the world's people, said "Amicus," and thus gave aid and comfort to the deists in their effort "to cut off the whole human family from any union or communion with God."[19] But such insights seldom glittered among the dreary discussions of well-worked over Bible verses.

On June 8, 1822, "Paul" began his series on the Trinity, the subject that was to cause the most concern among evangelical Friends in Philadelphia, for Ferris was firm, if somewhat snaillike, in avowing that Friends rejected Trinitarianism. "Paul" thought this unique Christian idea "vitally essential" as the base for the whole plan of salvation. "Take away this doctrine, and the Gospel has absolutely no foundation." Every system not built on it, he went on, "is falsely called 'the Gospel,' and is built upon the sand."[20] When "Amicus" delayed responding, he taunted his opponent for his evasion, linking Friends with heretics who "love to appear, *en masque*," trying to pass as true Christians.[21]

Thus goaded, "Amicus" the snail was transformed into Ferris the fierce. The notion of the Trinity was "vulgar," "absurd and unscriptural," "incomprehensible," "contradictory," "blasphemous," in short, "an impossibility."[22] Gilbert's Trinitarianism was nothing more than "Tritheism," less scriptural than the Catholic's transubstantiation, an inventive relic of the abysm of apostasy into which the early church had fallen. Unable to ground their doctrine on the Bible, the Trinitarians had "been forced to resort to the fallible standard of *human reason* for support," yet their idea "is not only *above* reason, but *contrary* to reason."[23] This heated discussion about the Trinity seemed to renew Ferris's self-confidence, while the vigor of his argument pushed him into making more personal attacks than he had heretofore dared. Claiming he knew nothing more about "Paul" than that he was a Calvinist priest, he appealed to his readers to dig deeply, "through the vile rubbish of human tradition, accumulated by Priestcraft," until they located the true cornerstone, the Christ whose spirit brought salvation.[24]

As the series drew to a close in late 1822, "Amicus" predicted the advent of the oft-retarded reformation that would restore the "primitive beauty" of the early church, so long effaced by passing ages of darkness.

Protestant reformers, though loyal to their measure of life and knowledge, had left many things undone. Now the time was ripe to pick the "*fruits of Apostasy*," especially "the absurd and pernicious doctrine of a 'Trinity of person in a Divine nature.' "[25] The work of reformation, he had already conceded, progressed slowly. "We are not to expect the meridian splendor of the gospel sun when it first emerges from the misty horizon of types and shadows," but as the morning advanced, spiritual truths became "more and more distinct," and the new and living way, the mists now removed, shone plainly visible.[26] In the present age, he reaffirmed, the notion that Christians should follow the opinion of "frail erring men," who in a "very dark night" introduced "theological Philosophy," had been replaced by a new era with new possibilities of reform. Now people could seek the truth for themselves in a world that had loosened the fetters of mercenary priesthood that for fifteen thousand years had shackled believers.[27]

Such mixed images represented Ferris's struggling attempt to convey the hopes of Quaker reforms to a larger audience. The debate spread their theological position abroad and was almost an immediate success. Copies of the *Christian Repository* sold so rapidly that the publisher began to advertise that he would buy back recent numbers at six times their original cost. And plans began at the same time to republish the letters in a small volume for wider distribution.[28] Hicks and those who sided with him sensed, as he put it, that "some of the main pillars of antichrists kingdom will be shaken to their base." Another future Hicksite rejoiced at the "success which has evidently attended us in this discussion."[29]

Others, though they might not agree totally with Gilbert's theology, were not so sure; they deplored the impact of the letters on the larger population, as well as among Friends themselves. John Comly worried that the controversy was "not only improper—but as likely to lead to difficulties."[30] Another wrote to the *Repository* to deny that "Amicus" represented the Society of Friends and to protest against publishing his essays without "authority and sanction previously obtained."[31] The editor of the *Repository* added to the forebodings of evangelicals by excerpting a letter from an unnamed Philadelphian to a friend in Wilmington. Cataloguing the heresies of Elias Hicks, which he tied to "Amicus," he listed that "Jesus Christ was no more than celebrated apostle—that people may be as good as he was—that many Friends are quite as good," that all are born holy, that there is no devil, that there is no need to observe the Sabbath, "that the Bible should not be made the guide!!!" "The Quakers here, the Hicksites deny every thing like christianity," he concluded; "they are blind, *spiritually*, as the Mussulman or the Hindoo."[32] A Ferris in-law expressed his uneasiness with the contest, and another evangelical complained that he envisioned the result as "laying waste all order—& giving up to the impulse of a power that seems as if it would lead to libertarianism and fanaticism."[33] Yet another accused "Amicus" of masterfully disguising a "poisonous hook" that would be swallowed by unsuspecting Christians. One non-Quaker reader predicted that the waning of Friends would be traced to the "Amicus" essays.[34] Because "Amicus" was so clearly identified as a defender of Hicks's views, the general ferment produced by his discussion with "Paul" at once highlighted the reformers' intentions and emboldened the evangelicals to take action against the perceived threat.

The evangelical concern about the necessity for dealing with Hicks and his followers surfaced formally in Meeting for Sufferings. This most important and powerful body in American Quakerism had become a closed corporation dominated by evangelicals. Its membership totaled fifty-six, four from each of the eleven quarterly meetings and twelve appointed by the yearly meeting directly; the *Rules of Discipline* provided specifically that the latter should live "in or near Philadelphia for the convenience of getting soon together," and a quorum required only twelve members.[35] The influence of Philadelphians was further enhanced by the common practice of having outlying and distant quarterly meetings designate residents of the city as their representatives. The evangelicals did not hesitate to use this practice for their benefit. Once, for example, the Southern Quarter with meetings in Delaware and Maryland instructed two of its representatives, Abraham Lower and Caleb Pierce, to nominate a person to fill a vacancy. They decided on Isaac Lloyd, a well-to-do city merchant, but before sending the nomination on to the Southern Quarterly Meeting, they mentioned their choice to Jonathan Evans. Evans bristled. "A very unsuitable person, . . . not initiated into the concerns of the society," he coolly assessed Lloyd, who was considered to be sympathetic to Hicks; he mentioned Ezra Comfort as a possibility, despite the distance of his home at Plymouth. Pierce and Lloyd could not now unite on a choice, Pierce insisting on Comfort, Lower on Lloyd, so the former agreed to inform the relevant committee of their impasse. Instead, he dispatched a note nominating Comfort anyway. Lower found out about the subterfuge before the quarter acted and prevented Comfort's selection.[36] With such tactics, Meeting for Sufferings would remain the stronghold of the evangelicals.

Moreover, this meeting had long ago, in 1806, stepped into a vacuum left when the Second Day Morning Meeting of ministers and elders was discontinued, partially because of opposition from rural Friends, afraid of the power it gave those who lived in the city. Dating back more than a century to 1701, and patterned after a similar body in London Yearly Meeting, the Second Day Morning Meeting endeavored to control the visits of ministering Friends from other yearly meetings and exercised oversight of doctrinal statements issued in the name of the Society. When this powerful committee was laid down in 1806, the yearly meeting turned over responsibility for overseeing theological writings to Meeting for Sufferings, but consciously failed to transfer authority to set limits on the visits of traveling ministers. This action—or more properly, lack of action—demonstrated the yearly meeting's intention to reduce centralized power.

According to the testimony later of one Hicksite, Halliday Jackson from Delaware County, city elders still met informally, considered prospective visitors, and, if it disapproved of them, authorized a member to raise the matter in the monthly meeting into whose confines the visitor wanted to come. Hence, for all practical purposes, the Second Day Morning Meeting had been resurrected.[37]

Jackson recalled specific incidents in which visitors had been told that their ministries were not welcomed. One Ohioan received a severe reprimand from Jonathan Evans after the visitor, described as "very worthy and innocent," spoke about love and unity in Pine Street Meeting, the rather diffident countryman presently went home, his intentions realized. On another occasion, Samuel Bettle, the clerk of the yearly meeting, stopped the visit of a traveling minister.[38] No doubt these actions by leading elders grew out of their concern for the good of the Society and presented few problems in times of general unity, but with sharpening factions, personal animosities, and questions about doctrine coming to the fore, what had been accepted as a legitimate exercise of power came now to be viewed as a threat to traditional testimonies, spiritual freedom, and local autonomy. Meeting for Sufferings, in the minds of Hicks's followers, represented the heart of the opposition to their reformation.

Hence Meeting for Sufferings was the most likely body to deal both with Elias Hicks and his mouthpiece "Amicus." Because the "Paul" and "Amicus" correspondence still dragged on, Hicks became the most immediate problem, particularly since he had just received a certificate from his meeting to attend the fall 1822 Baltimore Yearly Meeting and visit families in Philadelphia "if way should open."[39] In May when New York Yearly Meeting gathered, Joseph Whitall, a minister from Woodbury, New Jersey, a cousin of Isaac Hopper and member of Meeting for Sufferings, heard Hicks utter sentiments that Whitall characterized as unitarian. Whitall was greatly astonished and concerned; after all, he claimed to have previously defended Hicks against rumors that had circulated about his theology. Whitall heard Hicks declare "that the same power that made Christ a Christian must make us Christians and that the same power that saved him must save us."

Afterwards, Whitall objected directly to Hicks for his "unsound & unscriptural" words, but the venerable minister, according to Whitall, maintained his position and, indeed, expanded on it. "Christ," affirmed Hicks, "was no more than a man liable to fall like one of us," and "if he was any thing more, . . . it would destory the effect of his example." Aghast, Whitall predicted that such views would produce a schism among Friends, the worst one that had ever taken place. Hicks did not seem perturbed by this prospect and quoted a letter from a Philadelphia elder, whose name he would not divulge, that such sentiments were spreading in Penn's city. Confidently, he said he expected his views to prevail. Hicks, recounted Whitall, went on to deny Christ's miraculous conception and birth and insisted that Jesus did not become God's son until he was baptized.

Whitall could not reconcile these views with either the Bible or what early Friends believed. To believe that Jesus the Christ needed to be saved amounted to denying all the Old Testament prophecies concerning the promised Messiah. It marked Hicks's teaching as "antichristian, and not to be countenanced by members of our society, but to be discouraged and disowned, as lessening and opposing the authenticity of the scriptures and tending to lay waste and destroy the very foundation of the Christian edifice." Finally, such alien ideas smacked of the same heresies that had been earlier condemned by Irish and New England Friends, because they tended "to destroy discipline and to produce ranterism."[40] Drawn to prove that Hicks's doctrines undercut discipline and authority, this indictment gave all the justification the elders needed to move against him.

The plan devised by Evans, Bettle, and Whitall, among others, was to convene about a dozen loyal evangelicals immediately following the

September session of Meeting for Sufferings and to prevent Hicks from spreading his message within the city. As they entered the spacious Arch Street meetinghouse, Bettle, at whose home the strategy had been decided upon, whispered to the persons previously selected, "to stop at the rise of that meeting." Apparently, they did not know Abraham Lower's sentiments, because he was included. After a period of worship, Evans, dressed as always in knee breeches, long stockings, and buckled shoes, his voice the cultivated one of a man who fancied English literature, laid the problem before the gathering. "Elias Hicks is coming on here on his way to Baltimore Yearly Meeting. Friends know that he preaches doctrines contrary to the doctrines of our society; that he has given uneasiness to his friends at home, and they can't stop him." The burden, Evans had decided, now rested on Philadelphia's stalwarts: "unless we can stop him here, he must go on."

Whitall then added that two-thirds of New York Yearly Meeting stood with Hicks as did almost all members of his monthly and quarterly meeting. Evans prodded a bit, and Whitall told of Hicks's public testimony, which, Lower agreed out loud, if true, would mark Elias Hicks as no Christian. As Whitall proceeded, his recollections confirmed by Richard Jordan, an aged and respected minister who had also heard Hicks in New York, Lower interrupted, saying that some of these ideas did not conflict with the Society's position. Moreover, he went on, they were supported by the Scripture. John Cox, at sixty-eight, twenty-three years older than Lower, his hair long and grey, his right eye covered with a dark patch, broke in to chide Lower for his impertinence. The indictment resumed.

Evans had heard that Hicks had sent *The Celestial Magnet* from New York to the West, books that were unsound and indicated the sender's own unsoundness. Lower explained in Hicks's defense that he had only answered a correspondent's request, and Samuel Powell Griffitts, a medical doctor who would remain with the Orthodox, came to Hicks's aid, asserting that he had never heard him preach false doctrines. As the meeting continued, someone suggested a committee be named to "take an opportunity with Elias" when he arrived in Philadelphia and "in a prompt way to put a stop to his traveling in the ministry." Apparently the committee, whose composition is unclear, never acted; its functions were superseded and enlarged upon by a committee of ten elders representing all the meetings of the city. The meeting ended with an admonition to keep its object secret.[41]

Additional evidence to fuel evangelical opposition to Hicks arrived in Philadelphia in October before the New Yorker's visit. Thomas Eddy, an Empire State evangelical with a penchant for sneaky dealing, forwarded to a friend a manuscript he had written with instructions to have it recopied in someone else's hand and circulated among influential leaders. He specifically wanted it shown to William and Thomas Evans, sons of Jonathan. The essay purported to be an assessment of the state of New York Yearly Meeting, but it amounted to a savage attack on Hicks and his theological position. Eddy emphasized, both in his letter and essay, that Hicks's appeal was to the lower and unschooled portion of the community, a patent effort to identify his own views with people of more substantial standing.

Eddy attempted to show that Hicks was following a preconceived plan "to destroy the whole system of the Christian religion." Knowing that the best way to achieve his grand goal was to proceed slowly and subtly, Hicks began by referring to Jesus as merely a great prophet among other prophets. That idea established, the imaginative Eddy went on, Hicks spoke more openly against Christ's divinity, suggesting that he might have fallen as had Adam, else why would the Devil have tempted him? Then, according to Eddy, Hicks moved to "loosening the divine authenticity of the scriptures," preaching unitarianism, disregarding Sunday observance, and venting himself against "Banks, East Indian trade, civil government, agricultural Societies, Chemistry, which he called 'the Black Art,' the grand [Erie] Canal, [and] charitable societies." Because Hicks's ideas appealed to the uneducated, Eddy maintained, his influence became such that "he dictated and completely directed all the business of the Yearly Meeting."[42]

Eddy clearly implied that once one ventured down the slippery slope of Hicksism, one more than likely ended up as a dangerous malcontent, opposed to practically every established insitution of an orderly and progressive society. Eddy's interpretation of Hicks and his message also explained some of the fear with which evangelicals approached their problem. William Evans complained about a spirit "that would overturn the order of Society" and that failed to exhibit a proper "condenscension" to those who tried to support that order.[43] Passed from hand to hand, Eddy's essay went far to explain the elders' vigorous opposition to Hicks when he neared the city.

Eddy's letter and attacks soon fell into the wrong hands; and, if they explained the elders' opposition to Hicks, they also served to unify his allies.

Seizing their opportunity, the reformers rushed the Eddy material into print, much to the evident chargrin of Hicks's enemies. One close observer, Joseph Rakestraw, destined to side with the evangelicals, concluded that publication of Eddy's letter had worked in Hicks's favor by calling out his supporters and creating a kind of phalanx for him. "I don't approve of divisions," he explained to Ferris, "but there has been so much expressed against him—that there seems to be a necessity to stand up for the dear old man."[44]

Meanwhile, Hicks had crossed the boundaries of Philadelphia Yearly Meeting—to his adversaries it must have seemed like an invasion of an alien force—passing west of the city proper and visiting meetings along his route to Baltimore. He stopped at Ezra Comfort's Plymouth Meeting and during the course of his message spoke of spies who act under the guise of friendship while lying in wait for the innocent. After spending nearly a month in the Old Line State, he turned back toward Philadelphia, again visiting meetings along the way. He reached Little Creek, Delaware, in time for Southern Quarterly Meeting on November 26. Comfort, still expecting to be appointed the quarter's representative to Meeting for Sufferings, and his cohort Isaiah Bell, had journeyed to Delaware from the other direction.[45]

One thing Comfort and Bell heard there was clear—the Southern Quarter had not followed Jonathan Evans's advice and tabbed Comfort as its representative—but the subsequent controversy surrounding Hicks's comments made it uncertain what the New Yorker actually said. Whatever they heard, they informed Evans and other Philadelphians that Hicks had said that Christ "had no more power given him than man, for he was no more than man. He had nothing to do with healing the Soul, for that belongs to God alone . . . that man being obedient to the Spirit of God in him, could arrive at as great or greater degree of Righteousness than Jesus Christ."[46] Hicks later charged that neither of his accusers approached him at the time but scurried back to the city to spread word of his "false doctrines," a point that Hicks's friends used to show how their opponents violated the Discipline they claimed to uphold so carefully.[47]

Almost immediately, as word of Hicks's coming spread and with it reports of what he had said at Little Creek, the evangelicals began to move. This time their plans to confront Hicks got out. "Infamous conspiracy," fulminated reformer Isaac Hopper when he got the news.[48] One of the

"Amicus" collaborators, Evan Lewis, encouraged Hicks to stand fast once he arrived in Philadelphia. *"The tradition of the elders,"* or an easy and unthinking adoption of the opinions of past Friends, Lewis wrote, "we must leave behind before we can be properly qualified to stand in the gap between priestcraft and liberty of conscience."[49]

At seven o'clock on the evening of the day Hicks rode into town, December 7, 1822, Samuel P. Griffitts and Ellis Yarnall, both elders, one from Arch Street, the other from Western District Meeting, paid a visit to Hicks, who had taken up his customary lodging with Samuel R. Fisher, a member of Evans's meeting. They explained that reports had circulated about his unsoundness, and they recapped the charges of Whitall, Comfort, and Bell. Having been forewarned and given time to consider his response, Hicks took his stand on the Discipline, denying that Philadelphia elders had any authority to question him about what he had said in New York and refusing to respond to the Comfort-Bell allegations because they had not come to him first and privately with their concerns, as their own rules dictated.

At that point, the old minister softened a bit—Griffitts, after all, had defended Hicks earlier in September—and promised to give them what satisfaction he could if they came as friends. Both said they did, implying if not saying explicitly that they were not acting officially, and Hicks informed them pointblank that all the charges were untrue. They discussed the matter candidly, at one point, Hicks asking if they believed in Christ's divinity. Answering affirmatively, the two elders refused to say in what way. They pressed Hicks to meet with his accusers, but, insisting that the Discipline should control, he declined until they made amends to their meetings for violating "Gospel order." As far as his doctrines were concerned, the elders left satisfied or at least so Yarnall acknowledged later to Benjamin Ferris. Griffitts remarked that he was "better prepar'd to hear Elias Hicks preach than ever."[50]

If in fact Griffitts and Yarnall were reassured after their fifty-minute conversation, the matter might have stopped there; but both Hicks and his antagonists were strong willed and determined. The visitor made the next move. His certificate from Jericho authorized him to pay family visits to members of the Green Street and Northern District meetings, the former alive with his active supporters. After his two inquisitors had gone, three Friends from Green Street, including Lower, came to Fisher's house to confer with Hicks. Because Hicks had been unable to attend their last monthly meeting and seek approval for his proposed visit, Lower suggested they might call together the elders, overseers, and some of the active members to lay the concern before them.

Although this course was unusual, it did not violate customary procedures, so the next day, on First Day morning before meeting, the three canvassed the officers about a meeting to hear Hicks at seven that evening. (Large numbers got a chance to hear him that afternoon, too, but many were turned away: the alleys and side streets were chocked with people.[51]) Leonard Snowden, one of two evangelical elders at Green Street, proffered his opinion that only a monthly meeting could give permission for family visits and added that he preferred not to do anything that would run counter to the plans of the city's elders. Nowithstanding this objection, the announcement was made, and that evening the informal gathering voiced its approval of the visits, with Snowden and Joseph Scattergood, the other evangelical elder, dissenting. The assembled Friends requested Snowden to accompany their distinguished guest, but, pleading age and infirmities, he forbore. At the rise of the meeting he did warn Hicks against engaging in "matters of speculation" during his visits. When Hicks commenced his rounds to the meeting's 140 families the next day with a more willing elder, Snowden refused to receive him, a course followed also by Joseph Scattergood. The opposition, now open, served to embolden Hicks and, he thought, unblock closed minds.[52]

Monday evening, the 9th, two elders again waited upon Hicks with the now expected request — that he meet with his accusers. The answer remained the same. At this latest rebuff, elders from the city's five meetings met and delegated Yarnall to intervene with Hicks once more. He had a mind to spurn their offer again, but his associates argued that an outright refusal might convince those not involved that he feared to confer with the elders. He also recognized, and told the elders, that while he was among them he was amenable to them. Accordingly, Hicks attempted to turn the whole business to his advantage by agreeing to a meeting at Green Street on Thursday afternoon. The reformers planned to confront the elders with a contingent of their own, whereas the examiners assumed they would have Hicks all to themselves.

The Hicksites lined up an impressive collection of leading Friends to stand by their man. (They wrote Edward Hicks, Elias's cousin, but he pleaded that tending a sick child would force him to stay in Newtown; he did guess that his presence would "stir up a greater degree of enmity" even Elias's. "The storm has been long time a brewing," he said.[53]) John Comly and James Walton came in from Byberry, Robert Moore from Easton, Maryland, and Evan Lewis and William Poole from Wilmington, as well as about fifteen members of Green Street Meeting itself, including Abraham Lower. David Seaman, the New Yorker who was traveling with Hicks, was present to testify to the statements that had caused Whitall such trouble. The Orthodox side was represented by all but three of the ten male elders of Philadelphia; Jonathan Evans was indisposed, and another evangelical had "become uneasy in his mind and returned home."

The meeting settled into a period of silent worship, which ended when Thomas Wistar, a prominent and wealthy gentleman acting as leader of the elders, commented on the large number of people present. They had expected, he explained, "an opportunity with Elias Hicks and his companion" from New York; if the large group "thought proper to keep their seats, they [the elders] had better withdraw." Someone spoke up, saying that, if they could not confer privately with Hicks, they "should take it for granted that the charges were true." Statements like this led Hicks to wonder why the elders were placing so much emphasis on "flying reports" when people were present who could give them the facts. But an elder insisted that they "might as well withdraw if the other friends chose to stay."

As the group wandered back and forth across the issues, Caleb Pierce warned, "friends had better keep to the one point, whether Elias would give *them* a private opportunity." Again Hicks declined, and Wistar asked directly, "are we to understand this to be thy answer?" Back came the expected "yes," and Wistar rejoined, "then we are to conclude the charges are true," a conclusion to which Hicks refused to accede. Seaman, able to contain himself no longer, blurted out that they had made no charges. Hicks said he was ready to hear their charges with his witnesses present. Isaac Lloyd, one of the elders, was too exasperated with the proceedings to understand them.

Finally the elders, seeing that Hicks and his friends intended to stand fast, rose to go. As they did so, Thomas Stewardson, whose wealth and vast holdings of land made him unaccustomed to opposition, flung out, "The *ministers* are *answerable* to the *Elders*." That comment summed up the basis of the disagreement, and Hicks retorted above the noise of feet shuffling and people mumbling, "I have a certificate from my *friends at home* and I am *answerable* to them." Another elder went out muttering that this "is very strange procedure indeed." Two elders, Isaac Lloyd and

Samuel Noble, the latter having been Hicks's escort to the meeting's families, remained behind.[54]

After the elders' departure, another brief period of silent waiting ensued and a sense of unity prevailed—at least that was the way one chronicler described the scene. Hicks picked up on elder Stewardson's remark, noting that "it was time for friends to assert their rights, and not suffer themselves to be imposed upon" by those who desired "to have the whole rule and government of *ministers*." The electrified Friends vigorously nodded their assent.

The Hicksite party of reform can be dated from this meeting of December 12, almost from this final assessment, for Hicks himself had thereby given the marching order to his supporters. Certainly the issues had been clarified and defined. The group had watched the elders in action and were chagrined at the way their spokesman, old and venerable as he was, had been treated. William Poole, Hicks's close friend from Wilmington, dashed off a note to Benjamin Ferris and Eli Hilles, both stalwarts in the cause back home. "Extreme agitation prevails," he scribbled, because "utmost injustice is practicing against Elias." "If all was known to the middle aged & younger part of Society," his words became frantic, "they could scarce be restrained from abuse—to the Elders."[55]

Still at Green Street meetinghouse, the assembly continued. Lower proposed that Robert Moore, who had been at the Southern Quarter, recount what had happened so they might respond to the Comfort-Bell charges. "Elias's services and gospel labours were very acceptable," reported Moore, and "friends had great unity with him at that Quarter and elsewhere and had not heard any such expressions [as Comfort and Bell alleged] from him;" nor did Moore think "they had been used by him." Hicks claimed Comfort had evinced no objection to him when they were both at Little Creek—indeed he "appeared to have a friendship for, and unity with him," and never asked for a private interview. The put-upon Hicks closed by observing that he had been improperly used—one report used the phrase, "cruelly treated"—since he came to the city, but he prayed that those who had retired might be forgiven. At the end, such a sense of unity prevailed that one attender remarked, "I had never been in a Meeting which seemed more evidently owned by the *Divine Presence*."[56]

Hicks continued his visits, and by the following Thursday, the nineteenth, when Green Street Monthly Meeting convened, he had nearly finished. The meeting formally endorsed his public and private ministry and instructed the clerk to so indicate on his certificate.⁵³ In almost all of his communications during meetings all over town, Hicks had carefully spoken to what was emerging as the principal allegation against him—that his views about Christ's divinity made him a deist or Unitarian. The controversy attracted large numbers who came to meetings both morning and afternoon. At Pine Street Meeting on December 15, twice as many milled around outside as could get in.⁵⁸

One of Hicks's auditors, apparently not a Friend, sent a report to the press when the celebrated preacher spoke in Chester County. "The Chester Plough Boy" confessed that he had never received so much instruction from a minister of any sect. The congregation had sat in silence for nearly thirty minutes when Hicks arose from his seat in the gallery and gazed across the audience with a "paternal tenderness." He looked like a "Shepherd of Israel." "His venerable appearance, his burden of years, his whitened locks, his simplicity of manner," joined to his simple, forceful, and clear arguments to hold his audience enthralled for an hour and a half. Taking as his text, "a work well begun is half done," he stressed that people's religious faith should be as simple as a child's; instead theologians corrupted simple religion, which he defined as "righteousness, justice and mercy." The great enemy of true religion was to blindly follow human ways. "I appeal to your understanding," he exclaimed, "and wish not that any man should believe anything because I assert it." People attain heaven as "the result of acting up the dictates of God in man," and hell comes when one's soul experiences the torment of transgressing those dictates. Rightly understood, he said as he came to his climax, Christianity involves no mysteries, for "it is so plain that the wayfaring man can not miss it."⁵⁹

Still remaining a mystery, however, were Hicks's exact views on the divinity of Jesus, or at least evangelicals wanted clarification. On the same day that Green Street Meeting approved his services, Hicks had a talk with Ezra Comfort, who left an account of their conversation. The principal topic centered on Hicks's doctrine of Christ, with Comfort repeating what he had told others about the Southern Quarterly Meeting. The evangelical Comfort expressed amazement at the novelty of Hicks's belief that "Jesus had no power given him to heal the soul, for that belongs to God only," and that he had no more power than man, "for he was no more than man." Hicks assented except that he believed Christ was more than man: He was the son of God and perfect man because—and this point literal-minded evangelicals could never comprehend about the way traditional

Quakers viewed Jesus—and only because "He fulfilled all righteousness and . . . lived without sin."

Each commenced to quote Scripture at the other, to no final conclusion. Comfort attempted to show that his antagonist thought Joseph was Jesus' father, but Hicks countered that, as he had not lived then, "he could not tell whose son he was." Should we pray to Christ, queried Comfort? Praying to him, Hicks replied, was like praying to an image, for Christ had been seen with the outward eyes. Hicks expressed his own surprise at those so ignorant that they could not understand his point, yet would presume to teach the people; such teachers "were so outward, and knew so little about spiritual things."[60] Hicks's harsh comment about his detractors was directed at Comfort, whom he considered "Too ignorant a man, to make a fair statement of any subject, he might hear communicated."[61]

The conversation reflected two different approaches to theological authority. For Comfort and the other evangelicals, Hicks depreciated the Bible and Christian orthodoxy; the objective events described in the New Testament had to be accepted by the believer—at the beginning, as the basis of one's pilgrimage of faith, according to the evangelicals. Indeed after one had accepted the authority of the Bible, hardly any pilgrimage was left. For Hicks, on the other hand, doctrines grew out of experience, the reality that one encountered beyond the printed word; they had to correspond with human sensibility. To Hicks's party, the Christ encrusted with nearly two millennia of doctrines had to give way to the Christ who had lived righteously and given other humans an example of how they too could live—a Christ, the Hicksites were presumptuous enough to insist, whose spirit could lead people in the present. Anything else was outward and misleading.

On the same day, December 19, ten elders addressed a letter to Hicks in which they rehearsed once more the charges that Whitall, Comfort, and Bell had leveled at him. After reviewing their efforts to secure the truth from him, they solemnly declared, "we cannot have religious unity with thy conduct, nor with the doctrines thou art charged with promulgating." Two days following, Hicks responded with his usual denials. Standing again on the Discipline, he averred that the certificates from his monthly and quarterly meeting, all issued after the yearly meeting where Whitall had heard him, demonstrated that he was in unity with the only Friends to whom he was amenable. As for Comfort, Hicks claimed he had violated gospel order in not conferring personally with him. "Your requisitions," Hicks closed, were "arbitrary and contrary to the established order of our Society."[62]

The authors of both letters composed them for public circulation and consumption, as a way to influence the opinions of Friends who were still on the sidelines. To the same end, three members of the Southern Quarter signed a letter dated December 21, the same day as Hicks's response to the elders, in which they added their testimony to rebut Comfort's charges of infidelity against their Long Island Friend. Two months later, twenty-two more of those who had been at Little Creek affirmed that he had preached "the Truth of the Gospel" while among them.[63]

Philadelphia, as might be imagined, was a hothouse of rumors surrounding the events of December—one report had it that Ezra Comfort had proposed to meet Hicks, but the latter supposedly replied that Comfort "was really too insignificant a person to be so indulged."[64] The news of developments in Penn's city spread to New York and encouraged supporters of the reformation there to hope that Philadelphia's "Rabbis" would be routed.[65] Some Friends who disliked open confrontations doubted that much good would come from all the agitation, but the more active reformers were of a different mind. William Poole, a close observer, saw dry bones shaken and the opposition overruled: More significant for one who sought a reformation, the old had been bypassed by the young and middle-aged, who received Hicks's doctrines gladly and gave both silent and vocal approval to them. "The intention of thy visit has therefore been accomplished," Poole informed his mentor.[66] From the public prints came a similar, if more jarring, analysis: Those leaders who opposed Hicks "are carried away in the pursuit of wealth, power, and fame; . . . their chief ambition shows itself in an eager pursuit of riches and honor." How can such men, asked this person who wrote under the name of "Berean," call "upon others to moderate their desires of worldly things, and follow a meek and crucified Saviour?"[67]

Those who pitched their tents in the evangelical camp had every reason to date the beginning of the split from Elias Hicks's visit in December 1822.[68] Hicks had recognized that opposition to his ideas was strongest in Philadelphia. While his friends and associates would carry some of the burden, Hicks had such a broad appeal and such a sure way of arousing his opponents that he was indispensible to the reformation cause. He became the symbol and rallying point for those wanting to promote a reformation. His adherents, of course, had no trouble seeing him as such a symbol, and defenders of evangelical orthodoxy grudgingly admitted the same thing. In a lengthy analysis published in the *Saturday Evening Post* after the separation occurred, one evangelical spokesman commented on his standing. Many who had joined the dissidents had picked up Hicks-like opinions from other sources and harbored "secret jealousies—personal prejudices—wounded feelings—and opposite views of men and measures, but whenever he has appeared, . . . these latent and hitherto inert elements of discord and separation, have . . . ranged themselves on his side." Thus as the Orthodox reflected on it, Hicks's influence was not surprising. His earnest and vehement oratory, "antique appearance," reputation for probity, boldness and simply-stated views, all served to overwhelm his listeners and win them to his cause.[69] His opponents simply had no one who could match him.

Hence everyone recognized that Hicks's visit to Philadelphia galvanized his supporters—Poole's letter to him mentioned one book and two pamphlets that were presently coming off the press—and demonstrated to them that they had broad support. By 10 P.M. on one night alone, an estimated 100 people showed up at Samuel Fisher's to speak a word with Hicks.[70] Just as important, the events of December boosted the reformers' self-confidence. With their own eyes they saw that the elders need not be feared, and they were encouraged to believe they could win.

History seemed to be moving in their direction,[71] and the reformers conspired to give it a big shove. They found the recently created *Saturday Evening Post* open to their communications, so almost weekly they sent some kind of letter to defend Hicks or attack his opponents. Even while Hicks was in the city—he departed on Christmas Day—the *Post* carried a long laudatory excerpt from a Friend's journal that referred to him as "the first minister of the Society."[72] Two weeks later, the reformers kicked off the first issue of the new year with an article that praised Hicks's "powerful ministry." He held "forth the great doctrines of Christianity in their purity, clearing them of their errors, the corruption and false expositions, inspired upon them by tradition."[73]

Because of such achievements, Hicks's friends expressed amazement and regret that a man so highly esteemed had been subjected to a "persecution at once so unmanly and unjust."[74] They quoted from writings of early Quakers to disprove charges that Hicks was "an innovator upon original principles and inclined to Unitarianism," and they deplored actions of the pacific descendants of Penn who now seemed wont to follow other sects and unsheathe the sword of persecution.[75] The articles went on and on, until in June 1823, the editor confessed that he had never intended his paper to be a vehicle of religious controversy; but the reformers' pieces continued to appear.[76] The editor conceded that Hicks's opponents were "all honorable men," but he also expressed his own satisfaction that the misrepresentations concerning the New Yorker and the treatment he had received "savoured strongly of Persecution" — the "trials that all reformers had been subjected to."[77]

Not only had the elders to endure such criticism in the press, they were presently confronted by a new challenge, a woman minister from Indiana whose theology paralleled Hicks's and whose appeal rivaled his. Priscilla Hunt had been at Little Creek during the Southern Quarterly Meeting on her way northward and eastward, and now with Hicks gone, she took up where he left off. Her messages provoked bitter controversy — the elders claimed she had been dealt with by her own quarterly meeting for unsoundness, while her supporters described her as "that dear precious servant" of the Lord. Practically every place she appeared the meetinghouses overflowed with people unable to find seats. On Sunday afternoon, February 23, she came to Pine Street Meeting and spoke on Christ feeding the multitudes in the wilderness.

Her address on this occasion revealed the way traditional Quakers allegorized their messages. When the master commanded the people to be seated, he was, she said, recommending that they take on a humble air and leave behind the "city of confusion and the mountains of exaltation." At that point Jesus would "break the bread that was meet for them and hand it to his disciples & they to the multitudes — they all would be sent away rejoicing — and they would come to know their wilderness to be an eden and their desert as the garden of the Lord." She took her seat but in a few moments rose again to continue her message, speaking for about an hour all told. She touched on parties and the differences between creaturely and godly zeal — the former heated, irritable, and easily ruffled, the latter cool, mild, temperate, and full of love and good works. Recognizing that she was upsetting some evangelicals in her audience, she concluded with "now beloveds, this seems plain, but I must speak it," for she claimed nothing of her own. Afterwards, one who had previously appeared prejudiced was "broken and tendered" and went up to shake her hand with praise on his lips: "This is like healing oil."[78]

For better than four months, Hunt stayed in Philadelphia and its environs, visiting all the monthly meetings. She was able to "thresh the mountains of formality, with a sharp threshing instrument."[79] The reforming element trumpeted that the city's Quakers had been called to "virtue's shrine in strains so enchanting that even angels might have leaned from heaven to hear." At Merion she complained of too much external show without the inner reality of religious faith, a situation producing self-righteousness like wool to hide the wolves' actual nature.[80] Over the opposition of Jonathan Evans she was back at Pine Street on March 16. There she attacked the folly of those who would judge their brothers and sisters to protect the cause of truth: "the truth—it needed no defence." Let people regulate themselves, she advised; all one could do for another was "to admonish in the Love of God." "Schism & confusion" resulted from judgment.

Then Hunt spoke about doctrine and promptly stepped into the arena. Proceeding gingerly, she compared reason to the star that had guided the wise men to the infant Jesus and affirmed her belief "that reason would lead us to Christ & Christ to God." Reason, she went on, could not discover God nor was it sufficient for human salvation unless people attended "to the precepts of him to whom it led." William Evans arose as soon as Hunt took her place and warned, "Friends, Those are not the Doctrines which this Society professes—we never believed that Reason led to Christ;" only the Bible did that. Hunt waited for Evans to finish and then knelt in prayer, the customary signal for all in the meeting to rise; some on the high seats did so slowly and reluctantly—Evans had to be reminded by a touch on the arm, and one elder kept her seat throughout.[81] The reformers saw nothing wrong with this emphasis because they held that reason was not separate and distinct from God's inner revelation to each individual. One of them wrote later that reason, feeble as its light may be, "is altogether sufficient to shew the *unreasonableness*" of Orthodox pretensions.[82] The evangelicals, as Evans's comment indicated, worried that giving reason such a large role usurped the place of the Scriptures and led to unitarian infidelity.

Those accustomed to manipulating the levers of power were disturbed, perhaps taken aback, at the acclaim that greeted Hicks and Hunt, but they were not beaten. The visiting English minister William Forster and one of the "signing elders" followed Hunt as she visited scattered meetings.[83] One reformer, not knowing what they might plan, compared them to the "monster of deep when he has the harpoon fixed in his flesh."

Each local meeting became a miniature battleground between the two factions. When reformer John Mott preached at Green Street in January, a woman Friend rebuked those who espoused Hicks's doctrines and finally attacked that "man who had so unprofitably drawn the lighter parts of Society together at his meetings!" From the back of the room a young man called out, "are friends prepared for such backbiting and calumny as this?" An older Friend then observed that such communications as these "*would have a tendency to divide in Jacob and scatter in Israel.*"[84] This first public reference to the possibility of a schism highlighted the seriousness that now marked the conflict between the two parties.

With disagreement mounting into such open hostility, the elders became more determined to reassert their power. On January 4, 1823, nine of the ten elders who had signed the earlier letter to Hicks sent him another one. As before, they lamented his refusal to meet them and clear up the controversy over his views, "very different from those which are held and maintained by our religious society." Still, they promised no action themselves, recommending only that his Friends at home give the matter their "weighty attention." Jonathan Evans added a postscript uniting with the letter and its concern that the Society "not be under the imputation of holding doctrines which do not accord with the testimony of the Holy Scriptures."[85] Hicks answered, but did not mail his letter to the elders directly; instead he sent it to a confederate with instructions to distribute it as he saw fit. He did not change his position that the Philadelphia elders had violated the Discipline.[86]

On January 17, the Meeting for Sufferings moved to defend the "interests of Truth" — this quaint phrase harked back to the days when Quakers were called "Friends of the Truth" — by intervening in the "Paul" and "Amicus" debate. The most immediate concern was the approaching publication of the newspaper articles in book form; the meeting simply could not allow "Amicus' " views to go abroad representing those of the Society. The elders took two actions: They delegated one of their number to go to Wilmington and secure from the publisher a promise that he would include a disclaimer both in the *Christian Repository* and the book. Porter agreed only to the first request, perhaps because some subscribers to the book had threatened to withdraw if the minute were added. Then they approved a statement describing the theological position of Quakers on the matter of Christ's divinity, the Trinity, and the Bible.[87]

Entitled "Extracts from the Writings of Primitive Friends, concerning the Divinity of Our Lord and Saviour, Jesus Christ," the eleven-page pamphlet carried Jonathan Evans's signature and a statement that it would be distributed across the yearly meeting to illustrate "doctrines of the Christian religion, which have been always held, and are most surely believed by us." The authors of the excerpts were not listed, nor were the sources from which they came, although the compilers relied heavily on Robert Barclay's *Apology* of 1676. The statement affirmed that the Scriptures "were written by divine inspiration" and "cannot be subjected to the fallen, corrupt reason of man," even when "all our doctrines be tried by them." Jesus Christ, said the meeting, "is the beloved and only begotten Son of God who . . . through the Holy Ghost, was conceived and born of the virgin Mary." He "is the propitiation for our sins" and those of the world. Despite these firm evangelical sentiments, the meeting narrowed the distance between themselves and their opposition by declaring that "the way to come to that faith, is to receive and obey the manifestation of [Christ's] divine light and grace in the conscience, which leads men to believe and value, and not to disown or undervalue Christ."[88] The meeting divided about how to distribute the pamphlet, and not until a second session in the afternoon of the seventeenth was unity found to approve printing ten thousand copies but awaiting yearly meeting action in April before distributing any.[89]

To Hicks's followers, the statement represented an attempt by the evangelical elders to impose on the Society a "creed" that reflected their theology. A "combination" had now surfaced from its secret conclaves and seemed determined to use the dispute between "Paul" and "Amicus" as a pretext for their scheme and to cut off their opponents. Benjamin Ferris, whose writings spread this interpretation, saw the effort as one designed to make "*the Trinitarian faith*, in its most objectionable features" the standard for Friends.[90] Before long some evangelicals in New Jersey were heard saying that there ought to be a separation; things would be all right "if all the Unitarians would go off together."[91]

In all truth, Ferris's interpretation distorted reality and read back into the past an interpretation inevitably colored by subsequent events. The elders acted as people with power always act. They perceived a problem, and they moved to deal with it in accustomed ways. They expected to succeed. They might have to compromise—in this case, wait a bit over three months to send out their statement of belief—but they *would* send it out and they *would* put down this threat. That approach, which had always proved adequate in the past, represented the tradition of the elders. The only thing that this ruling elite did not expect, because they were not blessed with foresight, was that their opponents would use the cry of "creed" to mobilize the reforming element at the upcoming yearly meeting.

CHAPTER 7

"No outward law,"
OR
The Reformers React

A TRADITION EXISTS AMONG FRIENDS of Philadelphia Yearly Meeting that it always rains during the April week it is in session. The storms that broke out during the 1823 sittings within the impressive Arch Street meetinghouse proved much more damaging than anything the heavens brought that year. The principal topic was the "confession of faith" or "creed"—its proper title was "Extracts from the Writings of Primitive Friends"—that Meeting for Sufferings proposed to issue as a definition of the Quaker faith. Ever since its approval in January, the reformers and followers of Elias Hicks had organized to defeat the proposal and, if possible, win approval for other reforms aimed at reducing the authority of those who wanted to move the Society firmly into the evangelical fold. Yearly meeting in 1823 promised, as one observer predicted, "to be a trying time."[1]

Thunder rumbled already in the distance. In March, John Comly, assistant clerk of the yearly meeting who had served on the committee that recommended the controverted statement and who had acquiesced in its adoption, confronted Jonathan Evans, leader of the evangelical elders. Comly laid "things pretty close home" to Evans about the intolerance that had been shown to Hicks during his December visit.[2] Also in March, Stephen Grellet, the aristocrat refugee from the French Revolution, moved with his family from New York to Burlington, New Jersey, motivated in part by the expectation of trouble in Philadelphia. "The little dark cloud," he told his journal, that once hung only over Jericho "is now like a thick darkness over the land."[3] Some overzealous reformers wrote anonymous letters to Hicks's opponents, producing "too much warmth."[4]

Of a more substantive nature, the reformers were already planning to use the existing uneasiness with the proposal of Meeting for Sufferings to modify the rules and appoint elders for limited, rather than life, terms in meetings and on that body.[5] In Green Street Meeting, the overseers of this strongly Hicks-leaning group prepared to labor with Leonard Snowden and Joseph Scattergood, their two evangelical elders, and require them to abjure the rudeness they exhibited to Hicks during his late visit.[6]

Less active, apparently, were the evangelicals. They did have the strong support of William Forster, a British minister of evangelical bent. Forster's personality was not as trying to the reformers as those of some of the other English visitors who were in Philadelphia in early 1823, but they eschewed what one called his "English theology" or the "old presbyterian notion" about Christ the eternal son of God. Although he visited all the meetings in Philadelphia, he spoke only at Pine Street, where he admonished the younger set to respect their elders and avoid thinking that they needed no mediator with God. Hicks's supporters commented on the small attendance Forster drew and concluded that fears he would be a major force at the yearly meeting were unfounded. George Withy, another English visitor, put in circulation a "little pitiful pamphlet," as one reformer described it.[7] Williams Evans, Jonathan's more active son, toured the city's meetings in March, found a party spirit prevailing, and returned to mourn that some were working to "subvert the order and principles of the Society."[8]

On Monday, April 21, the one hundred-forty second yearly meeting of Friends in Philadelphia convened and immediately the two sides squared off. One of the first, and usually perfunctory, orders of business was to read the minutes of the past year's sessions of Meeting for Sufferings. As they were being read, it suddenly dawned on the reformers what the evangelical strategy was, for the "Extracts from the Writings of Primitive Friends" was included and, after approval of the minutes, would be distributed as part of that year's business. It amounted to a kind of back door way of endorsing the statement as approved by Meeting for Sufferings.[9] Many of those who spoke were not considered by the evangelical clerk, Samuel Bettle, to have any weight or influence: In fact, he testified later that he had never heard some of them before, either in yearly meeting or any other meeting.[10] Certainly Bettle never witnessed the kinds of raucous assaults on the leaders of the Society that would pound his ears in the next two days. One participant said the controversy "spread like a fire among light rubbish."[11]

First, John Comfort of Falls, a relative of the sainted John Woolman, but described by one evangelical as "a man of no religious weight," asked point blank, referring to the reading of the "Extracts," "who hath required this at your hands?" One Friend said he could not unite with the doctrines in the "Extracts," another averred that they were contrary to reason, Scripture and revelation, yet another engaged in an exegesis of Scripture to disprove that "there are three that bear witness in heaven" and quoted Sir Isaac Newton, much to the amazement of Bettle who said he had never encountered such an ill-suited approach in a Friends gathering. Those accustomed to making decisions were amazed at the opposition their plan had unleashed. After three hours, the meeting recessed until the following morning, undoubtedly with the evangelicals hoping the storm might subside during the night.[12]

Next morning at nine o'clock, however, things got worse for those in power. Dr. Robert Moore of Easton, Maryland, in the Southern Quarter, one of those who had signed the statement in December defending Hicks, asked that the "confession of faith" be expunged from the record. A chorus of assents greeted this suggestion, then someone else proposed a committee be appointed to investigate the actions of Meeting for Sufferings. That, too, won the assent of some Friends, including the combative Abraham Lower, a member of Sufferings; he announced his own support for even more radical change, specifically for appointing elders to designated terms. Edward Atlee, a medical doctor known for his outspoken opposition to clerical influence, shouted out, "liberty, rational liberty!" Coach and signpainter Edward Hicks, echoing his better-known cousin, maintained creeds had caused divisions and quarrels in the church and that "Meeting for Sufferings cannot and dare not urge or saddle this creed upon the Society." Before sitting down he appealed to young people to speak as God's oracles on the subject. According to Bettle, who sat at a table in front of the room and could readily see those who spoke, every single person who opposed the "Extracts" was associated with the Hicks group of reformers.[13]

Bettle was in a quandry. As clerk, he had to sum up the sense of the meeting, but as a prominent evangelical and member of Sufferings, he favored issuing the statement. To one side, John Comly, the assistant clerk, leaned over and whispered every few minutes that he ought to go ahead and make a minute removing the "Extracts" from the record. From the other side, Jonathan Evans took the floor to plead that Meeting for Sufferings had done nothing more than select some quotations from the writings of early Quakers and publish them, as with similar material in the past. Certainly, he confided, no one wanted to impose anything on the Society. One Friend countered that he had hoped no member of Meeting for Sufferings would speak on the matter; their actions had spoken clearly enough already. An evangelical put in that "a society without principles was a nonentity," a view with which Bettle agreed but one offering little immediate guidance to him. Finally, he proposed that the pamphlet not be published but that its text remain in the minutes. Late into the second day and after a bit more debate, the meeting approved this solution.[14]

On balance the reformers, those opposing doctrinal innovations and creedal statements along evangelical lines, carried the day. They had prevented issuance of the "Extracts"—the Orthodox group would not publish them until after the separation—and, more important, they had demonstrated that a significant number of members were ready to side with them against the powerful Meeting for Sufferings. Edward Hicks wrote his cousin that the evangelicals had been humbled by their setback and "seem willing to sine articles of peace on almost any conditions." Hicks was especially pleased that younger Friends had taken such a leading role. True, the reformers had not cleared the record—some remarked that leaving the statment in the minutes amounted to acknowledging it as the doctrine of Friends, but others pointed out that primitive Friends had, in fact, written what was contained in the document. Moreover, the yearly meetings' action prevented the "Extracts" from being used formally as a standard of faith.[15]

The rest of the meeting dealt with routine business, except that the younger element among the reformers initiated a discussion of slavery and the use of products made with slave labor, the latter an embarrassing topic for the well-to-do city elders. The pugnacious Edward Hicks, during a period of prayer on the last day, decided that his "heavenly father" required him to "take up my cross [and] not partake of the produce of slavery." Both Abraham Lower and Jesse Kersey joined Hicks in his testimony to the meeting; Hicks was so unnerved by his first attempt to speak on the subject that he could hardly push his words out.

The meeting appointed Hicks also to the epistle committee that was responsbile for drawing up an address to be sent to other yearly meetings throughout the world. Though he had wanted to include a statement condeming the recent caucuses of the elders, other members overruled him and took "all the kernal out of my Epistle & left nothing but the Shell." As the meeting drew to a close on the afternoon of April 25, William Forster delivered himself of a long prayer informing the Lord that all was lost for the evangelical cause.[16] A woman Friend, carried away by the attacks on authority, was heard to say that she hoped never to see the Bible in the hands of her children.[17]

Everywhere they looked or journeyed following the stormy 1823 yearly meeting, the evangelicals saw the hand and activities of those, as one characterized them, "so deluded as to believe they are engaged in the work of reformation." At the next quarterly select meeting of ministers and elders in Philadelphia, William Evans uncovered once more the same party spirit that he feared would overturn the order of Friends, and after visiting Moorestown, New Jersey, with Forster on May 7, he left heavy of heart because of the rampant theological speculation there. Forster, according to Evans, carried a heavy burden because of the unsoundness of doctrine he had witnessed.[18]

When she arrived in August 1823, Anna Braithwaite discovered the same baleful weaknesses. Unlike Forster, she displayed no reluctance to do open battle against Hicks's influence. Braithwaite claimed she came to America with little advance knowledge of the theological disputes then going on, but once she encountered them, she leaped into the fray and rapidly became one of the sharpest disputants.[19] Her efforts, as well as those of her followers, would fuel the debate and lend the evangelical cause a force that the more staid and proper Philadelphia elders had no taste for. Such foreign "embassadors," one Hicksite-leaning commentator wrote, "have . . . again kindled up the coals of disunion among us nearly to a blaze and by continual fanning them are kept alive to the grief of a large portion . . . both in N York and Pennsylvania."[20]

Braithwaite's coming had been much bruited about, and she was quickly taken under the care of Stephen Grellet, a development that foreshadowed the course her visit would take.[21] She spoke forthrightly against what the evangelicals called the "new doctrines" of those advocating "religious *liberty* and *reformation.*" Pamphlets were put out and rumors spread about her efforts; her champions responded in kind. When Hicks visited some of the same meetings after Braithwaite, he described them in a "mixed and unstable state" caused by teachers who had not kept to "the original foundation, the *light and spirit of truth*" but relied instead on "mere tradition." From the opposing camp, Grellet looked and saw the thick clouds emanating from Jericho about to overcome the land.[22]

The mutal recriminations grew directly out of two visits the English visitor paid to Hicks at his home in Jericho, the first in January 1824, the second in March. Hicks's reputation and striking appearance—Braithwaite described him as a tall, thin person, dressed as Friends of one hundred years before, and looking quite venerable—and the fact that she had come to visit *him*, all combined to put her nerves on edge. The support of her two companions, one of them the clerk of New York Yearly Meeting, Samuel Parsons, as well as her sense of divine help, stiffened her resolve.[23]

Their first conversation, following dinner at the Hickses, lasted for nearly two hours and began, as the host recalled it, with Braithwaite asking about one of his remarks in the quarterly meeting of ministers and elders held earlier in the day. Hicks had commented then on the absence of three-quarters of the representatives appointed earlier to attend the meeting. He suggested that a more careful attention to the unerring Divine Spirit would likely lead to naming representatives who would carry out their responsibilities. To Hicks, such an approach was an elemental one for Friends, and when Braithwaite disagreed, he expressed his surprise, pondered her obvious deficiency, and told her she might, on reflection, see the correctness of his position.

Hicks tended to dominate any conversation of which he was a part, and it appeared from recollections of both that Braithwaite made few substantive comments; instead her occasional interjections only served to goad him on. He maintained that the Scriptures were regarded too highly by most professing Christians—she remembered he said "Friends"—resulting in wars, hireling ministers, and "mere relics of the Jewish laws," such as water baptism and the "passover supper." When he emphasized the traditional Quaker position that the Spirit was before and over the Bible, thus "the primary and only rule of faith and practice," she took him to mean that paying attention to the Spirit would reveal all that anyone needed. And he certainly implied, if he did not say explicitly, that most use of the Bible had done more harm than good because it weaned humans away from the Spirit of truth whom Jesus had promised. Statements like this quickly led him into strong attacks on Bible societies and other organizations satisfied with outward forms.[24]

Braithwaite returned to Jericho and took tea with Hicks in March. This time the conversation commenced with the Trinity, with Hicks asserting that people should not be expected to believe what they could not understand, a common expression among the New England New Lights. According to Braithwaite, but explicitly denied by her host, Hicks asked if she were "so ignorant as to believe in the account of the creation of the world, as given in the Scriptures?" He declared it absurd to believe in an outward sacrifice for sin, for the same Spirit that was in Christ was the "*alone means* of *redemption* and salvation." He acknowledged, said Braithwaite, and Hicks agreed later, that he did not believe the Crucifixion could expiate his sins: "I never have known anything to effect that for me but the Grace of God that taught me agreeably to the apostle's doctrines to deny all ungodliness and the world's lusts, and to live soberly, righteously, and godly in the present world."

The climax of his near-monologue, at least in Braithwaite's memory, was Hicks's statement that the "fulness of the God-head was in *us* and in every blade of grass," that attending to the Spirit's leadings would open to people the Almighty's dealings, and that the Spirit offered the only test for governing the Society of Friends. Braithwaite queried how her understanding of the Spirit could be so markedly different from his; how should a choice between the two interpretations be made? Hicks responded that he did not know but that he hoped the day would come when the Discipline would deal not with doctrines but only with immoral conduct. What would happen to Friends, pressed his visitor, if one minister said one thing and one another? "He said he should like to see it tried."[25]

In a pamphlet produced by her supporters, Braithwaite gave the accepted evangelical answer to what for her must have seemed the height of infidelity; indeed at one point she recommended that a minister holding such views should be cut off from the Society in the same way parents, anxious to save a child's life, would amputate the diseased limb of their young one. The Scriptures were authentic, she insisted, and the Spirit's leadings would never conflict with them. She affirmed her belief in "the plain historical narration of facts [of the Bible] as having really taken place" as reported. Her special concern involved the unsoundness of those who professed to be guided by the Spirit but denied "such sacred truths as the miraculous birth and death of our Saviour for our sakes."[26] In a later communication directly to Hicks, she charged that his denial of Christ's propitiatory sacrifice was the "foundation on which infidelity stands" and was contrary to the views of ancient Friends.[27]

The discussion between Hicks and Braithwaite focused the issues for a wide audience. Now, thanks to the rapid circulation of copies of a memorandum that she wrote after her second visit, a barrage of pamphlets became available for any who wanted to participate vicariously in the discussion. As a matter of fact, Braithwaite undoubtedly returned to Jericho in order to refresh her memory of Hicks's position. Neither side was above exaggerating and misstating the opposition's posture. Hicks and his followers took swipes at the "distinguished Quakers" from across the seas who hobnobbed with "Dukes, Lords, and Levites" and supported Bible societies and other interdenominational charities, arguments sure to encourage rural distrust of foreigners, nobles, and the wealthy. Braithwaite's champions drew upon the kind of external evidence, in this case the Bible and Christian tradition, that made Hicks's tenets seem new and radical and quite beyond the pale of respectability. The anonymous editor of one pamphlet concluded his contribution by averring that to convert to Hicks's ideas, "we should divest our minds of all regard to, or belief in, those plain and positive truths which we have been taught to revere from our childhood; which holy men of all ages and of different countries, since the Christian era, have held most sacred."[28]

One of the more thoughtful disciples of Hicks agreed. "I think," wrote Thomas McClintock after Braithwaite had appeared in Penn's city,

> that both the rigid principles of Calvinism, and their opposite extreme, those of a too skeptical philosophy, are giving way to more sober and just views. And, what is still more important, people are beginnng to perceive and acknowledge that the best proof of a sound heart, is a sound life. May the Lord God Almighty prosper his own work, and liberate the world from the shackles of priestcraft and supersitition—false theology, and false philosophy, that men may come to an experimental knowledge of the *realities* of the kingdom of God.[29]

Hicks, of course, could not agree more. During the sessions of New York Yearly Meeting in late May 1824, he complained that those attacking his alleged "new doctrines" were themselves responsible for introducing novel and strange ideas among Friends. Cataloguing them, he listed such notions as: "our victory over sin is not to be known on this side of the grave, . . . the humanity of Jesus Christ, prays to his own divinity," and to be a Christian one had to affirm that Jesus' crucifixion was sufficient for the atonement of the whole world.[30]

By 1824, the reformers appeared to be succeeding in defining the issues—at least when Anna Braithwaite arrived in Philadelphia after her visits to Jericho, she found the story widespread that Hicks had "entirely converted" her to his views, a rumor she took pleasure in scotching.[31] On his ministerial rounds in early 1824, William Evans found contrary ideas at almost every stop. During Philadelphia Quarterly Meeting in February, one reformer came right out and told the gathering that the Scriptures had produced hireling ministers and puffed-up people; as for him, he was uneasy calling the Bible "holy." In Concord, Evans pondered how elders who had been led astray by "uncertain speculation" could hope to judge the soundness of their ministers, victims likely of the same malady.[32] And for one of the few times, he went to the public prints to rebuke a Friend who had rejected the evangelical notion that there existed three persons of one substance in the Godhead. God, allowed Evans, should be referred to more reverently—"a too frequent repetition of the Holy names amalgamated in the Immaculate Godhead is not only sinful, but tends to lessen the awe and veneration naturally attached to them."[33] He complained about the subtlety of the reformers in clothing their unsound sentiments with sanctity and orthodoxy even as their efforts led to "libertinism & disorganization," thus threatening to bring on both ranterism and a loss of the elders' power.[34]

To judge from their letters and redoubled public activity, the reformers were growing ever more confident about their progress. A more political, even divisive tone began to creep into their correspondence. William Poole, one of Hicks's stalwarts, compared the Philadelphia elders' cabal and the Holy Alliance of Europe, each threatening to stamp out the religious and civil liberties of the people. "Kingly, Aristocratic, & Clerical power" linked to the "Rich and influential" among Friends seemed determined to rule no matter what.[35] Confronting such authority, he wrote Hicks, had the effect "to *narrow the ground* on which opposition stands, & eventually bring the struggle *for power* to a mere point, wherein the *Body* of the Society will be opposed to the assumption of the Elders, & when this shall be the case, we can scarce doubt of the result of a question whether 'the few shall controul the whole or the whole guard in their own hands the Religious rights & liberties.' "[36] The reformation of righteousness would come, a pseudonymous "Lucus" told the readers of the *Saturday Evening Post*, when people attended to the divine illumination within themselves rather than relying on creeds and confessions of faith. Then reformers "will not be tied down to old customs, nor old systems, any further than they are sanctioned by the revelation of truth, independent of the testimonies or traditions of the church."³⁷

To promote the reformation cause, Friends in Wilmington, the second largest city in Philadelphia Yearly Meeting, initiated the first Friends' periodical in the world. Named the *Berean* after the town in which the apostles Paul and Silas preached, the magazine was a polemical biweekly owned and edited by Dr. William Gibbons, who brought out the first issue on February 23, 1824. Among its agents were Benjamin Lundy of Baltimore, editor of the *Genius of Universal Emancipation*, an early abolitionist newspaper, and Benjamin Webb, who after the separation would publish the *Delaware Free Press*, which among other things scandalized timid Friends by advocating public celebration of Tom Paine's birthday. Just as surely as the reformers widely touted the *Berean*, their opponents coupled it with free-thinkers and radicals such as Fanny Wright and Robert Dale Owen, the former a feminist notorious for her support for abolition, birth control, and abortion, the latter a Scottish utopian socialist.³⁸

The *Berean*'s constant theme was to promote religious reformation and attack Orthodoxy; every issue carried at least one article devoted to these topics. In the first number an unsigned piece distinguished between "professors" and "possessors" of religion. The author described the professors or "pretenders" as true religion's "worst enemies" and left no doubt that he identified them with evangelicals, whose faith was based on books, creeds, catechisms, and abstract propositions. The possessors of religion, on the other hand, "looks at *actions* more than *opinions*," and "believes in *his* [articles of faith], because he has 'the witness in himself' of their truth."³⁹

In April 1824, "E" exposed for *Berean*'s readers "a MONSTER whose depredations on human happiness have been confined to no society." That "MONSTER" was "ORTHODOXY," pouring her maledictions on every religious community" and covering the land "like the frogs of Egypt." The Orthodox had "beaten their ploughshares into swords and their pruning hooks into spears! and thus converted that religion, whose very essence is love, into a pretext for the bitterest animosities." Turning the oft-repeated phrase used by evangelicals against the reformers around, "E" charged that Orthodoxy was "founded on a *human* interpretation of the holy Scriptures" with "no better basis than *speculative opinion*." Was that any wonder that the Church "became like a stagnant pool, producing loathsome creatures, and diffusing poisonous exhalations?"⁴⁰ The Orthodox even stooped to murder, as witnessed the execution of the Unitarian Michael Servetus who happened to fall into John Calvin's hands in 1553 and suffered burning at the stake.[41]

Three months later, "R" revealed that something more elevated had emerged from the "stagnant pool," namely, a demand for reformation, from a line of men seeking to "dissipate the thick moral darkness, in which Christendom was shrouded." Despite their labors, however, reformers like Wycliff, Luther, and Calvin did "little more than demolish the outward pillars of the temple of superstitition." "R" applauded the Pilgrims who came to the New World to practice their religious convictions, even as he condemned the creedal intolerance into which they slipped. They had failed to watch the divine "light which lighteth every man that cometh into the world," the light that searched the "secret chambers of his heart, . . . which only can give him a knowledge of himself, and of his duties to God and his fellow men." So, "R" decided, the time to extend the Reformation had arrived. Jesus' promise — "I have yet many things to say unto you, but ye cannot hear them now. Howbeit when the spirit of truth is come, he will guide you into all truth" — showed the way to the "spirituality of Christianity — its *practical* character — its simplicity — its entire rationality."[42] Not every Quaker reformer agreed with all this listing, especially the last one, but it remained one of the most succinct versions of what the reformers envisioned for their Society.

The reformers had little use for an intellectual approach to religion, which they felt was as divisive in the history of the church as the Bible. They also preferred homely and agrarian images as a way of conveying their points of view to readers familiar with rural ways of life. In an editorial on October 3, 1825, Gibbons combined the two in an attack on speculative theology. Like briars and thorns that choked out food plants, speculation created thickets where people were condemned to wander, endlessly and hopelessly, seeking the tree of life. Gibbons warned such seekers against "sutstituting opinions for faith, the traditions of the elders for the teachings of the spirit, and the influence of education for the lessons of experience." Genuine religion, he wrote, aimed "to bring all its subjects into a uniformity of *practice*, by operating upon the heart, rather than the head, and thus establishing love and good works." With such a faith, "uniformity of *opinion* is not essential, nor can it be attained in all points." "To witness in our own experience the truth of this declaration: To KNOW thee, the only true God, and Jesus Christ who thou hast only true God, and Jesus Christ who thou hast sent, is life eternal" summed up the essence of true religion for this follower of Elias Hicks.[43]

To those associated with the *Berean*'s point of view, however, the history of Friends since the beginning of the eighteenth century was a "Retrogression," the title of a series of editorials from Gibbons's desk in 1826 and 1827. The true religion had declined because the emphasis on the light of Christ within had been replaced as the primary rule. Instead of the "law written on the heart," Quakerism had come to be characterized by the outward letter, its primitive unity scattered, its numbers in decline, its missionary effort stymied, and its peculiar practices compromised by the search for social respectability. Although these editorials concentrated on the state of Friends in Britain, the lesson for Philadelphia Quakers was plain: The reform required was to reverse history and become "an inward and spiritual people" once more.[44]

Twice monthly, the evangelicals endured such verbal assaults on their stewardship of the Society. Despite the help of visiting English ministers, there seemed little that could stop the advance of the reformer's view. William Evans, bull-necked and heavyset, with an established reputation for being constitutionally unable to see the lighter side of life, discovered gloom wherever he looked. When he attended the 1826 sessions of New York Yearly Meeting, he encountered the same "disorganizing" tendencies that existed in his own branch of the Society. He saw Friends led by those with little or no religious weight and headed straight toward ranterism.[45] Even in the Tract Association of Friends, a semi-official body dominated by evangelicals, Evans witnessed "the mischiefs done by Elias Hicks & his wild adherents." Unable to unite on reprinting a new edition of a pamphlet that one member insisted inculcated incorrect views of three distinct persons in the Diety, the Association had to lay the matter aside.[46]

The Tract Association's pamphlets and the *Berean* were only part of the verbiage the two sides unleashed against each other. Polemical works, like the *Berean* and the Braithwaite-Hicks conversations, were obligatory of course, but since Friends had an unusual addiction to dredging up the past, the debate inevitably took on a historical cast. The Hicks party published Job Scott's *Salvation by Christ*, written thirty years before, but suppressed after the author's death when the sponsoring yearly meetings came under evangelical influence.[47] The reformers found Scott's spiritualizing theology quite appealing, and one of them, "A Lover of Truth," rebuked the evangelicals opposed to its publication as those "who wish to be considered the sole judge of doctrine."[48]

Scott's essay captured the attention of a British pampleteer, Luke Howard, a leading evangelical thinker in London Yearly Meeting and a world-renowned scientist and meteorologist. His 1825 *Letter from Luke Howard to a Friend in America* argued that Scott came to his subject with an "excess of the imagination and the feelings." With an empirical approach perfectly suited to the laboratory but just as perfectly misplaced when dealing with matters of the spirit, Howard proved unable to deal with the traditional Quakerism that marked Scott's efforts. Instead he emphasized the historical Christ and his sacrifice as an atonement for sin, a central doctrine of evangelicals. And he concluded by predicting that Friends "must merge . . . into the great assembly of the visible Church," a course Howard himself took when he joined the Plymouth Brethren a decade later.[49]

In the charged atmosphere of American Quakerdom, such views did not escape censure, particularly since the reforming element saw them as exemplifying the decline of the Society from its original purity. Howard's "carnal scheme of redemption," alleged Benjamin Ferrris, posing as an anonymous critic, "has been adopted by some of the wealthy, influential, leading men and women" in England. A love of the world and a reluctance to bear the cross, coupled with acquiring great wealth and association with the world's people, had, according to Ferris, led some Friends on both sides of the Atlantic to join coalitions of the nobility and clergy to preach charity and send Bibles over the world. To make themselves more acceptable to their new partners, these Friends proceeded to adopt alien doctrinal positions, Trinitarianism, the outward Atonement, and the Scriptures as the Word of God. Finally, asserted Ferris, ministers of the Society began taking the figurative language of Scripture and applying it in a literal sense, as Howard had done in his essay. Then let some "honest hearted, *practical* Friend" rise and deny the new interpretation, and he or she would as likely as not be rebuked for unsoundness. Was it any wonder that "*genuine* Quakerism" had receded and was now approaching the "Lifeless, irrational, and barren theology" of the reformed churches? Howard's essay, Ferris charged, was being distributed from house to house to blacken "the religious character of a faithful minister of Christ" and take American Quakers down the sorry road their British cousins had already traveled.[50]

Inevitably, the discussion degenerated into a contest of citing Scriptural passages and asserting that one essayist was more right than the other. As Ferris put it, the Englishman was reduced to saying, "I, Luke Howard, have the most correct view of the meaning of 'that which is written,' I am right and Job Scott is wrong." At this level, it was difficult to see how an uncommitted Quaker seeking certainity could ever decide. For traditional Friends, those eschewing evangelical theology, Ferris gave the answer: "Job Scott depended upon the illumination of the Holy spirit, for his view of scripture truth, thou depends on thy own understanding, aided by critics and commentators."[51] This answer might not convince outsiders, but it reflected the faith of Hicks's reforming coterie in the superiority of the inward voice of God's spirit to reveal truth. No outward law could ever do the same.

Tying themselves to Scott's traditional Quaker theology in this fashion bolstered the reformers' belief that they were walking in the path of primitive Friends. It led them to charge that the evangelicals held "modernized views of Quaker principles," making them unable to bear the unalloyed and pure light of truth. A slashing attack on "the reverend divines" in the *Saturday Evening Post* of December 1824 by an "F.P.B." made this point quite explicit. Latter-day Friends, in this view, had refused to complete the reformation begun by their forebears; instead, they were content to settle down on previously laid foundations rather than "proceeding to build the superstructure designed to be erected thereon." When he saw this happening, Elias Hicks, moved by his "Samson-like spirit," sought "to arouse the carnal-minded from their spiritual slumber and to turn them from the dark mazes of tradition to the unalterable light of Truth within"; neither "the *formal* Quaker" nor "the *formal* Presbyterian" could successfully resist him. Such "traditional Christians," having been long accustomed to dwell in darkness, had become handicapped by eyes "too sensitive to bear the *light*, so much so that they wince and are offended at the very mention of it."[52]

As this conflict ebbed and flowed, a localized struggle took place within monthly meetings. In fact, contention was so widespread that meetings free of squabbling occasioned comment from observers.[53] The bitterest division occurred in Green Street Meeting, where the reforming element associated with Hicks was most powerful. Sparked by outspoken leaders like Abraham Lower, the meeting's seven hundred members were already conscious of their isolation within the predominately evangelical Philadelphia Quarter. Green Street was in a working-class area whose rapid growth made for instability and fed a feeling of being alienated from the dominant group of prosperous and self-assured Quaker grandees.[54] Lower complained that the evangelicals represented an aristocracy, rich from inherited wealth or the largess of high-paying government bonds. Leonard Snowden, a prominent evangelical at the center of Green Street problems, once opined to him, "wealth gives power." Such men enjoyed influence independent of any merit on their part, or so Lower saw it.[55] Hence it was quite natural for Green Street Friends to insist that each meeting had the right to control its own affairs without interference from superior bodies.

That position quickly led to trouble. The meeting's overseers, charged with the responsibility of exercising discipline within the local body, decided to treat with Snowden, one of their elders and, at seventy-three, one of the oldest evangelical leaders. Because of his opposition to Hicks during his 1822 visit, Snowden had signed the statement issued by the city's other leaders, and rumor had it that he had called the New York minister a "messenger of Satan" who would "show his cloven foot yet." The overseers interpreted such actions as violating the Discipline's proscription against "Detraction," especially because they involved a recognized minister of a sister yearly meeting. His attitude also reflected a basic disunity with the local meeting. Snowden resisted lengthy attempts, stretching over the better part of a year, to get him to moderate his position. Finally, he and three supporters, including his wife Jane and two women elders, Mary Taylor and Ann Sattergood, petitioned the ministers and elders of the quarterly meeting to intervene. Abraham Lower and Samuel Noble, the latter one of the more ardent reformers, tried to prevent the appeal on the ground that there was no difficulty in Green Street Meeting which the select quarterly meeting needed to take cognizance of.

The ministers and elders of the quarter, however, proved more than ready to step into the dispute and assist one of their embattled comrades, for the select meeting, if anything, had a more stellar and powerful membership than even Meeting for Sufferings. Thomas Stewardson, its clerk, controlled the extensive collection of land, stocks and bonds, while others like Thomas Wistar, Ellis Yarnall, Jonathan Evans and his son William, Caleb Pierce, and Samuel Bettle, not to mention their wives who were also ministers or elders, completely outranked in both wealth and prestige the likes of cabinetmaker Lower.[56] Analyzing the situation later, Benjamin Ferris concluded that in the previous twenty years no poor man in the city had been raised to the level of elder.[57] Given this background, no one was surprised when the select meeting appointed a committee of nine to visit Green Street.

In February 1823, this high-powered committee met with the ministers and elders of Green Street. Following usual practice, the group convened in silence with the expectation that someone from Green Street would explain the problem, but silence continued, even after the committee prodded. One committee member, Samuel Bettle, his voice taking on a pleading, whining tone, pressed Noble to relate the details of the problem, but the latter remained mute. Exasperated and denying that there was any difficulty, Lower pointed to Snowden and suggested that he explain. After still another silent delay, Snowden ventured that he had been "visited *as an offender* by the Overseers of Green Street Monthly Meeting," implying it was because of his opposition to Hicks.

There ensued from this conflict an almost incredibly lengthy process of appeals, arguments, and counterclaims, dragging on for nearly three more years. To the reformers in Green Street, the matter involved whether the overseers had the independent right to correct and counsel backsliders—the *Rules of Discipline* clearly stated that no meetings of ministers and elders "are in any wise to interfere with the business of any meeting for discipline."[58] To the evangelical elders, the Discipline's guarantee of a right to appeal from decisions of monthly meetings meant that the select quarterly meeting had every right to consider the Snowden case.[59] Like Snowden, they wanted to establish the principle that overseers had no right to question an elder for his official action.[60]

A new complication emerged six months later, and more than a year and a half following Hicks's visit, when the overseers recommended to their meeting that Snowden be removed as an elder. The dominant group, believing that elders served at the pleasure of the meeting, considered this move to be in perfectly good order, so the meeting concurred in the request. Neither Snowden nor the select quarterly meeting, however, shared this opinion; accordingly Snowden filed a protest with the quarterly body, which in turn joined him in a remonstrance to Philadelphia Quarter against the Green Street action. The rules were not entirely clear regarding removal of elders, although they implied that a quarterly meeting could assist a monthly meeting to bring a recalcitrant officer to submit to the meeting's wishes, a provision designed to favor established authority.[61] In this case, unfortunately for the evangelical ministers and elders, power rested firmly in the hands of the reformers, men determined to resist their authority.

As discussion of the case continued at the quarterly meeting level, the reformers extended their purge to two other evangelicals in their midst. Mary Taylor and Ann Scattergood, who had stood with Snowden in his resistance to the Green Street activities, were both relieved of their posts as elders in June 1826. Scattergood, Joseph's widow, particularly irritated the leaders in Green Street because of her habit of turning around from her place in the gallery and glaring at preachers with whom she disagreed. The two women claimed they had not been visited nor conferred with, in violation of the *Rules of Discipline*, and had suffered dismissal when two unnamed male Friends appeared in the women's meeting and pressed for their removal. An appeal to the monthly meeting brought no relief, so the two aggrieved women sought the quarterly meeting's help.[62] The quarter designated a committee consisting of some of the most high powered men, both religiously and economically, in the city.[63] Green Street Friends, of course, rejected the notion that a newly appointed committee might inquire into what they regarded as a purely internal affair of who was to serve as elder. "Whom we appoint, we can remove," summed up the embattled and increasingly united meeting's position.[64] Whatever the meeting's stance, the committee recommended that Taylor and Scattergood be reinstated.[65]

In quieter times, procedural disputes like this one would have been settled amicably; in fact, in quieter times, such disputes never came up. The *Rules of Discipline* was unclear. Elders, it provided, were appointed by monthly meetings, and their names then forwarded to the select quarterly meeting of ministers and elders, a procedure suggesting some oversight.[66] With no clear-cut outline for removing elders, the matter required sober consideration, an unlikely prospect in the mid-1820s in Philadelphia. The *Rules of Discipline* presupposed a broad agreement, not only on procedural questions, but on good will, points of doctrine, and acceptance of authority. All these fruits of a common religious experience seemed in short supply by 1826. Those who insisted that they were bound by no outward law simply did not intend to submit to the authority of those who lorded it over them and wanted to impose such a law. In November 1826, Philadelphia Quarter received a recommendation from the women's meeting that a committee be named to visit all the monthly meetings in the quarter, a previously common and uncontested practice. But not now: In the men's meeting the discussion lasted four hours, with Hicks's adherents asserting that the proposal would only lead to more division and discord, the evangelicals seeing it as a salutary attempt to heal open wounds. Already division and discord were rampant. Lower remembered how Green Street Friends trying to defend their actions to the quarterly meeting were told that they had "no right to be heard" and to "sit down." Once Bettle rose from his seat in the gallery and while Lower was speaking, in his most condescending manner, put his hand on Lower's shoulder and asked if the group wanted to hear him out; about twenty voices shouted, "Sit down" to Lower, but others asked him to go on.[67] It was no wonder that Hicks's followers outside the city viewed their Green Street comrades as living in a constant state of siege.[68]

Under such pressure, the clerk of the quarterly meeting acquiesced in naming the visitation committee, despite objections from what the reforming element considered the larger part of the meeting. No matter that Green Street's members persistently declared that the quarterly meeting lacked authority to investigate its actions when there was no legitimate appeal before it, the committee advised that Green Street Meeting be laid down and its members be shifted to the nearby Northern District meeting. There the matter rested until after the separation took place in 1827.[69]

Once again this particular dispute over elders at Green Street reflected fundamental disagreements between the Orthodox evangelicals and the Hicks party over authority in the Society of Friends. Samuel Bettle, longtime clerk of the Yearly Meeting, offered a quite explicit statement of the evangelical position. "A Monthly Meeting is strictly subordinate to a Quarterly Meeting—the power of the Quarterly Meeting extends to the annulling of the acts of the Monthly . . . and if the Monthly Meeting will not submit to the power of the Quarterly Meeting, . . . it has been the practice to lay down such refractory meeting." He did not cite the case of Green Street to prove the quarterly meeting's broad power, he merely assumed it existed because, as he read the *Rules of Discipline*, they provided for the subordination of an inferior body to its superior. For the Orthodox party, the superior body's authority extended to any matter that threatened the good order of the Discipline.[70]

The reformers, acutely aware of their lack of actual power no matter how large their numbers, denied the legitimacy of this broad construction of the *Rules of Discipline*. They insisted on local autonomy except in those few cases where superior meetings were granted express authority over inferior bodies. James Cockburn, a Hicksite who compiled a volume reviewing various documents incidental to the separation, explained that the superior meeting had only appellate functions to decide cases when "they are regularly brought before it . . . It possesses in itself no legislative or executive functions." Certainly it had no original power to review acts of subordinate bodies, as Bettle claimed.[71] Or, as another Hicksite undertook to clarify it for a secular court, the "Quarterly Meetings are merely a larger meeting of the members of the Monthly Meetings, and established by them, . . . and occasionally ask advice and aid, in cases of difficulty." The superior power "remains in the individual members of the several meetings," and larger meetings possessed only the power expressly granted in the book of Discipline.[72]

In the reformers' view, any outward law should be applied, if applied at all, at the lowest, or monthly meeting, level so as to guarantee the rights of each individual member. Hicks phrased it as succinctly as any other: "no literal law or Creed can take place under the Gospel, except in Moral, or outward things, — for no outward law can bind the soul, as the government of the Soul is exclusively the prerogative of God, and not of man."[73]

On the other hand, however much they contended that the basic issue involved doctrine — Bettle considered the "ground of the unhappy schism in the Society of Friends, is the difference in doctrine"[74] — the evangelicals who controlled Meeting for Sufferings revealed by their actions that the essential question finally became: who possessed the power to determine what the correct doctrine would be?

CHAPTER 8

"More for victory than truth,"
OR
The Public Struggle

EVERY YEAR ON THE TWENTY-FOURTH of September, his birth date, Thomas White Pryor noted his age—in 1826 he was sixty-three—and his weight—this year the scales revealed 286 pounds, up a bit.[1] This Green Street Friend, sympathetic to Elias Hicks as were most other members of his meeting, continually took stock of himself and events he observed. He did not take an active part in the agitation that spread throughout Philadelphia Yearly Meeting, but he carefully kept his journal up-to-date and made insightful comments as time passed.

On the last day of 1825, Pryor noted the ephemeral—the season was dry, the weather mild, the streams so low that the mills could not grind—and, for the historian, more important developments. "The divisions which have unhappily arisen among Friends," he penned in his aggressive hand, "appear not to show the least hopes of subsiding. The 4 Monthly Meetings in the City are much perplexed with a variety of debate. . . . But O Green Street thou favoured little Meeting how pleasing would it be if all in the City enjoyed the Love and harmony that prevails within thy walls."

In Pryor's next entry, twelve days later, he commented on the appearance of Anna and Isaac Braithwaite in Philadelphia and New York. From Pryor's description the Braithwaites seemed almost to look for ways to stir dormant animosities. Their messages reeked with the spirit of opposition to traditional Quakerism (Pryor subsequently remarked that Anna's denomination ought to be the Church of England, she was such a "great sticker for the Scriptures and of the body & blood of Christ"[2]). They lorded it over average Americans by riding in an ornate carriage with a servant girl perched in the box beside the driver, a practice which "if tolerated in England, in America [it] is too tyrannical, &c, &c."³ The Braithwaites' appearance and the ensuing controversy gave added credence to an exasperated Friend's outcry that the conflict was "more for victory than truth," so that it was impossible to know whom to believe.⁴

Nearly a year before Pryor's evaluation, the main reform strategist, William Poole of Wilmington, lamented his own unwillingness to trust anyone, even himself, "at this time when division of sentiment so much prevails." "It may be difficult," he told Elias Hicks, "to find a person to sit by as an umpire of truly independent character & on whom we can fully rely for a Report of the truth." Poole reported stories of agitation in New York, Baltimore, and Ohio yearly meetings—the latter involving a pamphlet by Elisha Bates—and of course in Philadelphia. In the City of Brotherly Love, Friends "are upon the whole in a very disjointed state. Thus it would seem as if the whole body almost is tending toward some material change." Poole, however, looked for a kind of purification, to come out of it all *closer examination* into the principles & practices that we have professed."⁵

To the evangelicals, on the other hand, conflict spelled trouble: unbelief, infidelity, and threats to the established order. The chronically worried William Evans could not even find comfort when the yearly meeting of 1825 rejected the reformers' now perennial suggestion that all officers be selected for a limited term. Evans viewed such proposals as demonstrations of the desperate lengths to which Hicks's followers were willing to go to retaliate against Philadelphia's elders for trying to discipline the Long Islander. Let such proposals be approved, Evans dreaded, and Elias Hicks's "unsound principles might be propagated with impunity and libertinism and ranterism would overrun the Society in places."⁶ Hence, Evans and Poole agreed that "material change" was in the offing—they just as surely disagreed about whether or not it was needful.

The conflict between the two Quaker factions was producing by 1825 a deluge of pamphlets presenting the case of each side. Just why this onslaught took place at this time remains unclear. It had something to do with Anna Braithwaite's ministerial tour and publication of her interview with Hicks; the volume of material picked up considerably after that, as the reformers hurried to get their version out.⁷ Perhaps the pamphlet war developed also out of a realization among the evangelicals that Hicks and the reformers were not going away and that they had a significant challenge on their hands. Perhaps the success of their appeals to traditional Quakers emboldened the reformers and in turn fed a backlash from the evangelicals. Moreover, the reformers had one periodical of their own and access to others, while the evangelicals had to make do with their power. All these factors no doubt played a part in increasing the tensions of the mid-1820s.

For example, one of the principal evangelicals in New York Yearly Meeting, the elderly Gideon Seaman, a Long Island neighbor of Hicks, wrote Jonathan Evans in early 1825 to express his misgivings about a proposal originating in Philadelphia's Western District Meeting to censure Hicks formally. Such a step would have little hope of success, Seaman explained, for "I very much doubt whether the Monthly Meeting of Jericho [Hicks's home meeting], will take much notice of such a communication." Seaman instead proposed that since Hicks's sentiments had already been widely disseminated, perhaps a broader select meeting of Philadelphia's ministers and elders would be the proper forum to pronounce an anathema against him; there was little hope for such a stand in New York because of "the indefatigable perservering of the other side."[8]

"The indefatigable perservering" was the same thing Isaac Braithwaite referred to as "strokes of generalship" on the part of Hicks. In order to quiet Hicks's "horribly blasphemous preaching," Braithwaite counseled another prominent New York evangelical, John Griscom, "not to be lulled into supiness under the idea that if we will only be quiet things will work out all right." Braithwaite, in fact, was quite explicit: He considered it high time for Hicks's local meeting to move, ignoring any charges of detraction that the reformers might bring. And the evangelicals should continue to produce the kinds of pamphlets that had already been forwarded to him in England — "well written & the arguments sound & clear."[9]

Symbolizing the breakdown of unity was Jonathan Evans's open affront to Hicks during the old minister's trip through Philadelphia on his way home from Baltimore Yearly Meeting in December 1824. Hicks attended Pine Street Meeting on the morning of the 14th and, after its rise, moved along the gallery greeting and shaking hands with the strongly Orthodox leaders there. When Hicks came to Evans, the Philadelphian refused the proffered hand, and Elias said, loud enough to be heard, "I am sorry to see thee fallen so far below the dignity of the man." Evans ignored the remark. That afternoon when Hicks attended Arch Street Meeting, another evangelical bastion, only one elder deigned to speak to their visitor. On Tuesday, at the Northern District Meeting, the reception on the part of the leaders was the same, but the general membership welcomed him warmly.[10] After his visit to Philadelphia, his enemies there sought ways to silence him and exclude him from the ministry. They decided to inform Jericho Meeting of the unsoundness of Hicks's doctrine, as the first step in dealing with him.[11] From Wilmington, Poole reported that Philadelphia's "union is at an end almost, & that a complete revolution must take place before it can be restored."[12]

At the same time, some young reformers counterattacked against charges that they were "Deists, New Lights, and Disorganizers." They published a collection of extracts from the writings of early Quakers to prove that they, not their evangelical opponents, were the true heirs of the tradition begun by George Fox and William Penn.[13] Although it was not clear who got out this anonymous pamphlet, circumstances pointed to Thomas McClintock, who had an intense interest in publicizing the reform cause.[14] The extracts themselves consisted of an edited version of Penn's *The Sandy Foundation Shaken*. The title page trumpeted that they would refute Orthodox notions of the Trinity, of the necessity for a blood sacrifice to appease God's wrath, and of the justification of "unpure persons" by Christ's righteousness. Affirming their intention to walk in "THE GOOD OLD WAY." the editors averred that the pamphlet proved that Hicks and his supporters were "*avowing and defending the same views and belief, which are now rejected as dangerous inovations*" by the evangelicals.[15] After he perused his Philadelphia cohorts' efforts, Poole exulted, "it proves decisively, I think, that the sentiments of our friend EH. are in accordance with the most divinely enlightened sons of the morning of our Gospel day."[16]

Stung by this addition to the debate and no doubt mindful that it did make a strong case for traditional Quakerism, an anonymous evangelical sought to parry the reformer's thrust with one of his own. The result, *A Defence of the Christian Doctrines of the Society of Friends*, made a significant contribution to the evangelical cause in that it revealed one heavy charge that could be leveled against the reformers. Although they denied being disorganizers, the reformers obviously rejected the lead of the recognized and constituted authorities of the Society; they wanted to substitute their own reading of the Christian experience for the one championed by the leadership. And while it might be true that the evangelical elders represented accurately neither the Quaker tradition nor the majority of contemporary Friends, the fact that they generally exercised their power in accordance with the rules could scarcely be denied. They had power and used it, something that should have surprised no one, least of all reformers.

The anonymous defender of Christian doctrines found the most vulnerable spot in the reformers' position, a sore spot that, not coincidentally, had plagued Protestantism from its very beginnings. In recognizing no leadership beyond their individual experiences (though Quakers like John Woolman, Job Scott, and, yes, Elias Hicks, affirmed that the Spirit could bring unity to people humble enough to be so guided), the reformers destroyed authority. Said this evangelical pamphleteer, with an excess of rhetorical flourishes:

> How many are there, who, deceived by specious pretences to greater spirituality, and to the guidance of the Holy Spirit; lured by the unlawful love of novelty, and a restless desire to be prying into the inscrutable mysteries of God, have left that precious state of humble dependence and holy faith, that true tenderness of spirit, that teachableness and conscientious fear of doing wrong, which they knew something of in the day of their early visitation; and are now determined to choose for themselves; to believe what they please, and deny what they dislike, — until they have at last come to reject the doctrines of Holy Scripture, to deny the Lord that bought them, and are "rapidly merging into the popular doctrines" of infidelity.[17]

"To believe what they please, and deny what they dislike," that was the obvious tendency of the Hicksite reformation, as well as of Protestantism generally. And that was why the Orthodox elders resisted it so sternly and strenuously. (The reformers spoke better than they knew when they sneered that the elders acted like bishops in the established church.) The elders were hardly people of charm or tact, but they controlled and exercised power and represented authority within the Quaker community. Remove them, destroy their prestige, and few limitations would remain on what individuals might believe. Constantly echoing the same theme — that they were resisting Hicks's unitarian doctrines — the elders failed to see that Hicks personally refused to exalt reason, but they rightly divined the potential for others to do so once reason was applied to the principles he laid down.[18] The rest of the *Defence* was an unexceptionable polemical work, amounting to little more than countering the reformers' quotations form Penn with the evangelical's own selection; again, about all disinterested readers could do was to throw up their hands in dismay or tally up the number of citations and declare as winner the one who marshalled the greatest number. The true grounds of the controversy could be found by examining the assumptions about authority that the antagonists brought to the discussion.

The public debate, of course, seldom proceeded on this level. Usually slogans, name-calling, and innuendo characterized the publications that emerged from Philadelphia's busy printing houses. In an evangelical pamphlet dotted with italicized words comparing Hicks's sermons with the sentiments of selected early Friends, the author hinted that the New Yorker's outspokenness might incur the wrath of the government. Hicks's doctrines would "in the end, *require a check*, from the civil magistrate; who . . . *beareth not the sword in vain*; but—*for the punishment of evil doers.*" But the state, the same evangelical warned, in words preshadowing the controversy over property that broke out after the separation, would not allow schismatics to enjoy a joint division of common assets. Then to cap his attack, the anonymous editor directed his readers' attention to a new edition of the notorious Thomas Paine's writings that cited "Elias Hicks, a celebrated Quaker preacher" for his views on the Atonement.[19]

The lowest level to which the evangelicals stooped was best represented in a short and scurrilous tract, "Sixteen Reasons Why I Cannot Be a Hicksite." The catalogue of reasons ranged from the reformers' alleged denial of the Scriptures through their rejections of the Atonement to their "loose hollow kind of morality, of that sly specious kind, which just clears them from the laws, while they will generally break the Sabbath, and practice any kind of dissimulation and misrepresentation, to carry their points, and promote their own selfish interests." With the straightest of faces, this hugger-mugger pensman called them not Friends but "Enemies"—to God, to Christ, to the Bible, to truth, to Christians and all mankind—"for if their doctrines should prevail, there *would be no Christianity, Bibles, Missionaries, truth, or morality, law or government in the world.*"[20]

The reformers took pains to assert that their opponents were men of wealth whose only interest, as one pamphleteer put it, was "a thirst for popularity and worldly aggrandizement" that led them "astray from the power of the living testimony." They strummed the strings of American nationalism by reminding readers that the elders had permitted themselves to be brought under British influence by "*self-stiled orthodox Quakers* from beyond the great waters"; hence had been quenched "the spirit of gospel liberty, and free inquiry." Such leaders stood aloof, praying wordy prayers, and "do not even congregate with the people." No wonder a "night of apostasy" had fallen upon a society heretofore noted for its *"industry, economy*, and simplicity." In a pamphlet vaguely resembling an Old Testament story, an anonymous "scribe" offered forty-two counts of apostasy against the Orthodox. One charged "Jonathan, who rules with a rod of iron," of falsely accusing others of lying, another pointing out that the clerk of Sufferings tried to prevent a stenographer from coming to meeting lest he record the proceedings. Still a third noted that certain "great sticklers for 'sound doctrine' " busily imported the newest fashions "to suit the taste of the bucks and dandies of the first water in our city" and permitted their own children to "take lessons in the dancing, fencing, and boxing schools, attend the theatre, circus, balls, cotillion and other fashionable parties, where the midnight hour is spent in revelling and vain amusement." Better, concluded the scribe, that such people attend to their own household needs.[21]

Such attempts at irony were almost totally absent from the evangelicals' writings, which were adust in tone and uniformly devoid of humor or creativity; it was almost as though they believed humor would detract from the solemnity expected of men of their station writing about matters of such great weight. The Hicksite reformers could be dry also, but they found somewhere or other an occasional bit of wit to relieve the tedium of discussion. Better than their opponents, they realized that humor was a sharp weapon, particularly when used against pretentious individuals trying to hold on to their positions of power. Thus the only creative moments in the long-winded and redundant pamphlet discussion came from the Hicksite fold.

The reformers, for example, published at least five pamphlets updating parts of the Bible with accounts of how God's chosen people were being oppressed by their enemies, the evangelical elders. The first verse of "A Chapter of Modern Chronicles" set the tone:

> And it came to pass that there were troubles in Israel, by reason of many having turned aside from the worship of the true God; and made unto themselves idols after the fashion of *men* and *women*, whereby they sought to overcome their enemies as in days of old when men rebelled against the commands of the Most High.

The familiar story was rehearsed, of how Elias the prophet went into the land of Penn, there only to be beset by his enemies, of the tribe of

"Backbites, who knew not George [Fox]." Valiantly, Elias proclaimed against those who laid up earthly treasures "in the place called Arch, and in Pine, and whersoever he taught them." When they conspired against him, with their allies from across the waters, "many turned from following after the elders, and went no more with them."[22]

The most creative Hicksite publication, tinged with humorous references to the foibles of the evangelicals, was a Shakespeareanlike drama, *The Intolerants*, that purported to reveal the interworkings of a trans-Atlantic conspiracy. Eight Orthodox Friends in the play were pictured as well-to-do, worldly-wise, and popularly acclaimed opponents of Elias Hicks, or "Paul." The anonymous playwright cleverly, if sometimes crudely, wove the personal traits of real-life evangelicals into his characters. "Professor Grum," modeled after John Griscom, a well-known Quaker scientist and evangelical of New York, was described as "he who with strength/Of mind Herculan, and intellect/Gigantic, his huge carcase up the steep/Hill of science having dragg'd," and as a man "by an enlighten'd world/Being styl'd a second Franklin." "Thomas Eddrington," or Thomas Eddy, confessed that he was a member of the church, but complained that he had been forced by the dominant reform faction to "worship in the Outer Court," and this indignity despite the fact that his name "riffl'd on the grand canal."

Eddrington emerges as the play's leading figure, whispering to William Forster ("William Loiterer"), who has just arrived from England when the play opens, about Paul's heresies. Another New York evangelical, Richard Mott ("Richard Mite"), to whom Jonathan Evans was "deeply attached," appeared as the evangelical plant among the reformers.[23] With Grum, the two plotters compose a letter to warn Philadelphia Friends of the approach of Paul, strong of arm and dauntless of heart. As they write, Grum blurts, "Say also that he is a cannibal." They furnish Loiterer, who promised to inform the "Mother Church" in London of Paul's "downright blasphemy," with a list of contacts in Philadelphia.

As actually happened, Eddrington's letter falls into the wrong hands and is published, leading him to threaten to take all down with him if they do not agree to stand together. He promises to expose Stephen Grellet, "deserter from Napoleon, . . . Namesake of nobler martyr than ten thousand such as he," and asserts, "we must/Stand, or fall together." The Orthodox march across the Hicksite stage as a cunning cabal, pursuing their own carefully calculated interests. "Samuel Peron," *né* Samuel Parsons, clerk of New York Yearly Meeting and described by a co-conspirator as "the veriest weathercock of all," is made to soliloquize:

> It surely is
> A villainous thing, to turn against him;
> But I was ne'er so brainsick, nor ever
> So romantic—to remain in doors when
> Earthquakes rock'd, until the house fell on me;
> Simply, because I lov'd it— . . .
>   Which was the
> Wiser, Napoleon or Talleyrand?—
> The former gain'd a name, the latter gain'd
> A Life—The former's in his shroud—the latter
> Rolls in stately pomp—be him my model— . . .

With no climax and no conclusion, the play just wound down, its closing lines a warning from the cautious Mite that the conspiritors should bide their time lest they be consumed by Eddrington's zeal.[24] But as a creative vehicle revealing the reformers' view of the evangelicals and their plans, it stood out above all the other ephemera produced in the controversy. Moreover, the literary and historical references suggested that the play was the work of a person of some learning who could stand back, put the controversy into a broader perspective, and then engage the opposition in a fashion different from the more predictable pamphlets.

Hicksite reformers found it easy to attack such men as Eddy, Mott, and Evans, for they did appear self-serving. As defenders of established authority, they were trying to maintain their prerogatives and power and quite naturally assumed that the good order from which flowed their influence was worth saving. Unlike other Christians, Quakers had never had a creed and had always permitted, nay insisted upon, individual interpretation. Thus the evangelicals could not fall back, as could more creedal groups, on past statements of faith. This did not prevent the evangelicals from rummaging through the writings of earlier friends to defend their position, but it did mean that their opponents could do the same thing and to equal effect.

The Orthodox, as might be expected, seldom indicated that they understood this situation; they simply wrote as men with rightful authority. Perhaps, therefore, it required a self-styled "Demi-Quaker" to clarify the point. In an "Address to the Society of Friends," issued in 1825, "Demi-Quaker" maintained that preachers in other sects "walk in a prescribed path, and are confined by doctrines and observances to which they are bound." Friends, on the other hand, believing that "a secret and divine impulse" moved their ministers, had to take especial care "lest they mistake the operation of other causes for a call to duty." Because most people sometimes strayed from the right path, the Society named elders to attend to the doctrines and conduct of ministers. "Such a superintendence can never be burdensome to one who is duly impressed with the solemn duty he is called upon to perform: on the contrary it will be a source of satisfaction and encouragement, [for the minister] to find he had around him faithful and friendly monitors, to caution and advise." Should he grow impatient under such "salutary control," then that would be evidence enough that he did not have the correct temper for a minister in the first place. Not surprisingly, a "Demi-Quaker" advised that traveling ministers should expect to be under the discipline of the elders in the places they visited.[25]

The same publicist, in an open letter to Hicks, enlarged upon what he viewed as a tendency of the reformers to lay waste every institution that stood athwart their "disordered" imaginations and proud hearts. Culling an example from the English Revolution, he asserted that such imaginations would abolish the Sabbath, tithes, ministers, the Bible, and ruling magistrates (because Christ was present now among his followers and had erected his kingdom to replace the tyrants who oppressed his saints). Hicks had intruded himself into a society "united in love and harmony" and had disturbed its peace with a "wildness of enthusiasm" and "mystical visions."[26] In a subsequent pamphlet, "Demi-Quaker" denominated this "ranting spirit . . . more injurious than infidelity itself" because those so infected believed themselves "above the advice of men" not only in religious duties "but in all the temporal concerns of life." Only the elders, "who are, and always have been, the true and efficient support of the society," could bridle such wanderings to prevent Hicks's reformers from running rampant over the received institutions that Friends had evolved.[27]

These letters to Hicks were direct responses to an effective strategy the reformers settled on. They sent stenographers to take down in shorthand the New Yorker's sermons and transcribe them for publication. The first volume appeared in 1825 with an initial printing of two thousand copies; in a ten-day span, the edition was more than half sold and a second planned. Everyone concerned entertained some doubts about their accuracy as transcriptions—indeed, errors did inevitably creep in—but they agreed that the sermons were having a powerful effect on Friends' thinking.[28] Even the secular press noted the book's appearance, with one paper printing long extracts from it.[29]

Marcus T. C. Gould, the stenographer who traveled with Hicks and took down most of his addresses, edited a kind of periodical, called *The Quaker*, which went through four volumes in 1827 and 1828, as well as other collections of sermons. Occasionally Gould would include a statement from one of the evangelicals or even a letter from one or another of the antagonists, but he usually apologized for so doing, justifying the departure because of the intrinsic interest that the material possessed.[30] In all cases, the material served to show the reformers in the best light, the evangelicals as intolerant and haughty.

Publishing such sermons inevitably forced Friends to take sides. Hicks himself always spoke forcefully, and firmly—and not a little dogmatically. At the climax of one of his sermons to a crowded meeting in Philadelphia, he seemed to try to rub the opposition the wrong way. "The blood of Christ—the blood of Christ—why, my friends, the actual blood of Christ in itself was no more effectual than the blood of bulls and goats—not a bit more—not a bit." He paused, the audience momentarily quiet, and then canes began to thump the floor in angry disagreement. Other listeners simply rose in their places as a silent protest. Mutterings came from all sides of the hall. Some left, and others, their eyes wide and faces flushed, stayed to see if there would be more.[31] It was no wonder that Thomas Evans, one of Jonathan's sons, publicly declared that every sermon "teemed with infidel and anti-christian principles."[32]

Personal accounts of such meetings spread, as this one did, by word of mouth, and transcripts of Hicks's sermons broadcast them even farther. He knew what words would inflame the opposition, and he was not reluctant to speak them. At Arch Street Meeting in November 1824, he told a gathering that "nothing can be a son of God but that which is immortal and invisible" and that "spirit cannot beget flesh and blood."[33] Near Dover, Delaware, two years later, Hicks explained "that if we would believe as we ought, the knowledge of that book called the scriptures cannot be anything necessary." How little Christendom had benefitted, he exclaimed, from a knowledge of the Bible, for "no external thing ever made a Christian," but only following the example of Jesus and each person's inward guide.[34] Words like "rational" and "reason" were often on his lips and, although he usually stressed the inadequacy of reason alone as a way to know God's will, his use of the words gave opponents a golden opportunity to charge him with unitarian views, or worse.[35]

Hicks did not bear the entire burden of preaching the word of the reformation; others carried their share. A sermon by Edward Hicks in May 1825 at Rose Street Meeting in New York City, for instance, compared the ruling elders with the New Testament's scribes and Pharisees—men of ambition, seduced by worldly temptations and oblivious to the call of Jesus. *"Those who fill the highest stations in the Church are,"* he spoke in italics, *"of all others the most wicked."* They opposed the saviour because he was contemptuous of their traditions and power, and so, fearful of the masses' support of their enemy, they sneaked around in the night to find ways to destroy him. Hicks traced this conflict between those with power and those who sought reform through the early church, to a "night of Apostacy," and right down to the present day. He never mentioned his cousin by name, but in the context of the raging controversy between the reformers and their evangelical opponents, the Lord's side was clear.[36] Later one Hicksite was overheard saying that "our friend Elias is as good and great a man as Jesus Christ."[37]

One of the most forceful and effective of all the Hicks allies was a transplanted Englishman, Thomas Wetherald, in 1826 a relative youngster of thirty-five. A butcher by trade and uneducated by worldly standards, he nonetheless charmed his audiences with his natural eloquence and carefully modulated accents. He lived in Alexandria, Virginia, a part of Baltimore Yearly Meeting, and in 1826 traveled in New York, Pennsylvania, and Delaware, where he spoke to the kinds of crowds usually reserved for Hicks alone.[38] His sermons represented traditional Quakerism at its purest—Fox, Woolman, Scott, and Hicks could have done no better. Boldly, he proclaimed that people could become God's children if only they would permit the spirit of Christ to circulate through them as the outward blood coursed through their physical bodies. Let no one, he told the grandees in Jonathan Evans's Pine Street Meeting in May 1826, think that external circumstances—wealth, education, heritage—could bring salvation. Only if the spirit of God acted within a person, producing honesty, mercy, and love, could that one know and live the true religion. "Let us remember that *Jesus* is a saviour, and that *Immanuel* is God with us: and we need not look for this divine power at a great distance, and beyond the grave.... It is in us a teacher; it is known unto all."[39]

Wetherald told another group that prejudice, education, and tradition had prevented people from seeing the real Christ and led them to speculate on "division and sub-divisions, about a Triune God, distinct persons, and I know not what."[40] In the best reformation tradition, he explained that "the gospel of Christ is simple," standing "in that power which is communicated immediately from God, the Father of lights and of spirits, into each of our spirits." What was communicated? Not words, but power, power that reproved and convicted people of their sin. "And I want us on these occasions to be still; and if we find the messengers of Christ, so called, are endeavouring to hatch up something—some declarations, whether from the scriptures or from tradition or former experience, believe them not." His testimonies were true, he announced, not because of Scripture, but because "they are recorded in the depths of my own experience." Where would one's understanding and experience stop? "I have never found a stopping place, and I don't want any of you to find a stopping place . . . we shall never come to an ultimatum in religion, and say, this shall be *my religion*, and *these* my doctrines." To attend daily to the spirit of truth was to possess an "experimental knowledge of God," without which true faith was impossible and with which one would be led into all truth.[41]

This brought Wetherald to the reformation. To Hester Street Meeting in New York, he embarked on a favorite Hicksite theme, the history of the church, which was to say, the history of apostasy. Creeds, dogmas, councils, theologies, traditions, and power inevitably led to confusion and error: "darkness was added to darkness, till mankind were brought into that dismal state of apostasy" that spread over Europe. However much Luther and Calvin "were stepping stones to the revolution and reformation which was brought about in public sentiment," their followers settled down and were content with the outward forms of true religion. "But if we come under the baptism of the Holy Ghost . . . , we shall not come under the influence of a teacher whom men can pay, whose god is his belly, whose glory is his shame, who minds earthly things." The true teacher was "Christ in you, the hope of glory," who reproves for sin, empowers for righteousness, and rules for his kingdom.[42]

Wetherald was in the Empire State to attend the 1826 sessions of New York Yearly Meeting. William Evans was also present and watched in dismay as views such as Wetherald's brought the "lighter" and "looser" part of the Society into a controlling position over "age, experience, soundness of judgement, or clearness of discerning." Why, one "pretended

Anna Braithwaite (1788–1859).
(Friends Historical Library, Swarthmore College)

Benjamin Ferris (1781–1867).
(Friends Historical Library, Swarthmore College)

reformer" had even shouted out during the reading of London Yearly Meeting's epistle, "my Saviour was never crucified," and rumors circulated that Hicks had expressed the same thing in one of his messages. To Evans's eye, unbelief and a "light estimate" of the Bible had taken deep root among New York Quakers.[43]

As 1825 closed, the two factions within American Quakerdom had almost come to a parting of the ways, neither side displaying much respect for the other. The pamphlet tug-of-war, as well as secular newspaper articles, had publicized the conflict and left each side suspicious of the other's motives and self-righteous about its own. The incursion of English evangelicals had sharpened tensions and left the impression that the powerful elders had the approval of English Friends for their course. Emboldened by their popular acclaim, the reformers' preaching missions heightened the evangelicals' insecurity about their grip on power. This evident softness encouraged the Hicksites, who were better at attack anyway, to push harder. For some time, the question, "Is thee a Hicksite or an anti-Hicksite?" had been bunted around in private correspondence;[44] now, with lines of division widening at every level, an answer was being required of more and more Friends. What had been primarily academic had taken on a personal, even existential quality.

Members of practically every monthly meeting had to confront the question about what to do with those in their midst who disagreed with the dominant faction. Friends who wore their Quakerism lightly were not so deeply touched by the divisions—though they could hardly escape the repercussions when one antagonist or another paid a ministerial visit—so the burden was borne by those active in local meeting affairs. In some influential meetings, like the one in Wilmington, dissenters from the dominant group laid low and said little, but those in charge were well aware that the discord elsewhere would sooner or later surface among them. When questions of doctrine or authority were agitated at quarterly or yearly meeting levels, the people who listened to the discussions and assented to the decisions were the same ones who exercised power at the local level.[45] They could hardly leave behind what they had heard or seen earlier.

Thus, at local levels conciliation had become nearly impossible in meetings where active participants in the debate regularly worshipped. Green Street Meeting maintained the unity that Thomas Pryor liked to crow about because the reformers there had a continuing struggle with Philadelphia Quarterly Meeting to remove Green Street's recalcitrant evangelical elders. In this case as in others, the immediate issues disappeared amid the appeals, counterappeals, and technicalities worthy of the most steadfast Philadelphia lawyer. Indeed, an impartial observer might have wondered if a flock of black-coated lawyers were not behind the whole struggle between Green Street and its quarter.

In the atmosphere then prevailing, the system Friends had evolved seemed almost to promote disharmony. Each meeting had a "select meeting" of local officers that convened to give answers to a stated series of queries about the state of the meeting. The questions were so broad and general that in good times they never elicited any controverted responses; in fact, the answers had become so routine that they never varied from meeting to meeting. For example, part of the second query asked, "Is love and unity maintained amongst you?"[46] Normally the meeting responded that love and unity was indeed maintained.

In discordant times like the middle 1820s, however, such customary replies only satisfied the dominant faction. Unfortunately, almost none of the discussions in which answers were formulated have survived. One that did, from a Green Street select meeting of six on January 13, 1825, richly reveals the dynamics of separation. Two of the participants were Mary Taylor and Ann Scattergood, the staunch evangelicals whose disagreement with the reformers in Green Street would lead to efforts to remove them from their positions as elders the following year. The transcript of the discussions, as recorded by an unknown secretary, demonstrated how questions of doctrine and authority became intermingled and were complicated by personality differences and the tendency of each side to hark back to previous discussions and personal confrontations. Of course, with insistent, strong-willed, and blunt-speaking reformers like Abraham Lower involved, such recriminations were almost inevitable.

After Samuel Noble, a local shoemaker and active reformer, took the table as clerk, the group began to consider each of the queries in turn. The first, concerning regular attendance and unbecoming behaviour in meeting, provoked no remarks, but Mary Taylor was primed for the next one. Outright, she inquired about the men's reaction to the ministry they had heard lately. None of the men—Lower, Noble, George Wooley, and John Lancaster—had any reservations and allowed that the usual answer, "ministers are mostly sound in word & doctrine, & generally careful to minister in the manner queried after," was adequate. Ann Scattergood demurred and thought that unsoundness in word and doctrine had popped up. Lower, assuming that Scattergood had reference to his own messages, averred that he did not intend to be instructed by Aquilas and Priscillas until they had followed "gospel order" and met with him privately. Noble interjected that Friends had no creed—he "hoped we never should"—so ministry should be judged "by our feelings while sitting under it." Asserting that she had been pained by ministry that denied the existence of a personal Devil, Scattergood worried about young members who were forced to listen to such notions. And she also said that she had had a discussion with the offending minister but had not brought up the Devil matter because it had slipped her mind.

Clearly nettled, Lower denied she had talked with him. Instead he had spoken to her when they passed in the street, and she had not acknowledged his greeting. Moreover, he revealed, "I never have told you frd that when I went to see her to talk to her about Slander she slammed the door in my face."

"Oh Abraham Abraham do have compassion on us," pleaded the usually silent but now exasperated Lancaster, a lumber merchant accustomed to more harmonious dealings.

Mary Taylor, trying to move the discussion back to the query, asked, "whether our men frd were altogether easy with what they had heard" and confessed that the usual answer did not satisfy her.

After Noble reminded the meeting that the word "mostly" qualified the answer, Scattergood said her mind was relieved; "let the answer go as it was."

But Taylor was still unhappy. "Mostly" failed to assuage her discontent. Although "things have been said, which I could not say was unsound, yet I believe had there been waiting for the attitude queried after [love and unity] they would not have been said."

The clerk ignored these comments, proceeded to minute the usual answer, and then inquired if the meeting would agree that "more of that unity which would qualify for an harmonious labour for truths honour is desirable & some of our members are not in unity with our mo. meeting." That query set off a donnybrook.

Lower, looking straight at Mary Taylor, charged, "you are not in unity with your mo. meeting." The air was tense.

Taylor broke the silence: "Who says so it's a charge I believe they cant substantiate."

Indicating that the reformers had already prepared a case against Taylor,

Noble answered, "Women frd say you are not in unity with your Mo: Meeting."

Pushing, Lower asked point-blank, "are you in unity with your mo: meeting."

Taylor tried to deflect the charges and retorted, "I am in unity with our discipline & our mo: meeting is founded on our Discipline of course I am united to the mo: Meeting."

Then Scattergood, who realized that the questioning of her evangelical sister was also aimed at her, interposed, "I can say the same I am united to the discipline & the order of Society."

"They say they unite with the discipline, the query is not whether we unite with the discipline, but are we in unity with our Monthly Mtg." Lower said. "Our meeting has acted agreeably to discipline in every case."

Both women affirmed that they were. Like a prosecutor rather than a cabinetmaker, Lower used the two elders' previous attack on Elias Hicks to remind them that they had condemned a minister with whom the meeting had formally united. With that, Taylor and Scattergood withdrew their objections to the clerk's minute.

When the next query, dealing with Friends' habits, was read, it was Lower's turn to question the traditional answer, "We are in good measure examples in uprightness temperance & moderation." He wanted to know whether women Friends who had evaded the question of being in unity with their meeting were examples of uprightness or not. Somewhat taken aback, Scattergood said she thought "the friends mind had been made easy," a view concurred in by the other embattled elder. Muttering agreement with Noble that the "answer [was] very low," Lower dropped the question and the select meeting proceeded to adjournment.[47] The six Quakers who went home tired that evening had personally experienced a healthy dose of the bitterness that now increasingly marked the controversy among Friends.

Comparatively minor matters bloomed into major issues. One February evening, for instance, Edwin A. Atlee, a physician, recognized minister, and reformer, set out to attend a meeting at the Green Street meetinghouse, accompanied by his wife. About seven or eight blocks from their destination, they happened to see a man wearing a plaid coat hurrying along up the street. Both Atlees took it to be a Friend and overseer, Isaac Davis, perhaps returning the garment to his brother-in-law, since Davis himself wore only plain clothes. Atlee did mention the occurrence, and the story got back to Davis, who with two others, including a leading evangelical, Thomas Stewardson, immediately waited upon Atlee and charged him with trying to blacken Davis's reputation. There were heated words—Davis claimed to have more than twenty persons ready to testify that he was at the meetinghouse fifteen minutes before the couple's arrival—and Atlee, known for his quick temper anyway, exclaimed that regardless of any outward evidence he was convinced that Davis "*was the guilty man.*" Though Atlee went by the very next morning to apologize to his previous night's visitors, Davis laid the matter before the monthly meeting. Some of the more ardent evangelicals seemed intent on disowning the doctor for his admitted imprudence and convinced the meeting to carry the matter over, a tactic denying Atlee the right to serve as a minister or participate in meeting affairs—and, not coincidentially, preventing him from advocating the reform cause at the upcoming April sessions of the yearly meeting. The matter dragged on for over a year, until one First Day morning Atlee stood up without warning in meeting and announced he was resigning his membership; he took his hat and left, much to his compatriots' chagrin.[48]

Outside the city and beyond, other purges also occurred. Maria Imlay, a member of Mount Holly Meeting in New Jersey, was removed as a minister in early 1826 after she preached that the "light within" was the only means of redemption necessary. Among other things, she denied that salvation could be expected from "a man who was hanged between two thieves."[49] A female firebrand, Phebe Johnson, who lived in New York and was infected by the eastern New Light disease, suffered the same fate. Her meeting's elders accused her of speaking too often, ignoring earlier advice to bridle her tongue, and charging Friends with departing from the truth. Her defense that she spoke only when led by the divine Spirit failed to move the elders.[50] In Elias Hicks's quarter, the reformers did not shrink from using the same methods against three of their opponents. In justification, Hicks himself explained that "cutting off two or three opposing and refractory members . . . never failed in restoring order and harmony" among Friends; he thought the present crisis no worse than the time when those who refused to free their slaves were disowned.[51] If such sentiments seemed strange coming from an acclaimed "tolerant," they revealed something of the pervasiveness of the perverse willingness to sacrifice ideals in the interest of victory.

As 1825 played out, the lines of division were so firmly drawn that respect for traditional authority was seriously eroded and even family and personal relationships suffered. In August at Pine Street Meeting, Jonathan Evans was challenged while he was speaking by an intemperate Friend so lacking in position that his name was not recorded. The meeting broke up in confusion with members streaming out the doors before the august Evans could finish. "Would he have believed it if he had been told seven years ago, that he would one day so far loose his influence in *his own* meeting that Friends would not remain to hear him out?" asked a commentator.[52] Another prominent reformer, active in Easton, Maryland, Meeting, related how he and his wife had been snubbed by some former intimates when they visited Salem, New Jersey. These erstwhile friends, now in the Orthodox fold, "turned their backs on us, and took no notice of us in any friendly way, but on the contrary treated us with great coldness and apparent contempt."[53]

Another reformer, more thoughtful than many, surveyed the deterioration and found the hope for reconciliation fading. Thomas McClintock was at Pine Street Monthly Meeting in June when an acrimonious, embarrassing set-to occurred. Provoked by widely circulated printed sermons, an evangelical overseer called Elias Hicks an "infidel" and a "deist"; a reformer shouted in response that "this was not *common* slander, but *slander by wholesale*." Then one of the stalwarts warned that if the propagation of Hicks's doctrines did not stop, "things would be beyond remedy." Shot back one longtime friend of Hicks's, Thomas Fisher: "It was already *too late* — . . . the day had passed by when any thing like a creed, or inquisitorial proceedings could be established."[54] Such deep divisions and sharp attacks indicated how volatile and tense the situation had become by the end of 1825. Separation was not necessarily in the cards—after all, people had surmounted larger disagreements before—but a full measure of charity and good will, not then plentiful commodities among Quakers, was needed. Clearly not needed was added fuel on the fires.

CHAPTER 9

"Painful indeed the spectacle,"
OR
Political Posturing

IN 1831, A PERSPECTIVE OBSERVER noted that "Philadelphia is a city to be happy in. . . . Everything is well conditioned and cared for. If any fault could be found it would be that of too much regularity and too nice precision."[1]

Orthodox Friends in Philadelphia in 1826 longed for things—Quaker things—to be well conditioned and cared for, regular and precise. How disappointed they were destined to be, for the citadel of the elders was under siege. Of course no one knew what 1826 would bring, but it was not hard to see that established authority in Philadelphia Yearly Meeting had been weakened. At Pine Street Meeting, where Jonathan Evans and family were members, where, if anywhere, things should have been well cared for, a committee to propose a clerk and assistant clerk reported on February 1 that it could reach no decision. The always gloomy William Evans groused in his journal about the three "unsound" members who had subverted the regular order. Evans took some comfort that "those restless people" had been thwarted and "could not do as they wished." Moreover, "if Friends keep firm to their religious exercise, and to the cause of Truth," he continued in words he no doubt repeated publicly, "they will prevail over those disorganizing spirits."[2]

Whether Evans's disorganizing spirits would prevail or not remained an open question, but that they continued to exist no one could deny. A self-described "weak one," an ordinary member come to Philadelphia to visit, was dismayed by the acrimony she found. She heard William Gibbons, her trusted physician, remark that "religion was a progressive work—

therefore we ought to be at liberty." "That," Margaret Hilles from Wilmington commented, "has always been the railing point of fanaticks in our society—as to individuals this certainly is true, but how is society to be held together without some restraints." Hilles disapproved of "ranterism," but she admitted she liked the discussion of "serious & interesting subjects" so much that some falsely identified her with the New Lights. For Margaret Hilles, a devoted young mother and loving wife, the spirits of disorganization were not limited to the business of the Society—indeed not, for she felt their fierce pulls and tugs within herself. That experience, which she considered her own unique problem, would come to be shared by an increasing number of Friends.[3]

Contributing most to this disquiet were the perambulations of English evangelicals who agitated meetings all over the country. Anna and Isaac Braithwaite, Ann and George Jones, Elizabeth Robson, Isaac Stephenson, and Thomas Shillitoe all visited the New World in 1826 and 1827 and thrust themselves like a sharp lance into the debate between the reformers and the Orthodox. It would have been bad enough for them to have preached their evangelical doctrines and then moved on to the next stop, but Friends had a longstanding practice that played right into the hands of any controversialist. Each traveling minister carried a letter from home, which the clerk of the meeting visited was asked to endorse. In normal times, some attestation of the meeting's approbation was affixed. Now when the clerk asked if the meeting approved the visitor's ministrations, the ensuing debate could stop all business and drag on until only the most committed remained behind to exhaust the question. In January 1826, Anna Braithwaite showed up at New York Monthly Meeting, presented her certificate, and refused to withdraw while the meeting considered it. Four hours of turmoil later, the only business concluded was to pass the marriage of a young couple and to decide that the clerk should simply note that the travel document had been received and read.[4]

Practically every meeting attended by the visitors erupted into an unseemly dispute, if not over signing the certificates, then dealing with what one side considered false doctrine. When George and Ann Jones descended upon Philadelphia in mid-September 1826, they were confronted by Maria Imlay, a minister from Mount Holly, New Jersey, widely acclaimed by the reform set but already disowned by the evangelicals. One evening at Northern District Meeting, in a surprising development, Imlay united with an earlier message from Ann Jones, a commendation the latter refused to accept. Referring to a "deistical" statement of Imlay's at another meeting, Jones exclaimed that she failed to understand how the "pure & impure" could flow from the same fountain. "I cannot leave this meeting," she continued, "without publicly declaring, that we have no fellowship with her, and testify against that specious and deceitful spirit, which, under the show of speaking in the name of the Lord, blasphemes God and his son Jesus Christ." With that she picked up her bonnet and left, while her husband and Samuel Bettle shook hands to signal the meeting's close.[5]

On one occasion, in November, the Joneses' appearance at Arch Street provoked a near riot that required the summoning of the police. Intended for young Friends under the age of thirty, the meeting attracted a large crowd, including one lad of ten. Forty-five minutes before the meeting was to settle at seven o'clock, scores milled around outside the gate, which was secured by a previously appointed "committee to preserve order." There were hurrahs for Elias Hicks and repeated calls for all who favored him to gather at one side—practically everyone did, even though there were some non-Quakers in the horde. Shouts of "fire, fire" rippled up and down the street and were a signal for fifteen or twenty youngsters inside the house to troop outside. Appearance of the fire engine only added to the confusion, and threats of "Get Charles Roberts," "Knock down Charles Roberts," "Mob Charles Roberts" accompanied pushing the gate to get at the member of the committee who was barring it. At 8:30, when the meeting broke up and Ann and George Jones left, the constable had to clear a path for them amid hoots and insults of "there's the old goat." A special investigation committee reported that some of Hicks's youthful adherents had plotted the scene and carried it off: "in this we are conformed, not only from the circumstance of the pernicious tendencies of his doctrines, but from the fact of his friends having been the prime movers and instigators [?] of this atrocious outrage on the common decencies of civilized life."[6]

One bit of glue that had held the Society together was the warm personal relations that had heretofore existed among Friends. Now the pull of different doctrines and disputes over authority weakened this necessary adhesive. When Abraham Lower embarked on a short winter missionary journey uptown to Arch Street Meeting, he quoted the verse, "By their fruits, ye shall know them." Two elders accosted him as he left the gallery and expressed their dismay at his doctrine. The aggressive Lower called on one of them the next morning and informed him that he had been ill-treated, hinting that it was because he was a poor man and they were rich.[7] William Poole, whose declining health gave him time to reflect on the unfolding situation, complained about the way women Friends were being influenced by their emotions to support the crusades of the English evangelicals. Women—"bad captive silly women laden with sin"—were giving the Society much trouble. "Of the men I do not so much fear, as in general they required *more evidence* than women—who I am persuaded are often held captive by their *affections*. . . .Besides which I think that I have found men *not standing firmly and uprightly* in consequence of the *influence of women*.[8]

When Philadelphia Yearly Meeting convened for its annual week-long sessions on April 17, these tensions became more evident. Lower, whom William Evans called "a troublesome man," spoke first. Focusing on the Light within, he stressed that outward means such as the Bible were useful for knowing divine matters but that God's revelation to each person was the final authority. Richard Jordan, an elderly evangelical widely revered by all Friends, answered Lower. "Man," he believed, "by all his powers was unable to comprehend spiritual things." After London's epistle was read, a struggle followed over whether or not to authorize the usual printing of copies for distribution. Lower and his forces insisted that terms like "mediation" and "atonement" made it unacceptable, and it ought simply to be read and laid by. That this suggestion was approved pointed more to the flexibility of the evangelicals than it did to the power of the reformers.

The rest of the sessions concerned themselves with the evils of the slave trade, something around which all Friends could rally. Consideration of this subject seemed to have been a part of the elders' strategy of diverting attention from questions of authority. One observer noted that when sessions grew tense, the clerk and other evangelicals bore down and moved on. They took advantage of the natural caution that characterized the assistant clerk, John Comly, to keep the meeting on their task. On the women's side of the Arch Street meetinghouse, Elizabeth Robson and Anna Braithwaite continually held the floor to remind the women that unfaithfulness was loose among them. Concluded Thomas Pryor, a careful Friend from Green Street: "I had less satisfaction than I ever had before at a Yearly [Meeting]. . . .But it was observable that the Orthodox friends rather gained than lost ground."[9]

Pryor was not the only Friend who left the yearly meeting with some disquiet. Comly was also troubled by the acrimony that had crept in. Three days after the end of the annual gathering, on April 25, the unwillingness of elders to make any concessions was underscored for Comly in a revealing fashion. Jonathan Evans, it appeared, had rebuked a visiting reform minister, Nicholas Brown from Canada, for the "savour" of some remarks he had made at Pine Street Meeting on the 16th. During their discussion, Evans inferred from what Brown said that the latter believed it possible to live in a state of perfection and "be as perfect as Jesus Christ," but Evans denied he called Brown an "infidel." Since no one else was present during the interview, it was one Friend's word against another's. A group of "weighty" leaders gathered at Samuel Bettle's to try to resolve the matter. Comly, always the conciliator, suggested that each person should make some concession to the other, but Evans insisted that he had stood on the doctrine of Friends and would not compromise. The group broke up with nothing solved.[10]

Something was near being settled, however, in the mind of John Comly. On Tuesday, May 30, having let a month lapse since the yearly meeting and Evans's obstinacy, the assistant clerk asked his monthly meeting for permission to appoint a series of meetings "in several places, chiefly within the limits of our Yearly Meeting, as way might open." Once his request was allowed, Comly was free to travel, hold meetings, and make contacts. Less than two weeks later, on June 11, he started on his trip, crossing the Delaware River and going to Chopwell Meeting in New Jersey. Practically every First Day thereafter, Comly visited one or another meeting. Some of them he used to speak to non-Friends, but most were to settled communities of Quakers. Almost always he had with him another Friend, on occasion a leading reformer like Benjamin Ferris, who accompanied him to West Chester. The gatherings were not without controversy, even for the yearly meeting's second ranking official. At West Chester, for instance, a female elder undertook to instruct him on his failure to include all of a text he preached from. She exhibited, he thought, "anxiety and uneasiness," whereas he "felt calm and peaceful." He always stopped at the homes of acquaintances and timed his visits for the convening of quarterly meetings. Occasionally an old Friend would refuse to attend his meetings.

No clear records remain of what Comly said during these visits. At a select quarterly meeting in August at Goshen he unburdened himself about the need for elders and ministers to be charitable, uphold all for good, and assist the ministry in its work of edification—all commendable if not very specific aims. At two stops, he remembered that he fell silent when the conversation turned to controversial matters, but that may have been because he perceived speakers to be hopelessly on the other side.[11] Comly's travels did not escape the evangelicals' notice, and his visits were later used to prove that the reformers were plotting to separate,[12] although such a motive was contrary to Comly's natural caution. The assistant clerk no doubt spoke his mind—he was clearly troubled—and preached sermons that identified himself with the reformation cause against the elders. Later Comly did decide that separation was in the offing and said so. Events were moving in that direction, but they were not there yet.

The constitutional power struggle within Philadelphia Quarter involving the right of Green Street to remove its evangelical elders still exercised everyone concerned, especially those delegated to sit through the interminable meetings where the matter came up. The same kind of quarrel gave rural Quakers a taste of the controversy when Southern Quarter attempted to remove its representatives on Meeting for Sufferings, who normally served for life or until resignation. Two of Southern Quarter's delegates, Caleb Pierce and Isaac Lloyd, both well-to-do Philadelphia merchants, had joined the city's elders in the 1822 protest against Hicks and become unacceptable to the largely reform-minded rural Friends they represented; a third post was vacant, and Abraham Lower obstructed the best he could from the fourth. On August 30, 1826, the quarter named Joseph Parrish, John Wilson Moore, both doctors, and Halliday Jackson, a prosperous farmer from Darby, to fill the vacant position and the ones held by Pierce and Lloyd. These three new appointees promised to add significantly to the strong but outnumbered reform voice of Lower on Meeting for Sufferings, and that likelihood, of course, made them unacceptable to the dominant evangelical elders.

When the new representatives showed up in September for the regular meeting of Sufferings, they evinced no open doubt that they would be seated. They laid their minutes of appointment on the clerk's already cluttered table, took their seats, spoke to acquaintances, and waited for the meeting to commence. Jonathan Evans, to open the meeting, read his prepared minute containing names of the various representatives—the old list—and picked up one piece of paper, observing casually that it might be relevant to some forthcoming business. Indeed it was. Upon being examined by four members, it turned out to be a protest from Pierce and Lloyd against their removal by the Southern Quarter. An extensive discussion ensued, with temperatures rapidly rising. One side, evangelical, had the advantage of power: Samuel Bettle, clerk of the yearly meeting, Thomas Wistar, both strong of purse and influence, Jonathan Evans, and Joseph Whitall of New Jersey, accuser of Hicks for infidelity. They insisted that Sufferings was a permanent body whose membership was not representative in any secular, republican sense, and they denied the right of any quarter to remove a delegate except at his request or for delinquency. The other side, composed of relatively unknown country members, argued that there was really nothing to debate—Southern Quarter had communicated the names of its representatives, and that was that. Finally, so the body could conduct some of its usual business, a large committee of seven or eight was appointed to make recommendations. The three disputed representatives remained throughout, as did presumably the two men they were to replace.

Between its September meeting and December, when Sufferings again convened, the committee apparently took no action by way of a compromise settlement, for clerk Evans proceeded to open the meeting as he had done three months earlier—by reading the old list of members. This time he rose from his table and underscored the evident fact that two of the disputed members, Jackson and Moore, were present; perhaps, he suggested by way of studied conciliation, they ought to withdraw until the matter was finally settled. Recognizing that the longer the affair dragged on the more likely they were to lose their seats, Jackson and Moore left and went to tell Parrish, who joined in a letter explaining what had happened. Jackson also prepared to attend Southern Quarterly Meeting in February.[13]

In the meantime, Jackson spread the word of what had transpired to distant and interested Friends. One such was William Poole, the infirm strategist of the reform cause in Wilmington. Frustrated at his own inability to get news of what was going on, Poole shared Jackson's letters with others similarly situated. He also pondered proposing to Wilmington meeting that its members be permitted to divide their contributions between the monthly and yearly meetings, "for if we can not have an examination of the funds, some of us have thought of paying no more." Poole's immediate concern arose from a rumor that Sufferings controlled a fund from the now defunct Friends meeting in Charleston, South

Carolina, that they had not accounted for. Country Friends were belatedly beginning to see and feel for themselves; "I have long been persuaded, that if a thorough examination takes place, an unlooked for degree of corruption will be found to have long existed," he signed off.[14]

Friends of Southern Quarter certainly got an opportunity to examine things first hand when they converged on Little Creek, Delaware, in February 1827. Samuel Bettle, at his most ingenious, attended with two other evangelical elders from Philadelphia. Their proposed strategy—always the tactic of those with power and time to wait—was to delay and have the Quarter appoint a committee to confer with the three of them on a solution. Bettle tried to overawe the assembled rural worthies with debating points in support of his contention that Sufferings was a permanent body, but the Quarter had been long since prepared by its most ardent reformers and united behind their August appointments. Moreover, in an obvious rebuke to Sufferings, they decided to report the matter to the yearly meeting and get a final ruling on their right to name anyone they might choose as representative. On reflection, Jackson considered that the case produced a wider sensation than any other matter then before the Society.[15] Certainly it graphically demonstrated to rural Friends how urban elders were usurping their prerogatives, a practice that clearly ran counter to the broad, democratic spirit of the times.

Moves like these hardened the resolution of the reform party, and notes implying a refusal to submit crept into their letters. Hicks thought the agitation among Friends "has been productive of many living and substantial births." "Had the same state of supineness and ease continued, that for a long time been prevalent among us," many now reborn "might still have remained easy and secure admidst their worldly enjoyments."[16] "None ought to be neutral," he instructed Poole, "but stand forth openly and boldly for the promotion of truth's cause; for otherwise they will strengthen the hands of the opposers."[17] Poole needed little encouragement, for he was already active in finding new ways to thwart the evangelicals. Still, some extreme actions of the more disorderly reformers troubled him. He "would have been better satisfied if the impatience of those who *profess themselves his* [Hicks's] *friends* had been so contrould as to have suffered the orthodox opposers to express their sentiments freely."[18]

The hardening lines and the bitterness between the two factions were emphasized when Hicks decided that the cause of truth required him to visit the Philadelphia area in November and December 1826. Spending most of his time within Concord and Southern quarters, both predominately rural areas to the south of Philadelphia, Hicks remained in the city long enough to fuel calls that he be disciplined. The Hicks tour took on something of the character of a royal progress. Marcus T.C. Gould, an enterprising stenographer, went along, insinuating himself into a convenient corner of the meetinghouses they visited so he could take down and later publish Hicks's sermons. The easily impressed William Wharton was everywhere, crowing about Hicks's successes, as was Emmor Kimber, now in the government's employ as a postmaster, and looking to recoup his fortunes with a grand scheme for publishing a volume of Hicks's memoirs. The acclaim of the crowds that greeted Hicks, even in isolated areas, would have gone to the head of a lesser man.[19]

In the city, though, rancor emerged. Friends' meetings for worship, hitherto noted for their tranquility, were now fraught with malice. In early December at Northern District Meeting, the worship degenerated at least twice into shouting matches between speaker and audience, contests so loud Gould lost all track of what was said. Even Hicks momentarily succumbed to the nasty mood. Immediately after Othniel Alsop, a wealthy vinegar merchant, spoke for about fifteen minutes in an atmosphere rapidly souring, Hicks quieted his supporters and began, "now I have been learning all the time my friend has been speaking; for we can learn not only from things that are right, but by things that are wrong. . . . " His jab flung, he went on to appeal to the group to judge for themselves who had spoken the truth.[20]

The most serious clash came on December 10 in a meeting at Pine Street so packed with young supporters of Hicks that regular members could not find seats but had to jostle with outsiders in the aisles. Hicks was not openly provocative; at least his words seemed conciliatory enough without compromising his views. When the town clock sounded 10 A.M., he began to speak. His doctrine ran backward to invoke that of the earliest Friends; that it won the open and vocal disapproval of the elders symbolized the degree to which traditional Quakerism clashed with the new evangelical doctrines. His emphasis centered on the in dwelling of God's spirit—the "divine life" Hicks called it on this occasion—within every rational being. "Now this life is the first principle, and has been the first principle in every reformation since man's fall and disobedience to God." He affirmed that human beings had to be reborn out of their natural, first-born selves into the life governed by submission to God's spirit—and to nothing outward—

no law, no outward blood, no outward Scriptures, not even an outward faith. An inner transformation was required, an obedience to the divine life which the physical, material Jesus exemplified so totally and completely.[21]

When he had finished, the meeting stirred, and elder Jonathan Evans, at sixty-seven nearly thirteen years Hicks's junior, rose to his feet. Some in the brimming room made derisive sounds, but the silence then deepened, the assembled body fully aware that this occasion would be long remembered.[22] Here now were the founts from which two different streams of theological thought flowed, the older one looking back to articulate an ancient view long cherished by Friends, the other, aged but still junior, representing equally venerable doctrine with roots reaching even farther but new to the Society to which they both belonged. Hicks spoke for a traditional constituency that distrusted the new-fangled world, which was somehow—they probably could not explain how—bound up with the new doctrines. And Evans, despite his traditional clothing and his careful, even understated speech, spoke for those ready to compromise with an emerging dynamic, and complex world, those willing to embrace it and to surrender the Society's peculiarities for full acceptance in it. At least some of those there on that December First Day knew that Hicks and Evans had once been friends but had not spoken civilly to each other for years. The meeting must have waited for Jonathan Evans as few Quaker meetings had ever waited before. And he did not disappoint them even if his words sounded a bit prepared, not quite spontaneous. He joined the issue.

"I believe it my duty to say," he began implying that he took no pleasure in the task, "that our Religious Society have always believed in the Atonement, the Mediation, and the Intercession, of our Lord, and Saviour Jesus Christ—that by Him all things were created, that are in heaven, and that are in earth, visible and invisible, whether they be thrones or dominions"— here was an appropriate point for a pause, to permit the audience to appreciate that dominions, even the dominion ruled by the elders, had heavenly sanction—"or principalities, or powers, all things were created by him, and for him, he is before all things, and by him all things consist. Any doctrines which go to invalidate these fundamental truths of the Christian Religion we can not receive, nor have any unity with."

"Great efforts are now making to bring the people to believe, that our Lord Jesus Christ was no more than a man—this is not our belief—nor can we admit it. Our Society never held any such opinions, nor do we

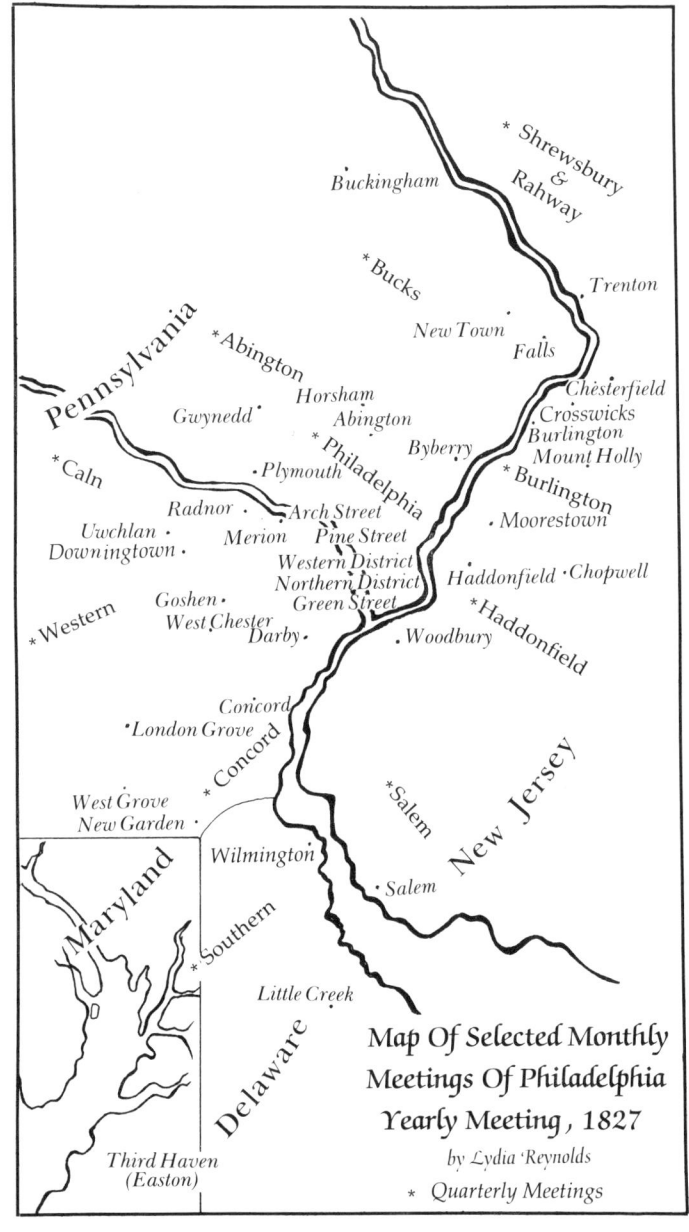

hold ourselves accountable for the sentiments of those who hold such doctrines." Evans then repeated three titles for Jesus used by the evangelicals, each one calculated to draw a line between them and the reformers, from whom he had already disassociated the Society: "King of Kings," "Lord of Lords," and "Judge of quick and dead." He closed on a defensive note in a reaffirmation that duty demanded his labor: "I think it right for me to mention this in order that the people may not suppose that we hold or approve such doctrines."[23]

As he finished, Isaac Lloyd, one of the powerful evangelical elders, was on his feet seconding Evans. "I unite with our friend Jonathan Evans. We as a Religious Society never did hold or believe, that our Blessed Lord and Saviour Jesus Christ came to be the Jews only, but that he was given for God's Salvation to the ends of the Earth."

Hicks added simply, "I have spoken; and I leave it for the people to judge—I can not exalt myself into the judgement seat."[24]

When the meeting arose, Hicks went to Evans and held out his hand, but the unbending elder replied, "no, Elias, I have not unity with thee nor with thy doctrines." Lloyd, still standing there, expressed his sorrow at the tone of Hicks's message, and Evans added, quoting the Bible, "He that denieth the Son, the same hath not the Father, let his profession be what it may."

Hicks flared back, "He that says I deny him or make him a mere man, is a liar."

But Evans stood his ground. "Elias, I am not afraid of thee, nor of thy abuse. Thou hast departed from the truth."[25]

The evangelicals boasted loudly of their victory over Hicks, an interpretation that the reformers naturally refused to accept, and forwarded minutes of disapproval to Jericho.[26] At Western District Meeting, where Hicks had spoken on the afternoon after the Pine Street confrontation, Thomas Wistar and Isaac Bonsall spearheaded an attack on "heterodox" followers of the now-absent Long Islander for their vocal abuse at that gathering. In a formal report they contemned the Hicksiste doctrines as tending "to the subversion of sound religious principles, and of the wholesome restraints of moral and domestic discipline." This extreme statement brought Jesse Kersey, a leading authority on Friends' practices, into the struggle; but the evangelical clerk ignored Kersey's argument, as well as the public opposition of twelve family heads, and minuted the meeting's acceptance. A similar action got under way at Pine Street,[27] where the evangelicals also moved against Thomas Fisher, brother-in-law of William Wharton, for some unspecified uncomplimentary remarks about Jonathan Evans.[28]

An influential group of evangelicals, led by Evans himself, and representing Meeting for Sufferings, waited on Marcus Gould shortly after his publication of Hicks's sermons. Upset at alleged omissions from his transcription, they complained that Gould's record of Evans's statement had distorted his views, although they mentioned no specific examples. The evangelical doyen also expressed wonderment that the omitted sections of Hicks's remarks were the ones that "were the most exceptionable." Gould stuck by his account, which fired up his inquisitors. Henry Cope, an up-and-coming young evangelical and clerk of Pine Street Meeting, demanded that Gould share his notes with them, but the stenographer refused, informing them that they had no right to make such a request. Well, one of the visitors retorted, "no individual has a right to go into the M. House of a religious Society & there take down what he heard & publish it for his emolument." The Society, they went on, "was a respectable body & many of its members in this city were well-known & esteemed & this evidence if laid before the public would go far. . . ." With Gould unwilling to back down, the visiting Friends left, their anger still not dissipated.[29]

While the evangelicals thus tried turning their prestige to advantage, the reformers were more and more dismayed at the state of things. John Comly, still paying visits to local meetings, arrived in Philadelphia the first of February. He was taken aback at what he witnessed at a select meeting of ministers and elders on Saturday, the 3rd. Strife and contention rent the meeting into contending parties. "Such a select meeting I had never attended," he exclaimed. "Painful indeed the spectacle!"[30] Comly attended Pine Street Meeting the next morning, Western District in the afternoon. Hostility toward him from once warm friends prevaded the very atmosphere.

That Sunday evening, February 4, he met with a group of reformers, including certainly Thomas McClintock, William Wharton, Samuel Noble, and Abraham Lower. Together they shared their gloom. No detailed record of what transpired survives, but pieced together from various sources, it is clear that the group moved toward making major decisions about the future. Comly had news about his travels, and as the city Friends recounted tales of their experiences, their gloom deepened. At one point, Comly asked straight out if there were any way the divisions could be healed, perhaps through mediation, perhaps by a more complete reliance upon the divine spirit, perhaps through some remedy he had not even considered. The assembled group could suggest nothing, and Comly, up to this point hopeful if not optimistic, felt his spirits sag. Then, like a revelation, he thought of a way to escape the problem; but as the group did not seem ready to unite around any program yet, he held his peace.

Next morning, Philadelphia Quarter gathered. From the first, ill will and division reigned. The meeting had as much noise, if not the festive air of a carnival. Sometimes five, six, or eight people tried to talk at once, and shouts of "order, order" interrupted speaker after speaker.[31] Four of the monthly meetings responded to the query regarding reading of pernicious publications in the usual general terms: Pine Street was more specifiic. It expressed concern that too many members were not only reading but circulating pamphlets tending to destroy the Christian religion and the authenticity of the Bible. The evangelical clerk, Thomas Stewardson, used the Pine Street report as the basis for the entire quarter's answer to the query, an indirect way of traducing the reformers' reading habits. Vocal protests led him to aver that he had no intention of modifying his summary unless the *"solid* part" of the meeting wished him to do so. During the raucous debate, Roberts Vaux, the most prominent Quaker in Philadelphia, who normally took little part in disputes like this one, lost his patience with Lower's assertions and vociferated, "I hope this meeting will not be turned out of its course by the flimsy sophistry of Abraham Lower." As many as one hundred members shouted at Vaux at one time, most of them from the back part of the house. John Comly sat by and watched while Friends were, as he phrased it, "stripped of the clothing of Christian meekness, forbearance, and brotherly kindness."[32]

Whipping up the debate, the evangelicals indicted those who failed to pay their debts — a violation of discipline which could subject the debtor to disownment — for continuing to take part in meeting affairs. "Monthly meetings," the argument went, "should not make use of those persons or their time who are not manifesting an honest exertion for paying their debts." Only those whose conduct corresponded to their religious obligations had a right to speak in meetings, they also asserted. This declaration amounted to an evangelical definition of the "solid and weighty" members and explained how clerks could ignore large numbers of Friends who did not meet their standard, yet could not be excluded outright from meetings.³³ Throughout the meeting, the clerk overlooked the "lighter" attenders, drawing minutes reflecting the views of more substantial members.³⁴ When dissidents could not be so silenced, a meeting's overseers could always undertake to "deal" with them, as in the case of a member of Pine Street charged later with making "misstatements" during the quarterly meeting.³⁵

Between the late recess on Monday and the 9 A.M. reconvening on Tuesday, something happened. No specific record survives of a meeting of the reformers that evening, but evidence points to a conclave of some kind. For one thing, as he sat silently in Monday's meeting musing on all that had gone before, Comly had his mind "opened to see more clearly that this contest must result in a separation of the two conflicting parts of the Society, as the only means of saving the whole from a total wreck." He began immediately to attempt to convince his colleagues not to expend their energies on a useless task, but to simply withdraw from the scene of contention and ask to be united to the country meetings. The urban Hicksites would have a home among peole who shared their desire that "the testimonies of Truth be again advanced and upheld."³⁶ Inevitably, Comly's plan provoked searching discussion of possible courses of action for the next day.

When the quarter reconvened on Tuesday, events also pointed to a change in strategy. Abraham Lower, leader of the dissidents, was a different man. No longer the pushy, angry militant determined to protect the rights of the average Quaker from powerful elders, Lower exhibited a calm but resentful reasonableness. On the very first question to be considered, he announced an unwillingness to continue the struggle. To explain this unexpected change of course, Lower told the meeting that it was clear the clerk intended to defer to those he considered solid Friends; in such a circumstance, others could hardly expect a fair decision. Therefore, the remarkably changed leader proposed, "without debate, we should patiently submit, & let the minute which was read yesterday pass." And so it went on every matter that came up. When the report on the Green Street elders was made, requiring them to be reinstated over the meeting's continued opposition, Green Street champion Lower explained that, for the reasons given earlier and because resistance seemed futile, the reformers would acquiesce. Anyway, he hinted, Green Street "had their *remedy*." Some reformers complained, but most followed Lower's lead. Samuel Noble, also in on the plan, suggested that a committee be appointed to consider the possibility of Green Street seceding from Philadelphia and joining nearby Abington Quarter. No one at the clerk's table paid any attention to this Noble gesture.[37] With the opposition quieted, the meeting ended by noon, something of a surprise considering the lengthy session of the previous day.[38]

The discussions during the meeting of Philadelphia Quarter set the reformers on a path to separation. Until they experienced the heavy-handed rule imposed during the quarterly meeting, and until a Friend as influential as Comly threw in his lot with them, the reform element had aimed at somehow convincing some of the elders of the justice of their position. Their vision of a reformation included the right of local meetings to enjoy the maximum autonomy and of individuals to work out their own statements of religious faith, all the while permitting them to be full participating members. These goals ran counter to the doctrinal position the evangelicals insisted on, just as they challenged the elders' authority.

The theological differences separating the two groups were not so great — Hicks and the reformers did not deny the historical Jesus a central role in God's plan of salvation, and they affirmed the work his mission called him to — but the words they used to define their separate positions had become more divisive than unifying. The moderate Comly, who must have appeared a temporizer to the more ardent reformers, experienced his greatest distress in the Quaker City when he watched silently and "beheld the confusion of language among them, so that they could not understand one another's speech." Such confusion and misunderstanding led to the incrimination of individuals, and that in turn made him lose hope. Separation became the only answer. He wanted it to be temporary, like a fast to restore health, but the step had to be taken regardless. Comly recognized that taking the course he was about to embark on would bring down censure, as he put it, "from those who could not understand the subject, or see it in the same light which has thus been opened to my view," but he saw no alternative.[39]

Shortly after the meeting's end while resting from the trauma of two days of struggle and long hours of intense discussion, Thomas McClintock sat down to write William Poole about recent happenings. In closing, he looked to the future in words that revealed Comly's influence and his general conclusions about the past. "The approaching Y.M.," he predicted, "will be an important crisis. . . . My own impression is, that it will be the last Yearly Meeting that will be held in Phil[a] in its present *joint capacity*, "He foresaw creation of one or two additional yearly meetings, one convening in Wilmington and consisting of quarters farther removed from Philadelphia, and perhaps another gathering at Green Street for suburban quarters; all this presupposed that the brittle "aristocracy" did not break in the meantime.

Then he went beyond Comly's more passive approach. "Without *another* clerk than the one we have had, the result of the Y.M^g must, in all human probability, be *impropitious*." This stronger position reflected the more determined attitude of one who had spent long years in the reformation cause to which Comly had only recently became a public convert. McClintock preferred to force out the evangelicals, leaving the yearly meeting in the hands of the reformers. "If the *aristocracy* which has got up amongst us is put down at our next Yearly Mg, it abittered, being high steel & brittle will fly off—which I could rather desire might be the result." For such an end, he applauded the pressure Abington Quarter applied when it doubled its usual number of representatives to the yearly meeting. *"Go ye and do likewise,"* he prodded Poole.[40]

Doubling the representatives from outlying quarters was part of a two-part strategy that unfolded after the Philadelphia conferences in early February. Comly took the lead in promoting a peaceful separation. The same day Philadelphia Quarter ended, he went to his own quarter in Abington, privately related his decision to work for a separation, and invited his friends to participate. On the 15th, he was at Green Street, carrying the same proposal; the next day he went to Wilmington and repeated his analysis in that hotbed of reform sentiment. On the 19th he showed up at Darby, Halliday Jackson's meeting, and found Friends there and visitors from Western Quarter nearly all receptive to his message. On the 22nd he attended Bucks Quarter and then Newtown, where he conferred with numerous acquaintances from rural meetings and recommended "a quiet retreat from the scenes of confusion and disorder which now agitate us." Among others, he worked on Edward Hicks, who did not completely forswear his personal intention to struggle with the "royal Americans."[41] In early March Comly convinced Emmor Kimber of the need for a separation and won his active support. When he went to Abington on March 4, he broached the need for that quarter to be prepared to take in Green Street Meeting when it finally split off from Philadelphia Quarter. After visiting Gwynedd on the 18th, where he ran into another itinerant,

Abraham Lower, Comly returned home to tend to some household affairs and await next month's yearly meeting.[42]

While Comly promoted a peaceful separation, another, more aggressive thrust was being readied. Lower, Samuel Noble, and Halliday Jackson, among others, traveled in the interest of limiting the terms of appointment for elders and members of Meeting for Sufferings—a proposal that the reformers in both New York and Philadelphia Yearly Meetings had championed unsuccessfully for years. The travelers also posed a more fundamental challenge to the evangelical power brokers: They wanted to double the number of official representatives to the yearly meeting from each quarter. Since any Friend might fully participate in the yearly meeting, representatives had only one important function: to nominate candidates for clerk and assistant clerk. Traditionally, each quarter sent two representatives for each monthly meeting within its confine. In doubling the number, they might assure that Samuel Bettle, clerk for ten years now, would be replaced by their most prominent adherent in the yearly meeting, assistant clerk John Comly. Lower had begun working to remove Bettle more than a year before, and he probably sired the plan to double representatives. Of course, it was by no means clear that this ploy would effect the desired result, for some of the extra ones chosen would undoubtedly be evangelicals; thus Abington chose 28, "21 heterodox and 7 of the Elderites." This possibility made Jackson rather less than an enthusiastic supporter of the idea, although he pushed it in Concord Quarter.[43] These efforts resulted in the doubling of representatives from Bucks and Abington quarters and an increase elsewhere—except in Philadelphia Quarter, the evangelical stronghold where the number remained twenty-four, until 1827 almost twice any two of the other quarters combined.[44]

In some meetings reform proposals prompted open confrontations between the two factions. At Bucks Quarter on February 22, Edward Hicks used the discussion to assail an English minister, Elizabeth Robson, as the source of the conflict for compromising the society's traditional testimony against "hireling priests." He charged that if American Quakers followed their English cousins into consorting with the hierarchy they would decline as surely as those in Britain. Afterwards, Bartholomew Wistar, one of Robson's Philadelphia companions, so vociferously assaulted Hicks that the latter's rural neighbors, unaccustomed to such set-tos, considered Wistar both insolent and impertinent.[45] Like the other country quarters, Bucks stood by its members' reform principles, sent twenty-four representatives to the yearly meeting—with only three or four likely to side with the Orthodox—and then added a fillip to the proposal to end permanent appointments to Sufferings. "If it shall be thought best to continue said meeting [for Sufferings]," they minuted, "the appointment of its members may be exclusively confined to the Quarterly meetings and subject to their removal." Bucks ventured this addition because word had just come from Philadelphia that one of the men they were then considering for Sufferings was unacceptable to the elders. The anger of the quarter was clearly rising.[46]

The bitterness in Bucks was matched elsewhere. From Southern Quarter, Dr. Robert Moore wrote about perceptions of "papal intolerance" on the part of the elders that would produce a backlash.[47] A rumor spread in Wilmington that Abraham Lower had been charged with unsoundness as a minister and was to be hauled before a select committee. "What will be the result?" wondered Benjamin Ferris. "When I look at the *Wealth* and *talent* and *industry* of our opponents I sometimes feel dismayed," but then "when I look toward that power that not only preserved David's life . . . but finally set him on the throne of Israel . . . I am encouraged."[48] After Richard Jordan, a highly repected minister, died in October 1826, the Haddonfield, New Jersey, Meeting prepared a disputed memorial minute for him; the reformers were convinced Meeting for Sufferings rewrote it to emphasize his opposition to their efforts. Said William Wharton: "I consider it a proclamation of orthodox views under the name of *R.J.'s memorial.*"[49] At Bucks's select quarterly meeting of ministers and elders, an evangelical elder and his wife forcefully tried removing a woman who attempted to deliver her message and got her to the door, only to have her relieve her mind of its burden by speaking from there.[50] When William Poole finally got his hands on a copy of the minutes that Pine Street and Western District meetings had dispatched to Jericho, he convened a group of ten or twelve Friends to discuss the charges against Hicks. Not one of the company, he reported, after reviewing what Hicks had actually said, but that believed the effort came from the "hand of that *master spirit*, of that man, who to destroy the character of Elias, is disposed to go to almost any length." Let the "young and middle-aged" know what was going on, he continued, and "it will produce such an excitement as scarcely has been known."[51]

Judging from their activities, the evangelicals in Philadelphia seemed bent on purging those who, as one observer commented, "dare to stand opposed to their proceeding."[52]

Optimism still reigned in the mind of assistant clerk John Comly, however. Satisfied that his labors in the field had been carried out under a divine leading and that he had demonstrated the faithfulness required of him, he evinced the surest conviction about what the yearly meeting would bring. "I looked forward to a trying Yearly Meeting," he recalled, "but felt no anxious care 'for the morrow.' " The only proper and reasonable solution was a peaceful separation, and he believed Friends would follow that course.[53]

The other reformers were not so sanguine—or perhaps not so convinced that their efforts had divine sanction. On the very day the yearly meeting opened, the infirm William Poole, unable to attend because he had to have his aching head shaved and bled, wrote a compatriot a letter that presupposed the struggle would go on; he did not forecast a split or write as though he anticipated a final resolution from the deliberations in Arch Street. Despite his illness, Poole had no plans to withdraw from the concerns of Society. To the contrary, he hoped that the yearly meeting would rebuff the evangelicals and listen to those who sided with Hicks, even as he plotted strategy for after the meeting's adjournment.[54] A letter from Hicks to Wharton exhibited the same commitment to continue the struggle.[55] For Thomas Pryor, not actively involved in the reform effort but an alert observer, the 1827 yearly meeting promised nothing out of the ordinary, a continuation of a conflict that all had come to expect if not always accept.[56]

On the eve of what turned out to be the most important session in their history, most Friends of Philadelphia Yearly Meeting foresaw no significant changes. Even those who had labored for the reformation the longest and who were prepared to unseat the clerk could not be sure. True, the ingredients for a split were present—the determined English ministers, the personal animosities, the differing theological positions, the struggles over power and questions of local autonomy, the abrasiveness of the Philadelphia grandees, the insecurities of the more rural and plebeian—but then they had all been there the year before and the year before that. This time the difference was that the reformers had hatched a plan around which they could rally and on which the evangelicals would find it difficult to compromise without surrendering a central symbol of their power. Philadelphia's Quaker order, then, was under serious attack, even if the relative strength of the contending parties remained unclear.

A vague and uneasy sense that such a struggle was impending infected average Friends as they prepared to attend the yearly meeting in April. Let Margaret Hilles, destined to side with the Orthodox, speak for them. On April 1, she wrote a friend, "I have not yet decided on going to Y. Meetg tho' my inclination points strongly that way—it is expected that it will be a time of great interest—but I hope the women's meetg will escape great part of the trial."[57]

PART III

From Reformation to Separation: Philadelphia, New York, Ohio, Indiana, Baltimore

CHAPTER 10

"Let us separate!"
OR
The Prime Division

AT THE CONCLUSION OF their yearly meeting in 1827, Philadelphia Friends followed custom and adopted a closing message, an epistle, addressed to other Friends. Traditionally, this document combined a brief account of what had transpired together with exhortations for readers to ponder. On April 21, after it had gone through the most divisive, the most bitter and painful sessions that any yearly meeting of Friends had ever experienced, Philadelphia Yearly Meeting approved a surprising epistle. This document read as though it had been composed in a vacuum, for it made no reference to a separation, the struggle over the clerkship, or the verbal abuse that had occurred within the four walls of the spacious Arch Street meetinghouse. Indeed, to read this letter alone, one would never have known that anything out of the ordinary had happened. It referred only to the "weak & deficient state of the various branches of this Meeting," an understatement if ever there was one.[1]

Yet, reading between its lines, in a curious, political way, the epistle was highly revealing and did help characterize the outcome of the 1827 yearly meeting, Philadelphia's one hundred and forty-sixth, and its last one as a united body until 1955. The epistle, after all, amounted to a perfunctory gesture when it came before the meeting on Saturday morning after nearly six days of off-and-on acrimony, and it was easy to win immediate approval for it from the tired and dispirited group. It also embodied the views of those who controlled the yearly meeting at that time and who would continue to control its machinery. For them, the branches were, in truth, weak and deficient and over the course of the next year would wither away to almost nothing. Philadelphia Yearly Meeting came to resemble a large, richly coiffured urban head with a weak and deformed rural body. The Orthodox did not mean their epistle to be read this way, but they had written more revealingly than they intended. Theirs was the classic position of powerful rulers whose subjects had left them behind, alone with their prestige, wealth, and talent.

All along the evangelicals had relied on their positions of superior power. They dominated Meeting for Sufferings, and the clerk of the yearly meeting was a charter member of their small group. In the city they controlled four of the five local meetings outright. Philadelphia Quarter generally reflected their wishes; and, because they resided close to the center of power, they kept abreast of developments and could respond to problems with alacrity. Moreover, for the past half-dozen years, the elders had enjoyed the active assistance of English evangelical ministers who had spread their newer version of Quakerism far and wide. Thus with the levers of power firmly in their grip and with the motive power supplied by visitors from abroad, they drove the machinery of the yearly meeting with only an occasional slip, as for example when they failed to win the 1823 yearly meeting's approval of their statement of faith. Like all those who exercise authority, they could afford to wait. And 1827 was the year they had waited for.

The yearly meeting officially began on the third Second Day of Fourth Month: in 1827, on Monday, April 16. But preliminaries foretold the future. This year on Friday the 13th, Meeting for Sufferings met to give final approval to the memorial minute for the much lamented minister, Richard Jordan. The minute's wording seemed unnecessarily partisan: that Jordan stood "as a watchman on the walls of Zion, sounded the alarm" against Friends who objected to observing the First Day and to reading Scripture as practices suited to "the normal, *traditional* professor, yet the enlightened and liberal-minded follower of *rational* religion, unshackled by the *prejudices of education*, or the force of *external evidence* had no need of them."[2] How could any but the most unfeeling oppose honoring a deceased saint? On the other hand, approval of the minute served to strengthen the hand of the evangelicals, whose power allowed them to recruit the dead to their banner.[3]

A clearer indication of the power of the evangelicals and the tactics they planned to employ came the next day at the select yearly meeting of ministers and elders; Jonathan Evans, in yet another of his incarnations, was its clerk. George and Ann Jones and Elizabeth Robson attended; as ministers from London Yearly Meeting, they were entitled to recognition. They hung back until Philadelphia Quarter tossed its bombshell. In answering the query concerning ministers, the quarter complained that some had come among them—everyone knew that "some" referred to ministers like Elias Hicks—who preached doctrines "tending to lay waste the fundamental doctrines of the Christian religion." Moreover, and this was a startling departure from customary practice, the quarter confessed that some "unsound ministry" existed in its midst. Seizing upon this opening, the English evangelicals proceeded to flay away at the entire yearly meeting, charging that infidelity was rampant. Then eighty-year-old William Jackson, who had been a rural minister for more than fifty years, in Chester County, proposed the formation of a committee to visit monthly and quarterly meetings to investigate these charges. This strategy was clever, since visiting committees were commonplace and normally unexceptionable, but this one would be charged to investigate and judge the theology of recognized ministers. With the right kind of committee making the right kinds of decisions, a purge could be initiated and unsoundness rooted out. Jackson himself made no secret of his belief that the Society had every right to disown members who could not affirm the divinity of Christ and the divine authority of the Scripture. Appointment of such a committee was approved over the active opposition of the reformers.[4]

John Comly left the session even more convinced that the evangelical party intended to dominate; that perception reinforced his conclusion that Friends could not longer remain together. Accompanying Halliday Jackson, whose own status on Sufferings was still not finally settled, he went to Darby and stayed for the meeting that third Sunday in April. At Green Street Meeting in the afternoon, Elizabeth Robson took a last opportunity before the yearly meeting to preach against those who did not believe that the precious blood of Christ was the means of salvation. Her lengthy message unsettled the meeting and caused a good bit of restlessness. Hugh Judge's daughter gave more satisfaction with her sermon that Friends must not rely on outward sacrifices. At the same time in Darby, a group of country Friends met with Comly, and another conclave of city reformers got together on the eve of the yearly meeting; both explored ways to deal with the deepening crisis.[5] Like the Orthodox, they would be ready the next morning.

The men and women who milled around the three front entrances at the impressive Arch Street meetinghouse had much to talk about. The winter just passed had been one of the coldest in years; ice had closed the Delaware River for thirty-one days straight into March, an almost unheard-of event. And someone was bound to remark that the winter was not over yet—April this year was colder than any for more than a decade. The crowd was large, and there were, thanks to the rural quarters' increased representation, more new faces than in previous years. These new participants stared and had pointed out to them the leaders of the Society as they hurried toward their places: Jonathan Evans, his hat turned up in the back; Samuel Bettle, wearing his modern trousers; the aged William Jackson; John Cox from New Jersey, with his sharp features, eye patch, and unusually long hair; Stephen Grellet, refugee from the French Revolution, whose speech still reminded listeners of his native country; and John Comly, short and plump with close-cut hair.[6]

As the 10 A.M. hour of convening neared, the town clock would strike, and the men and women would began to separate, the women gravitating toward the west side, the men toward the east. Despite the fact that men and women were theoretically equal in Friends' polity, the main business was considered on the east side of the house; indeed, the Women's Yearly Meeting would intrude only once in a major way in the deliberations of the week. Once in the meetinghouse, a newcomer, whether male or female, would see essentially the same facilities—a large room with high ceilings, at the south end three raised rows making the gallery for the ministers and elders, each seatback with a railing for ministering Friends to lean on, around the three other walls an upstairs balcony. In front of the top row of the gallery a table for the clerk and assistant clerk had been placed so they could look out over the entire room. The rooms had an air of openness about them, and even when crowded, as they were today, they tended to induce a quiet solemnity. Disrespect seemed out of order. The gallery this year, as in years past, was filled with powerful and substantial evangelicals. But a few reformers claimed places by right. Abraham Lower, the fiery cabinetmaker of Green Street, moved to his seat among his betters, as did a smattering of other reformers—William Wharton, young and close friend of Elias Hicks; Halliday Jackson, an aggressive farmer; and two medical doctors, Philadelphian Nathan Shoemaker and Robert Moore, from Easton, Maryland.

Tension rather than solemn silence united this yearly meeting, each side eyeing the other warily. As was custom, the meeting gathered in its traditional worship, broken by one Friend who spoke out three times to warn that God would surely withdraw his Spirit from his people if they turned from their inward guide. George Jones was next on his feet, speaking in his usual evangelical manner. Presiding clerk Bettle called the names of 163 representatives, most of whom were present and ready. Then a woman Friend entered to inform the men that Elizabeth Robson desired to address them at a suitable time. For the reformers, there was no such time, and some came right out and said so. But seventy-four-year-old John Cox spoke from the gallery in a cultivated and impressive tone calculated to silence them, "I am surprised that there should be a word of opposition to our Friend's concern." When Jonathan Evans gave the word that Robson might enter, the doors were opened.

For forty-five minutes she preached and prayed, centering on the divisions across the yearly meeting and the unsoundness of belief she had encountered. She referred to some as "light as chaff" and blown to and fro by every puff of wind. For the evangelicals, hers was sound testimony. The reformers believed she had permitted herself to be used by the other side, and they demonstrated their displeasure by refusing to rise or doff their hats when she prayed. When Robson withdrew close to noon, the meeting attended to some other routine business that kept it in session until nearly half-past one and then adjourned to permit the representatives to meet and select nominees for clerk and assistant clerk.

Nothing very troublesome had taken place so far, and Thomas Pryor thought that each side seemed "desirous of acting properly and consistent with the Master's will." A keen onlooker with Hicksite tendencies, Pryor was not close enough to the reform movement to know that the major confrontation of the week was about to occur in the representatives' meeting. The more urgent reformers had pinned their hopes on removing Bettle and making Comly clerk—a plan that the assistant clerk had come to accept if not totally embrace. With perhaps two-thirds of the representatives on their side, they had a realistic chance of success.[7]

As the rest of the yearly meeting hurried away to get some lunch, the representatives moved to the front of the room to engage in what had always been a mere formality, requiring no more than quick assent to continuing the incumbents as clerk and assistant clerk or ratifying noncontroversial substitutes. With Friends so sharply divided and determined, however, the kind of broad consensus that had worked in the past collapsed into a disorderly and heated row rivaling a hard-fought political convention. In fact, this meeting was worse because there apparently was no presiding officer, meaning that the person who could shout the loudest or hold the floor through personal prestige was the only one who could be heard. Because many representatives were new, most stood by as the tide of struggle surged around them and simply left it up to the ones who seemed more experienced and aggressive, or loudest.

The reform element pushed John Comly; the Orthodox, Samuel Bettle. A dispute commenced immediately over the order in which they were to be considered, some thinking that the first mention of Comly's name gave his candidacy priority, other arguing that the wisdom of removing the ten-year veteran Bettle ought to top the agenda. When the discussion finally returned to the merits of the two leaders, William Evans, for the evangelical wing, attacked Comly for the meetings he had held where separation had been discussed; no man who promoted separation, Evans advanced, had a rightful claim to the top post in the yearly meeting. The reformers used their preponderance of numbers to prove that Comly enjoyed broader support than one who sided with a minority of Friends; in this gathering, they reminded those who spoke of Bettle's prominence, every man was equal to every other. At this point, Abraham Lower got the floor and proposed that John Watson from Bucks Quarter should take the clerk's place and copy down the names of those favoring each candidate, a move vigorously rejected by some older members. When Watson himself declined, Lower suggested that those who favored Comly should join him on the other side of the house. But Daniel Stroud, a stout and influential Friend from Abington Quarter, stood in the aisle, his arms raised in warning, and protested: this is "like a political meeting, to decide by a majority." Lower's ploy had failed.

By this time, it was getting near 4 P.M., and sounds could be heard of Friends outside the meeting waiting to get in. One proposal that floated amid the confusion would have authorized John Cox to report to the afternoon session that the representatives could not reach an agreement. At another point, Lower renewed his suggestion that a young man from Bucks take down the names of those favoring each nominee, and Marden Wilson briefly occupied the table but only recorded a few names before the uproar overwhelmed him. A few representatives began to slip out one of the doors—Halliday Jackson met one hurrying through the yard muttering that he had to get something for dinner—and the sentiment grew that Cox should report the meeting's inability to agree. Lower, who had concocted the strategy to remove Bettle weeks before, got the floor and shouted, "Friends! Don't you realize that if this report is made Samuel Bettle will be clerk!"[8] Other ways out of the impasse were proposed — including resuming deliberations that evening or the next morning — but nothing was finally settled when the door on the southeast side of the building was pushed open and the crowd rolled in over the representatives. Lower believed his supporters expected him to submit Comly's name.[9]

Thus when the full body reassembled, the representatives had no agreed-upon report. Bettle went directly to his accustomed place, but Comly did not join him at the table, apparently awaiting the committee's recommendation. Two brief messages admonished the audience to exhibit love, patience, and quietness, but it was immediately clear that the injunctions had no impact. Cox arose in his place in the gallery and declared that the representatives had been unable to agree on the names of the two officers. Nothing like this had ever happened before, and the shock must have been considerable for those who did not know what had happened. Presently, William Jackson, the oldest member there, got to his feet and said he had attended every yearly meeting for sixty years and the practice had always been to continue the old clerks until new ones were appointed.[10] Since this statement sounded as though the appointments were only temporary, Halliday Jackson suggested that Bettle and Comly should retain their positions during the Monday session, with the representatives expected to come up with nominees who could, if it had to be that way, win the support of a majority. Some of the more prominent evangelicals, Thomas Stewardson and Thomas Wistar for example, quite warmly opposed any such concession to majority rule.[11] The more radical Lower proposed an immediate adjournment so that the representatives might bring in a recommendation. Jonathan Evans said that since the representatives had not named a clerk it was the duty of the meeting to do so; he thought Samuel Bettle would do well enough.

All three solutions were vigorously debated. Some representatives disclaimed any interest in having the matter tossed back to them. Bettle, of course, had his champions and, as the reformers recalled it, even more enemies. They rehearsed all of his supposed heavy-handed rulings, going back to the struggle in 1823 over what they called the "creed." Assertions about the "weightiness" and "lightness" of various members peppered the discussion. At one point, Wistar advised the overseers of Arch Street

Meeting to take note of one of the reformers who had, he considered, gone too far in criticizing Bettle. Such comments did not, it is safe to say, lessen the growing acrimony. Jesse Kersey led other reformers in iterating that the meeting was in no condition to conduct its business, a situation for which they were at least half responsible.

Finally, an evangelical member got the floor long enough to appeal to Bettle to prepare a minute, presumably conferring upon himself the clerkship for another year. Immediately, Lower exclaimed, "I warn the clerk not to do so, but to allow more time. A few are not to govern the Society. I hope the clerk will make no minute." He looked at Bettle, who was writing hastily. After the clerk glanced up, Lower went on, "I hope he will not read what he has written. It would be an act of injustice to continue the present clerk and I hope the meeting will not sanction an unjust act." Bettle, ignoring one with so little weight, read his minute confirming himself and Comly in their positions.

A loud, unbelieving gasp issued from scores of throats; and, if anything, the division became more bitter. Bettle made no effort to restore order but let the imbroglio go on. Each person who got the floor added to the chorus of complaints. Nathan Shoemaker and two or three others explained what "weighty" members had done to Philadelphia Quarter. Another Friend mentioned the select yearly meeting's visitation committee. Still others said that Bettle's minute was contrary to the will of the assembly. Occasionally an evangelical elder would interrupt a speaker to rebuke him for disorderly statements. Someone else pointed out that the evangelicals were trying to restrict the right of members charged with offenses to object to appointees on appeal committees. The cataloguing went on and on.

At one point, Bettle asked Comly, still sitting among the body, to come forward to the table. He demurred, and, like a fickle summer storm, the debate shifted to whether or not he should, or could, rightfully approach. After some further disputation, Comly indicated that the "brotherly kindness which once characterized our Society" had been lost; he wanted to adjourn. Surprisingly, John Cox agreed, but two or three leading Friends preferred to deal with some noncontroversial matters, such as the treasurer's accounts and the minutes from Meeting for Sufferings, and Comly, slowly and reluctantly, proceeded to the table. Although some of his supporters saw this move as a capitulation that strengthened the evangelicals' hands, Comly's move grew out of his desire not to be provocative. One Friend delivered a message in line with this intention, but another, a rural Friend who was deeply agitated, lifted his arms and yelled, "Let us separate! We had better separate! I told you so, Friends! Didn't I tell you so, long ago? Only look at the state we are in!" This ejaculation stirred the crowd into a frenzy of commotion, with younger Friends especially bobbing their heads and flaying with their arms until as much as one-third of the audience was quaking. Finally, enough order was restored to conduct some minor business, and the meeting adjourned to 9 A.M. the next day.[12]

After the meeting rose, Comly and Bettle lingered behind and engaged in an extended and friendly discussion based on the clerk's belief that Comly had advised a division at the meetings he had sponsored weeks before. Comly assured him that he had not promoted a division, but, recognizing that one already existed, he had counseled his friends that they should submit to the Orthodox and peacefully separate. Bettle, had not heard this side before, and he promised to tell his associates about the true situation.

Comly did not confer with any of the reformers that evening, if indeed they gathered then. But his spirit was so troubled that he could not sleep. Before morning on Tuesday, after tossing most of the night, Comly reached a conclusion that he wanted to share with John Cox, himself a former clerk of the yearly meeting. Hurrying to the home where the old elder was staying, he was disappointed that Cox was tied up with his fellow evangelicals, so he went on to the meetinghouse, composing a statement as he walked.

As soon as the meeting was gathered, the assistant clerk rose and drew the attention of his audience to the situation they faced. "At the last sitting I said I would go to the table in condescension to the wishes of some Friends. In that feeling I am now here." But it was clear that when it came to answering the queries, the body could not do so as a yearly meeting. How could we, he queried, say that love and unity were maintained among us?

> Two parties are striving for mastery, and inasmuch as I apprehend I see that if the Meeting proceeds with its business, it must be in that state of confusion and tumult which attends this strife, and one party must gain the ascendency and predominance . . . I cannot conscientiously consent to be the organ of a body made up of two conflicting parties, and I shall therefore request the Meeting to be permitted to retire into peaceful quiet. . . . I now propose that the Meeting suspend all further proceedings in the important business that was expected to come before it and adjourn, until time is allowed for such an

arrangement of our differences to be made, as will meet the views of the two parties, and enable each to proceed with the business with peace and quietness.

Comly finished and took his seat. He made no move to leave, nor did others of his party. Bettle turned to him and said, "why, John, you have mentioned no time to adjourn to, and it would be a dissolution." Comly said nothing and kept his seat. Some others expressed their approval of the suggestion, while others thought it premature. Nothing was settled and tempers rose.

Lower took the floor and reminded Friends of the action of the select yearly meeting to appoint an investigating committee who would "sit in judgment upon the consciences of their brethren and will decide who are orthodox and who are not." When Joseph Whitall objected, to this interpretation Lower was goaded into a near fury. He censured Philadelphia Quarter for its persecution of Green Street Meeting, as well as the select meeting for its actions. Though repeatedly interrupted by the clerk, Whitall, Thomas Wistar, and others, Lower continued, with other voices crying out—"Let him go on. . . . He shall speak. . . . Samuel Bettle, be quiet until Abraham Lower has done."

Meanwhile, the same overwrought rural Friend who spoke the day before sawed the air with his arms and shouted, "Don't you see that John Comly had the Spirit when he proposed to adjourn? . . . This Meeting is a disgrace to the Society. You had better adjourn, Friends. I told you so. We can't keep together to any advantage."

John North, an evangelical, struggled physically with a reformer in the aisle who was trying to make him keep his place. When he was finally able to speak, North reminded Friends that Elizabeth Robson's prayer had been answered: "she prayed earnestly that this dividing spirit might manifest itself fully, and now we see it. It is the same spirit that appeared in Ireland, and separated some there from the Society. It is the very same spirit. I told Friends so in this Yearly Meeting three years ago, and now it is showing itself. Friends, it is a dividing and separating spirit."

A vehement dispute then erupted about what the reformers called Philadelphia Quarter's "great oppression" of Green Street. Evangelical Thomas Cope flung back, "I am really surprised that any Friends should make such remarks," and reminded the gathering that two rural quarters had doubled their representatives and another had increased its from ten to fifteen; if Philadelphia Quarter had comparable numbers, it would have sent at least 150, not 24.

John Comly revived his proposal to adjourn, but the discussion could not be halted. For a third time, the assistant clerk tried to move to the original question, this time adding, "I am quite willing, after general approbation to determining the sense of the meeting on my continuing at the table, I shall entirely submit to the Meeting and proceed with the business." A number of Friends expressed their hope that he would continue, but Cephas Ross of Bucks Quarter launched into a long tirade about the "ruling party" and the oppressive situation. His frequent invocation of the name of God profoundly shocked many of the evangelicals. Comly took the general approbation of his request to be reconfirmed as assistant clerk as evidence of renewed unity and started to read the minutes of Meeting for Sufferings. When he got to the section indicating a committee had been dispatched to remonstrate with Marcus Gould for his version of Elias Hicks's sermons, the meeting again fell apart. One country Friend demanded to know where any meeting had gotten such authority, while others upheld the elders' decision. The debate became so bitter that Comly lost his composure and wept at the undisciplined state of the meeting. Watered by these tears, the meeting adjourned its morning session.

The afternoon was relatively calm, devoted primarily to answering the queries. Lower took exception to the way Philadelphia Quarter characterized some of the meetings at which Hicks had spoken. The real root of unrest, he asserted, was the elders; their party's oppression invited resistance. Ann Jones was admitted over some protest and, as Robson had done, sided openly with the evangelicals. She warned the meeting not to "be disorganized at the opposition so Manifest against the Truths of the Gospel." She came down strongly against those who did not believe in the Devil, despite the fact that he was "holding in his embrace many who were denying his existence." A Green Street reformer cried out, "Friends, beware of the leaven of the Pharisees," and the meeting recessed until the next morning at eleven, to permit the yearly meeting's ministers and elders to gather at eight.

Comly viewed this select meeting as a place where moderation might prevail. Perhaps events of the past two days had sobered the leaders of the Society, perhaps this gathering would reverse its decision of the previous week to commission an investigation of the state of the ministry. Of all the outstanding questions, this one was the most divisive. If it could be settled or compromised, Comly's hope for peace might be realized without a final separation. Whatever the likelihood, he decided to try one last time.

When he got to Arch Street, assistant clerk Comly discovered that Henry Hull, a New York evangelical and long-standing opponent of Hicks, had gotten out of his sickbed to attend; he spoke and prayed at length about the kinds of unsound doctrines that rejected the divinity of Jesus.[13] Then Comly got blunt with the meeting. He told them that reports of differences among ministers led to the existence of two parties as much as actual disagreements did, an analysis that seemed to point to the preachments of the traveling English ministers as the source of the present divisions. In phrases that would themselves become divisive, he averred that what one side judged to be sound doctrine, the other condemned as unsound. Since Friends "could only believe and judge according to the evidence and capacity with which we are funished," both sides could sincerely and honestly differ; hence to condemn ten quarters for unsoundness and hypocrisy could only widen and increase the breach in the Society. Unfortunately only a few were disposed to adopt his position, so Comly bade the meeting "farewell" — though he remained to the end — in a benediction that had a calming impact but failed to stop the rush to final separation. In fact, he henceforth considered the dominant party to be without any excuse in the whole business.

The select yearly meeting's early morning session was a watershed, as only the most ardent of the reforming element retained any hope of victory in the yearly meeting itself. Most saw now the wisdom of Comly's advice of acquiescence. The only bitterness on Wednesday came when slavery was discussed. The meeting agreed to solicit three thousand dollars from the quarters to assist North Carolina Friends in removing free blacks from their state. As he did annually, Lower grasped this opportunity to beard those who complained of the injury of slavery to Africans yet enjoyed the fruits of their enforced labor; his comments failed to elicit any open response or renewal of the conflict, but they did not sit well with the elders. Privately, Bettle and Comly agreed to give up the appeals involving elders from the rural quarters in return for Philadelphia Quarter's commitment not to push for a hearing of its reinstatement of the Green Street elders.

The yearly meeting did not convene on Thursday morning so that the traditional Fifth Day meetings for worship might take place in the five meetinghouses of the city. The principal reformers forsook these meetings to confer and prepare for a large meeting at Green Street in the evening, but they came back to Arch Street for the 3 P.M. session. The questions dealt with had little lasting significance, but sparks flew nevertheless. The report from Westtown School noted a painful insubordination, especially among the boys—a group of students had reportedly burned every Bible that could be found in the school—and laid responsibility for it to those who did not revere the Scriptures. The memorial for Richard Jordan was strongly opposed by the reformers, including Thomas McClintock, who said its wording committed the yearly meeting to a set of doctrines not accepted by the body of Friends. Even more infuriating, the clerk read a prepared minute approving the memorial before the discussion commenced—as Thomas Pryor informed posterity via his journal, it demonstrated the overbearing evangelical manner determined to have its way.

The Green Street conference on the evening of April 19 attracted nearly two hundred people eager to discuss the widening rifts. For some reason Abraham Lower was absent.[14] Comly pressed his long-held conviction that a separation was inevitable and that the reformers should submit so that the yearly meeting could go swiftly to its conclusion. This tactic had broad support, and the group moved to consider the broad outlines of an address to absent Friends sketched out earlier in the day. One participant expressed his pleasant surprise that so many "gray-headed patriarchs" had joined the predominately middle-aged crowd.[15] The meeting was relatively brief, its members agreeing to meet the following night to continue the discussion and to appoint a committee to sketch out their address.[16] Afterwards on his way to his lodging, Comly met Bettle, and they walked and conversed for nearly an hour. They agreed, recalled Comly, that a separation should take place, but when the assistant clerk broached the topic of an equitable division of property, Bettle was aghast. The Orthodox would do no such thing; they would not encourage separation by acceding to any plan reducing meeting assets.

Pryor noted a "wonderful change" in the state of the meeting the next morning. Previously each side had seemed to say to the other: "thus far canst thou go and no farther," but now a spirit of accommodation had emerged on what some hoped would be the last day of the meeting. This refreshing atmosphere reflected, no doubt, a widespread sense that the die had already been cast, that a calm retreat was inevitable, and that no excitement should disturb the process of peaceful division. The Comly-Bettle agreement of the day before to send the issue of terms for elders back to Bucks and Abington quarters, to treat Southern Quarter's dispute with Meeting for Sufferings in the same way, and to refer the reinstatement of Green Street elders back to Philadelphia Quarter won approval, but not without some dissent to the first two from discontented rural elements. Three vacancies on Meeting for Sufferings could not be filled. The epistle committee destroyed any hope that the meeting would finally end that evening when it reported its inability to complete its work and begged for another session the next morning, an unusual request that struck Comly as a bit too calculated. Perhaps something was up. Soon after 5 P.M., the weary members adjourned until Saturday.

Green Street meeting was the destination of more than six hundred Friends that evening. William Gibbons, the Wilmington physician and editor of the *Berean*, and Benjamin Ferris of "Amicus" fame served as joint clerks, as the conference considered the address presented from its committee. In contrast to the yearly meeting sessions, the meeting at Green Street exhibited a deep unity, for those who participated recognized that their decisions probably meant formation of a new yearly meeting. Comly was a little late in arriving and related that Bettle agreed a separation was about the only thing left to do.[17] The principal point of discussion was purely tactical: to and from whom should their explanation be addressed. The Green Street conference had no legal standing, and, however justified in its members' minds, it had embarked on a course leading to secession. Aware of this situation, Comly wanted at first to give it an air of legitimacy by getting the designated representatives to sign as delegates from the quarterly meetings. But here the conservatism of the country Hicksites surfaced: they simply did not want to take such drastic action. The meeting haggled over this point almost the entire evening until its members agreed to adopt the address but wait and decide how it should be signed the next day. Samuel Noble, from Green Street, consented to hold the document and accept signatures of those who wished to sign in the meantime.[18] During the night, Comly concluded that the best solution would be to print the address, signed by a few leading Friends, and send it to all Quakers within the confines of the yearly meeting.

Saturday morning's session was expected to be short—chiefly, reading the remaining epistles and then leaving for home—so no one was quite ready for what transpired. William Wharton, apparently heady from last evening's decisions, preached on a text from William Penn, "Zeal tempered with charity is good, but without it good for nothing." Attacking some of the Orthodox directly, he reprobated "this dark spirit of bigotry" that raged like a roaring lion through Quakerdom. His tone took on a "see-what-you-have-made-us-do" air, and he predicted that he would never again attend a yearly meeting at Arch Street.[19] Robert Moore spoke along the same lines, only adding his hope that the separation would not produce ill will. When Bettle read the epistle addressed to London, Lower complained about a reference he took to mean that one could pray to Jesus, but the meeting was not unduly delayed, however exasperated it was by such carping.

As business wound down, Thomas Stewardson was sent across the building to inform the women's meeting that the men were nearing adjournment. He returned, followed presently by two evangelical women who reported that the women had united to appoint a committee to visit monthly and quarterly meetings to investigate the state of the ministry; they wanted the men to consider it. (It later came out that Ann Jones had introduced the idea.[20]) This suggestion added fuel to a fire that seemed nearly out. From every side of the house, the reformers protested, although given their stance of the night before it remained unclear why they were so determined in their opposition. Most likely, some saw the Green Street conference as another way of pressuring the evangelicals into making concessions, thus negating the need for a formal, permanent separation. Indeed, Bucks, Abington, and Southern Quarters had won, at least temporarily, their wish to have elders appointed for specified terms and members of Sufferings appointed (and removed) when quarters desired. Charges flew back and forth—that the women's meeting had not originated this plan, that it violated the Discipline, that the women should mind their own business, that the plan irrevocably poisoned future relations between the two groups. Both John Cox and Bettle expressed their view that the meeting was not united enough to risk appointment of a committee; at this point, Jonathan Evans tried to turn the matter around with a statement that, whatever the will of the present session, "I believe the concern is owned by that unity of the Spirit in the bond of peace."

Emboldened by this statement, Evans's twenty-five-year-old son Charles, who had attended the Green Street meeting the previous evening, made an electrifying revelation. The same people, he reported, who now opposed this deep concern were only last night at a conference that presumed to set up a separate yearly meeting. He mentioned John Comly as one of the conference's leaders, one who had even agreed to sign its address, and he directly asked Comly if he would disavow this charge. "In perfect composure and calmness," Comly sat moot. But then Jonathan's second son, Thomas, added his bit. Pointing straight at Comly, he reminded the meeting that only a few days before the assistant clerk had informed them that there were, "mark the words, Friends," two *irreconciliable* parties" within the yearly meeting. And he also recalled his rapt audience's attention to the fact that during this very sitting another Friend had said a separation must and would take place. What better reason, he demanded, for appointment of a visitation committee?

The debate soon degenerated into a dispute over whether or not the Green Street conclave had authorized its own committee to visit local meetings and encourage them to defect. Charles and Thomas Evans both claimed that such a committee had been named, a revelation that Thomas Wistar thought made that subject "one of far more importance to us than the concern of our Women Friends." The reformer John Comfort denied that there was a shadow of foundation for such assertions — "no such committee had been appointed." But Charles Evans repeated his allegations, and Edward Bettle, the clerk's son, reported that forty-six representatives had already agreed to sign the address.

This first open discussion of their meeting was damaging for the reformers, for their actions confirmed their opponents' accusations. The Green Street gathering had not been held behind locked doors, and it had clearly moved toward secession; yet now its members were trying to prevent their opponents from holding the line against reformation. Thomas Cope put it best. No one, he said, would deny another the right to withdraw from a religious society for whatever reason, "but having done so, it would certainly be unreasonable that he should wish to continue active in the Society from which he had thus withdrawn, and not being satisfied with his own liberty of conscience, seek to control the consciences of others." Samuel Comfort, a reformer from Bucks Quarter, echoed this view and united with the idea of a committee so long as those named to serve on it favored its purpose. By this time, Samuel Bettle had a minute ready; eleven of the staunchest evangelicals were designated for the committee, including Jonathan Evans, Samuel Bettle, Thomas Wistar, Hinchman Haines, William Newbold, and Thomas Stewardson. The reformers continued to grouse about what Comly saw as "this determination of arbitrary power to carry its point," but they could hardly have asked for the right to help set yearly meeting policy when they had already moved to leave the body itself. After a few moments of deep and impressive silence, Bettle read the final minute with its traditional wording: "the Meeting concludes to meet again at the usual time next year, if the Lord permit." It was nearly one o'clock in the afternoon. The yearly meeting of 1827 was over. No formal separation had yet occurred, but there was still the Green Street meeting set to begin immediately.

Green Street meetinghouse was nearly full, as most of the rural Friends delayed their return home long enough to take back word of the latest developments. The seceders made a few more changes in their address, gave it their final approval, and appointed ten Friends, from across the yearly meeting, to sign it. Addressed to individual "Friends within the compass of Philadelphia Yearly Meeting," the epistle tied the Green Street reformers tightly to the witness of early Friends that had ended a "night of apostasy": "the power of God unto salvation to them that believe in and obey it." Through obedience to this reformation, Friends "were made powerful instruments in opening the door of gospel liberty, and removing many of the fetters that had been formed in the dark night of superstition and error that proceeded them." The reformation principle, they affirmed, had dawned — "that GOD ALONE IS THE SOVEREIGN LORD OF CONSCIENCE," and no power, civil or ecclesiastical, should ever be permitted to interfere with it. As long as Friends remained faithful, "not to speculative opinions, but to the light of CHRIST within," they would be united and shine like a city on a hill.

All this was past, explained the address as it moved to the present, for the unity of the yearly meeting had been interrupted and a division had appeared, unable to be reconciled. "Doctrines held by one part of society, and which we believe to be sound and edifying, are pronounced by the other part to be unsound and spurious." Love and condenscension "have been blasted," and oppressive measures pursued. Disorder was the result, both in the yearly meeting and in many of the subordinate branches. Preaching no new gospel and advising no new discipline, the Green Street conference recommended to Friends "that the period had fully come in which we ought to look toward making a quiet retreat from this scene of confusion, and we therefore recommend to you deeply to weigh this momentous subject, and to adopt such a course as Truth, under solid and solemn deliberation, may point to, in furtherance of this object, that our society may again enjoy the free exercise of its rights and privileges."[21]

John Comly was the most prominent signer and headed the list; the sentiments were his, if not the exact words. William Wharton's name stood out as the only Philadelphian, the others being country Friends best known in their own quarters. The decision to omit the more avid reformers' names underscored the moderate nature of their undertaking and promised not to alienate the slower-moving rural Quakers. The conference announced another gathering, six weeks later, on the first Monday in June, a delay long enough to allow Friends to decide what course they should take in the light of subsequent developments. The decision to address Friends as individuals was a shrewd one and allowed monthly meetings to await the visits of the yearly meeting committees and the actions of those who retained power in the Society. Conciliatory moves, a willingness to compromise, and mutal restraint might yet prevent final separation. Within six weeks each monthly meeting would convene at least once, the factions might sort things out at the local level, and things could return to normal. Even the more ardent reformers did not consider that the yearly meeting had deprived them of exercising any of their rights; it had acted in an arbitrary fashion, but its members had expressed themselves, even though the reformers' large numbers had been ignored.[22] If the visitation committees moved judiciously and cautiously and determined not to alienate the mass of rural Friends—something that men like Lower could hardly conceive of[23]—then separation might be over with the yearly meeting.

The evangelicals, because they exercised power, had the future of the Society in their hands, as they had had all along. Most of the reformers, especially those from the country, wanted no rash acts and hoped things would continue along known paths. The Green Street address wisely appealed to the traditional ties that held the Society to its past. Men like Abraham Lower, Halliday Jackson, Benjamin Ferris, William Gibbons, and John Comly knew well that when the yearly meeting's epistle spoke of "the weak & deficient state of [its] various branches" that the evangelicals were hinting at their course. Encouraged by the English visitors, the evangelicals would set out to strengthen the Society's branches, principally by lopping off those that were "weak & deficient."

CHAPTER 11

"A mistake if not a crime to be indifferent,"
OR
Everyone Decides

THE DISCORDANT BUSINESS SESSIONS of April 1827 marked the end of the beginning for the Quakers of Philadelphia Yearly Meeting. Although the basis for a separation had been laid long before, the final conclusion would not arrive until the slow-moving village meetings outside Philadelphia each came to grips with the issues that had convulsed the more activist urban Quakers and had now been tossed to them by the Green Street conference. During the next month, as quarterly and monthly meetings gathered, separation became more and more likely, only awaiting guidance from the second Green Street conference in June. Friends' polity, which stressed the independence of local meetings, practically required a struggle in each of sixty-one monthly meetings and forced individual Friends to take a personal stand with either the Hicksites or the Orthodox.[1] May 1827 was hardly a time for neutrality among the twenty-six thousand members of Philadelphia Yearly Meeting. As each meeting felt the wrenching conflict, so every family found itself pulled in one direction or the other. The personal tugging and tearing only increased the agony and acrimony that came to characterize the division.

The leaders of the reformation wing never doubted that the evangelicals would act as they had always done, arrogantly, with alienating aplomb, and exhibiting almost no political astuteness toward rural Friends whose allegiance they needed to win. William Poole, whose poor physical condition kept him away from meetings but left him plenty of time to think, expressed his amazement at the way the evangelicals had frittered away their influence. Such otherwise canny and artful men, he wrote, might have been expected "to create means of support and to bring to this support of their measures, all the influential members of Society. And yet we behold, not only that this prop has been struck from under them, but *how* the *influence* relied upon has been suddenly taken away, that now it has almost wholly ceased to exist."[2] The reformers, of course, did not sit still. They worked hard to promote their cause, but they enjoyed heavy-handed unintentional assistance from opponents unaccustomed to having to win friends in an untidy political arena. Their superior insights into the opposition's mentality lent the reformers a self-assured air that grated on evangelicals. William Evans recorded in his journal that when Abraham Lower proclaimed Green Street's independence of Philadelphia Quarter at the monthly meeting on April 26, Lower "seemed to glory in the prospect of being loosened from all restraint."[3]

The prize in the contest was the support of country Quakers, but the battleground was Philadelphia where Green Street's eager reformers worked the point, raised the issues, and took advantage of the ham-handed attempts of the Orthodox to keep power in their possession. The evangelicals, led by Elizabeth Robson and Stephen Grellet, descended on Green Street the very Sunday after yearly meeting ended and proceeded to flay unbelievers hip and thigh. At Pine Street, Ann Jones used biblical images to goad her auditors to put down the rebellion they faced. "The Lord will wet his bright Sword with one hand while he holds vengeance with the other and hurls damnation at your disobedience," she proclaimed. "Your stiff Necks is a Sinew of Iron and your brows are brows of brass. There are individuals here who believe that they have more Widsom than the God that made them."[4] Prodded by such preachers, the evangelicals took a firm stand against the dissidents—and drove the uncommitted straight into the Hicksite fold.

The Green Street reformers called together about 40 members of their meeting on Tuesday, April 24, to plan strategy. The yearly meeting had referred back to Philadelphia Quarter the question of whether Leonard Snowden should be returned to his position of elder. Since the quarterly meeting had already ordered his reinstatement and had taken the same course in regard to Ann Scattergood's and Mary Taylor's appeal against their own removals, everyone knew what Green Street had to look forward to. Moreover, fears existed that the quarter would try to merge Green Street Meeting into the more evangelical Northern District Meeting and perhaps even deprive them of their meetinghouse. Those attending this caucus unanimously agreed that the two women elders could not be accepted. The most significant action involved Green Street's relation to Philadelphia Quarter. The determined Friends assented to withdrawing from the quarter and applying for membership in the more congenial Abington Quarter.[5] Without approval of Philadelphia Quarter, this action amounted to an act of secession in clear violation of the Discipline, but this fact produced hardly a pause on the part of Green Street's radicals.

The Green Street meetinghouse on Thursday the 26th was the venue for the first open confrontation between the evangelicals and the reformers since the rise of the yearly meeting the previous Seventh Day. The three English ministers then in Philadelphia, the Jones couple and Elizabeth Robson, attended, as did a stellar delegation from the quarter, consisting of two Evanses, William and Thomas, Henry Cope, and Thomas Wistar. Adding to the crowd's numbers were visitors from other meetings in the city, anxious to see something of the conflict as a continuing drama. Clearly conscious of the significance of their actions, representatives of each side spoke as though everything being said was for the record — as indeed, it was, for three Orthodox scribes kept an eleven-page joint summary of the proceedings.[6]

Sparks first flew in the select meeting of ministers and elders, which convened early in the morning. Normally there were six members of Green Street's select meeting, four males who were reformers of varying intensity, and the two deposed women elders who were not expected to attend. But this morning they showed up, bolstered by a committee of evangelicals from the quarterly meeting. Upon their arrival, Lower immediately objected to proceeding further; the meeting, he claimed, was no longer "select" because it included the two women the monthly meeting had removed from their position. Thomas Wistar informed the group that the quarterly meeting had reinstated Scattergood and Taylor and that it had no right to exclude them. But the select meeting adjourned to meet the following afternoon, if the monthly meeting, after being informed of what had transpired, approved.

A few minutes later, at ten o'clock, the regular Thursday meeting for worship gathered, its overwhelmingly Hicksite membership being forced to listen to an Orthodox discourse from Elizabeth Robson that set their teeth on edge. The antagonism between the two groups, however, did not surface until the monthly meeting for business convened. The clerk, a determined reformer named Joseph Warner, started to read the minute that Tuesday's caucus had approved when George Jones, in his best evangelical style, interrupted to explain the need for monthly meetings to be subordinate to quarterly meetings. Warner once again started to read his previously prepared minute when Henry Cope rose in the gallery and requested to know where this minute had come from. No one, he told the meeting, had any right to meet "out of doors," compose a minute, and then try to press it as the meeting's conclusion. Warner simply ignored this advice and read his minute dissolving the connection between Green Street and Philadelphia Quarter and naming two Friends to carry the news down to Arch Street at the upcoming quarterly meeting.

Before the proposal could be approved, at least nine local adherents to the evangelical cause sided with Cope and objected to the minute, but, led by Samuel Noble and Abraham Lower, the reformers insisted that any Friend might bring to a monthly meeting a proposed minute for its consideration.[7] The three evangelicals officially representing the quarter, Cope, Wistar, and Peter Thompson, expressly warned the dissidents that they were seceding from the Society of Friends by embarking on this course. Undeterred, the meeting approved the proposed minute with Thomas Evans's words ringing through the hall: They had been forewarned and were fully aware that this action dissolved all connections they had enjoyed with the Society of Friends.

As if to answer Evans, Lower practically exulted in this step toward independence. Green Street Friends could withdraw, he proclaimed, to the Rocky Mountains if they wanted to, and no outside power had any say-so about what they might do. Yes, added Edmund Shotwell, one of the more outspoken reformers, Green Street denied the right of the quarter's committee even to express an opinion on the subject; another member, carrying this principle even further, announced that they had never recognized the committee. Astonished by this assertion, Wistar queried the meeting to see if this view was widely shared. Not quite, Noble responded, our group "had recognized the committee, but not as incorporated in the meeting and having a right to take part in its deliberations."

The clerk then read a second minute appointing five of the meeting's leading reformers, including Noble and Lower, to attend Abington Quarter and petition for admission. Interestingly, the first speaker after this minute,

Joseph Boustead, a tanner employed in the Scattergood tanning yards, turned around the poor man-rich man argument so often used by the reform element. Since many of us here, he stated accurately, were very poor and likely always to be so, it would really be a great hardship to have to go so far away to Abington. Boustead's concern reflected the traditional practice that members of a meeting should reside within its boundaries. Shotwell rushed to reassure the poor tanner that the meeting would grant a certificate of transfer to any other meeting within the city for those who wished. Another evangelical carped that the Discipline did not permit issuing certificates for those who were not moving near the new meeting, which complaint caused the usually reticent Thomas Pryor to blurt out, "you can go without them [the certificates] then." This brief set-to revealed how those involved in what William Poole had started calling a "revolution"were being forced to reorder their thinking.[8]

William Evans brought the discussion back to the constitutional issue when he reiterated that Green Street reformers could not act without the quarter's approval, since that meeting had created them and insisted on their continued subordiantion. Displaying his practical sense, Wistar wanted to know where Green Street would be if Abington refused to admit them. Lower, still flying high from the excitement of independence, refused to be worried and responded that they would still be Green Street Monthly Meeting. Now, he continued, there was a meeting in the city where ministers of the everlasting gospel might be received without censure, persecution, or abuse. Rather than disorder and anarchy, oppression and tyranny, and a domineering spirit such as existed elsewhere in the quarter, he shouted and gestured toward the evangelicals sitting near him in the gallery, Green Street would be a peaceful asylum. When the Orthodox tried to respond, Lower or some other reformer called on their supporters to take no notice but to continue with their own business.

A request for a certificate of transfer for a family moving to Ohio gave the evangelicals a chance to warn that, since the meeting had dissolved its relation to the Society, it had no power to issue transfers. One reformer shot back that such remarks were quite improper, and he wished the Friend would be quiet. William Evans, whose worries about libertinism were well known, countered, so "that was a specimen of the liberty thee plead for & the peace & love thee talked so much about." Angered at this sarcasm, a Hicksite parried with some personal reflections about Evans.

The dominant faction notified the women's meeting about their actions and indicated a readiness to adjourn, but word came back that the women were unclear about what had gone on and were discussing whether representatives should be named, as usual, to attend Philadelphia Quarter. Lower considered that the women might stay as long as they wanted — "no doubt," he allowed, "P.Q. would receive them & recognize them as Green St M Met^g" — but, the business of the meeting being over, he did not think it necessary to wait around. After he and Noble had been deputized to so inform the slower women and had left the room, two evangelicals ventured that those who did not approve of the course taken should remain behind and appoint representatives to the quarter. To encourage this sentiment, Thomas Evans rehearsed once again what had gone on. "It was as clear as any proposition could be," he claimed, "that whatever pretences they might make a large part of the Meet^g had virtually seceded from the Religious Society of fr^{ds} & joined another, by what name it was distinguished" he did not know; it was quite proper and in order for the loyalists to stay behind and choose representatives. When at least three of the reformers asked Evans to keep quiet — one thought it out of order for an outsider and such a young man to be so outspoken — Evans claimed he was only stating facts. Besides, he wanted to know, "where was the liberty of conscience, the freedom of speech, the quality & the love of Peace of which they had made so much profession." Appealing to the average member, Evans asked them to observe well what spirit was guiding their leaders and to think about where they would be led.

Thus, emboldened, an evangelical asked the clerk to leave behind the minute books so "that the members of the Society of fr^{ds} might proceed regularly with their business." The reformers tried to shout him down, but he finished just as Lower returned to hear the tail end of the discussion. In a mocking manner that reminded the evangelicals that he was in his element and they were out of theirs, Lower taunted: "oh yes, you can stay & apt your R[epresentatives], & there is no doubt but P Q Meet^g will receive them & recognize you as G St Meet^g. We know enough of their proceedings to tell you that — You know my fr^{ds} how they thrust those two women upon the Meet^g contrary to all discipline & in fact considered them as the Meet^g & if there were only one of you they would own that one as the M Meet^g." A visitor from Baltimore tried to renew the evangelical warning, but Lower cut him off by noting that he was a stranger and did not have all the facts. Why, he continued, Green Street had suffered such grievances, "which I'll venture to say were never heard of in this country."

With that clerk Warner picked up the minute books, declared the business concluded, and left the house. But exactly twelve evangelicals from Green Street lined up with eight from other meetings along one bench in the gallery and remained behind to conduct a rump session. As they sat in silence, some of the reformers drifted back in to watch and jeer.

The evangelicals could not find one of their number willing to act as clerk and take down the names of reprentatives to the quarterly meeting. First Joseph Snowden and then William Scattergood demurred, and then Boustead, perhaps a bit more practical than the professed authorities on the Discipline, remarked that he saw little reason to appoint representatives, the quarter's committee having witnessed the same disorder they all had seen. At this point the meeting's caretaker came in and asked the group to leave, as he had cleaning to do. Not a soul moved off that bench, even though others took up the cry to get them out. One agitated Friend reported that four of the trustees wanted them out, but the evangelicals took the high ground: "all the trustees in the city could not legally turn them out, that the house belonged to frd^s. The trustees held it for them & the members of the society had a right to remain there untill the business of the day had been transacted."

George Gibbons, whose occupation as a conveyancer gave him some familiarity with legal proceedings,[9] yelled out, "I will take down the names of every one of them & complain of them for a riot," and Morris Longstreth rushed up into the gallery and accosted William Evans and George Jones directly. They had, he allowed, been there long enough, to which Evans responded that he intended to stay as long as his associates remained. Sneered Longstreth: "the house does not belong to thee nor to any of thy family." Another reformer confronted Jones with the accusation that the whole problem resulted from English influence, while others mocked and laughed at the proud and portly foreigner. As they left the meeting, the evangelicals had to pass through a snorting, unruly mob of what one called "these wild creatures."

The women's rump meeting, clerked by Ann Scattergood, continued in session, even as they had to endure the ministrations of Lower, who opened the door, looked in, and called out that there could be only one monthly meeting at Green Street and that this one was "seditious." As he spoke, a reformer brushed past him and came back leading his wife out. Over the hubbub, Robson preached a sermon that appealed to the evangelicals but excoriated the reformers. When she sat down, Edmund Shotwell went up into the gallery and tauntingly inquired if she and Ann Jones would like to dine with him. As the meeting broke up, some of the reformers hooted and jeered at the departing women.

It would be hard to find, in the previous annals of Quakerdom, a more splenetic and rancorous meeting, but it would not be the last such. Indeed, as the process of division proceeded, the Green Street gathering became a kind of model, its ill will repeated, its personal aspersions multiplied, and its vitriolic aftertaste embittering. Whenever evangelicals like one of the Evanses appeared at a quarterly or monthly meeting where reformers were dominant, there were sure to be similar scenes as the Hicksites rose to take the bait. The handful of evangelical-dominated meetings was more sedate, but only because those who exercised the power in them used it to disown and administer discipline to people who had long since rejected their authority and in most instances were not even present.

Meanwhile, rural Friends of a reform inclination were girding up their loins for what they expected would be similar struggles when the yearly meeting's investigating committee made its appearance. The leading reformers knew they had to bring along with them the great mass of Friends who lived beyond the city's limits. Jesse Kersey, finally free from his addiction to drugs, saw in a clear-headed way that many "are not sufficiently aware of the dangers to which we are now exposed," or the circumstances that fully proved "it would be a mistake if not a crime to be indifferent." He suggested that special committees be named at quarterly meetings to inform monthly meeting of impending dangers.[10] William Poole, whose meeting at Wilmington seemed to be pretty well united in the reformation cause, proposed working from the other direction. He thought a large committee in Wilmington should suggest revisions to the discipline. Then this report could go up to Concord Quarter to stem the progress of "the evil spirit from Phil^a" that had taken hold there.[11]

John Comly busily labored from both ends. On April 30, he "felt an openness" to attend Abington Monthly Meeting, where the reform element introduced and read the Green Street address, which was then forwarded to the quarterly meeting. Simply reading this document, of course, was educational and, for the Orthodox, inflammatory and tantamount to rebellion, but opposition proved minimal. When Comly got back to Byberry that afternoon, a conference of local Friends met to discuss the general situation and agreed to accept "suffering Friends" from the city into membership without certificates of transfer. Because such a course specifically violated the Discipline, that it received approval demonstrated that the reform cause had strong support among the rural element. On May 2, Comly went to Horsham Meeting, where, once again, the Green Street address was read, and sentiment increased for a peaceful separation. A week later, Comly ran into his first major opposition when he returned to Horsham for the meeting of Abington Quarter. In the select quarterly meeting of ministers and elders attended by members of the yearly meeting's investigating committee, a local evangelical, David Comfort, tried to force Comly's removal on the ground that he had signed the Green Street statement and had thereby forfeited his right to be a minister in the Society. Lower, who had been dropped as a minister by Philadelphia Quarter only four days earlier, also put in his appearance and was faced with the same demand. Both men kept their seats throughout the two-hour debate, and Comly, at least, remained absolutely silent.[12]

The general meeting of Abington Quarter the following day was reminiscent of the last Green Street Meeting. It attracted a large crowd— a vast number from a 30- to 40-mile radius, as well as the yearly meeting's committee, a committee from Philadelphia Quarter dispatched to oppose Green Street's request for membership, and George and Ann Jones, the English bulldogs of evangelicalism. A spring thunderstorm set in at the 10 o'clock meeting time and lingered most of the day. The farmers and their wives listened to the Green Street address and, unawed by the presence and warnings of such worthies as Jonathan Evans and Stephen Grellet, proceeded to welcome Green Street Meeting as a part of their quarter. Significantly, the clerk who favored the Orthodox refused to make the necessary minute and was temporarily displaced by a clerk more sympathetic to the majority. If that were not enough of an affront to the evangelicals, the controlling faction refused even to record the presence of the yearly meeting's committee.[13] When the word got back to Philadelphia, William Evans growled to his journal, "this disorderly meeting was a practical comment on the call to retreat from the confusion which the Comly party asserted prevails in the Society."[14] The members of the committee from Green Street were greeted as conquering heroes when they returned victoriously, while the evangelical contingent "was almost ashamed to be seen in the Streets" — or so a reformer described it.¹⁵

Whether or not they were ashamed to appear in the street's, the Orthodox still maintained their power within the city's meetings. Just before the Horsham gathering, Philadelphia Quarter moved with vigor against the reformers. Lower was removed as a minister, because he "had lost his gift as a gospel minister"; and Stephen Stephens, an elder of Radnor Meeting who had signed the Green Street address, was also expelled. Green Street Meeting itself was laid down, its members ordered transferred to the Northern District Meeting, and its record books demanded.¹⁶

To make sure they observed the letter of the Discipline, a committee of seven from the quarter attended Green Street's Monthly Meeting on May 17 to inform them officially. The city's leading reformers compared themselves to the children of Israel who had been freed from their bondage "with their wives, their Children and their little ones, their Goods and utensils in order to have a quiet retirement"; they "felt no disposition to return back or give up any of their professions." When the few Orthodox members withdrew with the committtee, the meeting seemed no smaller but instead enlarged by a tender mood of common purpose, an esprit de corps. In Quaker terms, the meeting was "broken." Lower was so moved that he could scarcely utter a word. The women in their meeting experienced the same spirit until Ann Scattergood, who stayed after all the others of her party had gone, reminded them that if they did not abide by the quarterly meeting's directives they would be disowned. This first actual separation was not marred by unseemly actions; the leaders warned members to show that they could "love those who did not love us even our enemies.'¹⁷

Any doubts the evangelicals Brahmins might have harbored about the seriousness of the reformers was surely dispelled when the small group of about thirty arrived at the Pine Street meetinghouse for their regular monthly meeting on May 23. They found there a large number of members who seldom attended business sessions, these Friends augmented by others from the country as well as from other meetings in the city. After a few preliminaries, William Wharton presented a letter signed by forty-five of Pine Street's members asking for a division of the meeting's property so they might build a new meetinghouse. In seeking to separate, the letter read, they wanted to remain Friends but did not desire to change their residences so as to live within the boundaries of another meeting. The signers claimed to be "actuated by a desire to promote liberty of conscience and peace and good will to all." Wharton had reviewed these intentions, but the clerk did not permit him to read his carefully composed letter and instead referred it to a committee.[18]

The clerk's purpose, of course, was to bury an idea likely to feed other opposition, a course anticipated by Wharton, who had traveled to Byberry the day before to inform that meeting of the activities of those he called "our trinitarian friends." On May 29 he and his wife were back at Byberry for its monthly meeting. Wharton asked for membership without the requisite certificate for himself, his family, and three other reformers. Though somewhat reluctant to accept the other three, whom they had no knowledge of, the meeting acceded to the request after Wharton vouched for their character. Even more significant was Wharton's next request—that Byberry oversee a new meeting for worship in the city, an act representing a clear encroachment on Philadelphia Quarter's province and the evangelicals' power to control things there. With only one evangelical voicing feeble objection to the plan, Byberry Friends appointed a committee, including Wharton, to superintend the new meeting on June 3. The Whartons and Abraham Lower had every reason to exult when they rode back to the city that evening.

Not all reformers were so happy. Joseph Parrish, a forty-seven-year-old doctor, thought they ought to wait until after the scheduled conference at Green Street on the 4th before starting a new meeting. Wharton, however, insisted that it would be "sort of a nucleus" around which simililarly minded Friends might collect. They had not even found a suitable place to meet and Sunday was only four days off.[19] Of all the reformers' moves, this one embodied the most fundamental challenge yet to the entrenched power in Philadelphia—a good reason for keeping the plan tightly under wraps. It was one thing, after all, for Green Street, made up of a batch of known radicals like Lower and Noble, to declare for independence, but it was still another for a quarterly meeting to encroach on the territory of a coequal body; no wonder William Evans called it an "invasion."[20]

As the dissident reformers looked around for an appropriate place to hold their new meetings, quarterly meetings outside the city continued to be scenes of conflict. The presence of one or another of the yearly meeting's committees always guaranteed a confrontation, as did the reformers' determination to read the Green Street address and appoint representatives to the upcoming conference.[21] Rural opposition proved so vigorous, indeed, that a rumor spread that Samuel Bettle had conceded it was more determined and extensive than anyone had thought likely.[22]

When avid reformers like Lower and Noble appeared, their rural counterparts were galvanized to firmly resist the evangelicals on the visitation committees. At Buckingham on May 31, Bucks Quarter's select meeting sat from 10 A.M. to 5 P.M. without conducting any business because the two Green Street emissaries refused to leave when Jonathan Evans demanded they do so. At one point a proposal to put Lower out forcefully died when he refused to cooperate, and no one came forward to wrest him out; Lower promised to leave promptly when his friends asked him to do so, but that occasion never arose. After his fellow ministers from the quarter had grown weary and left the house, only Edward Hicks remained to receive the full force of the committee's wrath against the unsound ministers of the area, but the reformers savored their victory when they finally sat their opponents out. At the general quarterly meeting the next day, with the reformers in complete charge, the group united with Bucks's twenty-two (of twenty-four) representatives to the yearly meeting and protested against the disorderly proceeding that had taken place there. Needless to say, neither the committee nor the handful of local evangelicals could prevent the Green Street address from being read and formally minuted.[23] Such stinging defeats must have seemed like nearly lethal doses of ratsbane to the evangelicals.

To add to Orthodox woes, it was public knowledge by Friday, June 1, that Abington, Bucks, Western, and probably Southern quarters would have official representatives at the Green Street conference and that the dissenters in the city would have a new meeting at Carpenters' Hall on Sunday. In the short run, the new meeting proved most irritating. Wharton and party chose their site well. Rife with symbolism, Carpenters' Hall had housed the meeting of the First Continental Congress that began the process of unifying the American colonists against British power in 1774; the reformers saw themselves resisting the same species of arbitrary rule. On the first meeting day, the building teemed with reform-minded Friends from the city, country supporters in town early for next day's conference, and the merely curious. Well-known Friends such as Jesse Kersey and John Comly ministered to the crowded meeting and lent an air of continuity with the past. Attendance at the Orthodox meetings in the city was noticeably down, particularly, as one ruefully noted, among the men.[24]

Within three months, the Carpenters' Hall meeting had become a monthly meeting, the nucleus of the Cherry Street (later Race Street) Meeting, and religious center for Hicksite Friends until 1955.[25] Its nine hundred seats were filled nearly every Sunday.[26]

The Green Street conference lasted two days, closing on Tuesday, June 5. William Gibbons and Benjamin Ferris occupied the clerk and assistant clerk positions and presided over a meeting that occasioned no dissent; if evangelicals were present, they uttered not a word. (A story circulated immediately after that Anna Braithwaite, who had been in New York for the yearly meeting there, had hurried back in the hope of arriving prior to the adjournment; but she did not make it.[27]) It quickly appeared that sentiment was strongest for establishing a new yearly meeting in Abington, Bucks, and Southern quarters, with reported majorities in all but Philadelphia ready to join it. The conferences adopted another epistle, this one addressed to "Friends of the Quarterly and Monthly Meetings" within Philadelphia Yearly Meeting, and appointed a committee of forty to advise and assist meetings as they considered a likely course of action.[28]

The address was markedly different in tone from the first Green Street message six weeks before. The earlier statement recommended that individuals ponder what courses the cause of truth required of them, while this one proposed that Friends, acting together in monthly and quarterly meetings, proceed to create a separate yearly meeting. It charged that more than five years before some individuals had become infected with a disorderly spirit that had spread to meetings and resulted in unjust charges against "faithful Friends in the ministry" — allegations of being unfaithful, "denying the Divinity of Christ, and undervaluing the Scriptures." More recently, the address went on, this spirit surfaced in the yearly meeting, overruled the greater part of the representatives, and imposed a clerk on the body. The reformers had hoped that those caught up in this evil business might see the error of their ways, but instead the "spirit of discord and confusion has gained strength." Thus separation had become the only alternative for those who held "principles of the early professors of our name." In a politically sharp move, the reformers got twenty-two rural and generally obscure Friends to sign the address;[29] not a single Philadelphian added his name, a fact that amazed the evangelical Henry Cope when he reviewed one of the seven thousand copies the meeting had printed.[30] Unlike Cope, the reformers knew they had to win holdouts outside the city.

In preparation for the new yearly meeting, called for October 15, four months hence, an advisory statement was issued the following week by the newly constituted committee. In essence, the group requested that Friends favorable to the views in the epistle confer at monthly and quarterly meeting levels, determine their numerical strength, and secue control of their meetings if the larger number was so inclined; if a local group was unable to "move as a body," those who were reform-oriented should attach themselves to a nearby meeting or request the forthcoming yearly meeting to recognize a new quarter. Contrary to the Orthodox threat to disown all opponents, the Hicksites demonstrated a more tolerant approach. Their statement specifically recommended "that such Friends as do not unite with us be permitted quietly to withdraw, or have their right of membership transferred to some other meeting, as they may desire."[31]

The official Orthodox response to these developments was embodied in an epistle approved by Meeting for Sufferings and signed on July 20 by Jonathan Evans. In this statement, they abandoned almost all the doctrinal arguments they had pursued over the years. The principal issue now, expressed both explicitly and in tone, involved insubordination against established authority. They quoted William Penn on early Friends, always a clincher—"they were bowed and brought into subjection, . . . we did not think ourselves at our own disposal; to go where we list, to say or do what we list, or when we list." They cited Robert Barclay—"they cry out *breach of liberty, oppression, persecution*! we will have none of your order and government; we are taught to follow the light in our consciences and not the orders of men." And they concluded—"although they have attempted to cover their real designs, it is evident that a difference in principles and doctrines from the Society of Friends, and a thirst for unlimited liberty, are the original and leading motives for their separation." Like every opponent of every reformation, these nay-sayers, until recently secure in their exercise of power, demonstrated that the issue involved power and who should wield it.[32]

In outlying sections, the few Orthodox seemed more moderate, less anxious to enforce the letter of the law, than their city-bred fellow believers. William Jackson, for example, who had taken such a prominent role in the struggle over the clerkship in the yearly meeting, proposed at New Garden that the meeting peacefully divide. Each group would have new record books and access to the old ones retained by a generally respected member. Hicksite Friends would meet for business at New Garden, the

Orthodox about three miles down the road at West Grove. Although this agreement did not hold fast, particularly as time and distance exacerbated tensions, it did show a more conciliatory approach than was usual when the yearly meeting's high-powered committee succeeded in firing up their forces. In fact, a member of the committee insisted that New Garden's compromise, "without precedent in the annals of Ecclesiastical history," should be annulled. The meeting ignored him. One observer summed it up, "so I think our orthodox is not quite as stiff as the cityzens yet."[33]

The process of separating continued unabated, as Quakers across the yearly meeting awaited the convening of the new yearly meeting. West of the Delaware River, the undertaking was farther along, the meetings in New Jersey lagging somewhat behind. Just before the June conference, the *Berean*, Wilmington voice of reformer William Gibbons, estimated that at least three-fourths of Pennsylvania's Friends had lined up against the evangelicals and predicted that, as soon as those in New Jersey felt the Philadelphia elders' heavy hand, they too would join the right side.[34] Private reports from New Jersey suggested the reformers were not as confident and united as they were across the river. Moreover, influential New Jersey evangelicals like Joseph Whitall and John Cox made up for their small numbers by fully exercising the powers their positions gave them. Reformers in the four New Jersey quarters, Shrewsbury and Rahway, Burlington, Haddonfield, and Salem, proved unable to send official representatives to the yearly meeting but held out the likelihood of doing so for subsequent ones.[35]

It made no great difference that each local meeting struggled with the same issues that had been fought over earlier and elsewhere; the personal toll remained high. Close associates, long-time friends, and even members of families found themselves on different sides. In Wilmington, the Hilles brothers, Eli and Samuel, who operated a school together, followed paths so different that, as Samuel's wife Margaret put it in early 1828, "almost no conversation has occurred with them except upon common topics."[36] In some meetings, such as Wilmington's where the reformers were dominant but permitted the Orthodox to continue using the meetinghouse, the psychological price had to be paid weekly. Until a conclusive separation took place and the Orthodox built a new meetinghouse, the minority submitted. When an unsound person prayed, the evangelicals kept their seats and left their hats on. For the first time in her life Margaret Hilles experienced what it meant to belong "to a contemn'd & perhaps to some a despisd minority." One monthly meeting day in Decmber, she and two other women had to leave the meetinghouse in the rain. She evinced surprise "that it should cost me such an effort—but really the physical effect upon my strong frame comes very near to fainting. I hope time will assist in conquering my weakness—for now that these efforts are to be made nearly every week I do not expect to be entirely well until the task is somewhat lighten'd." A visit of an evangelical acquaintance "was itself an evidence & a consolation that repaid me for much suffering"; she was "well content" when they finally got a new meetinghouse.[37] Even hardened reformer William Poole grieved when a close relative—Poole referred to him as "brother"—announced that he and his family were going with the Orthodox; he was, the elderly Poole explained, "the man from whom *I least expected* such a line of conduct."[38] And a New Jersey Hicksite wondered if her brother, of the opposite persuasion, would even visit her again; "it is hard to nature to part with such friends," she sadly concluded.[39]

Such psychic pains were most often privately borne and silently suppressed, never becoming public knowledge. Much more visible were the continuing struggles at local and quarter levels. Each side supplied its own horror stories to convince waverers of the absolute perfidy of the other party. The *Friend*, the Orthodox weekly that first appeared two days prior to the October 15 Hicksite yearly meeting, related how the reformers at the August meeting of Abington Quarter had tried to prevent the evangelical element from carrying on as usual. The fundamental problem involved the overwhelming majority's determination to send an official delegation to the new yearly meeting, a move vigorously resisted by the old yearly meeting's committee of leading Quakers. After the Hicksite majority adjourned the meeting, the Orthodox remained behind, as the report had it, "to transact the proper business of the Quarterly Meeting." The Hicksites stood around, laughing, talking, jeering, and generally being rude. Unable to continue, the Orthodox postponed their efforts until the next day but found, upon arriving, that the door was locked and barred; the Hicksite who kept the keys refused to surrender them. An Abington trustee offered the use of the meetinghouse for worship but for not for a rump quarterly meeting. Gathered under a tree to worship, the evangelicals were interrupted by a number of reformers "irreverently keeping on their hats while a female minister was engaged in supplication." Afterwards the faithful 300—the Hicksites claimed the number was nearer 120—returned to a nearby millhouse where they concluded the business of what they considered the true and faithful quarterly meeting. Since the mill was private property, they invited only those in unity with the old yearly meeting. The same kind of scene was repeated across the yearly meeting, wherever the reformers were able to contol.[40]

Physical control of meetings by the reforming element did not deter the evangelicals; it only increased their resourcefulness and drove them to seek legal advice. Thomas McClintock related how one of the reformers rode home with an Orthodox relative, a leader of Abington millpond group. Reviewing the actions of the Orthodox meeting—preparing an epistle to explain the split and selecting a new clerk—the Orthodox Friend let it slip that they had followed the proper course of action to keep their quarterly meeting. When queried about what he meant, he explained that Samuel Bettle had directed them "according to *legal advice*." Then quickly catching himself, he refused to divulge anything more about his thoughtless indiscretion.[41] The evangelicals thus carefully followed the same course in all the quarters except Philadelphia, which they already controlled—first protesting against moves to read the Green Street epistle or to sending official representatives to the October meeting, then, when defeated, announcing that loyal Friends should remain behind to conduct the meeting's business. The same pattern applied also in monthly meetings. In this fashion, the evangelicals built their claim to be the true body of Quakers. Their legal counsel did in fact argue later that the reformers acted irregularly and outside established procedures and were consquently not entitled to recognition as the Society of Friends.[42]

The question of the ownership of meetinghouse property—as distinguished from control of it—did not immediately arise, although individuals on both sides carked about the problem.[43] For one thing, no one knew how permanent the divisions would be or how long meetings might have to be held under trees, beside the road, or in millhouses; in some cases, as at Haddonfield, New Jersey, the two parties uneasily shared the same meetinghouse as late as 1843.[44] For another, the Hicksites, with their predominately country backgrounds, were less sophisticaed about using the law than the opposing side, and they wanted to adhere to the Discipline's prohibition against suing in the courts. They also distrusted lawyers, whom Edward Hicks described as "those ravens who will croak the loudest for those who can give them the most of their favorite food, money."[45] Thus Hicksite tactics of locking the doors against the Orthodox, using their larger number to intimidate them, and altering meeting times remained standard modes of operation until the minority made new arrangements. Finally in 1829 the yearly meeting recommended discussions with the Orthodox on an amicable division of meeting assets.[46] Soon thereafter attorneys for the Orthodox filed suit to deny Green Street Meeting ownership of its property.[47]

Such a strategy had become about the only way the evangelical minority had to preserve its prerogatives in most of the yearly meeting, for the numbers were certainly not on their side. The division amounted to almost a two-to-one advantage for the Hicksites. At the time of the split, before the Orthodox disowned the Hicksites in a wholesale fashion, Philadelphia Yearly Meeting counted 26,817 members; about 17,379 went with the reformers and 9,009 sided with the Orthodox.[48] According to figures for ministers and elders collected by the latter, the percentages were a bit smaller but reversed in favor of the Orthodox: about 59 percent remained Orthodox, the other 41 percent united with the Hicksites.[49] The strongest Orthodox quarter was, of course, urban Philadelphia, while the reformers enjoyed their largest majority in the small, isolated, and rural Southern Quarter situated in southern Delaware and eastern Maryland—indeed, unlike the other ten quarters, the Orthodox never created even a show organization there. The New Jersey quarters of Haddonfield and Burlington, in close proximity to the Quaker City, apparently had small Orthodox majorities of 450 and 250 respectively; no other Garden State quarter sided with the evangelicals.[50] The Orthodox never took a complete census, not only bcause they probably did not want to reveal their minority status—an important disability in an age of Jacksonian democracy—but for the more practical reason that they did not have access to records in rural areas and hence had no way to count.

To reassure any waverers among their already hefty majority in rural areas, the Hicksites spread tales of the oppression of Green Street Friends by the Philadelphia faction and the haughty way the old yearly meeting's committee went about trying to hold the line for soundness. From Darby, Halliday Jackson exclaimed that the king of Israel had sent faithful servants against "Jonathan Evans & company . . . to cast down the image of Baal and stamp it to pieces and cast it as it were to the four winds." At this monthly meeting, Darby's clerk presented a prepared minute recognizing the evangelical quarter's claims, which action produced a three-hour debate and the appointment of a new clerk more in tune with the majority. Finally Jackson suggested that the reformers peacefully retreat from the scene of confusion, but he asked for copies of reports that were to be considered. At first this request brought forth only gasps of disbelief and more acrimony, but "at length as if actuated by some extraordinary human principal and remarkable spirit of accommodation brother Jonathan humbled himself so much as to condescend that *friends* should have a copy of the reports." The reformers left the small minority behind and proceeded to organize themselves into the only true and faithful meeting in the town, or so they saw it.[51]

If such matters did not possess a life-and-death urgency, others literally did. Since 1818, Philadelphia Friends had owned a cemetery, the Western Burial Ground, on a block of land between Arch and Cherry at Seventh Street. Surrounded by a wall, the cemetery was jointly controlled by a board of trustees from the city's five meetings and administered by a committee of ten, two from each. In addition, each meeting had a burial committee to authorize interment of deceased Friends. After Philadelphia Quarter dissolved Green Street Meeting, the gates to the burial ground remained closed for members of the renegade meeting unless application was made through the Northern District Meeting to which its members were assigned. Needless to say, no loyal Green Streeter would ever consider compromising the cause in any such fashion. In August 1827, when Ann Shotwell, a girl of seventeen, died, her parents refused to apply for a permit. One of the Green Street trustees went to the graveyard and requested admission. When he was refused, he used an ax to pull out one of the staples holding the lock and escorted workers in to dig the grave. Meanwhile, prodded by Henry Cope, Edmund Randolph, an evangelical elder from Northern Meeting, took a permit to the family of the dead girl, but they spurned the gesture. On August 30, the interment took place without further incident. Not only did the victory go to the Hicksites, but reports that the Orthodox were trying to prevent the burial of the dead circulated, according to William Evans, within a radius of forty miles of the city. Such stories did little to help the Orthodox cause, as Evans fretted.[52]

Acting by majority will, the burial ground's committee of ten excluded its two Green Street members and continued to bar the gate to members from the offending meeting. On one occasion a procession carrying a body to be interred was stopped at the gate, forcing one of the mourners to scale the wall and break the inside locks.[53] Five Hicksite trustees, moved by tales of those who had to go over the wall, then authorized construction of a new gate on the Cherry Street side. On May 31, 1828, a crew of workmen, led by one Green Street trustee and its members on the committee of ten, tore a hole in the wall for a new gate. Upon an Orthodox complaint, the mayor himself issued a warrant for the arrest of these trespassers, charged them with forcible entry and rioting, and had five of them jailed. Moreover, unwilling to raise bail — and desiring to be martyrs for the cause — the five remained in jail for five days until brought before a judge on a *habeas corpus* petition.[54] In voiding the arrest warrants, the judge's opinion dealt a severe blow to the Orthodox contention that they controlled the property. Nevertheless, the Orthodox filled up the new hole in the wall and continued to deny Green Street members use of the cemetery's old gate. Thomas Cope referred to the Democractic judge as a "low intriguing politician" who frequented taverns to drink with voters, a characterization that illustrated something of Orthodox social preferences and explains why they found it so difficult to attract support among rural Friends.[55]

Meanwhile the Orthodox commenced a systematic purge. In mid-September, a month before the new yearly meeting was to convene, overseers from the Northern District meeting started visiting members of Green Street, a move preliminary to mass disownment. Going from door to door, these Orthodox envoys charged members with holding monthly meetings outside the order of Society and encouraging establishment of a new yearly meeting. Thomas Pryor could scarcely contain the hostility he felt toward the overseers who visited him: "it was a tryal and a mortification almost beyond what flesh and blood could indure to see the presumption the arrogance and impudence of these two champions of Orthodoxy & aristocracy marching from house to house [,] their impudence too glaring to behold without feeling absolute contempt for them." In two other meetings, Arch Street and Northern District, long-time meeting employees received discharge notices, apparently because they were suspected of softness toward the Hicksites.[56]

As the date neared for the upcoming yearly meeting, Philadelphia's Quaker community was all abustle with activity of this kind. During one busy session, Pine Street Meeting disowned thirty of the reformers who had rejected all pleas to turn from their separatist ways. The three other Orthodox meetings were doing the same, disowning by tens and fifties. Usually reformers refused even to confer with committees sent to labor with them, though occasionally one might agree to see the inquisitors, only to insist that the reformation cause made disownment acceptable.[57]

Rumors circulated that the hordes of rural Hicksites would descend on the city in October to invade the Arch Street sanctum; the edgy elders ordered night-and-day guards placed around their building.[58] Such worries turned out to be unwarranted, for there was enough wealth in the Carpenters' Hall Meeting to finance the $1,000 construction of a rough building across from Green Street meetinghouse in the Middleton and Wooley lumberyard. Measuring 100 by 45 feet, it would hut the men's yearly meeting, while the women gathered in more comfortable facilities across the street.[59]

The first part of October was wet and chilly, but providence seemed to shine on the reformers' efforts. On Thursday, the only clear day during the week preceeding the opening of the new yearly meeting, workers got the cedar roof on just in time for the next day's drizzle.

Thomas Shillitoe, the English evangelical fresh from labors in New York and New England, arrived the same day. He did not show up for the historic developments on Green Street, spending his time instead ministering among the Orthodox, who, it was rumored, were not altogether pleased with the plainness of his testimony.[60] Thomas Wetherald, the young Friend from Alexandria, Virginia, who had so enthralled reformers with his eloquent preaching the year before, came bearing a certificate from his meeting that specifically commissioned him for service at this yearly meeting: It amounted to the first outside endorsement of what the reformers were about. When he spoke at Green Street Meeting on Sunday the 14th he set the tone for the week's activity. Advising Friends not to depend on Fox, Penn, and other early Quakers unles they experienced the same baptizing power, Wetherald attacked the "first day Saints and every day Devils" who relied on human doctrines.

Estimates varied of the number of those present for the new meeting. Five quarters, Abington, Bucks, Concord, Western, and Southern, had designated official representatives, as had Mount Holly, Chesterfield, and Radnor meetings; these totaled 130. William Poole, whose headaches kept him at home, heard there were only a few short of 3,500 — 1,700 to 2,000 men, and 1,200 to 1,500 women[61] — while John Comly guessed nearly 1,800 men. The June conference clerk, William Gibbons, plagued by illness and struggling to get the *Berean* out on time,[62] asked to be relieved of his post; and so Benjamin Ferris got the clerk's seat.

As might be expected, the main topic involved how to proceed through the agitated state most of the Society was in. A large committee, consisting of Friends from every quarter, was delegated to meet Monday evening at Carpenters' Hall and make recommendations. Although some sentiment existed to modify the book of Discipline, particularly so as to ratify what meetings had done in admitting disowned members without certificates of transfer, the less provocative course of maintaining the old rules prevailed.[63] Essentially the committee suggested appointing a continuing body of men and women to attend to the concerns during the year, when the yearly meeting was in recess. A select yearly meeting of ministers and elders was also established with the pointed reminder that it did not have supervisory powers over meetings. Both moves marked a major departure from past practices, for the "representative committee," a renamed Meeting for Sufferings, would have women members, something never before allowed, and the limitation of the select yearly meeting's role would help prevent power over meetings from gravitating into the hands of a group of insiders. The yearly meeting firmly rejected a proposal from one of its committees that the next year's assembly be scheduled for the same third week in April when the Orthodox would gather. This expression of moderation, a rather surprising unwillingness to challenge the old yearly meeting, led the Hicksites to choose the second week in April as their time to convene.

After preparing an epistle to Baltimore Yearly Meeting, the only Quaker body so favored, the assembled Friends approved an epistle to the several meetings within its confines. At least seven times, this document admonished Friends to act humbly toward, and live peacefully with, those who might differ in opinion with them, and it specifically advised against contending with the Orthodox over matters regarding property. "Retire then, we entreat you, from all airy speculations on religious subjects—from all light and chaffy conversation. Enter into your closets—shut the door—commune with your hearts and be still. Thus you will learn in the school of Christ." And in what its authors must have guessed would infuriate the Orthodox, the epistle closed with a quotation from a book of advices "published under the direction of our Yearly Meeting in 1808."[64] Having so directly connected themselves with the main line of Quaker tradition, Benjamin Ferris, clerk of the men's meeting, and Rebecca Comly, wife of John Comly and clerk of the women's meeting, affixed their names, and the meeting ordered ten thousand copies printed.

The first yearly meeting of the Hicksite Friends was now history. Publicly, however, they denied that they were a new yearly meeting. James

Cockburn, a Hicksite who had come to the United States from Scotland nearly three decades before, prepared a full 281-page defense of the movement. His views reflected what others said. "There was no new ground taken," he asserted, "no new pretensions claimed, nor any rash declarations made." The new yearly meeting, in a careful understatement that distorted the facts, was merely "an extra session" called by a "general conference," which itself had represented "the voice of the members of the yearly meeting."[65]

The Hicksites knew the truth even if for political reasons they did not speak it aloud. Thomas Pryor summed up the yearly meeting in his journal. "Thus began & so ended the first Yearly Meeting ever held in the Northern Liberties [the old name for that section of Philadelphia] and the first in the New order of things among the Tolerant friends."[66] Even before the yearly meeting, Poole was searching for ways to protect "the new Society," and while it was going on, he commented on "our reasons for the separation." Similarly, Elias Hicks wrote Poole and referred to "the new Yearly M^g held last week in Phila^{ia}."[68] Others, more cautious, like McClintock and Comly, carefully used the same words in private correspondence that they used when addressing the public, but everyone involved understood that a phrase like "the new yearly meeting" referred to the October gatherings.[69]

Cockburn was nevertheless fundamentally correct when he explained that no new ground had been broken, just as Pryor was profoundly mistaken when he, enthusiastic and optimistic, saw a new order of things unfolding. For the new yearly meeting differed only minimally from the old. Something had happened to the reformers on their way to becoming Hicksites. The reform impulse, the hope of a new order, simply evaporated. Benjamin Ferris, thoughtful clerk of the new yearly meeting and the most scholarly of all the reformers, saw what was likely to happen, even if he failed to apply his insight to the movement he had done so much to foster and which he now headed. In writing to Halliday Jackson to express his appreciation for all the Darby farmer had done for the cause and to warn him of slanderous attacks against him, Ferris remarked,

> there always had been in every revolution having for its object a reformation either in religion or politics some timid calculating kind of people who are more influenced by the *event*, than by the *principle* of action. These people will, if you succeed, join with you in rejoicing—if you fail, they will blame you,

and even go so far as to cast our your name as evil. For my own part, I care very little for such, whether they be against us or for us—they may so far be an advantage to us as they increase our numbers, but otherwise cannot increase our joy.[70]

Ferris' principle of action," other than seizing power from the urban elders, had never been very clear. Elias Hicks, and perhaps William Poole, may have envisioned the contours of a thoroughgoing reformation; other reformers did not. Having separated from their opponents, they had little more than a negative vision to sustain them and knew not what to do with their new power. Using old Quaker ideas and slogans, they had opposed the emerging, disruptive modern world. With the exception of a handful of leaders from Wilmington, champions of free inquiry and broad tolerance, most reformers were unable to do more than try to resist a world that was destroying theirs. Of course, they failed and over the years came to embrace the new secular order. Because they had not raised a standard firmly based on the social realities that made them different from the urban elders, nothing finally remained for them save merging with their former opponents. That came in 1955.

CHAPTER 12

"As soon have half their Teeth pulled,"
OR
From Four, Eight

WITHIN THE YEAR FOLLOWING organization of the new yearly meeting in October 1827, four other yearly meetings would undergo the same trauma. Two of them, Baltimore and Indiana, were relatively minor affairs, representing small numbers and little dislocation. In New York and Ohio, on the other hand, the separations partook of the character of battlegrounds in which the contending parties, each long nurtured by its own champions, squared off to see which would best the other. In all four instances, separations would not have occurred without the example of Philadelphia and the active encouragement of partisans from the City of Brotherly Love. Philadelphia marked the way, setting the example and giving an air of legitimacy to rending asunder the fabric of unity among Friends. The process of separation began at the local level and tore slowly upward until the 1828 sessions of the yearly meetings confirmed what had transpired below. Naturally, the bitterest struggles occurred in the meetings where the two factions were most completely divided.

To maintain what they knew was strong reform sentiment in Baltimore Yearly Meeting, the first of the four to convene following adjournment of the new meeting in October, the Hicksites dispatched a special epistle to the south.[1] The second eldest yearly meeting on the continent, Baltimore covered meetings in all but Maryland's eastern shore, part of Virginia, and into central Pennsylvania. Although small in size—the total number in the yearly meeting did not exceed 2,500 at the time of the separation[2]—Baltimore occupied a pivotal position because it oversaw development of early meetings in Ohio and was in a position to influence developments among western Friends.[3] The area of the yearly meeting was overwhelmingly rural, with its only two cities, Baltimore and Washington, D.C., hardly more than overgrown southern towns. Elias Hicks's concern for Friends there pulled him again and again toward the region, and he paid seven visits in the thirty years prior to 1827.[4] His determined stands on internal issues facing Quakers there did not always win universal approbation, but even detractors recognized that his presence commanded attention and surely influenced events.[5]

Hicks's influence showed itself when Ann Braithwaite and Elizabeth Robson visited the yearly meeting sessions of 1825. The two preached what one attender called "established Church doctrines," attacked lack of belief in the atoning blood of Jesus, and made themselves so obnoxious that the yearly meeting united and instructed the elders to have a private session with their English visitors.[6] Braithwaite and Robson's lack of appeal to Baltimore Quakers was undoubtedly due to the long-standing influence that Hicks's partisans had cultivated in the yearly meeting. One of them, Edward Stabler of Alexandria, Virginia, for example, served as clerk and assistant clerk for years up to the time of the separation. A friend of Hicks and a traveling minister himself, he led a circle of six or eight that reportedly met until midnight each night during yearly meeting to settle the issues to come before the body the next day. The fact that some whispered about his "unitarian" principles, making him a "Jew's believer" in their eyes, tarred the reform movement and blackened its proponents' reputations in the eyes of people like Robson and Braithwaite, not to mention some few locals who chafed under the reformers' domination.[7]

The urban-rural divisions so common in Philadelphia existed also in Baltimore, exacerbated in 1827 by the presence of Thomas Shillitoe, the plain-dressed and plain-speaking English minister. As so often happened, the principal point of discussion was the kind of picky and technical one that Friends seemed to delight in: whether to receive and read the Green Street message and one from the Orthodox Meeting for Sufferings. Sentiment strongly opposed reading the latter, both in Baltimore's own Meeting for Sufferings, where the split was 20 to 3, and in the yearly meeting itself. Shillitoe, who said he dreaded attending the meeting, called the epistle from Green Street "illegitimate," but his assessment won no support and provoked the eloquent Thomas Wetherald to dispute with him openly on the question. The upshot was approval of an epistle directed to all the yearly meetings in the world that announced unity with the new Philadelphia group. It was, wrote the clerk of the women's yearly meeting, "a bold step (not Nicodemus like) not only to own to you that we were your sisters but to spread it far and wide." John Comly, who watched these developments from the gallery, must have gone home with a sense of accomplishment.[8] The Hicksite bandwagon was rolling.

It stopped next in New York, where divisions at the local and quarterly meeting levels made it increasingly likely that a separation would occur when New York Yearly Meeting began its sessions during the last week of May 1828. In geographical reach, this yearly meeting was the largest in the country with eleven quarters stretching into Connecticut and Vermont in the East and then on to western New York and southern Canada in the West and North. The largest concentration of Friends centered in New York City, which could boast a bit more than 2,000, slightly better than one-tenth of the total of 19,000.[9] New York's Quaker history ran back to the visits of George Fox in the 1670s, with formal organization occurring in 1695.[10] New York, of course, was also the home of Elias Hicks, the venerable and widely acclaimed patriarch of traditional Quakerism. Over the long years of his life, he had traveled time and again the backroads that led into the rural recesses where Friends assiduously guarded the light they had experienced. His following was a large one, particularly in these rural regions, and it lent him an eminence that placed him above his contemporaries. That eminence was precisely the reason, of course, that the evangelical opposition complained so much about him. Henry Hull, for example, saw him as having almost dictatorial powers. Hicks could still a group of his clamoring supporters by merely standing and asking for quiet; concluded Hull: "it afforded sorrowful evidence of their being under the control of a mortal man."[11]

As in Philadelphia, Hicks's critics resided in the city. There his traditional and popular message frightened Friends already acclimated to the compromises of sophisticated urban life. His attacks on Bible and benevolent societies, voting, and courting public opinion were bad enough.[12] Even worse was an air that observers had long ago noted and even called to his attention. He evinced a kind of cocksureness that easily shaded over into censoriousness of people who disagreed with him. Even when he preached against using products made with slave labor, one observer wrote him, his "severity of expression" made it less "likely to bring about the desired end of convincing others, and bringing them over to a disuse of those articles."[13] Calling people's motives into question might square with traditional Christian approaches to converting sinners but it certainly was not calculated to appeal to those who already felt themselves to be virtuous and who were so acclaimed by others. As his harshest New York critic, Thomas Eddy, a man of wealth and noted public philantrophy, told a friend in 1821, Hicks "would ruin Society by his preaching against the clergy & particular popular institutions, the offspring of great minds, such as Missionary, Bible Societies, &c, &c, which deeply prejudiced the Clergy & great men against our Society."[14] It was no wonder that a man like Eddy took up his pen to warn others about Hicks's influence. And it was also no wonder that Hicks's large army of disciples presently took critics like Eddy "under dealing," the Quaker term connoting discipline.[15]

Hicks's preeminence and power in New York made it an obvious target for all the English evangelicals who wanted to beard the old lion right in his den. Thomas Shillitoe, who did not arrive until late 1826, exemplified their strategy. He always stayed with evangelicals, so he might avoid contact with the reformers except to excoriate them for their unsound doctrines. At one place after another, he encountered inroads made by the "enemy of all righteousness," "disesteem for Sacred Writings," and, worse, a "careless posture by which some took and kept their seats."[16] During the 1827 yearly meeting, he could hardly stand the affronts heaped on him and other English visitors. In a meeting of ministers and elders, when the evangelicals pushed one of their pet schemes to order a committee down to quarterly meetings so as to stir up the faithful, he was shocked when a women left her seat and grabbed the clerk's elbow to prevent him from making his minute.[17] The evangelicals made no attempt to heal the divisions and, in fact, alienated more and more of the rank and file from their position.[18]

The Philadelphia split inevitably had its impact in neighboring New York. Some saw the Philadelphia experiment as a model. "On the whole," wrote one reformer, "I am of the mind that the fate of the Society very much hangs upon the procedure of friends who are attached to the Meeting of Green Street—if they should be favored with strength to continue in the right ground—the society will gradually approach to the same point."[19] Even routine business contained the seeds of acrimony. In August 1827, a couple requested to be married under the care of New York Monthly Meeting, but the evangelicals would not give their approval because the groom was a member of Green Street Meeting and to grant a certificate of clearness would amount to recognizing a meeting the Orthodox had dissolved. The followers of Hicks, of course, were just as insistent: they wanted to teach the evangelicals, both in New York and in Philadelphia, a lesson. The couple finally passed only because the clerk acquiesced.[20]

The same kind of issue occasioned the first actual separation in New York. In September at Rose Street Meeting, a young man requested a certificate of transfer to Green Street Meeting and thereby provoked a real donnybrook. To grant the request, the evangelicals reiterated, would amount to doing business with a disorderly meeting—not to do so, responded the Hicksites, would be to turn against a great body of Friends. The clerk, less compliant this time, refused to make the minute, and a tug-of-war commenced over the minute books. Upon losing the struggle, the Hicksites procured some loose sheets of paper, made their minute, and adjourned, leaving the Orthodox behind to complete what they claimed was the real business of the meeting.[21] In Cornwall Quarter, on the west side of the Hudson, discussion of appropriate answers to the queries had the same affect, with "tolerants," as the reformers sometimes styled themselves, sending up one set of answers, the Orthodox another.[22] Some day soon, someone would have to sort out these conflicting factions and decide which one was the Society of Friends.

Were a Westchester reformer to have his way, the sorting-out party would be the reformers. Evan Lewis, a journalist and schoolteacher, checked in with Benjamin Ferris in February 1828, three months prior to New York Yearly Meeting. Reflecting on the example of his fellow believers to the south, Lewis averred that his only criticism was that they had permitted themselves to be put in the position of withdrawing, instead of forcing the minority to do so. "If the liberals had marched in solid column," he considered, "and by dint of strength and numbers affected a breach in the ranks of their opponents, they would have been compelled to yield and would have left the field." When New York Quakers divided, "which will not be long," he forecast, "the *minority* will leave the *majority* in possession of the field—*and this is as it should be*." The failure of the Pennsylvanians in this respect gave the Orthodox an unmerited advantage among western Friends. Lewis closed by advising Ferris to send to the west *Bereans* chock full of information for the use of "plain matter-of-fact people" rather than "the Logician and the Metaphysician."[23]

Meanwhile, in Indiana, the Orthodox were busy shoring up their threatened edifice. Only six years old, Indiana Yearly Meeting covered a sparsely settled but rapidly growing region nearly bereft of roads or places of public accommodations. The Friends there, who settled first along the Whitewater River and seemed to explode westward across the central part of the state, emigrated not only from Ohio, Pennsylvania, and Maryland, but also from the slave-holding South, North Carolina especially. Starting with five quarterly meetings, Indiana Yearly Meeting had eight by 1828. Wholesale disownments suggested they viewed their meetings as bulwarks against the surrounding wilderness, as institutions to prevent their members from running off and chasing every alluring will-o'-the-wisp that lurked in the unknown.[24] Moreover, their isolation led them to associate with members of other denominations—"Priests of Bale," old Hugh Judge called them—who inevitably tempted them to compromise their peculiar Quaker testimonies and produced few "doers of the word."[25] Hence these Friends, whose rural setting might otherwise have made them ready recruits to the cause of the reformation, had reason to fear what they considered innovations and a threat to what the Orthodox called "sound Quakerism."

More importantly, the Orthodox had in Elisha Bates one of the most vigorous and creative Quaker activists in the country. Temperamentally, he more nearly resembled the reformers than the evangelical grandees of the eastern cities: A born scrapper with a keen sense of what would appeal to the common folk of the Midwest, he published a monthly journal, the *Miscellaneous Repository*, that propelled the doctrines of evangelicalism deep into what was to be the heartland of American Quakerdom. That he was a grassroots theologian who could hold his own with the widely read eastern reformers could only earn him more respect from his rural clientele and add to his stature.

Bates burst on the previously placid scene in Richmond, Indiana, even before Indiana Yearly Meeeting met in October 1827, as did a brood of English evangelicals, Anna and Isaac Braithwaite and Ann Jones. Jonathan Taylor, the clerk of Ohio Yearly Meeting, and Jeremiah Hubbard, a North Carolinian of pronounced evangelical views, also showed up. Together, they put the pressure on. Did the Indiana Friends know, asked the visitors, that Elias Hicks had been preaching doctrines that were inimical to Christianity? No? Then perhaps Friends should consider his letter to Dr. Edwin Atlee[26] or some quotations from his sermons published in Philadelphia. Now were Indiana Friends troubled about the direction their Society was taking? Yes? Then perhaps they would appoint a committee to confer with others looking toward a common discipline for all the yearly meetings; perhaps they would also approve a testimony against the new-fangled doctrines. The three relatively minor Hicksite-types present from the east could do nothing in the face of this onslaught—indeed, their certificates were not read, and the yearly meeting went on to approve both the requested committee and a lengthy "Testimony" that condemned Hicks by name. Circulation of four thousand copies increased when Bates's paper and the Philadelphia *Friend* trumpeted the document in their pages to illustrate the Hoosiers' soundness and to influence hold-outs. The Ohio Meeting for Sufferings weighed in a month later with a statement explicitly commending the Testimony and bemoaning efforts to destroy a belief in Jesus' divinity, his propitiatory atonement, and the Bible's authority.[27]

Indiana's Testimony, like one issued in November by North Carolina Yearly Meeting,[28] purported to hold the line against the incursion of alien doctrines and warned Friends against reading pernicious books and pamphlets. The Testimony referred directly to the *Berean* and Hicks's published sermons. By long quotations from George Fox, the epistle endeavored to demonstrate that Friends had always affirmed evangelical doctrines and that those of Hicks and the *Berean* were aberrant. And, in referring to the separation in the East, the Hoosiers announced their refusal to "acknowledge a connexion with these separate meetings, nor religious fellowship with individuals who compose them." If Evan Lewis had learned something from the Philadelphia split, Elisha Bates and party had also been instructed—they did not intend to sit by while their influence and power were eroded right out from under them. Their ability to hold their positions suggested that if someone as resourceful and talented as Bates had piloted the Philadelphia elders, things might have turned out differently in the East.

Unfortunately for the unity of the Society, Quakers in New York were short on Elisha Bateses. The clerk of the yearly meeting, Samuel Parsons, from Flushing, had little popular appeal. As the 1828 sessions approached, he was ending twenty years at the table, ever since he was a relatively young thirty-four. He proudly noted that both his parents and grandparents were Friends, making him a birthright member, and he gave others the impression that he considered most rank-and-file Friends as disorderly rabble. Needless to say, he usually deferred to a handful of weighty members. Anticipating trouble at the first session, he prepared some minutes ahead of time, which in itself was not unusual, but he also took the precaution of leaving behind the minute books and the originals of reports from the quarters, lest he be required to surrender them.[29] John Griscom, a professor at Rutgers Medical College, a leading evangelical, and a philanthropist, made arrangements for the use of a meeting room at the college in case the Orthodox minority needed another gathering place.[30] "Timid minds," one Friend noted, "are alarmed at the prospect ahead."[31]

The Orthodox in New York followed Evan Lewis's plan, so that the separation at the yearly-meeting level was swift and relatively painless. By this time, the two sides had their respective roles down to perfection. Some of the upstate quarters and Westbury Quarter on Long Island increased their number of representatives, while excluding those with known evangelical views.[32] When the select meeting of ministers and elders gathered at the Hester Street meetinghouse on Saturday, May 24, an evangelical immediately complained that there were unqualified visitors present from Philadelphia. Of course, they refused to leave. The meeting divided sharply over whether its Hicksite clerk, John Barrow, should continue; unable to reach a conclusion, it had to permit him to keep his place. The meeting sat, discussed, sat, debated, sat, and then, after several hours, adjourned. The next day, Thomas Shillitoe attended two meetings, both of which seemed overrun with Hicksites.[33]

Shillitoe initiated the action that provoked the actual separation. As soon as the Monday morning session was quiet, he rose and protested the presence of those from the new meeting in Philadelphia—one Orthodox estimate inflated the figure to a hundred.[34] Hicks, to the surprise of no one, identified himself with the visitors, pointing out that he had attended the sessions in Penn's city the previous month and that they were members of the only yearly meeting there with which he was in unity. They were, he thought, "*the cream of the society.*" For nearly two hours the meeting debated the status of their disowned guests, until an evangelical proposed that the sound part of the meeting retreat to the basement so the meeting's legitimate business might be concluded. Nicholas Brown, an itinerant minister and reformer from Canada, immediately charged that the minority had planned a separation and, since they had a clerk who sided with them, he proposed that the meeting select a replacement. As Samuel Mott's name was called out, Parsons stood up to read a minute. From all corners of the house, shouts rang out in protest because the followers of Hicks assumed that Parsons was about to adjourn the session.[35] Some yelled, "Don't let him read it," others, "pull him down," still others, "he is not clerk of the Yearly Meeting."³⁶ At one point, Hicks turned to quiet the crowd, but the noise of hisses, shouts, and canes and umbrellas banging the floor nearly drowned him out. Parsons read his minute into this din—with what volume, no one recorded—and the Orthodox filed out on their way to the basement.³⁷

After Mott tried unsuccessfully to reach the clerk's table through the surging mass of Friends, his supporters passed him bodily along above their heads. When he got to the gallery, Hicks reached out his hand to help, but, losing his grip, watched helplessly as the new official inaugurated himself by tumbling into his seat.³⁸ But Mott knew what to do. One of his first acts was to read a minute abolishing the Meeting for Sufferings, which, because of the broad territory of the yearly meeting, was dominated by urban evangelicals.³⁹

Down in the cellar, the evangelicals found they could not get in, for the doorkeeper sided with the Hicksites and refused to surrender his key. They milled around in the yard while John Griscom went upstairs to request another, but he was hooted down with shouts of "turn him out," "turn him out." Upon his return, Parsons lent an air of legitimacy to the courtyard caucus by making a minute to continue the session at Rutgers Medical College, to which the group marched so gravely that bystanders wondered if it were someone's funeral procession. When they arrived, an evangelical suddenly remembered that they had left the women in their yearly meeting and hurried to get them, but found the gate locked; it was not until the next morning that the Orthodox women could reconvene at the African Methodist church.⁴⁰

On Wednesday morning, many in the two yearly meetings attended what would be their last worship together at the Rose Street meetinghouse. Thomas Wetherald, the firebrand from Alexandria, was in rare form, and Hicks was "favored," in the Quaker phrase. Shillitoe said he dreaded getting up, but felt led to preach about the power of "Christ who died outside the gates of Jerusalem." Whereas Hicks and Wetherald stressed the inward revelation of Christ, Shillitoe recommended that his auditors procure and review a just-published booklet on the "true doctrines of Friends." As he passed out of the house at the rise of the meeting, he repeated over and over to those he passed, "beware of that man, beware of that man." But the lines seemed too tightly drawn already for anyone to pay much heed to this parting advice.⁴¹

A good bit of sorting out remained. The numerous yearly meeting committees were handicapped by clerks who had taken the record books over to the opposite party or treasurers who refused to surrender the funds. Each side tried to have its own committee meetings at the stated times and places, a determination that was bound to engender conflict.[42] Formal separations spread across the yearly meeting, as the majority installed locks on meetinghouse doors where they had never been before or made fragile arrangements to share tiny rural meetinghouses. Most such attempts at accommodation proved short lived, with each party presently going its own way with claims to be the only true meeting of Friends in the area. Each yearly meeting dispatched its committee to visit subordinate meetings, a development that promoted division in the process of trying to strengthen the locals on the scene. "This is hard times for a timid old man," lamented one reluctant reformer as he viewed the requirements made of him by the changing situation.[43] At the end of the shake-down period, the Hicksites remained in possession of most of the meetinghouses and claimed about 12,500 members to nearly 6,000 for their opponents.[44]

The next contest between Hicksites and evangelicals now emerged in Ohio. Since before the split in Philadelphia, evangelicals there had girded themselves for the coming struggle. Meeting for Sufferings had endorsed a lengthy defense of the new evangelical approach to Quakerism in 1825,[45] and in early 1827, Elisha Bates brought out the first issue of his periodical. The *Repository's* pages crackled with attacks on the Hicksites, particularly as represented by Gibbons's *Berean*, and defenses of its editor's own works. For the aggressive Bates, the supporters of Hicks had themselves introduced a "new scheme of religion," and he published critiques that were almost parodies in their absurd renderings of Hicks's doctrines. Although even some of his own supporters expressed their misgivings at the extremity of his interpretations, Bates stuck by his pen and continued his crusade. Because Hicks argued that the Saviour was within rather than without, Bates decided that he meant that everyone had a separate Saviour and that Christ could not have had an existence independent of the individual. Friends in the West, he concluded about this view, "should seriously and awfully pause before they enter upon it."[46]

The Hicksites in Philadelphia addressed an epistle to their fellow believers to the West that recounted their side of the separation and tried to woo readers to the reformation cause.[47] But without someone on the scene with enough influence to counteract Bates, the epistle was like so much spume on a great sea's surface; it could have little impact on the strong currents running below. The Hicksite faction did have a paper, the *Informant*, heralding its cause for a brief period, but patronage was so shaky that its editor and publisher had to constantly dream up schemes to keep it alive.[48] Hampered by their opponents' power in the yearly meeting and often in local meetings, as well as by their own insufficiency, the Ohio reform element had every reason to feel dispirited.[49]

One Hicksite moaned that "Calumny and detraction—invective and abuse—contempt and sarcasm, are the weapons wielded against us, not merely in our houses, streets, and highways, but in our solemn meetings."[50] Mounting in intensity after Meeting for Sufferings endorsed the Indiana Testimony in November 1827, these attacks came mainly from roving evangelical ministers, a gaggle of British visitors, a North Carolinian or two. Committees dispatched to Ohio's five quarterly meetings to warn Friends against consorting with Hicksites—and recommending disciplinary measures if they did—also aggravated an already tense situation. The most caviling Carolinian, Jeremiah Hubbard, pronounced all as "Deists" or "Infidels" unfavorable to his evangelical views on the Atonement and Christ's divinity and warned his party to resist the temptation to appoint them to committees or any other service. To the Hicksites, the committees from above smacked of European brands of priestcraft because they judged the faith of Friends and advised excommunication for those who could not measure up to the evangelical mark. If a meeting refused to receive visitors like Hubbard or a committee, it immediately became a target for discipline. By the end of 1827 Friends who would not have entertained thoughts of separation earlier had changed their minds. Concluded a Friend of Somerton: "now a Separation is the only alternative; not only because 'peace and tranquility can never be restored, whilst the two parties remain connected together in one body,' but because it is a determination of the Orthodox party to disown all who cannot embrace their dogma."[51]

Informal conferences of owned and disowned Hicksites began to be held to discuss the situation and plan strategy. The dissatisfaction centered in Belmont County, just west of the Ohio River, where Quaker settlements had their longest history. A conference at Somerset in January 1828, for example, lasted three or four hours and resulted in a decision to form a new monthly meeting. The gathered Quakers talked about the "creed," their name for the Indiana Testimony, and decided that their overzealous opponents "are making *Hicksites*, as they call us, faster than all the books before could do."[52] In other meetings, the appearance of a visiting committee or the reading of the Indiana Testimony would provoke a walkout. After such a secession at Concord, site of the oldest monthly meeting west of the Ohio, the quarter laid down the meeting and attached its members to the staunchly evangelical Short Creek group. Needless to say, the Concord Hicksites refused to recognize these proceedings, conferred, and petitioned for admission to another quarter. Nor did these moves end the conflict, because each party tried to use the same meetinghouse—in one instance resulting in a shoving match between two overwrought individuals.[53] These activities, which by the end of April had spread to at least three quarters, reminded evangelicals of a "leprosy over our society." They grumbled about the lack of religious experience among the Hicksites, who, said Benjamin Ladd, arch-evangelical and former clerk of the yearly meeting, "boast much of their numbers."[54]

As the September date for the yearly meeting neared, leading Friends from all over the country began to think of visiting Ohio. The Orthodox planned a conference a week before the yearly meeting at Mount Pleasant to set a common course of action toward the Hicksites. This gathering attracted a stellar delegation of Philadelphians; led by Jonathan Evans and Samuel Bettle, it included William Evans, Thomas Stewardson, and three other lesser lights. Even from far-off New England, three Friends decided to come.[55] The most famous of the visitors, however, were Elias Hicks, whose eighty-year-old bones somehow survived the bump-bump of the ride across the seemingly endless hills and valleys of Pennsylvania,[56] and Thomas Shillitoe, who started a bit after his rival but caught up just before reaching Ohio. Both old men—Shillitoe was six years Hicks's junior— honed their rhetoric to a cutting edge as they stopped at meetings along the way.[57]

Both sides feared disorders at Mount Pleasant. As early as June, Bates's *Repository* was spreading word that the purpose of recent conclaves was to plot the seizure of the commodious meetinghouse at Mount Pleasant.[58] While such rumors had no substance, some of the language of the reformers could but encourage them. One Hicksite wrote an eastern correspondent about the evangelicals' "iron rod" and noted, "the struggle [at the yearly meeting] will be a violent one I believe, but we not withstanding their threats of the law are quite undounted & intirely diehard to stand our ground in definance of their law."[59] With all the Orthodox leaders from the East in town, the Hicksites expected their opponents to be so powerfully reinforced that they would give no quarter. "That they will leave the house I have no prospect," wrote one observer, "for I have been ready to conclude they would as soon have half their Teeth pulled."[60]

The five hundred or so permanent residents of the prosperous village were accustomed to strangers traveling through, carting goods back and forth from the East, but they had never seen anything like the mob of 1828.[61] Mount Pleasant's two inns overflowed with the influx of Quakers, always large when yearly meeting convened but this year straining the inns beyond capacity. One private home collected forty guests at one time. Visitors ate a meal at one house, lodged at another, and then rearranged themselves during the week.[62] Even the meetinghouse, at sixty by ninety-two feet the largest building in the state, was filled to bursting point.[63] When Shillitoe arrived on August 15, the roads were so deep in mud that he had to get out and help steady the carriage.[64] But the crowds continued to stream in, as Mount Pleasant prepared for a boom time and the Quakers their latest showdown.

Saturday, September 6, two days before the yearly meeting was to open, was the usual time for the select meeting of ministers and elders. This first gathering of Ohio Friends seemed inauspicious. In the morning a weighty committee of six waited upon Hicks at Israel French's, where many of the reformation leaders lodged. They asked him to stay away and presented documents they had procured from the rump meeting of Orthodox Friends on Long Island purporting to show that Hicks was a separatist and ordering him to return home. Of course, Hicks did not recognize any such group, so near the appointed hour of 10 A.M. he and his entourage left for the meetinghouse. Walking ahead, Halliday Jackson and Amos Peaslee came to the gate but were forbidden to enter by a committee that included a stout man who came outside and placed his body in front of the closed gate. Reasoning did no good, so the little group, swelled now by about twelve defecting members of the select meeting, found seats and sat in a meeting along the fence. That afternoon they met at a local school to discuss the situation and decide on a course of action.[65] Round one had gone to the powers that were, yet, as Jackson predicted, "they will get the *organs* but . . . we will get the *church*."

On Sunday, it seemed that practically everyone in town wanted to get into the meetinghouse. At ten o'clock, the hour to begin, the house was full, Shillitoe and Anna Braithwaite having arrived long before and seated themselves in the gallery with their adherents. Hicks and two other eastern ministers pushed through the crowd of five hundred who were milling around outside unable to get in; if some early arrivals had not moved to allow them to sit in the gallery, the ministers would not have found a place. Hicks spoke first, for about forty minutes, to an audience that seemed unusually quiet; every eye in the building, estimated Jackson, focused on him. Elisha Bates was next on his feet from high in the gallery. Hicks, he warned those who were not Friends, was not a recognized minister of the Society and his doctrines did not represent it; he did not believe in a Devil or a heaven and hell, except in some kind of spiritualized, internal sense. William Evans thought Bates's defense "an able exposition" of the rights of the Society. Braithwaite followed and repeated for forty-five minutes an account of interviews she had had with Hicks and explained how his docrinal position ran contrary to Scripture and Friends' history. Just as Hicks rose to defend himself, two evangelicals shook hands to close the meeting. Slowly the congregation rose, but its members refused to leave until Hicks started moving toward the door. Some remained inside to hold the house in the face of Bates's decision that it be locked between sittings.[66]

That afternoon Hicks, Mary Lukens, one of his supporters from Chester County, Pennsylvania, and others of a reform tendency went to the Short Creek meetinghouse about half a mile from the hamlet. With the Orthodox left behind, Hicks and Lukens "had good service." At Mount Pleasant, Amos Peaslee spoke longer than old Jonathan Taylor, the yearly meeting clerk, thought appropriate, and he requested that the minister be seated. When the Taylor request was ignored, Bates stood up and shouted at Peaslee to sit down, but that demand brought only hoots from the audience and a scattering of the Friends present. Jonathan Evans, nearly seventy years old, was unable to attend this meeting or very many others during the week since he had a high fever, a rapid pulse, and stomach pressure; a doctor prescribed bleeding and a heavy dose of calomel, and Evans slowly recovered his strength until by Thursday he could wobble out to the last session of the Orthodox conclave at Short Creek.

The main event opened the next day at 10 A.M., although the Indian Affairs committee convened at eight, thus giving the Orthodox first crack at filling the building — an important consideration, for Bates had promised to have it opened promptly at the stated time. According to Jackson, who had a long discussion with them on Sunday morning during a stroll around the meeting house, Bates and Taylor planned to use civil officers to keep the Hicksites out but expressed the hope that all would be peaceful.

Jackson shared the desire for peace, but he indicated "Friends are determined to enter the house and I am afraid there will be some violation of the peaceable principles." The evangelicals had consulted lawyers and, much to William Evans's gratification, had found that Ohio law was strict about punishing disorders in religious assemblies, even by members. Thus, early Monday, despite the rain that was pelting down, the trustees of the meetinghouse posted the property warning away nonmembers—which meant anyone who had been disowned, as the denizens of good order viewed it. That meant Elias Hicks and his reform contingent. The trustees delivered notices directly to Hicks, Jackson, Peaslee, and a few other leaders. Hicks inexplicably elected to stay behind in his room and missed all the excitement; perhaps he had had enough.

About 9:45, with the rain still coming down, the doorkeepers who had been inside discussing their plans opened the doors, and crowds of Orthodox Friends rushed in, leaving large numbers to stand in the rain and mud. Wet Quakers made for short tempers. The doorkeepers, appointed by the various quarters to exclude those disowned from their areas, could not stand against the press. One woman, claiming she had been pushed back twice, allowed as how she was going in because, regardless of what the guard said, she had not been disowned. Her husband lent his support, and she popped through the door in a hurry. An Irishman—perhaps one Jackson had thought of when he referred to "the zealous"—burst through the front door at the head of a phalanx of lunging Hicksites. The husband of another rebuffed woman threatened one guard, "keep thy hands off my wife. Don't thee touch her or I'll split thee down."

Inside, things were somewhat quieter, but only temporarily. On the women's side of the house, the Orthodox—referred to as "other dogs" by the Irishman—went on with business and paid no attention to the Hicksites, who went off to the back of the room; both groups adjourned after about an hour. On the men's side, Thomas Shillitoe commenced to pray before the meeting gathered; his were the last calm words before the storm broke. The rules provided that last year's clerk would serve until the first sitting on Tuesday, when the representatives should report their recommendation for a replacement. But the rule did not meet the needs of the reformers. Israel French therefore proposed, just as Taylor prepared to read the opening minute, that since the clerk had disqualified himself by his divisive actions over the last year—he had attended the Orthodox meeting in New York—a new one should be named. A voice immediately nominated David Hilles of Redstone Quarter, and shouts from all over the hall lent their approval, while Taylor called the roll of representatives and tried frantically to proceed in the accustomed order.

The meeting, however, was soon in an uproar. Some Hicksites circulated through the twelve to fifteen hundred people present[67] asking, "Friends, will you suffer your clerk to be kept from the table?" Others, standing on benches, shouted for the clerk to come down from his seat in the gallery. A number of Orthodox members stationed themselves around the incumbent as his assistant read the reports from the quarters. One rash Hicksite tried to leap up to where Hilles was sitting, but fell back, only to scramble up again until he and some others were able to push their man toward the table. Out in the audience, one young frenzied man climbed on the stove, yelling that the God of Love had left the gallery and the God of Mammon had taken over. A soundingboard ran above the gallery, with one row of seats above that. Whether from there or not was never really determined—with the noise and confusion it proved difficult to get anything straight—but a bench or board cracked with enough of a new sound that people paused and looked around. In the brief silence, someone shrieked, "the gallery is falling!" That bit of intelligence produced cries of alarm and a rush to get downstairs from those unfortunate enough to be on the second floor—at least one panicky person jumped out a second-story window. Shillitoe remembered seeing a cloud of dust and a piece of ceiling fall. In the midst of this chaotic scene, some unknown enthusiast bellowed, "Hurrah for Jackson."

Suddenly, for about five minutes, things got quiet, a kind of unannounced truce between armies, as people looked about them and probably wondered what they were about. Then someone saw that Jonathan Taylor still sat at his table, and young men rushed to yank it from its defenders' grip. Taylor held on, as the table was pushed toward him and then quickly pulled back, again, and again. The clerk's life seemed imperiled. William Evans asked some of the struggling evangelicals if they thought the cause of religion was promoted by such conduct. A small door to the outside just behind the table provided an entranceway for some on the outside to attack from the rear. With these reinforcements, the hapless walnut table was pulled apart and literally broken to pieces. Taylor tumbled back out the door and fell to the ground, his face slightly injured, his spectacles knocked off. In the only humor of the day, he looked around and asked no one in particular, "And what sort of religion is this?" David Hilles used the table drawer as his symbol of authority and began to read a minute opening the meeting. Benjamin Ladd, who had, by one account, bitten a man's shoulder in the melee, proposed that the meeting adjourn until ten the next morning. Before the evangelicals left, Jackson suggested that since a separation had obviously taken place the two parties should try to work out some accommodation, a remark that set William Evans's teeth on edge. The group remaining set the meeting time at 9 A.M.

At ten the next day, after the Hicksites had been in session for an hour, Bates and a trustee of the meeting entered and asked that the building be vacated so that Ohio Yearly Meeting might proceed. Told that Ohio Yearly Meeting *was* sitting and that they might enter to discuss common use of the property, Bates repeated his demand that his party have "uninterrupted possession." The Orthodox then retired to corners of the yard, the men on one side, the women on the other, and conducted their business, the most important item being selecting Bates as clerk. They also sent a group of Friends to the Short Creek meetinghouse to erect some temporary extension so they could conclude the rest of their meeting there.

In the afternoon, the sheriff of Jefferson County arrived from Stubenville with arrest warrants for some of the Hicksites. Jackson and two or three others were charged with trespass, and David Hilles and one associate with disturbing the meeting. Israel French and eight other Friends were charged with rioting. On October 25, Hilles and his codefendant were found guilty and sentenced to pay five-dollar fines and court costs; a higher court later dismissed their appeal. A jury convicted French and the others charged with rioting in April 1829; they received sentences of thirty mintues in jail and a fine of six and one-quarter cents. Cases against the others never came to trial.[68] Within a week, rumors reached the East that Hicks and three or four of his compatriots were in prison and had so seriously injured Jonathan Taylor that there were fears for his recovery.[69]

The Orthodox at Mount Pleasant amassed a healthy majority of the approximately 1,500 Friends who came to the first explosive session on Monday morning, and the Hicksites conceded that about 1,000 went to the Short Creek meetinghouse; since it could accommodate only 700 at best, rude plank shelters went up to shade about 300 more. Given that the nearly 8,900 Friends in the yearly meeting had already divided almost equally, the evangelicals' healthy margin resulted from the fact that Mount Pleasant was in an area replete with Bates's supporters.[70] That they did not use their superior numbers to contest Hicksite occupation of the meetinghouse after Monday morning underscored their commitment to legal remedies, their realization of the close division elsewhere, and their refusal to struggle physically. In subsequent years, thanks to a Hicksite decision to move the date of their annual sessions forward a week, a *de facto* arrangement permitted both groups to share the Mount Pleasant meetinghouse.[71]

The split in Ohio did not lessen the intention of Indiana evangelicals to maintain their tight grip. Indiana Yearly Meeting was the only one where the evangelicals had such broad support that they could act toward dissidents with almost complete freedom. Their control of the yearly meeting's machinery was never seriously challenged, and the disciples of Hicks were so isolated and weak that they did not even try to take over the old yearly meeting or contest with the evangelicals. Indeed, when Hicks arrived in Richmond, site of the yearly meeting, he did not attend its sessions, contenting himself with holding a meeting in an adjacent barn; this decision and his refusal to participate in the Ohio split suggested that he sensed his side was weak. No matter what kind of face the Hicksites tried to put on it, they could not disguise their feeble state nor avoid provoking the suspicion that the Indiana separation was propelled not so much by popular discontent as by a desire of some to leap on the bandwagon.

The puzzle of why such a small minority of rural Indiana Friends — one estimate had less than fifteen hundred out of a total membership of just under fourteen thousand[72] — were willing to join the reform cause was answered in part by a Hicksite leader. Referring to the resolutely Orthodox meeting at Geran's Creek, Noah Haines pointed out that "the members are mostly Southern people, and they generally have Closed up all avenues of obtaining correct information[.] our opponents are very kind to such by furnishing them with there declarations and the friend, and EB's papers, Cautioning them not to Read anything on the other side."[73] The Carolinians who flooded into Indiana — naming counties and creeks after those they had left behind — had never been touched by Hicks's brand of Quakerism as had Friends from Pennsylvania and Maryland, where over the years he had built up a solid core of supporters. Too, Indiana was still a frontier region, its settlements widely scattered, its communication with the East hampered by time and distance, and its people isolated and more concerned with bending the wilderness to their control than with religious controversy. To make the situation worse for the cause of the reformation, people on the frontier lived in a world where things—nature in particular—could quickly get out of control: one oldtimer wrote in the winter of 1828 about how an unexpected sea of mud, "Belly Deept to horses," had locked people in until spring.[74] Consequently, they valued the status quo and were reluctant to have things they took for granted disturbed. The same reformer who grumbled about the lack of correct information delayed for nearly five months in sending reports of the separation to the outside world because the "Publick mind was in so grate State of Excitement."[75]

What resulted was not so much a separation as establishment of a new denomination. The Hicksites, recognizing their weakness, never tried to capture the old organization and could lay no claims to continuing the yearly meetings. Centered in Miami Quarter, in western Ohio around the small town of Waynesville, the reform element had grown increasingly restive since the 1827 yearly meeting adopted its Testimony and the quarters began to enforce it at the local levels. Committees presently appeared at monthly meetings, using the Testimony as a standard to judge the members. They tossed around by now familiar labels such as "infidel" and "deist" for those who refused to asent to the Testimony, and they pressured meetings to reject transfers or communications from separatist meetings. At Richmond, the sound members named a committee of five who, after joining with the regular overseers, visited and "treated with" individual members.[76]

Indiana's Meeting for Sufferings gave official endorsement to these tactics at a meeting called in Richmond in March 1828. After ordering five hundred copies of the declaration of Philadelphia's Meeting for Sufferings for reading in all subordinate meetings, this sparse gathering of eighteen elders out of fifty-six forbade all correspondence with Baltimore Yearly Meeting, even though there had been no separation there. When Miami Quarter met in May, its members' expectation that the proponents of "modern orthodoxy" in Richmond would seek to deprive them of their meetinghouse proved correct. A delegation appeared with a written communication demanding that they vacate the premises. Instead of doing so, Miami Quarterly Meeting decided to form a new yearly meeting to meet in late September. "I verily believe," the postmaster at Waynesville wrote back East, "that unless we who are so much defamed to defend the ancient Principle of quakerism, it will be Lost, amongst the formal professors of the day . . . as they are much in favour of our orthodox quakers."

Although postmaster and schoolmaster Haines was grieved at having to take these steps, he experienced a kind of exhilaration he had never known before: "I have frequently Read and herd of separations in meetings but could form but little Idea of the feelings produced by the act when it comes to be Realized. When the fittings of orthodoxy came to be broken a heavy crashing of the chains was herd for the space of a few minutes, and then friends were quiet nothing herd but sobs and deep sighings for a short time." It might be presumptuous for part of one quarterly meeting to create a new yearly meeting, he explained, but he believed "without a shadow of a doubt that it was a Right move," which would surely attract other "tired minds."[77]

When the new yearly meeting convened on Monday, September 29, its star attraction was Elias Hicks himself, and people flocked in from up to thirty miles away just to hear him preach. Delegates attended from all but two of the eight old quarters, with four quarters—Miami, Whitewater, Center, and Westfield—having official representation. By Hicksite count, between six and seven hundred people sat through the sessions or listened from outside the overcrowded meetinghouse. With no Orthodox voices raised, the meeting began and ended with the uninterrupted solemnity that had always characterized Quaker meetings before the contest between reformers and evangelicals.[78] Thomas Shillitoe, making his way on to Richmond for the other Indiana Yearly Meeting, came though Waynesville on Tuesday but decided not to stop.[79]

In Richmond, some Hicksites refused to leave the yearly meeting, but the three thousand or so others who attended went on with their business and concluded quietly. The Hicksites gathered in a nearby barn at the same time the Orthodox scheduled their public meetings for worship. Reports indicated that attendance was large in both buildings, but, judging from the reformers' reluctance to challenge their opponents, they realized their minority position and did not raise a fuss.[80]

At the conclusion, Hicks set his path toward the East, but he could have had no hope of reaching it in the two weeks before the annual sessions of Baltimore Yearly Meeting, given his willingness to stop at practically every crossroads to deliver a message to waiting Quakers. The situation in Baltimore was the exact opposite of the one obtaining in Indiana. The reformers were poised to sweep all before them, and the opposition's weakness gave them little incentive to try and prevent the inevitable. There was little need for the Hicksites to separate because the monthly and quarterly meetings were so solidly behind them that they simply controlled things as a matter of course. When quarters appointed official representatives to the yearly meeting's sessions, for example, they succeeded in excluding all but two evangelicals, a clear testimony to the depth of reform sentiment there.[81]

The yearly meeting confirmed the reformers' nearly absolute power among the Friends within its boundaries. Two prominent Philadelphia evangelicals, Thomas Evans and Ellis Yarnall, found slight prospect for the separation they had come to effect, so they had to resort to what Evans referred to as "mischievous" actions to free sound Baltimore Friends from the thralldom of the Hicksites. The select meeting on Saturday, the 25th, hardly noticed the large number of separtists from Philadelphia, despite an attempt by an especially zealous evangelical female to provoke the unusually laconic Ann Jones into a display of antagonism. The shape of things to come was foreshadowed on Sunday afternoon when, instead of worshipping at one of the city's two meetings, the Jones duo made their appointment at a previously announced meeting in a Methodist church. The Hicksites chortled at the very idea of two Quaker ministers sitting easily behind a Methodist pulpit with its big Bible laid out before them.[82]

On Monday morning there was a minor skirmish or two over whether to accept the visitors and epistles from other yearly meetings, but the meeting agreed to allow the representatives to sort out the epistles and suggest responses, an unusual procedure that later provoked the fire of the evangelicals.[83] A walk-out of two Orthodox Friends on the first afternoon—George Jones led the grand procession—did not spark a withdrawal, forcing the remaining evangelicals to suffer under the oratory of Edward Stabler and Thomas Wetherald until Wednesday evening. Evans sat near the back of the meeting and listened to Wetherald's declamations about attempts of an ecclesiastical hierarchy to impose a Romish inquisition on Friends until he could hardly contain himself. When the yearly meeting recognized the Hicksite yearly meetings of Philadelphia, New York, and Indiana—Ohio's epistle had not yet arrived—the evangelical secession took place. The Hicksites counted forty-six men, women, and children who left to hold what Jackson described as "the British Y.M." in a nearby schoolhouse; only six or eight were from rural meetings.

The new group represented only five hundred of the Yearly Meeting's twenty-five hundred Quakers.[84]

With Baltimore's evangelical separation, the reform cause, at least institutionally, had clearly played out, its creativity gone. By this time, the players had practiced their roles so often that they had their parts down nearly to perfection. A minor separation drama on Nantucket Island had yet to be performed, but it offered no slips or surprises and followed the accustomed script down to appointment of a committee to visit monthly meetings and to divisive appearances by English ministers.[85] Only the actors and scenery changed from stage to stage, and the audience could retire with a sense that they had witnessed all this before.

EPILOGUE

"Cries down all laws both moral and Divine," OR The Seeds of the Future

IN ONE SENSE, QUAKERS HAVE ALWAYS been the most Protestant of all Christian sects, for they have carried to its logical extreme the doctrinal centerpiece of the Reformation—that religious faith must grow directly and immediately out of one's own experience of the divine word. Every Friend can easily understand the reformer Martin Luther's famous pronouncement in the debate at Worms in April 1521: "I will answer without horns and without teeth. . . . I do not accept the authority of popes and councils, for they have contradicted each other—my conscience is captive to the Word of God. I cannot and I will not recant anything, for to go against conscience is neither right nor safe. Here I stand, I cannot do otherwise."[1]

Elias Hicks and the reformers who accepted his traditional Quaker message saw themselves carrying on this Protestant tradition. To them, their evangelical opponents resembled all too closely the popes and councils that Luther, Calvin, and Fox had struggled against. It was not simply that they used history for their own purposes—partisans always ransack the past to find support for their cause—the truth was that these Quaker reformers were right. Their powerful adversaries were trying to move Friends' thinking in a new, un-Quakerly direction. The evangelical efforts amounted to a kind of reform from above, with too little concern about what the mass of Friends wanted or desired, certainly with an infuriating lack of political acumen and sensitivity. In an age of the common man, the power of such isensitive grandees was inevitably doomed to be contested.

Thus like all entrenched minorities, the evangelicals viewed their opponents as dangerous radicals, out to overturn the established order — *their* established order, let it be said. Thomas Shillitoe, of all the evangelicals the closest in simple plainness to the reformers, took obvious delight in finding an outsider who agreed with him about the dangers of the reformation cause. As he tagged along behind Hicks on their way to Ohio in 1828, he met an Episcopalian who had just attended one of the Long Islander's meetings and who was shocked at what he had heard and witnessed. "His doctrines will not do for me," the churchman reported; "he cries down all law, both moral and Divine; if people receive his doctrines, I should not be safe out of my house in the evening, nor in my bed at night." Shillitoe handed him some anti-Hicks pamphlets to wipe away at least some of the reproach the preacher had visited upon their Society.[2]

As often happens during the unfolding of human events, the reformers soon discovered that the principles they proclaimed could be turned against them, though they left no indication that they appreciated the irony. When Benjamin Webb, the Wilmington firebrand, frontally attacked his former Hicksite compatriots because they refused to honor his insistence that the cause of the reformation required "universal liberty of conscience," William Gibbons was livid. In words that echoed earlier evangelical warnings against the reformers, Gibbons demanded that Webb be dealt with and disowned if he did not recant. He called for a "prompt exercise of discipline," and asked, "why separate from disorder and confusion only to plunge into *greater*, and to permit *our very foundations to be sapped and undermined* by those of our own household?"[3] The reverberation from the evangelical camp could easily be heard: "Why, indeed?"

So the question was one of authority. The traditional Friends who opposed introduction of the evangelicals' "creed" in the name of individual liberty and in line with their historic faith helped feed discontent with established authority; in doing so, they were ushering deep into the heart of Quakerism a modern principle that would gradually crowd out the traditional idea that in the bond of truth unity could be found. The Hicksite principle, much to Gibbons's chagrin, put little stress on unity or authority. Instead, it allowed freer range to individualism and encouraged each Friend to interpret faith and practice in the light of each one's unique experience.

Individual Friends thus became masters of their own individual religious destinies, tending to believe whatever they desired and to act pretty much as they pleased. Ironically, the Wilmington wing of the Hicksite faction, of which Gibbons was a charter member, had taken the lead in introducing this tendency to the reformation cause. Rather than a new covenant, it amounted to a new freedom.[4] The Hicksites spawned the kind of Quaker, as critic Lewis Benson alleges, who sees the Society as "primarily a refuge for those who want freedom to follow their own individual bent in an atmosphere that is mildly religious and fiercely tolerant."[5]

Another irony emerges here, for the followers of Hicks were originally those who were most insistent upon Friends' maintaining their peculiar testimonies against the encroaching world. Once the Hicksites, however, overthrew the elders, their principle of tolerance permitted Friends of their branches to adopt the ways of the world and its people with no evident restraint. In fact, disownments among Hicksites became so infrequent that they practically disappeared, and the belief spread that they had always opposed disowning members. Thus, in the world of modern Quakerism, it has become unthinkable for a meeting to cut off a member, no matter the circumstance or the activity. It should come as a surprise to no one, therefore, that Richard Nixon, a birthright and life-long Friend, could proudly proclaim himself a "deeply committed pacifist, perhaps because of my Quaker heritage from my mother," even as he presided over the world's largest military machine, which was even then, in 1971, exercising its capabilities in Vietnam.[6] Nixon may not have been able to tell Hicksites from Amorites, but he followed in the reformers' footsteps.

If descendants of Hicks did their bit to provoke the ironist's chuckles—and tears—the evangelicals could not escape the mockery of history's muse either. Despite the fact that they correctly sensed where a victory for the Hicksites would lead, they were woefully unable to maintain the most obvious Quaker features of the faith once they succumbed to the lures of evangelical theology. Toward the end of his life, Jonathan Evans may have realized that in aligning himself with the English ministers he had gone too far, for he opposed the Gurneyite evangelical movement of the 1830s, in much the same way that Gibbons reacted against the extreme wing of his party.[7] But evangelicalism had its foothold and by the end of the century had torn through the midwestern heartland of American Quakerism, verily like a spring tornado, annihilating the Society's distinctive features. Today the majority of American Quakers go to churches with salaried pastors, choirs, and even creedal statements, making them all but indistinguishable from their Methodist and Baptist neighbors in many areas of faith and practice.

In 1955, the Hicksites and Orthodox in Philadelphia and New York Yearly Meetings reunited, and thirteen years later those of Baltimore followed. They thus put behind them better than twelve decades of lessening differences. Starting from different positions, they had come to the same Hicksite point and adopted the profoundly modern notion that people should be left free to do and believe what they pleased. The gripping conviction of Elias Hicks that the Spirit of God would renew the divine covenant with those who professed the truth had been lost along the way. It did not even enjoy the character of a relic, which at least might have been revered; instead, this traditional tenet could be found only in the dusty and dim archives of the past where it could trouble no one.

Notes

CHAPTER 1

1. *Christian Faith and Practice in the Experience of the Society of Friends* (London: London Yearly Meeting, 1960), para. 20.
2. For a contemporary statement of this problem, not limited to Friends, see Langdon Gilkey, *Message and Existence: An Introduction to Christian Theology* (New York: Seabury Press, 1980), 34–37.
3. Howard W. Brinton, *Friends for 300 Years* (New York: Harper & Brothers, 1952), 101.
4. Winthrop S. Hudson, "A Suppressed Chapter in Quaker History," *Journal of Religion* 24 (April 1944), 116–17.
5. Sidney E. Ahlstrom, *A Religious History of the American People* (New Haven: Yale Univ. Press, 1972), 210–11. For an extended analysis of the Keithan controversy, see J. William Frost, "Unlikely Controversialists: Caleb Pusey and George Keith," *Quaker History* 64 (Spring 1975), 16–36.
6. Arthur J. Mekeel, "The Founding Years, 1681–1789," in John M. Moore, ed., *Friends in the Delaware Valley* (Haverford, Penn: Friends Historical Assoc., 1981), 50.
7. Gilkey, *Message and Existence*, 24–25.
8. Frederick B. Tolles, *Meeting House and Counting House: The Quaker Merchants of Philadelphia, 1682–1763*, (Chapel Hill: Univ. of North Carolina Press, 1948).
9. See two articles by Arthur J. Mekeel, "The Founding Years," 49–50, and "The Relation of Quakers to the American Revolution," *Quaker History* 65 (Spring 1976), 3–18.
10. See Jack D. Marietta, *The Reformation of American Quakerism, 1748–1783* (Philadelphia: Univ. of Pennsylvania Press, 1984).
11. Job Scott, *The Works of that Eminent Minister of the Gospel, Job Scott* (Philadelphia: John Comly, 1831), I, 98,105.
12. Mekeel, "Founding Years," 51.
13. Hugh Judge, *Memoirs and Journal of Hugh Judge* (Byberry, Penn: John and Isaac Comly, 1841), 146–49.
14. Ibid., 147–48.

15. Roger A. Bruns, "A Quaker's Antislavery Crusade: Anthony Benezet," *Quaker History* 65 (Autumn 1976), 92.
16. David B. Davis, *The Problem of Slavery in the Age of Revolution, 1770–1823* (Ithaca: Cornell Univ. Press, 1975), 216–17, 237–40.
17. Phillips P. Moulton, ed., *The Journal and Major Essays of John Woolman* (New York: Oxford Univ. Press., 1971), 177.
18. Ibid., 139–40.
19. Ibid., 255.
20. Scott, *Works*, I., 31.
21. Ibid., I., 286, 312.
22. See, for example, Elbert Russell, *The History of Quakerism* (Richmond, Ind: Friends United Press, 1979), 237.
23. See description of James Moore, 1 mo. 4, 1790, reprinted in Henry J. Cadbury, *Friendly Heritage: Letters from the Quaker Past* (Norwalk, Conn.: Silvermine Publishers, 1972), 141–42.
24. Scott, *Works*, I, 15,17, 42–43. There is a brief review of Scott's theology in Edward Grubb, *The Historic and Inward Christ: A Study in Quaker Thought* (London: Headly Brothers, 1914), 54–58.
25. The essay is printed in Scott, *Works*, I., 476–531, quotations from 485, 499. For an excellent analysis of Quaker theology, particularly as it related to Calvinism, see J. William Frost, "The Dry Bones of Quaker Theology," *Church History* 39 (Dec. 1970), 503–23. An essay that concentrates on the experience of salvation is Mary C. Grimes, "Saving Grace Among Puritans and Quakers," *Quaker History* 72 (Spring, 1983), 1–26.
26. Scott, *Works*, I, 17.
27. Ibid., I, 190–92.
28. Ibid., I, 178–79.
29. Ibid., I, 179.
30. Jonathan Evans, comp., *A Journal of the Life, Travel, and Religious Labours of William Savery, late of Philadelphia, a Minister of the Gospel of Christ in the Society of Friends* (London: C. Gilpin, 1844), 292–94.
31. Peter Brock, *Pacifism in the United States, From the Colonial Era to the First World War* (Princeton: Princeton Univ. Press, 1968), 371–73; Russell, *History of Quakerism*, 294–95; Bliss Forbush, *Elias Hicks, Quaker Liberal* (New York: Columbia Univ. Press, 1956), 118–19; Henry Hull, *Memoirs of the Life and Religious Labours of Henry Hull* in William and Thomas Evans, eds., *The Friends Library, Comprising Journals, Doctrinal Treatises, and Other Writings of Members of the Religious Society of Friends* (Philadelphia: Joseph Rakeshaw, 1840), IV, 247.
32. On evangelicalism, see Claude Welch, *Protestant Thought in the Nineteenth Century, Volume 1, 1799–1820* (New Haven: Yale Univ. Press, 1972), 26–28; David E. Swift, *Joseph John Gurney, Banker Reformer & Quaker* (Middleton, Conn.: Wesleyan Univ. Press, 1962), xiv–xv, 49.

33. Welch, *Protestant Thought*, 28-29.
34. Arthur C. McGiffert, *The Rise of Modern Religious Ideas* (New York: Macmillan, 1915), 109-10.
35. Frederick B. Tolles, "Quietism Versus Enthusiasm: The Philadelphia Quakers and the Great Awakening," *Pennsylvania Magazine of History and Biography* 69 (Jan. 1945), 44.
36. For an excellent analysis of the impact of evangelical theology on the Society, see Elizabeth Isichei, *Victorian Quakers* (London: Oxford Univ. Press, 1970), 3-16, Gurney quotation from 5.
37. Swift, *Gurney*, 177-78.
38. Forbush, *Hicks*, 195.
39. Brinton, *Friends for 300 Years*, 11-12. For examples of early efforts to deal with this tendency, see Hugh Barbour and Arthur O. Roberts, eds., *Early Quaker Writings, 1650-1700* (Grand Rapids, Mich.: Eerdmans, 1973), 479-85.
40. David Sands, *Journal of the Life and Gospel Labors of David Sands; with Extracts from his Correspondence* (London: Charles Gilpin, 1848), 242.
41. Charles I. Foster, *An Errand of Mercy: The Evangelical United Front, 1790-1837* (Chapel Hill: Univ. of North Carolina Press, 1960), 33; Kenneth S. Latourette, *A History of Christianity* (New York: Harper, 1953), 1166-67; Swift, *Gurney*, 146; Frank Thistlewaite, *The Anglo-American Connection in the Early Nineteenth Century* (Philadelphia: Univ. of Pennsylvania Press, 1959), 39; Paul G. Faler, *Mechanics and Manufacturers in the Early Industrial Revolution* (Albany: State Univ. of New York Press, 1981), 109-38.
42. Edwin W. Rice, *The Sunday School Movement, 1780-1917, and the American Sunday School Union, 1817-1917* (Philadelphia: American Sunday School Union, 1917), 45-46.
43. Lawrence J. Friedman, *Gregarious Saints: Self and Community in American Abolitionism, 1830-1870* (Cambridge, Eng.: Cambridge Univ. Press, 1982), 11-13; Ahlstrom, *Religious History*, 424-25; Lois W. Banner, "Religious Benevolence as Social Control: A Critique of an Interpretation," *Journal of American History* 60 (June 1973), 23-41, quotation from 36.
44. On this important point, see Paul Tillich, *Prespectives on 19th and 20th Century Protestant Theology*, Carl E. Bratten, ed. (New York: Harper, 1967), 19, 21-22; Tolles, "Quietism Versus Enthusiasm," 44.
45. For example, see an editorial in *Reformer* 2 (1 July 1821), 24-25.
46. Jacqueline C. Reinier, "Rearing the Republican Child: Attitudes and Practices in Post Revolutionary Philadelphia," *William and Mary Quarterly* 39 (Jan. 1982), 155, 161.
47. Swift, *Gurney*, xiv-xv.

48. E.P. Thompson, *The Making of the English Working Class* (New York: Vintage Books, 1963), 30–31, 56–57.

49. Forbush, *Hicks*, 113.

CHAPTER 2

1. Quakers and Presbyterians did not get along well. The most extensive example in this period was a tome by William Craig Brownlee, *A Careful and Free Inquiry into the True Nature and Tendency of the Religious Principles of the Society of Friends, commonly Called Quakers* (Philadelphia: J. Harding, 1824). Future Hicksites set out to respond immediately. See Thomas McClintock to Friend, 9 Jan. 1824, George H. Burr papers, Friends Historical Library, Swarthmore College (hereinafter cited as FHL). There is some evidence that the reformers started the *Berean* for the specific purpose of answering Brownlee. *Saturday Evening Post* (Philadelphia), 15 Dec. 1827.

2. The Orthodox elders apparently wrote and collected relatively few letters. They simply did not feel called upon to prepare for something, a split, they could not imagine would take place.

3. For a description of the Orthodox, see Robert W. Doherty, *The Hicksite Separation: A Sociological Analysis of Religious Schism in Early Nineteenth Century America* (New Brunswick, N.J.: Rutgers Univ. Press, 1967), 38–39, 42, 67–72.

4. Alan M. Zachary, "Social Thought in the Philadelphia Leadership Community, 1800–1840," Ph.D diss., Northwestern Univ. 1974, 2.

5. Elias Hicks to William and Deborah Wharton, Sarah and Thomas Fisher, 14 Feb. 1825, Joseph Wharton papers, FHL.

6. William B. Evans, *Jonathan Evans and His Time*, 1759–1839 (Boston: Christopher Publishing House, 1959), 32, 38, 62: Moore, ed., *Friends in the Delaware Valley*, 258; Doherty, *Hicksite Separation*, 67.

7. William Forster, *Memoirs of William Forster*, ed., Benjamin Seebohm (London: Alfred W. Bennett, 1865), I, 379.

8. Evans, *Jonathan Evans*, 30, 131–32, 144; Thomas W. Pryor, Journal, II, 60, 95, Thomas W. Pryor papers, FHL.

9. Undated [McClintock] memorandum, Burr papers, FHL.

10. William Evans to Elizabeth Barton, 29 Nov. 1824, Charles Evans papers, Quaker Collection, Haverford College (hereinafter cited as QC).

11. Evans, comp., *Journal of Savery*, 271.

12. William Evans, Journal, 130, William B. Evans papers, QC.

13. *Extracts from the Writings of Primitive Friends, concerning the Divinity of our Lord and Saviour, Jesus Christ* (Philadelphia: Solomon W. Conrad, 1823).

14. Evans, Journal, 149–50, W. B. Evans papers, QC.

15. Ibid.

16. Forbush, *Hicks*, 189.

17. Evans, *Jonathan Evans*, 42. There is a tradition among Hicksites that Evans's embarrassment over his decision contributed significantly to his opposition to Hicks, a strong opponent of using products made with slave labor. See Emmor Kimber to Hicks, 25 Jan. 1829, Elias Hicks papers, FHL.

18. Evans, Journal, 147, W.B. Evans papers, QC; Evans, *Journal of Savery*, 271.

19. Jonathan Evans to Hicks, 17 Feb. 1800, Elias Hicks papers, FHL.

20. Undated [McClintock] memorandum, Burr papers, FHL.

21. Evans to Mildred Ratcliff, 24 Aug. 1838, Charles Evans papers, QC.

22. Swift, *Gurney*, 215–16.

23. Jeremiah J. Foster, *An Authentic Report of the Testimony in a Cause at Issue in the Court of Chancery of the State of New Jersey, between Thomas L. Shotwell, Complaintant, and Joseph Hendrickson and Stacy Decow, Defendants* (Philadelphia: J. Harding, 1831), I, 273, 274, 279–80; McClintock to Hicks, 8 Apr. 1828, Elias Hicks papers, FHL.

24. Thomas Evans to Henry Cope, 21 June 1829, Charles Evans papers, QC; Foster, *Authentic Report*, II, 401-402.

25. William Evans, *Journal of the Life and Religious Services of William Evans* (Philadelphia: Friends Books Store, 1870) 25, 30.

26. William Evans to Elizabeth Barton, 4 Dec. 1824, Charles Evans papers, QC.

27. Evans, *Journal*, 24.

28. William Evans to Barton, 29 Nov. 1824, Charles Evans papers, QC. Evans's reference was to Edward Hicks, apparently a particularly notorious practicioner of this art.

29. Ibid., 27 Oct. 1824, Charles Evans papers, QC.

30. *Hole in the Wall, or A Peep at the Creed Worshippers* (N.p.: Privately printed, 1828), 4–5, 30, 33.

31. "A New Confession of Faith," May 1825, Alfred Rodman Hussey papers, FHL.

32. "Samuel Bettle," "Dictionary of Quaker Biography," QC; Doherty, *Hicksite Separation*, 38.

33. Francis R. Taylor, "The Famous Case of Thomas Shotwell vs. Stacy Decow and John Hendrickson," *Bulletin of Friends Historical Association* 16 (Spring 1927), 12.

34. "Bettle," "Dictionary of Quaker Biography," QC; Eliza C. Harrison, ed., *Philadelphia Merchant: The Diary of Thomas P. Cope, 1800–1851* (South Bend, Ind.: Gateway Editions, 1978), 481–82.

35. Foster, *Authentic Report*, I, 35–59, 64; Samuel L. Knapp, *The Life of Thomas Eddy* (New York: Conner & Cooke, 1834), 284.

36. Samuel Bettle to Edward Bettle, 20 Oct. 1829, Bettle Family papers, Thomas Kite Diary, 27 Jan. 1827, Sharpless-Kite papers, both in QC.

37. John H. Griscom, comp., *Memoir of John Griscom, LL.D* (New York: Robert Carter & Brothers, 1859), 258.
38. "Ellis Yarnall," "Dictionary of Quaker Biography," QC; "John Evans vs. Ellis Yarnall and Others, 1810," *Bulletin of Friends Historical Association* 7 (May 1916), 50-54.
39. Foster, *Authentic Report*, I,72, 82.
40. Thomas Evans to Henry Cope, 31 Oct. 1828, Charles Evans papers, QC.
41. Doherty, *Hicksite Separation*, 38-39.
42. "The Society of Friends in Philadelphia," *Friend* 2 (14 Feb. 1829), 141.
43. Kimber to Hicks, 25 Jan. 1829, Elias Hicks papers, FHL.
44. Doherty, *Hicksite Separation*, 38-41, 67-68.
45. Thomas P. Cope to Henry Cope, 22 June 1828, Charles Evans papers, QC; Harrison, ed., *Philadelphia Merchant*, 215-16.
46. "Richard Humphreys," "Dictionary of Quaker Biography," QC.
47. "Thomas Eddy," "Dictionary of Quaker Biography," QC; Knapp, *Life of Eddy*, 156, 172-73, 341; A.T. Gary, "The Political and Economic Relations of English and American Quakers (1750-1785)," D. Phil. thesis, St. Hugh's College, Oxford Univ., 1935, p. 458.
48. See Thomas Eddy to John Warder, 18 Oct. 1822, in *The Cabinet; or, Works of Darkness Brought to Light* (Philadelphia: John Mortimer, 1825; 2nd ed.), 6-7.
49. *A Declaration of the Yearly Meeting of Friends Held in Philadelphia*, (Philadelphia: Thomas Kite, 1828), [3]. The copy in the papers of Benjamin Ferris, FHL, was annotated by him.
50. Ibid., 5-6.
51. Ibid., 19.
52. Ibid., 27.
53. Ibid., 32.
54. *Saturday Evening Post* (Philadelphia). 17 Nov. 1827.
55. For example, Bates is mentioned only once each in Errol T. Elliot, *Quakers on the American Frontier* (Richmond, Ind.: Friends United Press, 1969), 269, and in Jones, *Later Periods*, I, 506. Jones, though describing Bates as "one of the most famous of the American ministers and Quakers leaders of the time," says simply and in a note, he "afterwards left Friends." Bates was disowned when he defended, among other things, the rite of water baptism and was himself baptised. See the "Testimony of Disownment Against Elisha Bates," in *Journal of Friends Historical Society* 5 (1908), 28-29.
56. For a study of Bates, see Donald G. Good, "Elisha Bates: American Quaker Evangelical in the Early Nineteenth Century," Ph.D. diss., Univ. of Iowa, 1967. See also Good's "Elisha Bates and Social Reform," "*Quaker History* 68 (Autumn 1969), 81-92.
57. [Elisha Bates], "The Doctrines of Friends Defended," *Miscellaneous Repository* 1 (Feb. 1827), 25-28.

58. [Elisha Bates], "Controversy," ibid. (Apr. 1827), 94-95.

59. Elisha Bates, *The Doctrines of Friends: or the Principles of the Christian Religion, as held by the Society of Friends* (Mountpleasant, Ohio: Elisha Bates, 1825), 132-34.

60. Ibid., 10. Although Bates's discussion of redemption followed Barclay quite closely, to the extent of quoting him directly at times, his analysis represented an attempt to synthesize evangelical insights with traditional Quakerism. That was something that no other Friend of the time tried to do.

61. Donald G. Good, "Elisha Bates and the Hicksite Controversy," *Quaker History* 70 (Fall 1981), 105. Good interprets Bates's theology with little appreciation of its evolution. It is true that he held to a high evangelical view of Scripture after the separation, but it is a misapprehension to see him with the same view when he published his 1825 *Doctrines*.

62. George W. Banks, *Orthodoxy Unmasked; or All is Not Gold that Glitters* (Philadelphia: Privately printed, 1829), 47.

63. [Elisha Bates], "The Epistle of the Separatists," *Miscellaneous Repository* 1 (Feb. 1828), 217-22.

64. The Testimony of the Society of Friends on the Continent of America (New York: Richard & George S. Wood, 1830). On the authorship, see G[eorge] V[aux], "Elisha Bates," *Journal of Friends Historical Society* 5 (1908), 27.

65. *The Telescope* (New York), 5 May 1828.

66. Isaac Braithwaite to John Griscom, 29 Dec. 1824, Letters of English Friends, QC.

67. John Griscom, *A Year in Europe* (Philadelphia: H.C. Carey, & J. Lea., 1823), I, 34.

68. *Cabinet*, 73.

69. For a survey of evangelical developments in England, see Rufus M. Jones, *The Later Periods of Quakerism* (London: Macmillan, 1921), I, 274-313, and Isichei, *Victorian Quakers*, 3-16.

70. On Gurney, see Swift, *Gurney*, and Jones, *Later Periods*, I, 492-505.

71. Joseph John Gurney, *A Letter to a Friend, on the Authority, Purpose, & Effects of Christianity, and Especially the Doctrine of Redemption* (Bradford: T Inkersley, 1824; 15th ed.), quotation from 19.

72. Swift, *Gurney*, 177.

73. "George Withy," "Dictionary of Quaker Biography," QC; George Whity, *An Affectionate Farewell Address to Friends in North America* (Philadelphia: Solomon W. Conrad, 1823), 56. See also Evans, *Journal*, 69. Withy's address provoked a response from an anonymous New York Quaker who likened its author to those more interested in "pelf and popularity" than in obeying the laws of their religious community. He also suggested Withy had been snared by "idolaters, who always lie in wait to deceive." *The Antitypical Essay* (New York: privately printed, 1823), 9-10.

74. See George Withy, *A Sermon Preached at Friends' Meeting House, Burlington, New Jersey, on the 10th of the fifth Month 1822* (Philadelphia: privately printed, 1822), 12.

75. Jones, *Later Periods*, I, 324; Isichei, *Victorian Quakers*, 121; John Hunt, Journal, 8 May 1823, John Hunt papers, FHL.

76. "William Forster," "Dictionary of Quaker Biography," QC; Pryor, Journal, II, 200, Pryor papers, FHL.

77. Forster, *Memoirs*, II, 8, 9, 36; Pryor, Journal, II, 201, Pryor papers; McClintock to William Poole, 6 June 1825, Burr papers, FHL.

78. William Forster to Joseph John Gurney, 7 Dec. 1819, in Forster, *Memoirs*, I, 234–39.

79. Evans, Journal, 111, W.B. Evans papers, QC.

80. McClintock to Poole, 2 April 1823, Burr papers, FHL.

81. J. Bevan Braithwaite, *Memoirs of Anna Braithwaite* (London: Headley Brothers, 1905), 79–80; Pryor, Journal, II, 175–76, 222, Pryor papers, Edward Garrigues to Poole, 16 Jan. 1826, Ferris papers, both in FHL; "Anna Braithwaite, "Diary of Quaker Biography," QC.

82. George H. Gibson, ed., "William P. Brobson Diary, 1825–1828," *Delaware History* 15 (1972–73), 298.

83. Mary W. Brown to Moses Brown, 25 May 1826, Thomas W. Brown papers, QC.

84. "Anna Braithwaite," "Isaac Braithwaite," "Dictionary of Quaker Biography," QC; Swift, *Gurney*, 177.

85. "Ann Jones," "George Jones," "Dictionary of Quaker Biography," QC; William Chanceller to Benjamin Ferris, 23 Nov. 1826, Benjamin Ferris papers; Pryor, Journal, II, 225, Pryor papers, FHL.

86. McClintock to Poole, 29 Jan. 1827, Burr papers, FHL. Playing his little game, the overseers of this reformer-dominated meeting called on Jones to rebuke him for detraction.

87. Forbush, *Hicks*, 225.

88. Foster, II, 84–85.

89. John Hunt, et al, to [Ann Jones], 14 May 1826, Halliday Jackson papers, FHL. The evangelicals later used this letter to show that the reformers did not hesitate to adopt the same tactic they charged the Orthodox with misusing. Foster, *Authentic Report*, II, 88–89.

90. Foster, *Authentic Report*, II, 87–88.

91. Pryor, Journal, II, 228, Pryor papers, FHL. The rough and tumble of the separations may have led her to moderate her extreme stance, for at New England Yearly Meeting in 1829, she advised the men that in their zeal to uphold the outward saviour they should not lose sight of the reason for his coming—to put an end to sin and introduce practical righteousness. See Thomas Evans to Henry Cope, 21 June 1829, Charles Evans papers, QC.

92. Joseph J. Green, "Elizabeth Robson," *Journal of Friends Historical Society* 14 (1917), 75–79.
93. Forbush, *Hicks*, 224.
94. Marcus T. C. Gould, rpt., *Sermons by Thomas Wetherald and Elias Hicks* (Philadelphia: Marcus T.C. Gould, 1826), 159–82. After her hour-long sermon, the two evangelical ministers at the head of the meeting sought to end it by shaking hands, but none of the Friends present moved. Then Robson, seated in the gallery with Braithwaite, also essayed to close the session. Again no one moved. Whereupon Thomas Wetherald and Hicks spoke briefly and then shook hands. At this sign, the audience filed out. One observer, not a Friend, remarked that he thought himself surrounded by 2,000 statues. Ibid., 185; Hicks to Poole, 1 June 1826, Elias Hicks papers, FHL.
95. Chancellor to Ferris, 23 Nov. 1826, Ferris papers, FHL.
96. "Thomas Shillitoe," "Dictionary of Quaker Biography," QC.
97. Jones, *Later Periods*, II, 94–100.
98. Thomas Shillitoe, *Journal of the Life, Labours, and Travels of Thomas Shillitoe, in the Service of the Gospel of Jesus Christ* (London: Harvey and Darton, 1839), I, 230.
99. Hicks to Poole, 18 Nov. 1826, Elias Hicks papers, FHL.
100. Shillitoe, *Journal*, II, 424–25.
101. Edward Hicks to Hicks, 15 Oct. 1826, Elias Hicks papers, FHL. See also, Pryor, Journal, II, 224, Pryor papers, ibid.
102. Shillitoe, *Journal*, II, 164, 116–67.
103. Ibid., II, 311.
104. Ibid., II, 170.
105. Ibid., II, 157, 250.
106. Ibid., II, 249.
107. Samuel Wood, a retired publisher and philanthropist in New York, suggested to Hester Street Meeting that he be designated Shillitoe's companion, but the Hicksites insisted that Wood would not do. A compromise decision referred the matter to a committee equally divided between the two factions: it was leaning against Wood until Shillitoe informed the members bluntly that regardless of their decision he could not travel with someone with whom he could not unite. Wood was then tapped. Ibid., II, 160, 166–68, 171; *Dictionary of American Biography*, X, 471–72.

CHAPTER 3

1. Hugh Judge to Elias Hicks, 18 June 1812, Elias Hicks papers, FHL.
2. Judge to Hicks, 24 March 1813, ibid.

3. Judge to Hicks, 4 March 1818, ibid. On Judge, see Hugh Judge, *Memoirs and Journal of Hugh Judge* (Byberry, Penn.: John & Isaac Comly, 1841).

4. Hunt, Journal, 9 Jan. 1823, Hunt papers FHL.

5. Pryor, Journal, II, 140, Pryor papers, FHL.

6. Walt Whitman, *Prose Works* 1892, ed. Floyd Stovall (New York: New York Univ. Press, 1964), II, 643.

7. G.W.B., "The Schism among the Quakers," *Christian Examiner* 30 (May 1841), 248.

8. William Wharton to Deborah Wharton, 24 Nov. 1826, Wharton papers, FHL. At the small meetinghouse in Little Creek, Delaware, attendance was about fifty—"24 white males, 5 blacks, & the rest females."

9. Forbush, *Hicks*, 288.

10. Pryor, Journal, II, 143, Pryor papers, FHL.

11. Gibson, "Brobson Diary," 298; Pryor, Journal, II, 202–203, FHL.

12. The most extensive collection of these sermons is in a periodical, *The Quaker*, edited from 1827 to 1829 by Marcus T. C. Gould, a supporter of Hicks.

13. Whitman, *Prose Works*, 637–39, 642–43; Emanuel Howitt, *Selections from Letters Written during a Tour through the United States, in the Summer and Autumn of* 1819 (Nottingham: J. Dunn, 1820), 8–11; G.W.B., "Schism," 238.

14. Forbush, *Hicks*, 6–7, 11–12.

15. The two most satisfying analyses of Hicks's thought are D. Elton Trueblood, "The Career of Elias Hicks," in *Byways in Quaker History*, ed. Howard H. Brinton (Wallingford, Penn.: Pendle Hill, 1944), 89–93; and Charles E. Nelson, "The Hicksite Separation in the Society of Friends," B.A. thesis, Harvard Univ., 1952, 60–73.

16. *The Quaker* 3 (1828), 254–55.

17. Emmor Kimber to Hicks, 25 Jan. 1829, Elias Hicks papers, FHL.

18. *The Quaker* 1 (1827), 60–61. When Hicks finished, Jonathan Evans took the floor to assert that Friends held to Orthodox doctrines. Ibid., 72.

19. Ibid., 4, (1829). 9–27.

20. Elias Hicks, *A Series of Extemporaneous Discourses, Delivered in the Several Meetings of the Society of Friends* (Philadelphia: Joseph & Edward Parker, 1825), 61, 81–82.

21. William Evans to Elizabeth Barton, 4 Dec. 1824, Charles Evans papers, QC.

22. Hicks, *Extemporaneous Discourses*, 61.

23. Ibid., 129–31, 133.

24. Ibid., 60.

25. *The Quaker* 1 (1827). 131. Paul Tillich, in his discussion of the relationship between mysticism and revelation arrived at the same conclusion. He found rationalism to be the "daughter of mysticism. . . . Reason emerged within us out

of mystical experience, namely the experience of the divine presence within us." Tillich, *Perspectives*, 19.

26. *The Quaker* 1, (1827). 132–33.
27. Tillich, *Perspectives*, 28.
28. Gibson, "Brobson Diary," 296–98. For a brief sketch of Brobson, see ibid., 56.
29. Forbush, *Hicks*, 280–81.
30. *The Cabinet*, 14. Hicks's disgust with chemistry may have resulted from the fact that one of the staunchest evangelicals in New York, John Griscom, was a chemist.
31. Gibson, "Brobson Diary," 298.
32. L.H. Clarke and M.T.C. Gould, stenos, *Sermons Delivered by Elias Hicks and Edward Hicks in Friends Meetings, New York, in 5th month*, 1825 (New York: J.V. Seaman, 1825), 12, 28, 133–35.
33. For a vivid view of how country Friends regarded their urban cousins, see a poem, "The Last Day of the Yearly Meeting, 1813," in *Bulletin of Friends' Historical Association* 2 (March 1908), 82–84.
34. Ibid.
35. Edward Hicks, *Memoirs of the Life and Religious Labors of Edward Hicks* (Philadelphia: Merrihew & Thompson, 1851), 71.
36. Ibid., 101.
37. Ibid., 63.
38. Ibid., 58–61, 96, 110, 124, 128, 131.
39. David Tathem, "Edward Hicks, Elias Hicks and John Comly: Perspectives on the Peaceable Kingdom Theme," *American Art Journal* 13 (Spring 1981), 38.
40. "Halliday Jackson," "Dictionary of Quaker Biography," Evans to Thomas Evans, 2 Sept. 1828, Evans papers, both in QC; Foster *Authentic Report*, II, 35ff, 90–94, 460–61.
41. Halliday Jackson, "History of the Separation of the Society of Friends," 32–33 Burr papers, FHL.
42. Foster, *Authentic Report*, II, 118–19, 161.
43. "John Comly," "Dictionary of Quaker Biography," QC; John Comly to Isaac Hicks, 17 Dec. 1817, 11 Feb. 1818, Isaac Hicks paper, FHL.
44. John Comly, *Journal of the Life and Religious Labours of John Comly* (Philadelphia: T. Ellwood Chapman, 1853), 282–83.
45. "John Comly," "Dictionary of Quaker Biography," QC.
46. Comly, *Journal* 358–59, 363–63, 383.
47. Ibid., 324–25.
48. Nathan Shoemaker to Hicks, 6 Jan. 1827, Elias Hicks papers, FHL.
49. Jesse Kersey, *A Narrative of the Early Life, Travels, and Gospel Labors of Jesse Kersey* (Philadelphia: T. Ellwood Chapman, 1851), 17, 55, 62, 64–75. Kersey

explained that a prescription for a bout with typhus caused his addiction.

50. Emmor Kimber, "Dictionary of Quaker Biography," QC; Emmor Kimber, *Facts Stated, that the Truth May Not Be Blamed; with Observations upon Elders, Discipline, Disownment, and Appeals; in a Letter to an Appellant* (Philadelphia: William Brown, 1823), 1–12; Emmor Kimber to Hicks, 24 Jan. 1823, Elias Hicks papers, FHL; Harrison, ed., *Philadelphia Merchant*, 421, 480. Kimber was later restored to membership.

51. Priscilla Cadwallader, *Memoir of Priscilla Cadwallader* (Philadelphia: T. Ellwood Zell & Co., 1864; 2nd ed.). 6–8, 68–69.

52. Ibid., 18–19.

53. For an insightful sociological examination of the Hicksites, see Doherty, *Hicksite Separation*, 42–50, 77–89.

54. Foster, *Authentic Report*, I, 354–57, 401, 454; Doherty, *Hicksite Separation*, 40.

55. Edward Garrigues to Poole, 16 Jan. 1826, Ferris papers, FHL.

56. Hicks to Abraham Lower, 26 Feb. 1823, in [Isaac T. Hopper, ed.], *Letters of Elias Hicks* (New York: Isaac T. Hopper, 1834), 134–36.

57. Benjamin Ferris to Wharton, 6 Nov. 1830, Ferris papers, FHL.

58. Hicks to Lower, 26 Jan. 1824, [Hopper], *Letters of Hicks*, 146–49.

59. Foster, *Authentic Report*, I, 441.

60. Ibid., I, 383.

61. See Memorandum, Jan. 1826, in Miscellaneous Mss., Green Street Meeting, FHL.

62. Pryor, Journal, II, 213, Pryor papers, FHL.

63. For name of leaders, see Minutes, Green Street Meeting; and for occupation, Robert Desilver, *Philadelphia Index, or Directory for* 1823 (Philadelphia: privately printed, 1823) no pagination.

64. Evans, Journal, 146, W. B. Evans papers, QC.

65. Memorandum, Jan. 1826, Misc. Mss., Green Street Meeting, FHL.

66. McClintock to Hicks, 10 Jan., 14 March 1825, Elias Hicks papers, McClintock to Poole, 6 June 1825, undated [McClintock] memorandum, Burr papers, FHL.

67. McClintock to Poole, 16 Dec. 1822, Burr papers, FHL. In 1836, McClintock removed to upstate New York, where he became, in 1848, joint clerk of the progressive Yearly Meeting in New York. A. Day Bradley, "Progressive Friends in Michigan and New York," *Quaker History*, 52 (Spring 1963), 98–99.

68. "William Wharton," Dictionary of Quaker Biography," QC; Doherty, *Hicksite Separation*, 40.

69. Wharton to Hicks, 8 March 1827, Memorandum, 24 May 1827, Wharton papers, FHL.

70. Hicks to Wharton, 17 April 1827, ibid. Interestingly, to reassure his well-off supporter, Hicks related to him the story of a Long Island neighbor, probably

Thomas Willis, whose opposition to Hicks and to the cause of truth had been punished with bankruptcy. Be assured, Hicks wrote, "that all those who have risen up to accuse their brethren, in their self-righteousness, and creaturely wisdom, will ere long manifest themselves by their fruits, to the satisfaction of all who know them."

71. McClintock to Poole, 6 June 1825, Burr papers, FHL.
72. McClintock to Hicks, 8 April 1828, Elias Hicks papers, FHL.
73. Carol E. Hoffecker, "Nineteenth Century Wilmington: Satellite or Independent City?," *Delaware History* 15 (1972–73), 204.
74. Edward N. Vallandigham, *Delaware and the Eastern Shore* (Philadelphia: Lippincott, 1922), 159.
75. Hoffecker, "Nineteenth Century Wilmington," 4.
76. *Encyclopedia of Southern History*, David C. Roller and Robert W. Twyman, eds. (Baton Rouge: Louisiana State Univ. Press, 1979), 345–46; Vallandigham, *Delaware*, 163–64.
77. Benjamin Ferris, "A Sketch of the Proceedings," Martin A. Claver, ed., *Delaware History*, 13 (April 1968), 68–69. See also Jonathan Fairbanks, "Friends in Wilmington," *Quaker History* 58 (Spring 1969), 31–40.
78. For examples, see entry under William Poole in Ruthanna Hindes, "Delaware Silversmiths, 1700–1850," *Delaware History* 12 (Oct. 1967), 287–89; Willa G. Cramton, "Selleck Osborn; A Republican Editor in Wilmington, Delaware, 1816–1822," *Delaware History* 12 (April 1967), 214; Gibson, "Brobson Diary," 56.
79. Poole to Halliday Jackson, 22 Nov. 1827, Jackson papers, FHL.
80. Hindes, "Delaware Silversmiths," 287–89.
81. Poole to Hicks, 7, April 1820, Elias Hicks papers, FHL.
82. Poole to Hicks, 2 Aug. 1820, ibid.
83. Poole to Hicks, 16 Jan. 1821, ibid.
84. Poole to Jackson, 28 Feb. 1825, Jackson papers, ibid.
85. Anthony F. C. Wallace, *Rockdale* (New York: Knopf, 1978), 256–57; Fairbanks, "Friends in Wilmington," 38–40.
86. *Delaware Free Press* (Wilmington), 14 March 1832.
87. "Authority in Religion," *Berean* 2 (10 Jan. 1826), 209. Despite his cosmopolitan breadth, Gibbons considered novel-reading to be one of the serious evils of the day. William Gibbons, *A Review and Refutation of Some of the Opprobrious Charges against the Society of Friends* (Philadelphia: T.E. Chapman, 1847), 194.
88. "Evan Lewis," "Dictionary of Quaker Biography," QC; Evan Lewis to Hicks, postcript in Ferris to Hicks, 16 July 1821, Elias Hicks papers, FHL.
89. Lewis to Hicks, 18 Nov. 1822, Elias Hicks papers, FHL.
90. Quoted in the *Telescope* (New York), 15 March 1828.
91. See the unpublished paper by Jean McClure, "Benjamin Ferris and the Letters of Paul and Amicus: A Study of Liberal Thought in early Nineteenth Century Quakerism," Swarthmore College, 1956.

92. Ferris to Hicks, 16 July 1821, Elias Hicks papers, FHL; Benjamin Ferris, "Historical Review of the Rise and Progress of the Separation of the Friends of Philadelphia Yearly Meeting," 2, unpublished ms, Ferris papers, FHL.
93. Benjamin Ferris, "An Account of the Separation in the Society of Friends," 5, unpublished ms, Ferris papers, FHL.
94. Hicks to Phebe Willis, 19 May 1818, in Foster, *Authentic Report*, II, 416–19.
95. *Christian Repository* 1 (22 Dec. 1821), 145.
96. Ibid. (2 Feb. 1822), 169.
97. See the analysis identifying Hicksites with Unitarians in G.B.S., "Schism," 237–52.
98. Ferris, "A Sketch," 80; Foster, *Authentic Report*, II, 91–93, 199–206; *Delaware Free Press* (Wilmington), 3, 17, 24 March 1832. It was a fascinating development when reformer Gibbons took the lead in demanding that Webb be disciplined, with Ferris dragging his feet. See H. Larry Ingle, ed., " 'A Ball that Has Rolled Beyond Our Reach': The Consequences of Hicksite Reform, 1830, As Seen in an Exchange of Letters," *Delaware History* 21 (Fall-Winter 1984), 127–37.

CHAPTER 4

1. Membership figures and meeting locations may be found in Edwin S. Gaustad, *Historical Atlas of Religion in America* (New York: Harper, 1976; rev. ed.), 94, 96.
2. For the organization and a brief sketch of principal points of faith, see *Rules of Discipline of the Yearly Meeting of Friends, Held in Philadelphia* (Philadelphia: J. Mortimer, 1825), quotations from 48–49. For an account of the origins of "Meeting for Sufferings," see Mekeel, "Founding Years," *Friends in the Delaware Valley*, 39–41.
3. Elias Hicks, *Journal of the Life and Religious Labours of Elias Hicks* (New York: Arno Press, 1969), 279.
4. G.B.S., "Schism", 237–38.
5. *Rules of Discipline*, 78–79; Mekeel, "Founding Years," 38. On the use of queries to tighten discipline, see J. William Frost, "The Origins of the Quaker Crusade Against Slavery: A Review of Recent Literature," *Quaker History* 67 (Spring 1978), 56.
6. Joseph Scattergood, "Diary," 18 April 1815, Joseph Scattergood papers, QC.
7. Frost, "Origins of Quaker Crusade," 56.
8. Doherty, *Hicksite Separation*, 73; Brinton, *Friends for 300 Years*, 186.
9. Thistlewaithe, *Anglo-American Connection*, 79.
10. Russell, *Quakerism*, 296–97; Arthur J. Mekeel, *Quakerism and A Creed* (Philadelphia: Friends Book Store, 1936), 48–49.
11. Barbour and Roberts, *Early Quaker Writings*, 467, 513.

12. Scott, *Works*, I, 221.
13. Jones, *Later Periods*, I, 311–12.
14. Evans to Hicks, 24 May 1804, Elias Hicks papers, FHL.
15. Joseph Kite, "Notes on Philadelphia Yearly Meeting in 1830, 1831, 1832, 1833," 20 April 1830, in Sheppard Family papers, QC.
16. See, for example, Williams Evans's account of his visit to North Carolina Yearly Meeting in 1830, in Larry Ingle, ed., "An Orthodox Friend's Visit to North Carolina," *Southern Friend* 5 (Spring 1983), 8–11.
17. Scott, *Works*, I, 526.
18. Hicks to unknown, 10 Aug. 1810, Elias Hicks papers, FHL.
19. Scott, *Works*, I, 114, 178, 449.
20. Hicks, *Journal*, 141–42. D. Elton Trueblood has suggested that the most critical period for Hicks's understanding of the failure of the outward institution of the church came when he read Johann L. Mosheim's *Ecclesiastical History of the Fifth Century* during the summer of 1815. It seems more likely that Mosheim merely confirmed and gave added credence to a tendency already clearly developed in the sixty-seven-year-old Hicks. See Trueblood's essay, "Career of Hicks," in *Byways in Quaker History*, 77–93.
21. Hicks, *Journal*, 353.
22. James Cockburn, *A Review of the General and Particular Causes Which Have Produced the Late Disorders and Divisions in the Yearly Meeting of Friends, Held in Philadelphia* (Philadelphia: Philip Price, Jr., 1829), 18–19.
23. Evans to Hicks, 17 Feb. 1800, Elias Hicks papers, FHL.
24. Evans to Hicks, 24 May 1804, ibid.
25. Hicks to Jemima Hicks, 10 Aug. 1808, ibid.
26. Stephen Grellet, *Memoirs of the Life and Gospel Labours of Stephen Grellet*, ed. Benjamin Seebohm (Philadelphia: Henry Longstreth, 1860), I, 1, 11–13, 28–29, 34, 41, 46, 58; William W. Comfort, *Stephen Grellet 1773–1855* (New York: Macmillan, 1942), 30.
27. Grellet, *Memoirs*, I, 35.
28. Hicks, *Journal*, 126–27.
29. Grellet, *Memoirs*, I, 141–43.
30. Hicks, *Journal*, 127.
31. Grellet, *Memoirs*, I, 144, 147, 168.
32. Ibid., I, 169, 185–86, 195–96; Comfort, *Grellet*, 78–79.
33. Grellet, *Memoirs*, I, 173–74.
34. Henry Tuke, *The Principles of Religion, as Professed by the Society of Christians, Usually Called Quakers* (New York: Collins, Perkins, and Co., 1805); Jones, *Later Periods*, I, 285–87.
35. Ferris, "Account," 25, Ferris papers, FHL.
36. On this point, see also Isichei, *Victorian Quakers*, 10–11.

37. *The Reformer*, a monthly published in Philadelphia, was filled with articles expressing this viewpoint. See, for example, "Editorial Remarks," *The Reformer* 2 (June 1, 1821), 122-23. See also unsigned and undated essay in Ferris papers, Box 12, FHL.

38. Hicks to unknown, 5 June 1817, Elias Hicks papers, FHL.

39. Grellet, *Memoirs*, I, 215-16, 477.

40. *The Reformer* 2 (April 1821), 89-93.

41. Hicks to *The Reformer*, 11 May 1821, in *The Reformer* 2 (June 1, 1821), 134-40.

42. Evans, *Journal*, 23-24.

43. Scattergood, "Diary", 10, 26 Sept., 22 Oct. 1815, 1 Jan. 1818, 4 July 1819, Scattergood papers, QC.

44. Thos L. Moore to Hicks, 29 Jan. 1785, Elias Hicks papers, FHL.

45. James Mott to Hicks, 5 Aug. 1805, ibid.

46. Whitman, *Prose Works* 1892, II, 645.

47. Edward Hicks to Elias Hicks, 23 April 1818, Elias Hicks papers, FHL.

48. Foster, *Authentic Report*, I, 377, 380-82; II, 72-73.

49. Edwin B. Bronner, "Distributing the Printed Word: The Tract Association of Friends, 1816-1966," *Pennsylvania Magazine of History and Biography* 101 (July 1967), 344-48.

50. Evans, *Journal*, 43-44.

51. Jones, *Later Periods*, I, 460.

52. Mekeel, *Quakerism and a Creed*, 48; Isichei, *Victorian Quakers*, 26-27.

53. Minutes, Philadelphia Yearly Meeting, 23, 24 April 1817. John Comly, Abraham Lower, Jesse Kersey, and Emmor Kimber were all on the committee. Kersey, interestingly enough, was one of the warmest suporters of the idea. See Kersey to Comly, no date, Joseph Turner papers, QC.

54. Edward Hicks, *Memoirs*, 96-97.

55. Ferris, "Account," [30]-31, Ferris to Fannie Ferris, April 1817, Ferris papers, FHL.

56. Hicks to unknown, 5 June 1817, Elias Hicks papers, FHL. Hicks himself served on the committee to review the proposal. Minutes, New York Yearly Meeting, 26 May 1817.

57. Judge to Hicks, 11 Sept. 1817, Elias Hicks papers, FHL.

58. Ferris, "Account," [32]-33. Jordan was remembered as being among the first to raise the alarm about those who professed "superior light and religious advancement." *A Biographical Memoir of Richard Jordan, A Minister of the Gospel, in the Society of Friends* (York: W. Alexander & Son, 1828), 37-38. The Hicksites interpreted Jordan's regular attendance at New York Yearly Meeting as a way the Philadelphia junto tried to check Hicks's influence. Kimber to Hicks, 25 Jan. 1829, Elias Hicks papers, FHL.

59. Pryor, Journal, II, 39, Pryor papers, FHL.

60. Edward Hicks to Elias Hicks, 23 April 1818, Elias Hicks papers, FHL.
61. Ferris, "Account," [32].

CHAPTER 5

1. Hicks, *Journal*, 334–35; Forbush, *Hicks*, 19–22, 182.
2. Foster, *Authentic Report*, I, 173.
3. Ibid., I, 109.
4. Ibid., I, 165–66.
5. Hicks to Willis, 19 May 1818, in ibid., II, 416–19.
6. *Saturday Evening Post* (Philadelphia), 15 March 1823.
7. Hicks to Willis, 19 May 1818, Foster, *An Authentic Report*, II, 416–19.
8. On this point, see also Robert P. Falk, "Thomas Paine: Deist or Quaker?" *Pennsylvania Magazine of History and Biography* 62 (Jan. 1938), 52–63, comparison of Hicks and Paine, 58–60.
9. Foster, *Authentic Report*, I, 67.
10. Evans, *Journal of Savery*, 271.
11. Knapp, *Eddy*, 283.
12. Foster, *Authentic Report*, I, 358. Bettle himself testified that about this time he had some reservations about Hicks, but they were not serious ones. Ibid., I, 81.
13. Evans, *Journal* 54–55.
14. Foster, *Authentic Report*, I, 354. Abraham Lower, who reported that Bettle had told him about the incident, was confused about the timing of the confrontation (Ibid., I, 358).
15. Hicks, *Journal*, 380–82.
16. Evans, *Journal*, 54; Foster, *Authentic Report*, II, 39.
17. *Saturday Evening Post* (Philadelphia), 13 Oct. 1827. Although this source, written by a defender of Hicks in a polemic aimed at the Orthodox, is not contemporaneous with what it describes, an evangelical champion who responded to it directly did not disagree with its account of Hicks's visit; he did, significantly, label Hicks a *"leveller* as well as a *reformer"* (Ibid., 12 Dec. 1827). A problem of dating remains, but from internal evidence it appears that Hicks's statements here were made before the Pine Street Meeting.
18. Elias Hicks to Valentine Hicks, 28 Oct. 1819, Elias Hicks papers, FHL; Forbush, *Hicks*, 189, 320, n 29; Foster, *Authentic Report*, I, 354, II, 39; Cockburn, *Review*, 60; Elias Hicks, *Observations on the Slavery of the Africans and their Descendants, and on the Use of the Produce of Their Labour* (New York: S. Wood, 1814).

19. Foster, *Authentic Report*, I, 409, II, 39–40; Jackson, "History of the Separation," 37–38, Burr papers, FHL; Ferris, "Account," 35–37, Ferris papers, FHL. Interestingly, when Hicks wrote home the next day, he failed to mention the incident. Hicks to Valentine Hicks, 28 Oct. 1819, Elias Hicks papers, FHL. Even more interesting, when they issued a historical survey of the causes behind the split in 1828, the Orthodox Yearly Meeting did not mention what had happened at Pine Street. See *A Declaration of the Yearly Meeting of Friends*.

20. Ferris, "Account," 35, Ferris papers, FHL; Forbush, *Hicks*, 189.

21. Cockburn, *Review*, 61; "Free Produce Among the Quakers," *Atlantic Monthly* 22 (Oct. 1868), 491–92; L. Maria Child, *Isaac T. Hopper: A True Life* (Boston: John P. Jewett & Co., 1853), 276. *Saturday Evening Post*, 13, 20 Oct., 22 Dec. 1827; Ferris, "Historical Review," 8, Ferris papers, FHL.

22. William Poole to Hicks, 8 Dec. 1819, Elias Hicks papers, FHL.

23. See, for example, *The Reformer* 2 (March 1821), 61–65.

24. Theophilus R. Gates, *The Trials, Experiences, Exercises of Mind, and First Travels of Theophilus R. Gates* (Philadelphia: David Dickinson, 1818), 239–62, and *A Measuring Reed; to Separate the Precious from the Vile* (Philadelphia: D. Dickinson, 1819), 250–51; *The Telescope* (New York), 11 Feb. 1826.

25. *The Reformer* 2 (1 July 1821), 147. Points of view like this one were endemic to rural and small town elements distrustful of urban elites. See Bertram Wyatt-Brown, "The Antimission Movement in the Jacksonian South: A Study of Regional Folk Culture," *Journal of Southern History* 36 (Nov. 1970), 501–29.

26. *The Reformer* 2 (April 1821), 89–93.

27. Joseph Rakestraw to Hicks, 5 May 1821, Elias Hicks papers, FHL. There are biographical sketches of Allen and Forster in Jones, *Later Periods* I, 335–47, 367–69.

28. *The Reformer* 2 (1 June 1821), 122–23.

29. Hicks to *Reformer*, ibid., 135–40.

30. Hicks to William B. Irish, 15 Jan. 1820, Elias Hicks papers, FHL.

31. Hicks to Poole, 8 April 1822, ibid.

32. Whitman, *Prose Works*, 1892, II, 639.

33. On this point, see Hugh S. Barbour, *The Quakers in Puritan England* (New Haven: Yale University Press, 1964).

34. Hicks to Poole, 14 Feb. 1820, Elias Hicks papers, FHL.

35. Comly, *Journal*, 400.

36. Hicks to Poole, 14 Feb. 1820, Elias Hicks papers, FHL.

37. Hicks to Gideon Seaman, 3 March 1822, ibid.

38. Hicks to Irish, 11 Feb. 1821, ibid. This letter contains the first reference to schism, and that in rebuttal, that I have found among Hicks's papers.

39. Hicks to Poole, 14 Feb. 1820, ibid.

40. Hicks to Poole, 28 Dec. 1820, ibid.

41. Hicks to Poole, 14 Feb. 1820, 3 March 1823, ibid.

43. *A Letter from a Friend in the Country to a Friend in the City, containing Remarks on Late Reviews of Some Letters of Elias Hicks* (Philadelphia: privately printed, 1825), 4.

44. Hicks to Poole, 28 Dec. 1820, Elias Hicks papers, FHL.

45. D. Elton Trueblood in his essay, "Career of Hicks," in *Byways in Quaker History*, 77–93, went too far when he labeled the Long Islander "incapable of systematic, reflective thought." Hicks's correspondence on theological issues, which Trueblood apparently had not reviewed, is enough to refute such assertions.

46. Hicks to Irish, 11 Feb. 1821, Elias Hicks papers, FHL.

47. See, for only a few examples, *Saturday Evening Post* (Philadelphia), 26 April, and 10, 24 May 1823; "Divinity of Christ," *Berean* 3 (3 April 1827) 273–74.

48. Hicks to Poole, 8 Feb. 1822, Elias Hicks papers, FHL.

49. Hicks to Thomas Willis, 16 Nov. 1829, in Foster, *Authentic Report*, II, 432. Hicks's letters to Willis were printed and widely circulated (see ibid., I, 119).

50. Hicks to Thomas Willis, Oct. 1821, in ibid., II, 422, and I, 110.

51. The basic study of this group is Frederick B. Tolles, "The New-Light Quakers of Lynn and New Bedford," *New England Quarterly* 32 (Sept. 1959), 291–319. For one evangelical reaction, see Evans, *Journal*, 71–72.

52. Poole to Hicks, 11 June 1821, Elias Hicks papers, FHL; Comly, *Journal*, 267–68.

53. Hicks to Poole, 26 Dec. 1821, Elias Hicks papers, FHL.

54. Ibid. Hicks thought pamphlets one and three were most lucid.

55. David B. Slack, *The Celestial Magnet* (Providence: Miller and Hutchens, 1820–21), quotation from third pamphlet, 7.

56. Hicks to Poole, 26 Dec. 1821, Poole to Hicks, 27 Jan. 1822, Elias Hicks papers, FHL; Foster *Authentic Report* I, 112, 356, 411–13; Hicks to Moses Brown, 30 March 1825, in *Letters of Hicks*, 171–76. Slack's fourth pamphlet did confirm Hicks's belief that Joseph was Jesus' father, for he grew bolder in asserting it after digesting the Rhode Islander's argument. See Hicks to Thomas Willis, Oct. 1821, in ibid., II, 421–22.

57. Hicks to Brown, 30 March 1825 in *Letters of Hicks*, 172.

58. Hicks to Poole, 8 April 1822, Elias Hicks papers, FHL.

59. Poole to Hicks, 2 Aug. 1820, ibid. See also Issac T. Hopper to Ferris, 7 Nov. 1822, Ferris papers, FHL.

60. Poole to Hicks, 7 April 1820, Rakestraw to Hicks, 5 May 1821, Elias Hicks papers, FHL.

61. Ferris to Hicks, 16 July 1821, ibid.

62. Poole to Hicks, 16 Jan. 1821, ibid.

CHAPTER 6

1. Elias Hicks to Edward Hicks, 9 April 1822, Elias Hicks papers, FHL.
2. Hopper to Ferris, 30 Aug. 1821, Ferris papers, FHL. Hopper asked Ferris to burn his letter after reading it, but the recipient noted, "I was not easy to commit this to the fire but have preserved it for future reference." On Hopper, see Child, *Hopper*.
3. Evans, *Journal*, 63.
4. Poole to Hicks, 15 Feb., 18 April, 1822, Elias Hicks papers; Joseph Whitall to Poole, 19 June 1822, Burr papers, FHL.
5. Report, "To the Yearly Meeting from William Jackson, Richard Jordan, Jona^n Evans, John Cox, Hinchman Haines, John Comly, and Samuel Bettle," 16 April 1822, Bettle family papers, QC.
6. Poole to Hicks, 11 Jan. 1822, Elias Hicks papers, FHL.
7. McClure, "Benjamin Ferris and the letters of Paul and Amicus," 21-22, FHL; *Christian Repository* 2 (24 Jan. 1823), 165. Gilbert estimated that two-thirds of Wilmington's inhabitants were Friends, well over twice the likely number (Ibid. 2 [14 Feb. 1823], 177). The "Paul" and "Amicus" disputation just about kept the *Repository* alive. Toward the end of the series, Porter noted that he had only 600 subscribers and appealed to Friends, who had had a "large indulgence" in the paper, for support (Ibid. 2 [17 Jan. 1823], 163). But within six months the *Repository* printed its last issue.
8. *Christian Repository* 2 (24 Jan. 1823), 165; Ahlstrom, *Religious History*, 465-66.
9. Poole to Hicks, 11 June, 15 Oct. 1821, 11 Jan. 1822, Elias Hicks papers, FHL.
10. Poole to Ferris, "without date but was written about 6 mo 1821," Ferris papers, FHL.
11. Fairbanks, "Friends in Wilmington," 34-38.
12. *Christian Repository* 2 (24 Jan. 1823), 165.
13. Ferris to Hicks, 16 July 1821, Hicks papers, FHL. *Christian Repository* 1 (26 May 1821), 27.
14. *Christian Repository* 1 (12 May 1821), 9.
15. Ibid., 1 (30 June 1821), 46.
16. Ibid., 1 (19 and 26 May 1821), 24, 26.
17. Ibid., 1 (28 July, 11 Aug. 1821), 64, 72.
18. Ibid., 1 (17 Nov., 22 Dec. 1821), 126, 145-46.
19. Ibid., 1 (19 Jan. 1822), 161-62.
20. Ibid., 2 (8 June 1822), 33.
21. Ibid., 2 (22 June 1822), 41.
22. Ibid., 2 (29 June, 15 Nov. 1822), 45, 125.
23. Ibid., 2 (10 and 24 Aug., 7 Sept. 1822), 69, 77, 85.

24. Ibid., 2 (15 Nov. 1822), 125.
25. Ibid., 2 (1 Nov. 1822), 117.
26. Ibid., 1 (11 Aug. 1821), 70.
27. Ibid., 1 (22 Dec. 1821), 145–46.
28. Poole to Hicks, 15 Oct. 1821, Elias Hicks papers, FHL.
29. Hicks to Poole, 26 Dec. 1821, ibid.; Hopper to Ferris, 22 Nov. 1822, Ferris papers, FHL.
30. Poole to Ferris, no date, Ferris papers, FHL.
31. *Christian Repository* 2 (27 Dec. 1822), 149. To allay such concerns, "Amicus" added a note to his final essay averring that he spoke only for himself. Ibid., 2 (17 Jan. 1823), 161–62.
32. Ibid., 2 (27 Dec. 1822), 152. The letter contains the earliest reference I have been able to discover to the "Hicksites."
33. Poole to Ferris, no date, Richard M. Smith to Ferris, 25 Jan. 1822, Ferris papers, FHL.
34. *Christian Repository* 2 (28 Feb., 7 March 1823), 187–88, 191–92.
35. *Rules of Discipline*, 48.
36. Foster, *Authentic Report* I, 354–55; Ferris, "Account," 51–53, Ferris papers, FHL; Doherty, *Hicksite Separation*, 115.
37. Foster, *Authentic Report*, II, 35–36, 73–75; *Rules of Discipline*, 49; Doherty, *Hicksite Separation*, 134.
38. Foster, *Authentic Report*, II, 37–38, 76.
39. Hicks, *Journal*, 390–91.
40. Joseph Whitall to Poole, 19 June, 9 Aug. 1822, Burr papers, FHL. Poole replied to both letters, but his second response, as he noted on the letter from Whitall, produced no further answer. Communication was breaking down.
41. Foster, *Authentic Report*, I, 247, 355–57, 411, 418–19; Evans, *Jonathan Evans* 30, 132, 163; Jackson, "History of the Separation," 43, Jackson papers, FHL; "An Account of the Proceedings which took place in relation to Elias Hicks, before and during the late visit to Philadelphia," 2, Burr papers, FHL.
42. *The Cabinet*, 6–20.
43. Evans, *Journal*, 79.
44. Rakestraw to Ferris, 8 Nov. 1822, Ferris papers, FHL.
45. Hicks, *Journal*, 392–93; Ferris, "Account," 53–55, Ferris papers, FHL; Foster, *Authentic Report*, I, 359. For one example of the evangelical reaction, see Evans, *Journal*, 74.
46. Ezra Comfort and Isaiah Bell, "Expression of Sentiments uttered by Elias Hicks," 9 Dec. 1822, in Papers relative to Hicksite Separation in Baltimore Yearly Meeting, QC.

47. "An Account of the Proceedings," 16, Burr papers, FHL; Ferris, "Account," 55, Ferris papers, FHL. Comfort and Bell were disowned by their rural, Hicksite-leaning meeting, a decision upheld by Abington Quarter, but overturned by the yearly meeting. Jackson, "History of the Separation," 47, Jackson papers, FHL.

48. Hopper to Ferris, 7 Nov. 1822, Ferris papers, FHL. This letter contains the first use of the term "orthodox" to describe Hicks's opponents that I have found.

49. Evan Lewis to Hicks, 18 Nov. 1822, Elias Hicks papers, FHL.

50. [Memorandum], Asa Matlack papers, QC; "An Account of the Proceedings," 3–4, Burr papers, FHL; Ferris, "Account," 57–59, Hopper to Ferris, 9 Dec. 1822, Ferris papers, FHL; Jackson, "History of the Separation," 48, Jackson papers, FHL.

51. Hicks to R. and Martha Aldrick, 12 Dec. 1822, Elias Hicks papers, FHL.

52. "An Account of the Proceedings," 4–5, [10], Burr papers, FHL. Foster, *Authentic Report*, I, 359, 427; Hicks, *Journal*, 394; Hicks to Poole, 10 Dec. 1822, Elias Hicks papers, FHL.

53. Edward Hicks to David Seaman, undated, David Seaman papers, FHL.

54. "An Account of the Proceedings," [6]–9, Burr papers, FHL; Foster, *Authentic Report*, I, 359–60; [Memorandum], Matlack papers, QC; Doherty, *Hicksite Separation*, 67–68, 120; Seaman to Sarah Seaman, 17 Dec. 1822, Seaman papers, FHL. One recollection had it that the leaders had Hicks's three accusers waiting nearby and intended to bring them on if they could have forced Hicks into a "select" meeting. Ferris, "Historical Review," 19, Ferris papers, FHL.

55. "An Account of the Proceedings," 9, Burr papers, FHL; Poole to Ferris and Eli Hilles, [13] Dec. 1822, Ferris papers, FHL.

56. "An Account of the Proceedings," 9–[10], Burr papers, FHL; [Memorandum] Matlack papers, QC.

57. "An Account of the Proceedings," [10–11] Burr papers, FHL.

58. Thomas McClintock to Poole, 16 Dec. 1822, ibid.

59. *Saturday Evening Post* (Philadelphia), 4 Jan. 1823.

60. Ezra Comfort, "Substance of a conversation between Ezra Comfort and Elias Hicks," 19 Dec. 1822, in "Papers Relative to Hicksite Separation," QC.

61. Hicks to Jonathan Evans, 27 Jan. 1823, Elias Hicks papers, FHL.

62. Cockburn, *Review*, 68–73.

63. McClintock to Poole, 16 Dec. 1822, Burr papers, FHL; Cockburn, *Review*, 73–75, 78–79.

64. Kimber to Hicks, 22 Dec. 1822, Elias Hicks papers, FHL.

65. Samuel Hicks to Hicks, 24 Dec. 1822, ibid.

66. Poole to Hicks, 20 Dec. 1822, ibid.

67. *Saturday Evening Post* (Philadelphia), 25 Jan. 1823.

68. See ibid., 15 Sept. 1827; *Declaration of the Yearly Meeting*, 7; Evans, *Journal*, 77.

69. *Saturday Evening Post* (Philadelphia), 4 Aug. 1827.

70. Poole to Ferris and Hillis, [13] Dec. 1822, Ferris papers, FHL.

71. A writer in the *Saturday Evening Post* suggested that the "tumultuous scenes" accompanying Hicks's visit administered "a pretty severe shock to shake their false heavens of theory, and put the people in a way to think for themselves." Such events "are the necessary effects of evils previously existing, and will continue to operate so long as the cause remains to produce them." *Saturday Evening Post* (Philadelphia), 5 April 1823.

72. Ibid., 21 Dec. 1822.
73. Ibid., 4 Jan. 1823.
74. Ibid., 1 Feb. 1823.
75. Ibid., 8, 15 Feb. 1823.
76. Ibid., 28 June 1823. The *Post*'s editor was Thomas C. Clarke.
77. *Saturday Evening Post* (Philadelphia), 22 Feb. 1823.
78. Forbush, *Hicks*, 212; McClintock to Poole, 24 Feb. 1823, Burr papers, FHL; Foster, *Authentic Report*, II, 77.
79. McClintock to Poole, 2 April 1823, Burr papers, FHL.
80. *Saturday Evening Post* (Philadelphia), 5 April, 10 May 1823.
81. Thomas Fisher to Hicks, 17 [March] 1823, Elias Hicks papers, FHL; Foster, *Authentic Report* I, 419, II, 38–39. There is some discrepancy in dating this meeting at Pine Street. Benjamin Ferris ("Account," [92]–93), Halliday Jackson ("History of the Separation," 67), and Abraham Lower (Foster, *Authentic Report*, I, 421) indicate the meeting was on February 16, the first day Hunt went to meeting in the city, but from the letter of McClintock (see note 78) and Fisher, whose letter has the date partially torn off, I have concluded the more probably date is a month later, March 16.
82. McClintock to Hicks, 8 April 1823, Elias Hicks papers, FHL.
83. Ferris, "Account," [98], Ferris papers, FHL.
84. Kimber to Hicks, 24 Jan. 1823, Elias Hicks papers, FHL.
85. Cockburn, *Review*, 76–78. Richard Humphreys signed the first but not the second letter. One of the horns of the bull had fallen off, one reformer commented. McClintock to Poole, 11 Feb. 1823, Burr papers, FHL.
86. Hicks to Jonathan Evans, 27 Jan. 1823, Elias Hicks papers, and McClintock to Poole, 11 Feb. 1823, Burr papers, both in FHL.
87. Foster, *Authentic Report*, I, 71–72; Evans, *Journal*, 76. The Meeting's disclaimer appeared on February 7. *Christian Repository* 2 (7 Feb. 1823), 175. For the threat to renege on the subscription, see ibid., 2 (21 Feb. 1823), 183.
88. *Extracts from the Writings of Primitive Friends*, 4–10.
89. Evans, *Journal*, 76–77; Forbush, *Hicks*, 219.
90. Ferris, "Account," [76], Ferris papers, FHL.
91. Unknown to Seaman, 1 March 1823, Seaman papers, FHL.

CHAPTER 7

1. Poole to Hicks, 14 March 1823, Elias Hicks papers, FHL.
2. Edward Hicks to Hicks, 24 March 1823, ibid.
3. Grellet, *Memoirs*, II, 149-50.
4. McClintock to Poole, 2 April 1823, Burr papers, FHL.
5. Samuel Noble to Hicks, 13 Feb. 1823, Elias Hicks papers, FHL.
6. Kimber to Hicks, 24 Jan. 1823, ibid.
7. McClintock to Poole, 2 April 1823, Burr papers, McClintock to Hicks, 8 April 1823, Elias Hicks papers, FHL; Withy, *A Sermon*.
8. Evans, *Journal*, 77.
9. Foster, *Authentic Report*, I, 368. It required nearly thirty minutes for the clerk to read the relevant section of the minutes. Pryor, Journal, II, 156, Pryor papers, FHL. In his unpublished history of the separation, Benjamin Ferris charged that the evangelicals of Meeting for Sufferings wanted to avoid the *Rules of Discipline*'s prohibition against meddling "with any matter of faith or discipline which has not been determined by the Yearly Meeting." By placing their doctrinal statement in the minutes they would be free of the charge that they were meddling in a matter of faith that had "not been determined by the Yearly Meeting," and then they could issue the 10,000 printed copies stored in the book room. Ferris, "Account," [82-84], Ferris papers, FHL. While this interpretation has an aura of plausibility about it, particularly when viewed in the light of subsequent events, it seems more likely that the evangelicals expected some of the agiation to die down by the time of yearly meeting and then hoped to win approval of the document, particularly if the matter came up in the round-about fashion they planned.
10. Foster, *Authentic Report*, I, 82.
11. Evans, Journal, 108, W. B. Evans paper, QC.
12. Ibid.; Evans, *Jonathan Evans*, 69; Edward Hicks to Hicks, 24 Sept. 1823, Elias Hicks papers, FHL; Foster, *Authentic Report*, I, 72, 82. Throughout this account of the 1823 yearly meeting, I have reluctantly relied on Evans's biography of his ancestor for names of the participants. I have been unable to discover any other source that is as detailed as Evans's book in linking names and specific comments that were made. Even the unpublished portion of William Evans's journal in the William Bacon Evans papers in QC, with sections marked through to indicate to the printer that they were to be omitted, does not have some of the names that William Bacon Evans supplies.
13. Evans, *Jonathan Evans*, 70; Foster, *Authentic Report*, I, 72; Evans, *Journal*, 77-78; Evans, Journal, 109, W. B. Evans papers, QC. On Atlee, see *The Reformer* 4 (1 April 1823), 73-78.
14. Evans, *Jonathan Evans*, 70-71; Foster, *Authentic Report*, I, 72, 368; Jackson, "History of the Separation," 74, Jackson papers, FHL.

15. Edward Hicks to Hicks, 25 April 1823, Elias Hicks papers; Jackson, "History of the Separation," 75, Jackson papers, FHL.
16. Edward Hicks to Hicks, 25 April 1823, Elias Hicks papers, FHL; Evans, *Journal*, 79.
17. [Margaret Hilles] to Samuel Hilles, 4th Day evening, G.M. Howland papers, QC.
18. Evans, *Journal*, 79.
19. Braithwaite, *Memoirs of Anna Braithwaite*, 138.
20. Pryor, Journal, II, 181, Pryor papers, FHL.
21. Hicks to John Comly, 16 Aug. 1823, McClintock to Hicks, 6 May 1824, Elias Hicks papers, FHL. English visitors naturally tended to find lodging with well-to-do urban Friends. On her second trip in 1825, for example, Anna Braithwaite and her husband Isaac stayed with Thomas Stewardson, and when she came in 1824 Elizabeth Robson resided at John Warder's. Pryor, Journal, II, 190, 214, 224, Pryor papers, FHL.
22. *Examination of a Pamphlet, entitled the Misrepresentations of Anna Braithwaite, in relation to the Doctrines Preached by Elias Hicks*, (New York: privately printed, n.d.), 8-9; Hicks, *Journal*, 394-95; Hicks to Poole, 27 Aug. 1824, Elias Hicks papers, FHL; Grellet, *Memoirs*, II, 150.
23. Braithwaite, *Memoirs*, 139.
24. Foster, *Authentic Report*, I, 166; "Examination of a Pamphlet," 21-23, 39-45.
25. "Examination of a Pamphlet," 23-37, 47-50.
26. *Letters and Observations relating to the Controversy respecting the Doctrines of Elias Hicks* (n.p.: privately printed, 1824), 9-13. One account has it that the commentary in this production was written by Joseph John Gurney. Russell, *History of Quakerism*, 305.
27. Anna Braithwaite to Hicks, 13 Nov. 1824, Elias Hicks papers, FHL.
28. *Examination of a Pamphlet*, 18; *Letters and Observations*, 50. Hicks was angry, even bitter, about Braithwaite's attacks on him and refused to see her once the open warfare started. Hicks to Poole, 27 Aug. 1824, Braithwaite to Hicks, 13 Nov. 1824, Elias Hicks papers, FHL.
29. McClintock to Hicks, 6 May 1824, Elias Hicks papers, FHL.
30. Hicks to Poole, 25 May 1824, ibid.
31. Braithwaite to Hicks, 13 Nov. 1824, ibid.
32. Evans, *Journal*, 84-85.
33. *Saturday Evening Post* (Philadelphia), 15 May 1824.
34. William Evans to Elizabeth Barton, 27 Oct 1824, Charles Evans papers, QC.
35. Poole to Jackson, 3 Aug. 1824, Jackson papers, FHL.
36. Poole to Hicks, 27 Dec. 1824, Elias Hicks papers, FHL. Poole's reference here to "the struggle *for power*" is the first time I have discovered its use.

37. *Saturday Evening Post* (Philadelphia), 23 Aug. 1823.
38. Foster, *Authentic Report*, I, 90-91, II, 473.
39. "Differences between a Professor and a Possessor of Religion," *Berean* 1 (23 Feb. 1824), 5-6.
40. "E," "Orthodoxy," ibid., 1 (20 April 1824), 74-76.
41. "Servetus," ibid., 1 (24 July 1824), 139-40.
42. "R," "On the Progress of Reformation," ibid., 1 (24 July, 17 Aug., 1824), 137-39, 172-75.
43. "Speculative Theology," ibid., 2 (3 Oct. 1825), 97-98.
44. "The Retrogression," ibid., 3 (5 and 19 Dec., 1826, 2 and 16 Jan. 1827), 145-46, 162-63, 178-79, 193-95.
45. Evans, *Journal*, 100-103; Evans, *Jonathan Evans*, 158-59.
46. Evans to Barton, 4 Dec. 1824, Evans papers, QC.
47. Jones, *Later Periods*, I, 312.
48. *Saturday Evening Post* (Philadelphia), 3 July 1824.
49. Jones, *Later Periods*, I, 310-11; Isichei, *Victorian Quakers*, 52; *A Letter from Luke Howard*, quotes from 4, 19.
50. [Benjamin Ferris], *A Letter from a Friend in America to Luke Howard, of Tottenham, near London, in which the Character of Our Late Friend, Job Scott, Is Vindicated and Defended*, (N.p.: privately printed, 1826), 16-21. Ferris's authorship is confirmed in Hopper to Ferris, 20 March 1826, Ferris papers, FHL.
51. [Ferris], *Letter from Friend in America*, 23.
52. *Saturday Evening Post* (Philadelphia), 11 Dec. 1824.
53. Poole to Hicks, 2 Feb., 8 July 1825, Elias Hicks papers, FHL.
54. Doherty, *Hicksite Separation*, 48-49.
55. Foster, *Authentic Report*, I, 388.
56. My account of the Snowden affair is taken from Ferris, "Account," 103-125, Ferris papers, FHL, and Foster, *Authentic Report*, I, 361-66, 419-21, 426-53. On the Philadelphia Quakers' economic and social power, see Doherty, *Hicksite Separation*, 38-41, 67-68.
57. Ferris, "Account," 113, Ferris papers, FHL.
58. *Rules of Discipline*, 59.
59. Ibid., [4]. For the evangelicals' point of view, see appeal by Taylor and Scattergood to Quarterly Meeting, 4 Nov. 1826, Scattergood Diary, QC.
60. Cockburn, *Review*, 113-14. Cockburn was a member of the select meeting's committee of nine (Ibid., 112).
61. *Rules of Discipline*, 59. Green Street leaders considered theirs a relatively mild rebuke, since they had not deprived Snowden of any right he enjoyed as a Friend (Cockburn, *Review* 114).
62. Taylor and Scattergood to Monthly Meeting, 20 Sept. 1826, Taylor and Scattergood to Quarterly Meeting, 4 Nov. 1826, Scattergood Diary, QC; Jackson,

"History of the Separation," 93, Jackson papers, FHL; Foster, *Authentic Report*, I, 450. This action against the women may have been taken in retaliation for the decision of Philadelphia Quarterly Meeting in May to refer the whole matter to the next yearly meeting (Ferris, "Account," [124], Ferris papers, FHL). To be consistent with their repeated assertion that they were not punishing their evangelical officers for their views but for their disunity with the meeting's actions, the dominant group in Green Street did not take action against Snowden's wife Jane because she was a minister. To move against a minister could justify moves against Hicks. Moreover, she was aged and infirm (Foster, *Authentic Report*, I 448–49).

63. The committee included Thomas P. Cope, Isaac Davis, Jonathan Evans, and Ellis Yarnall, among others (Philadelphia Quarterly Meeting, Minutes, 6, 7 Nov. 1826, 9–10).

64. Jackson, "History of the Separation," 94–95, Jackson papers, Pryor, Journal, II, 213, Pryor papers, FHL.

65. Cockburn, *Review*, 124; Foster, *Authentic Report*, I, 365.

66. *Rules of Discipline*, 55–56.

67. Foster, *Authentic Report*, I, 364, 440–41.

68. Comly, *Journal*, 306–307.

69. Cockburn, *Review* 126–27. Cockburn reprints a full account of these developments adopted by Green Street Meeting after the separation (see ibid., 144–67). Interestingly, William Evans, who attended and spoke at one of the meetings in which the matter was agitated, did not mention the effort to discipline Green Street; instead, he dwelt on the principles of infidelity that arose from shunting aside portions of the Bible that a person found disagreeable because he or she could not understand them (Evans, *Journal*, 95–96).

70. Foster, *Authentic Report*, I, 62–63, 84.

71. Cockburn, *Review*, 127. See also the brief of Green Street in ibid., 144–67.

72. See brief of Stacy Decow in Foster, *Authentic Report*, I, 40–55, quotation from 44–45.

73. Hicks to Poole 7 Dec. 1823, Elias Hicks papers, FHL.

74. Foster, *Authentic Report*, I, 67.

CHAPTER 8

1. Pryor, Journal, II, 224, Pryor papers, FHL.
2. Ibid., II, 222.
3. Ibid., II, 213–14.
4. Isaac Comly to Hicks, 23 May 1826, Elias Hicks papers, FHL.
5. Poole to Hicks, 14 Jan. 1825, ibid.

6. Evans, Journal, 126–28, W. B. Evans papers, QC.
7. McClintock to Hicks, 14 March 1825, Elias Hicks papers, FHL.
8. Gideon Seaman to Jonathan Evans, 31 Jan. 1825, Charles Evans papers, QC. On the move to censure Hicks, see Cockburn, Review, 93–96.
9. Braithwaite to Griscom, 29 Dec. 1824, Letters of English Friends, QC.
10. Hicks to Roger Brooke, 9 Feb. 1825, Elias Hicks papers, FHL; Pryor, Journal, II, 192–93, Pryor papers, FHL.
11. Noble to Hicks, 16 Feb. 1825, Elias Hicks papers, FHL; Cockburn, Review, 93–96.
12. Poole to Hicks, 16 Feb. 1825, Elias Hicks papers, FHL.
13. Noble to Hicks, 16 Feb. 1825, ibid.
14. See McClintock to Hicks, 14 March 1825, ibid., and the McClintock defense of the pamphlet in its third edition, The Sandy Foundation Shaken (New York: Isaac T. Hopper, 1832), ii–viii.
15. Sandy Foundation, xi.
16. Poole to Jackson, 28 Feb. 1825, Jackson papers, FHL.
17. A Defense of the Christian Doctrines of the Society of Friends (Philadelphia: privately printed, 1825), viii.
18. Ibid., xii–xiii.
19. A Comparative View of the Sermons of Wiliam Penn, Robert Barclay, and other Primitive Friends, with the lately Published Sermons of Elias Hicks (Philadelphia: privately printed, 1825), 57–58, 65. Paine's editor grouped Hicks's comments with those of Jefferson, Franklin, Robert Dale Owen, and Napoleon—no mean company (Thomas Paine, The Theological Works of Thomas Paine [Boston: privately printed, 1840], 12–13). An evangelical response to the second edition of The Sandy Foundation Shaken also connected Hicks to Paine in the same way (Strictures upon the Second Edition of a Pamphlet Recently Published in Philadelphia, by the Followers of Elias Hicks, Entitled, The Sandy Foundation Shaken, &c. &c. [Philadelphia: privately printed, 1825], 15).
20. Sixteen Reasons Why I cannot be a Hicksite (n.p.: privately printed, n.d.) FHL.
21. Matters of Fact relative to Late Occurrences among Professional Quakers (Philadelphia: privately printed, 1827).
22. A Chapter of Modern Chronicles; The Second Book of Modern Chronicles; Chronicles of Quakerism, or Modern Apocrypha; The Book of the Two Apostles; The General Epistle of Ahilud (Philadelphia: privately printed, n.d.). These pamphlets were obviously written after the separation.
23. "Richard Mott," "Dictionary of Quaker Biography," QC.
24. The Intolerants, A Drama (Philadelphia: privately printed, 1827). Because all the action takes place in New York and all the characters are either New Yorkers or from England, it seems probable that the play came out of the struggle there

rather than in Philadelphia where it was published. The copy in FHL decodes the "Dramatis Personae" but mistakes "Thomas Wilful" for Thomas Stewardson of Philadelphia; from the description of Wilful, the author was clearly referring to Thomas Willis, a close neighbor of Hicks's.

25. "A Demi-Quaker," *Seven Letters to Elias Hicks, on the Tendency of His Doctrines and Opinion, with an Introductory Address to the Society of Friends* (Philadelphia: privately printed, 1825), 4–6. This pamphlet, as well as a similiar one published the following year, has been attributed to Richard Waln, member of a prominent Quaker family. The author, however, expressly denied being "in profession with the people called Quakers" (Ibid., 7). Elizabeth Robson said the author was "Robert" Waln. Elizabeth Robson, "Journal," 307. Library, Friends House, London.

26. "A Demi-Quaker," *Seven Letters*, 8, 15–16.

27. "A Demi-Quaker," *Observations on the Sermons of Elias Hicks in Several Letters to Him; with some Introductory Remarks, addressed to the Junior Members of the Society of Friends* (Philadelphia: privately printed, 1826), 4–5.

28. McClintock to Hicks, 14 March 1825, Elias Hicks papers, FHL. While it may be true, as Bliss Forbush wrote (Forbush, *Hicks*, 230), that Hicks did not immediately consent to the publication of his sermons, other reformers, as McClintock's letter indicates, agreed that they should be brought out, and Hicks later came around to this view as well. See Hicks to M.T.C. Gould, 28 March 1828, in *The Quaker*, 4 (1828), vii.

A puzzling reference in McClintock's letter suggests that the editors of Hicks's sermons may have permitted the opposition to review the manuscript before final publication. McClintock referred to an "unpleasant" sentence from Hicks's discourse at Arch Street on November 14, 1824 ("Spirit can not beget anything but spirit; it cannot beget flesh and blood." Hicks, *Extemporaneous Discourses*, 11). The sentence, said McClintock, was not in the stenographer's notes, "but was insisted upon by the opposite party; honestly I presume under the conviction that it was spoken." It seems unlikely that the reformers would have wanted Hicks's sermons passed on by the evangelicals, yet as careful a man as McClintock would have hardly referred to one of his own group as the "opposite party."

29. *Saturday Evening Post* (Philadelphia), 19 March 1825.

30. See, for example, *The Quaker* 3 (Jan. 1828), 18, (Oct. 1828), 224.

31. Whitman, *Prose Works* 1892, II, 645.

32. McClintock to Poole, 6 June 1825, Burr papers, FHL.

33. Hicks, *Extemporaneous Discourses*, 11. For an evangelical attack on this idea, see *A Review of Elias Hicks' Letter to Thomas Willis, on the Miraculous Conception of Our Lord Jesus Christ* (Philadelphia: privately printed, 1824), [27]–28.

34. *The Quaker* 4 (1828), 115–16.

35. One Congregational magazine used the labels Unitarian, Universalist, and "as we say, Infidel" to describe him (*The Spirit of the Pilgrims*, 1 [Aug. 1828], 433).
36. Clarke and Gould, *Sermons by Hicks*, 36–51.
37. *Spirit of the Pilgrims* 2 (Jan. 1829), 64.
38. "Thomas Wetherald," "Dictionary of Quaker Biography," QC; Gibson, "Brobson Diary," 299.
39. Gould, *Sermons by Wetherald and Hicks*, 20–23.
40. Ibid., 70.
41. Ibid., 185–98.
42. Ibid., 246–59.
43. Evans, Journal, 140–41, W.B. Evans papers, QC.
44. M. Pennock to S. Vickers, 10 Jan. 1822, quoted in Doherty, *Hicksite Separation*, 51.
45. Poole to Hicks, 14 Jan. 1825, Elias Hicks papers, FHL.
46. *Rules of Discipline*, 78.
47. Desilver, *The Philadelphia Index*; Green Street Meeting minutes, 18 July 1822, Memorandum, 13 Jan. 1825, Miscellaneous Mss, Green Street Meeting, FHL.
48. McClintock to Poole, 28 March 1825, Burr papers, FHL; Nathan Shoemaker to Hicks, 29 March 1825, McClintock to Hicks, 5 March 1826, Elias Hicks papers, FHL. Atlee apparently joined the Swedenborgians (Comly to Hicks, 23 May 1826, Elias Hicks papers, FHL). Evangelicals heard rumors that Atlee had lamented his inability to get Friends to adopt Swedenborg's doctrines (Evans, Journal, 140, W.B. Evans papers, QC).
49. See the collection of documents on this case in Edward W. Smith papers, QC.
50. Phebe Johnson to Hicks, 23 Feb. 1825, Elias Hicks papers, FHL. Johnson's was a fascinating case. After the separation, she was disowned also by the Hicksites, giving her the rather unusual distinction of winning the disfavor of both branches of Friends. She later associated herself with an unorganized group of free thinkers on the fringes of Quakerism (See *Delaware Free Press* [Wilmington], 20 Nov. 1830 and 9 Apr 1831).
51. Hicks to Brooke, 6 Feb. 1826, Elias Hicks papers, FHL.
52. Shoemaker to Hicks, 8 Aug. 1825, ibid.
53. Robert Moore to David Seaman, 30 Dec. 1825, Seaman papers, FHL. Some evangelicals, Moore reported, were congenial.
54. McClintock to Poole, 6 June 1825, Burr papers, FHL.

CHAPTER 9

1. Quoted in Russell F. Weigley, ed., *Philadelphia: A 300-Year History* (New York: W.W. Norton & Co., 1982), 258.

2. Evans, Journal, 133, W.B. Evans papers, QC.
3. [Margaret Hilles] to Hilles, 4th day evening [April 1823], Howland papers, QC.
4. Hicks to Brooke, 6 Feb. 1826, Elias Hicks papers, FHL.
5. Pryor, Journal, II, 224-25, Pryor papers, [McClintock], "Ann Jones attacks Maria Imlay," undated memorandum, Burr papers, FHL. Jonathan Evans had interrupted Imlay at Pine Street the previous Thursday to inform her that she was disturbing the meeting's quiet.
6. "Manuscript Book Containing Rough Notes on the Disturbance at Arch Street Meeting House, 1826," QC.
7. Edward Garrigues to Poole, 16 Jan. 1826, Ferris papers, FHL.
8. Poole to Hicks, 12 May 1826, Elias Hicks papers, ibid.
9. Evans, Journal, 136-37, W.B. Evans papers, QC; Pryor, Journal, II, 216-18, FHL.
10. Evans, Journal, 139, W. B. Evans papers, QC. This incident and how it was handled later took on a divisive and legendary character. See Foster, *Authentic Report, II,* 82-83. The fact that Evans omitted this incident from his published journal suggests that it conflicted with the Orthodox view, advanced by Evans, that Comly, as even-tempered and magnanimous as anyone could be, was bent on promoting a split. For this view, see Evans, *Journal,* 107; Foster, *Authentic Report,* I, 68, II, 323; Evans, *Jonathan Evans,* 82.
11. Comly, *Journal,* 294-301.
12. See note 10.
13. My account of this affair is taken primarily from Jackson's testimony in Foster, *Authentic Report,* II, 46-47, 96-102, and Jackson, "History of the Separation," 106-13, Jackson papers, FHL. For wealth and occupations of leading Friends, see Doherty, *The Hicksite Separation,* 38-41. Unfortunately data on some of the leading participants are omitted or unavailable.
14. Poole to Jackson, 26 Dec. 1826, Jackson papers, FHL.
15. Foster, *Authentic Report,* II, 47-48; Moore to Jackson, 14 Jan. 1827, Joseph Turner to Jackson, 27 Jan. 1827, Jackson papers, FHL; Minutes, Meeting for Sufferings, 381-82.
16. Hicks to McClintock, 14 Aug. 1826, in [Hopper, ed.], *Letters of Hicks,* 194-96.
17. Hicks to Poole, 10 Feb. 1827, ibid., 196-98.
18. Poole to Jackson, 13 Dec. 1826, Jackson papers, FHL.
19. Wharton to Deborah [Wharton], 24 Nov. 1826, Wharton papers, FHL; Kimber to Hicks, 18 Oct. 1826, Elias Hicks papers, FHL.
20. *The Quaker* I (1827), 124-33; Doherty, *Hicksite Separation,* 38.
21. *The Quaker* I (1827), 54-72; Evans, Journal, 149, W.B. Evans papers, QC.
22. Evans, Journal, 149, W. B. Evans papers, QC.
23. There are at least four mildly variant version of Evans's statement; I have

followed the version in Evans Family papers, QC. See also, *The Quaker* I (1827), 72, Evans, Journal, 150, W. B. Evans papers, QC, and Hannah Rhodes (Evans's daughter), Memorandum, Miscellaneous Mss, FHL.

24. Evans Family papers, QC; *The Quaker* 1 (1827), 72; Evans, Journal, 150, W.B. Evans papers, QC.

25. Evans Family papers, QC.

26. Jackson to Seaman, 3 Jan. 1827, Seaman papers, FHL.

27. Shoemaker to Hicks, 6 Jan. 1827, Hicks papers, ibid.; Cockburn, *Review*, 98–102. When emissaries from both meetings arrived in Jericho with their mintues, they were received cordially—Hicks even invited them to his home for dinner—but nothing was done about their requests. Indeed, minutes of approval for Hicks's ministry at Byberry and Green Street, as well as endorsements from Southern and Concord Quarters, came in (Hicks to Wharton, 27 Feb. 1827, Wharton papers, FHL).

28. Wharton to Poole, 23 Dec. 1826, Burr papers, FHL; Hicks to Wharton, 8 Jan. 1827, Wharton papers, FHL.

29. There are two memoranda of this conversation, dated 10 Feb. 1827, in Charles Evans papers, QC. Gould was not a Friend and kept his own notes of the discussion. See also Wharton to Poole, 11 Feb. 1827, Burr papers, FHL; and Pryor, Journal, II, 241, Pryor papers, FHL.

30. Comly, *Journal*, 307; Foster, *Authentic Report*, I, 372. Interestingly, William Evans also was disturbed by this meeting. Evans, *Journal*, 104.

31. Pryor, Journal, II, 235, Pryor papers, FHL.

32. Comly, *Journal*, 308–11; McClintock to Poole, Feb. 1827, Burr papers, FHL.

33. Evans, Journal, 153, W.B. Evans papers, QC.

34. McClintock to Poole, Feb. 1827, Burr papers, FHL.

35. Wharton to Poole, 11 Feb. 1827, ibid.

36. Comly, *Journal*, 309–10; Pryor, Journal, II, 235, Pryor papers, FHL.

37. McClintock to Poole, Feb. 1827, Burr papers, FHL; Evans, *Journal*, 105.

38. Pryor, Journal, II, 235, Pryor papers, FHL.

39. Comly, *Journal*, 307, 311.

40. McClintock to Poole, Feb. 1827, Burr papers, FHL. The exact date of this important letter defies discovery. See H. Larry Ingle, ed., "The Hicksite Die Is Cast: A Letter of Thomas McClintock," *Quaker History*, forthcoming.

41. Hicks, *Memoirs*, 106–107.

42. Comly, *Journal*, 312–17; Foster, *Authentic Report*, II, 108–109.

43. Wharton to Poole, 11 Feb. 1827, Burr papers, FHL; Foster, *Authentic Report*, I, 358, II, 115–16, 120–21.

44. Foster, *Authentic Report*, I, 274–75.

45. Edward Hicks to Elias Hicks, 27 Feb. 1827, Elias Hicks papers, FHL; Hicks, *Memoirs*, 109. Hicks did invite Robson to his home for dinner, but she questioned his Christian profession and rejected his invitation.

46. Wharton to Hicks, 8 March 1827, Burr papers, FHL; Foster, *Authentic Report*, I, 465-66, II, 486.
47. Moore to Jackson, 14 Jan. 1827, Jackson papers, FHL.
48. Ferris to Jackson, 4 Feb. 1827, ibid.
49. Wharton to Poole, 8 March 1827, Burr papers, FHL; Comly, *Journal*, 317; "Scrutator," "Spirit of Orthodoxy," *Berean* 3 (12, 26 June 1827), 353-55, 372-74. Jordan's published journal did not reflect the extreme evangelical Orthodoxy that the memorial espoused. See, for example, the statement, "he early perceived the buildings of the seeds of skepticism, and a disorganizing spirit, secretly endeavouring to insinuate itself among Friends, under the plausible and sanctimonious profession of superior light and religious advancement." *Biographical Memoir of Richard Jordan*, 37. Even the "Testimony of Haddonfield Monthly Meeting Concerning our Beloved Friend Richard Jordan, Deceased" was not so strongly evangelical as the "Addenda," probably heavily edited by a committee of Meeting for Sufferings. See Richard Jordan, *Journal of the Life and Religious Labours of Richard Jordan* (Philadelphia: Thomas Kite, 1829), 3-11, 164-72.
50. Wharton to Poole, 8 March 1827, Burr papers, FHL.
51. Poole to Jackson, 21, 26 March 1827, Jackson papers, FHL.
52. Pryor, Journal, II 237, Pryor papers, FHL. One of those referred to was Isaac T. Hopper.
53. Comly, *Journal*, 317.
54. Poole to Jackson, 16 April 1827, Jackson papers, FHL.
55. Hicks to Wharton, 17 April 1827, Wharton papers, FHL.
56. Pryor, Journal, II, 236-37, Pryor papers, FHL.
57. Hilles to Morris Smith, 1 April 1827, Howland papers, QC.

CHAPTER 10

1. Minutes, Philadelphia Yearly Meeting, 1827, 21 April 1827.
2. *Memoir of Richard Jordan*, 38.
3. Comly, *Journal*, 317.
4. Ibid., 317-18. Foster, *Authentic Report*, I, 98-99, 372; Membership on this committee overlapped significantly with the one appointed by the yearly meeting the following week. Ibid., II, 107.
5. Comly, *Journal*, 318-19; Pryor, Journal, II, 237-38, Pryor papers, FHL.
6. Pryor, Journal, II, 237, Pryor papers, FHL; Evans, *Jonathan Evans*, 163, 167; Samuel Alexander, "Personal Recollections and Reminiscences of some of the American Friends who travelled in these Countries on Religious Service from 1828 to 1852," *Journal of the Friends Historical Society* 4 (April 1907), 91. My account of events of yearly meeting week, unless otherwise noted, is drawn from Pryor

Journal, II, 237–48, [Thomas Evans], "At a Yearly Meeting held in Philada in the 4th mo. 1827," Bettle family papers, QC; Comly, *Journal*, 319–32. Evans presented the most detailed account, but its bias toward the Orthodox is evident. I have followed Evans, *Jonathan Evans*, 84–127, in putting some speeches in the first person. The testimony contained in the two volumes of Foster's *Authentic Report* is also invaluable; it must be read as a whole.

7. Lower estimated that 100 of 147 representatives present favored Comly (Foster, *Authentic Report*, I, 458).

8. Two and a half years later, Lower claimed to have no recollection of this statement, but it certainly sounds like him. For his denial, see ibid., I, 459.

9. This account follows [Evans], "At a Yearly Meeting," Bettle papers, QC, supplemented by Foster, *Authentic Report*, I, 372–73, 458–59, II, 52, 332–34, 338–44. On the question of counting members, committees charged with hearing appeals did often present reports signed, not by all, but by a majority. In fact, in the case of Ezra Comfort's appeal to his quarterly meeting against a decision of his monthly meeting disowning him, a majority of one reportedly upheld him (Foster, *Authentic Report*, I, 275–76, II, 343). Such precedents, in this case involving a decision by an evangelical majority, bolstered Lower's position (ibid., I, 367, 458).

10. What Jackson's exact words were it is impossible to say, but his phrasing was extremely important. I have used the wording that would have given his statement its greatest appeal. See Cockburn, *Review*, 194. Jackson's point was correct, but it overlooked the fact that it was the representatives' responsibility to report out a recommendation. Until they turned the matter over to the yearly meeting itself or the meeting assumed its admitted right to select its officers—neither of which had yet been done—then the meeting should have adjourned or appointed the old clerks to serve temporarily until replacements were decided upon.

11. Foster, *Authentic Report*, II, 53.

12. Ibid., I, 68–69, II, 54.

13. For Hull's views, see his *Journal* in Evans, eds., *The Friends' Library*, IV, 308–309.

14. Foster, *Authentic Report*, I, 473. Halliday Jackson's testimony that "perhaps fifteen or twenty Friends" attended seems unrealistically low (ibid., II, 137).

15. *Saturday Evening Post* (Philadelphia), 9 July 1827.

16. Halliday Jackson, William Gibbons, Joseph Churchman, Joseph Foulke, and Jesse Kersey were among those named to this committee. The principal author of the address is unknown. Foster, *Authentic Report*, II, 138–39.

17. Ibid., II, 139.

18. *Berean* 3 (15 May 1827), 322.

19. A bit more than a month later, Wharton wrote from memory what he had said in this final session. He included no reference to the prediction that this would

be his last yearly meeting at Arch Street. See Memorandum, 24 May 1827, Wharton papers, FHL.
20. Foster, *Authentic Report*, II, 56.
21. The address can be found in Comly, *Journal*, 627-30.
22. Foster, *Authentic Report*, II, 141.
23. Ibid., I, 371.

CHAPTER 11

1. *An Examination of an Epistle*, 18.
2. Poole to Jackson, 4 June 1827, Jackson papers, FHL.
3. Evans, Journal, 158, W.B. Evans papers, QC.
4. Pryor, Journal, II, 249, Pryor papers, FHL.
5. Ibid., 249-50. This kind of "out-of-doors" caucus did not win the approval of all the reformers. William Poole reminded one of his correspondents that such pre-meeting gatherings caused complaints against Philadelphia's "Trinitarians," enough reason, said he, that Wilmington Friends "shall not pursue it" (Poole to Jackson, 31 May 1827, Jackson papers, FHL).
6. My account of this meeting is taken primarily from this summary, filed under Green Street Meeting, Miscellaneous Mss, supplemented by Pryor, Journal, II, 251-52, Pryor papers, FHL; Evans, Journal, 158-59, W.B. Evans papers, QC; and Foster, *Authentic Report*, II, 383-84, 488-89.
7. The reformers noted that except for two of the objectors, Joseph Rakestraw and John Lancaster, all had some connection, either by blood, marriage, or trade, with the deposed elders, Leonard Snowden, Mary Taylor, and Ann Scattergood (Pryor, Journal, II, 251, Pryor papers, FHL).
8. Poole to Jackson, 29 May 1827, Jackson papers, FHL.
9. Doherty, *Hicksite Separation*, 124.
10. Kersey to Gibbons and Ferris, 30 April 1827, Ferris papers, FHL.
11. Poole to Ferris, undated, but probably early May 1827, ibid.
12. Comly, *Journal*, 333-34; Jackson to Ferris, 10 May 1827, Ferris papers, FHL; Evans, Journal, 159-60, W.B. Evans papers, QC. Jackson described Comfort as a "tool" of the committee.
13. Comly, *Journal*, 335; Pryor, Journal, II, 254-55, Pryor papers, undated [McClintock] memorandum, Burr papers, FHL.
14. Evans, Journal, 162, W.B. Evans papers, QC.
15. Pryor, Journal, II, 255, Pryor papers, FHL.
16. Ibid., 253; Evans, Journal, 160, W.B. Evans papers, QC.
17. Pryor, Journal, II, 256-57, Pryor papers, FHL. The caliber of the quarter's committee was definitely second-rank, as none of the prominent evangelicals

served. This suggested that the leaders did not take the committee's duties very seriously. Despite the withdrawal of the Orthodox on this occasion, some of them came back the following week for the regular Thursday meeting (ibid., II, 259).

18. Wharton, *et al*, to Monthly Meeting of Friends of Philadelphia for the Southern District, 16 May 1827, Wharton papers, FHL; Pryor, Journal, II, 259, Pryor papers, FHL; Evans, *Journal*, 109.

19. Wharton to Poole, 30 May 1827 Burr papers, FHL; Doherty, *Hicksite Separation*, 41.

20. Evans, *Journal*, 110.

21. Jackson to Ferris, 10 May 1827, Ferris papers, FHL.

22. Poole to Jackson, 29 May 1827, Jackson papers, FHL.

23. Pryor, Journal, II, 262-63, Pryor papers, FHL; Wharton to Poole, 1 June 1827, Wharton papers, FHL; Hicks, *Memoirs*, 124-25. Interestingly, Bucks Quarter did order its monthly meetings to raise money and fulfill the commitment made by the yearly meeting to send funds to North Carolina Friends in order to pay for transporting freed slaves out of that state (Jackson to Ferris, 1 Jun 1827, Ferris papers, FHL).

24. Pryor, Journal, II, 261, Pryor papers, FHL; Cope to John Sheppard, 13 June 1827, Henry Cope papers, QC; Evans, Journal, 163, W.B. Evans papers, QC. The relative weakness of male support for the evangelicals can be seen also in Evans to Townsend, 10 Sept. 1827, and Jackson to Ferris, 28 Oct. 1827, Ferris papers, FHL.

25. Wharton to Poole, 24 Sept. 1827, Wharton papers, FHL.

26. Rebecca Turner to Joseph Turner, 4 Oct. 1827, Turner family papers, FHL.

27. Wharton to Poole, 8 June 1827, Wharton papers, FHL.

28. Pryor, Journal, II, 265, Pryor papers, FHL; Cockburn, *Review*, 213.

29. Foster, *Authentic Report*, II, 455-56. Only three, Halliday Jackson, Robert Moore, and Edward Garrigues, were active reformers.

30. Cope to Sheppard, 13 June 1827, Cope papers, QC.

31. Printed letter signed by John Watson, 12 June 1827, Wharton papers, FHL. The question of what the Hicksites should do about disowning the Orthodox was discussed in the higher echelons of the reform movement. The matter was not settled finally until John Comly came out strongly for a tolerant policy that permitted the Orthodox to bear the odium. See Comly to Poole, 2 Dec. 1827, Poole to Jackson, 13 and 22 Nov., 19 Dec. 1827, Jackson papers, FHL.

32. *An Epistle to the Members of the Religous Society of Friends* (Philadelphia: Solomon W. Conrad, 1827), 4, 12, 14.

33. Mabel Hoopes to Jackson, 12 Dec. 1827, Jackson papers, FHL; Ezra Michener to McClintock, 15 Jan. 1828, Ferris papers, FHL.

34. "The State of Society," *Berean* 3 (29 May 1827), 237-38.

35. Poole to Jackson, 10 Sept., 13 Dec. 1827, Jackson papers, FHL.

36. "Samuel Hilles," "Dictonary of Quaker Biography," QC; Hilles to Stewardson, 28 May 1828, Howland papers, QC.

37. Hilles to Stewardson, 2 and 16 Dec. 1827, 17 July 1828, undated, Howland papers, QC. Hilles noted charitably that the "separatists" conducted the meeting "with much propiety & kindness."
38. Poole to Jackson, 13, 22 Nov. 1827, Jackson papers, FHL.
39. Hannah Warrington to Hannah Warrington, 16 Nov. 1827, Evans family papers, QC.
40. "Communication," *Friend* 1 (27 Oct., 3 Nov. 1827), 15, 21; undated [McClintock] Memorandum, Burr papers, FHL.
41. Undated [McClintock] memorandum, Burr papers, FHL.
42. See the pleadings in Hendrickson *vs* Shotwell, Foster, *Authentic Report*, I, 1-11, and W. Rawle, et al., memorandum, 19 March 1828, Cope papers, QC.
43. See especially, Poole to Garrigues, 11 June 1827, Poole to Jackson, 28 June, 21 July 1827, Jackson papers, FHL; Evans to Townsend, 10 Sept. 1827, Ferris papers, FHL; Thomas P. Cope to Henry Cope, 22 June 1828, Charles Evans papers, QC.
44. Thomas Redman to Thomas Evans, 7 Aug. 1843, Henry Albertson papers, QC.
45. Hicks, *Memoirs*, 110. At least one reformer, William Wharton, apparently considered using the courts. See memorandum in Wharton papers, FHL.
46. Foster, *Authentic Report*, II, 176-77, 462.
47. William Yardley to "Esteemed Friend," 28 Nov. 1829, Ferris papers, FHL.
48. Exact numbers for those on each side are difficult to verify. Judging from their figures, Orthodox interest centered in the quarters where they were strongest, in Philadelphia, Caln, and those in New Jersey. They condemned the alleged distortions of the Hicksites, whose count benefitted from having access to the records, but offered no figures in rebuttal (Foster, *Authentic Report*, II, 404, 495). Incomplete Hicksite figures may be found in *Berean* (N.S.) 1 (July, Aug., Sept., 1828), 145-54, 159, 177-78. There is also a count of the New Jersey quarters in "Statement of members at the Separation," in Albertson papers, QC. For polemical purposes, the Orthodox cited approximately 20,000 as the total in the yearly meeting (*Examination of An Epistle*, 18). To reach the totals indicated, I have assumed that the faction controlling each quarter was more likely to have access to the most accurate figures; hence I have used the Orthodox figures in Philadelphia and have given them the 222 additional members they claimed over the Hicksites in their two New Jersey quarters as well as Caln. Neutrals amounted to about 429. For a description of how the Orthodox compiled their figures, see Foster, *Authentic Report*, II, 404; for the Hicksites, see ibid., 176. The Hicksite figures are in ibid., 461-62.
49. "Society of Friends in Philadelphia," *Friend* 2 (14 Feb. 1829), 141-42. The Hicksites, who never published a full count of ministers and elders, found a slight majority for themselves in two-thirds of the meetings (*Berean* [N.S.] 1 [Sept. 1825], 177-78).

50. Foster, *Authentic Report*, II, 461–62, 495.
51. Jackson to Ferris, 28 Oct. 1827, Ferris papers, FHL. The emphasis he gave to *"friends"* indicated that Jackson wanted to highlight Evans's admission that the Hicksites were Friends. For another example, see "Spirit of Orthodoxy," *Berean* 3 (12, 26 June 1827), 353–55, 372–74.
52. *Friend* 1 (28 June 1828), 293–95; Evans to Townsend, 10 Sept. 1827, Ferris papers, Pryor, Journal, II, 286–87, Pryor papers, FHL.
53. Foster, *Authentic Report*, I, 394.
54. *Friend* 1 (14, 28 June 1818), 280, 293–95; Foster, *Authentic Report*, I, 399. It is doubtful that the two black workmen shared the same conscientious grounds for refusing bail as the three Quakers.
55. Thomas P. Cope to Henry Cope, 22 June 1828, Charles Evans papers, QC.
56. Pryor, Journal, II, 290, 296, Pryor papers, FHL.
57. Samuel Allinson to Mary Allinson, 31 Aug. 1827, Allinson family papers, QC; Turner to Turner, 4 Oct. 1827, Turner papers, FHL.
58. Poole to Hicks, 26 Oct. 1827, Elias Hicks papers, FHL.
59. Wharton to Poole, 24 Sept. 1827, Wharton papers, FHL; Pryor, Journal, II, 301, Pryor papers, FHL; Allinson to Allinson, 31 Aug. 1827, Allinson family papers, QC.
60. Shillitoe, *Journal*, II, 249; Poole to Ferris, 16 Oct. 1827, Ferris papers, FHL. Unless otherwise noted, my account of the yearly meeting is drawn from Pryor, Journal, II, 297–304. Pryor papers, FHL; Cockburn, *Review*, 225–37; Comly, *Journal*, 341–44; and Minutes of the meeting, 15 Oct. 1827, Ferris papers, FHL.
61. Poole to Hicks, 26 Oct. 1827, Elias Hicks papers, FHL.
62. Poole to Hicks, 28 April 1827, ibid.; Wharton to Poole, 28 July 1827, Burr papers, FHL.
63. Characteristically, Poole had been a firm supporter of a thoroughgoing revision as a way to break up the old society so "that a better state of things may be introduced & become the hedge around the new Society." Poole to Jackson, 4, 28 June 1827, Jackson papers, FHL. During the yearly meeting itself, however, he reversed himself and opted for adoption of the old Discipline to take the sting out of Orthodox charges that the reformers were trying to get free of the law. But he still wanted a committee appointed to consider a lengthy list of revisions. Poole to Ferris, 16 Oct. 1827, Ferris papers, FHL.
64. The Orthodox rose to the bait. A correspondent in the *Friend* complained that it was "ungenerous" for the new yearly meeting to so identify itself with a meeting with which it was in opposition and from which it had separated (*Friend* 1 [8 Dec. 1827], 62–63).
65. Cockburn, *Review*, 240.
66. Pryor, Journal, II, 303–304, Pryor papers, FHL.
67. Poole to Ferris, 16 Oct. 1827, Ferris papers, FHL.

68. Hicks to Poole, 21 Oct. 1827 Elias Hicks papers, FHL.
69. See, for example, McClintock to Hicks, 12 Nov. 1827, ibid.; Comly to Poole, 2 Dec. 1827, Jackson papers, FHL.
70. Ferris to Jackson, 28 Oct. 1827, Jackson papers, FHL.

CHAPTER 12

1. Philadelphia Yearly Meeting Minutes, 19 Oct. 1827, Wharton papers, FHL.
2. Jones, *Later Periods*, I, 480; Bliss Forbush, *A History of Baltimore Yearly Meeting of Friends* (Sandy Spring, MD: Baltimore Yearly Meeting, 1972), 68.
3. Elliott, *Quakers on the Frontier*, 66–67.
4. Forbush, *Hicks*, appendix II.
5. Ely Balderston to Hicks, 6 Feb. 1818, 6 May 1820, Elias Hicks papers, FHL.
6. Isaac Wilson to Jackson, 24 Nov. 1825, Jackson papers, FHL.
7. Balderston to Hicks, 6 May 1820, Elias Hicks papers, FHL; Bliss, *History*, 158.
8. Rachel Mason to Jackson, 6 Nov. 1827, Jackson papers, FHL; Pryor, Journal, II, 305, Pryor papers, FHL; Shillitoe, *Journal*, II, 254–55.
9. Foster, *Authentic Report*, II, 463–64.
10. Russell, *History of Quakerism*, 113–14.
11. Evans, eds., *The Friends Library*, VI, 309–10.
12. Foster, *Authentic Report*, II, 271–72.
13. Mott to Hicks, 5 Aug. 1805, Elias Hicks papers, FHL. See also John Murray to Hicks, 3 Feb. 1808, ibid.
14. Aaron Legett to [unknown], Dec. 1827, Burr papers, FHL.
15. Samuel Hicks to Elias Hicks, 24 Dec. 1822, Elias Hicks papers, FHL. Other Hicks opponents also were dealt with. See *Friend* 1 (16 Feb. 1828), 142–43.
16. Shillitoe, *Journal*, II, 177, 187–88, et passim.
17. Ibid., II, 225.
18. Andrew Cock to Ferris, 27 June 1827 Ferris papers, FHL.
19. Ibid.
20. Hicks to Poole, 22 Aug. 1827 Elias Hicks papers, FHL.
21. Shillitoe, *Journal*, II, 245–46; Turner to Turner, 4 Oct. 1827, Turner family papers, FHL.
22. Hicks to Valentine and Abigail Hicks, 4 Nov. 1827, Elias Hicks papers, FHL.
23. Lewis to Ferris, 19 Feb. 1828, Ferris papers, FHL.
24. Elliott, *Quakers on the Frontier*, 79–84.
25. Judge to Hicks, 4 March 1822, Elias Hicks papers, FHL.
26. Hicks's letter to Edwin Atlee on September 27, 1824, was used widely by

the evangelicals to show that Hicks depreciated the Bible and the substitutionary theory of the atonement. See *Letters and Observations*, 4, 14-19.

27. Joseph P. Plummer to Seaman, 14 Oct. 1827, Seaman papers, and Plummer to Hicks, 9 Nov. 1827, Elias Hicks papers, both in FHL; *Miscellaneous Repository* 1 (Nov. 1827), 169-79; *Friend* 1 (10 Nov. 1827), 29-31. The *Friend* printed an additional 1,000 copies of its issue carrying the testimony so its readers could distribute extra copies. The Hicksites believed Bates wrote the testimony (Thomas White to Jackson, 7 Jan. 1828, Jackson papers, FHL).

28. The North Carolina statement was reprinted in the *Friend* 1 (29 Dec. 1827), 86-88.

29. Cock to Ferris, 27 June 1827, Ferris papers, FHL; Foster, *Authentic Report*, I, 169, 178-79, 182.

30. Foster, *Authentic Report*, I, 188.

31. Cock to Ferris, 27 June 1827, Ferris papers, FHL.

32. Foster, *Authentic Report*, I, 175.

33. Shillitoe, *Journal*, II, 310-11; Foster, *Authentic Report*, II, 270.

34. Foster, *Authentic Report*, I, 113.

35. *Friend; or Advocate of Truth*, 1 (June 1828), 187-88.

36. Shillitoe, *Journal*, II, 312.

37. Foster, *Authentic Report*, I, 181.

38. Shillitoe, *Journal*, II, 312-13.

39. *Friend* 1 (28 Jun 1828), 291.

40. Shillitoe, *Journal*, II, 313-14; *Friend* 1 (31 May 1828), 264.

41. Shillitoe, *Journal*, II, 315; Turner to Turner, 30 May 1828, Turner papers, FHL.

42. Turner to Turner, 30 May 1828, Turner papers, FHL.

43. Samuel Titus to Seaman, [4?], 11 Jul 1828, Seaman papers, Jacob Willetts to Hicks, 18 Aug 1828, Elias Hicks papers, FHL.

44. Foster, *Authentic Report*, II, 463-64.

45. Bates, *The Doctrine of Friends*.

46. "The New Doctrines," *Miscellaneous Repository* 1 (Feb 1828), 215-17, 222.

47. See the undated "To Friends Within the Compass of Ohio and Indiana Yearly Meetings," Ferris papers, FHL.

48. John Williams to Leggitt, 18 May 1828, ibid.

49. Irish to Ferris, 25 Sep 1827, ibid.

50. William Schooley to Ferris, 22 Dec 1827, ibid. This lengthy letter was copied and circulated in the east to give a first hand view of the Ohio situation.

51. Ibid.; Thos. Wickenshan to Jackson, 28 Jan, 1828, Jackson papers, William Thomas to Ferris, 27 Apr 1828, Ferris papers, FHL.

52. Hezekiah Thomas to Ferris, 30 Jan 1828, Ferris papers, FHL. Thomas reported that his copy of the *Berean* had been read so much that it had almost worn out.

53. "The Separation in the West," *Miscellaneous Repository* 1 (April 1828), 226-29, 256.

54. Elliott, *Quakers on the Frontier*, 397; Benjamin Ladd to wife, 14 April 1828, Ladd to Thomas and Amos ladd, 27 Apr 1828, Benjamin Ladd papers, QC.

55. William Procter to Brother and Sister, 17 Sept. 1828, *Journal of the Friends Historical Society* 19 (1922), 9; Ladd to Thomas and Amos Ladd, 24 April 1828, LADD PAPERS, QC.

56. Hicks to Wharton, 24 July 1828, Wharton papers, FHL.

57. Shillitoe, *Journal*, II, 324-32.

58. *Miscellaneous Repository* 1 (June 1828), 312.

59. Samuel Swayne to Jackson, 4 Aug 1828, Jackson papers, FHL.

60. William Thomas to Ferris, 20 July 1828, Ferris papers, FHL.

61. Randal M. Miller, "The Union Humane Society," *Quaker History* 61 (Fall 1972), 92; *Fifth Census; or Enumeration of the Inhabitants of the United States, 1830* (Washington: Duff Green, 1832), 128-29.

62. Susan D. Pierce to Cidney Darlington, 17 Sept. 1828, Miscellaneous Mss, FHL.

63. Daisey Newman, *A Procession of Friends: Quakers in American* (Garden City, NY: Doubleday & Co., 1972), 84.

64. Shillitoe, *Journal*, II, 339.

65. My account of the yearly meeting, unless otherwise noted, is based on Shillitoe, *Journal*, II, 343-47; Jackson to Jane Jackson, 7, 11 Sept. 1828, Jackson papers, Jackson to "Esteemed Friend," 9 Sept. 1828, Ferris papers, Hicks to Valentine Hicks, 10 Sept. 1828, Elias Hicks papers, Pierce to Darlington, 17 Sept. 1828, Misc Mss, all in FHL; William Evans to Thomas Evans, 12 Sept. 1828, Evans papers, QC; "The Separation in the West," *Miscellaneous Repository* 1 (Sept. 1828), 370-81; "Ohio Yearly Meeting," *Friend; or, Advocate of Truth* 1 (Oct. 1828), 249-75, (Nov. 1828), 276 [misnumbered]-81.

66. Marcus T.C. Gould reported in the *Friend; or, Advance of Truth* that Bates, et al, remained behind to confer with the village lawyer whom they had just hired. If so, there were Hicksites present and the lawyer-client relationship was breached. Susan Pierce wrote shortly thereafter that her mother and father, both staunch followers of Hicks, stayed in the house to hold it and had vituals carried to them "by wholesale."

67. "The Opinion of Judge Hallock," *Miscellaneous Repository* 2 (1 Jan. 1829), 13.

68. Ibid., 12-15 and (16 Jan 1829), 46; Israel French to Friend, 1 May 1829, in *Friend; or, Advocate of Truth* 2 (20 May 1829), 166-67.

69. Procter to Brother and Sister, 17 Sept. 1828, *Journal of Friends Historical Society*, 8.

70. For the total number of Friends in Ohio Yearly Meeting—the exact figure was 8,873—see "A Map of the Meetings of Friends in Ohio Yearly Meeting, 1827,"

in Map Collection, FHL. On the equal split, See French to Jackson, 5 July, 13 Sept. 1829, Jackson papers, FHL. Bates published a series of computations that not only inflated the total number of Friends to 9,575, but gave the Hicksites only 1,344, or less than one-seventh of the total. It is not clear how he arrived at these figures since he referred to them variously as "estimates" and "an exact enumeration." ("Friends and Hicksites in Ohio Yearly Meeting," *Miscellaneous Repository* 2 [8, and 15 May 1829], 299–301, 308–13.

71. French to Jackson, 5 July, 13 Sept. 1829, Swayne to Jackson, 3 Sept. 1829, Jackson papers, FHL. The Hicksite committee charged with opening the house for the 1829 sessions did have to climb through a window because the key with which they had locked the house would not work.

72. Harlow Lindley, "A Century of Indiana Yearly Meeting," *Bulletin of Friends Historical Society of Philadelphia* 12 (Spring 1923), 13. The 1827 figure for the yearly meeting was 13,945.

73. Noah Haines to Jackson, 26 May 1829, Jackson papers, FHL.

74. Matthew Coffin to Jackson, 10 Dec. 1828, ibid.

75. Haines to Jackson, 20 Oct. 1828, ibid.

76. Joseph Plummer to Hicks, 29 Dec. 1827, Elias Hicks papers, FHL.

77. Haines to Jackson, 26 May, 21 June, 31 Aug. 1828, Jackson papers, FHL; Charles F. Coffin, "The First Yearly Meeting in Indiana," *Bulletin of Friends Historical Society of Philadelphia* 2 (March 1908), 7.

78. Haines to Jackson, 20 Oct. 1828, Jackson papers, Hicks to Valentine and Abigail Hicks, 3 Oct. 1828, Elias Hicks papers, Rebecca Silver to Phoebe Eldridge, 13 Oct. 1828, Jennings Family papers, all in FHL.

79. Shillitoe, *Journal* II, 350.

80. Ibid., II, 353; Hicks, *Journal*, 417; Silver to Eldridge, 13 Oct. 1828, Jennings papers, FHL.

81. Hicks, *Journal*, 417–20; William Stabler to Jackson, 17 Sept. 1828, Jackson papers, FHL.

82. My account of the yearly meeting, unless otherwise indicated, is taken from "A Narrative of the principle part of the events which transpired at Baltimore Yearly Meeting held in the year 1828," in Hicksite Separation in Baltimore Yearly Meeting papers, Evans to Cope, 31 Oct. 1828, Evans papers, QC; Pryor, Journal, II, 365–66, Pryor papers, Jackson to Jane Jackson, 28, 31 Oct 1828, Jackson papers, FHL.

83. "Baltimore Yearly Meeting," *Friend* 2 (15 Nov. 1828), 39.

84. Forbush, *History*, 66; "A member of Baltimore Yearly Meeting," *A Narrative of the Causes Which Led to The Separation of The Society of Friends* (Baltimore: William Woody & Son, 1852), 25.

85. Robert J. Leach, "The Hicksite Separation on Nantucket," *Quaker History* 71 (Spring 1982), 31–53.

EPILOGUE

1. Roland H. Bainton, *Here I Stand: A Life of Martin Luther* (New York: New American Library, 1955), 144.
2. Shillitoe, *Journal*, II, 324.
3. This fascinating matter can be followed in Ferris to Gibbons, 4 Sept. 1830, and Gibbons to Ferris, 22 Sept. 1930, Ferris papers, FHL.
4. On this point, see Ingle, ed., " 'A Ball that Has Rolled Beyond Our Reach' "127–37.
5. Lewis Benson, *Catholic Quakerism: A Vision for All Men* (Philadelphia: Philadelphia Yearly Meeting, 1968), 2.
6. *New York Times*, 10 March 1971.
7. Evans, *Jonathan Evans*, 135–36.

Bibliographical Essay,
OR
Whence the Story

WHEN I FIRST BEGAN THE RESEARCH on which this study is based, I had reviewed—too cursorily as it turned out—many of the secondary works on the Hicksite separations, books such as Robert W. Doherty, *The Hicksite Separation: A Sociological Analysis of Religious Schism in Early Nineteenth Century America* (New Brunswick, NJ: Rutgers Univ. Press, 1967), Rufus Jones's account in the first volume of *The Later Periods of Quakerism* (London: Macmillan Co., 1921), Elbert Russell, *The History of Quakerism* (Richmond, IN: Friends United Press, 1979), J. William Frost's excellent essay, "Years of Crisis and Separation: Philadelphia Yearly Meeting, 1790-1860," in *Friends in the Delaware Valley*, John M. Moore, ed. (Haverford, PA: Friends Historical Association, 1981), as well as such older works as Samuel M. Janney, *An Examination of the Courses which Led to the Separation of the Religious Society of Friends in American, 1827-1828* (Philadelphia: T. Ellwood Zell, 1868), and Edward Grubb, *Separations, Their Causes and Effects: Studies in Nineteenth Century Quakerism* (London: Headley Brothers, 1914). Biographical studies like Bliss Forbush, *Elias Hicks, Quaker Liberal* (New York: Columbia Univ. Press, 1956), William B. Evans, *Jonathan Evans and His Times, 1759-1839* (Boston: Christopher Publishing House, 1959), and David E. Swift, *Joseph John Gurney, Banker, Reformer & Quaker* (Middletown, CT: Wesleyan Univ. Press. 1962) added personal dimensions to the controversy. I incorrectly assumed that these works, despite Doherty's own explicit disclaimer to the contrary, amounted to a full and complete study of the separation, especially in Philadelphia.

Imagine my surprise, therefore, when in the summer of 1982, I asked the helpful attendants at Friends Historical Library at Swarthmore College to bring up the first box of the papers of Benjamin Ferris, and I found material that had never been used extensively. Although I thought I had examined the footnotes of the above secondary works closely, one of the first items I saw was new to me: one of Ferris's two unpublished histories of the separation. My reaction, as I turned page after page and came upon mounting evidence of a partisan group organized to promote a reformation, resembled that of an old grizzled prospector who had finally stumbled onto his long-sought mother lode. For me, at least, the riches steadily increased, and I realized that I was the first person to mine these resources and extract from them the story of the Hicksite reformers and their reaction to the intrusion of evangelical theology into the Society of Friends.

With its Hicksite antecedents, the Friends Historical Library possesses the largest and best-organized collection of manuscript materials on the reformation cause. First in importance were the Elias Hicks manuscripts, followed closely by the papers of Ferris, Isaac Hicks, Halliday Jackson (which also include an unpublished history of the separation), Joseph Wharton, Samuel Comfort, Elliott Richardson, and David Seaman; the George H. Burr papers includes letters and reports from a large number of people from whom Thomas McClintock wheedled materials on the separation. Housed here also are monthly, quarterly, and yearly meeting reports and minutes, many of which have been microfilmed for easier access; these were a singular disappointment, for they contained little of the substance of discussion and only sketches of the formal action. A particularly valuable source, never before used, was the manuscript journal of Thomas White Pryor, an active observer of the passing scene. To enhance the richness of the Library's resources, there are even miscellaneous collections that include material from individual meetings.

The less efficiently organized Quaker Collection of manuscripts at Haverford College possesses more separate collections but fewer gems, apparently because the Orthodox either did not save their letters or because they were a small and closely knit group who could confer orally as they went on their daily rounds. Still more exciting discoveries awaited here, however, the most important being portions of the manuscript of William Evans's journal, in the William Bacon Evans papers, from which the editors of his printed journal worked, marking through potentially embarrassing entries usually lightly enough so later students could detect Evans's uncensored reations. Thomas Evans's account of the 1827 yearly meeting, its date of composition unclear, is a part of the Charles Evans papers. Other collections examined in the Quaker Collection included: the papers of Henry Cope, Benjamin W. Ladd, the Sheppard family, the Bettle family, Moses Brown, Thomas Brown, Richard Mott, Joseph Turner, the Evans family, the Allinson family, Joseph Scattergood, the Talcott family, the Matlack family, Henry H. Albertson, G.M. Howland, Edward W. Smith, the Taylor family, and Sharpless-Kite. There are also a few useful items in a collection relating to the separation in Baltimore Yearly Meeting.

Friends House Library in London contains two collections of note that illuminate the evangelical side of the controversy: the Braithwaite manuscripts and the diary of Elizabeth Robson.

Supplementing such manuscript resources are published journals and memoirs of many of the participants, particularly the Hicksites: Most valuable were those of John Comly, Edward Hicks, Elias Hicks, and William Evans. Others consulted included John Griscom, David Sands, Job Scott, Hugh Judge, Priscilla Hunt Cadwallder, Charles Osborne, Joseph Hoag, Edward Stabler, Stephen Grellet, Anna Braithwaite, William P. Brobson (in *Delaware History*, 15 [1972-73]), Thomas Shillitoe, Thomas Cope, George Fox, John Woolman, William Forster, William Savery, Henry Hull, and Jesse Kersey. The memoirs in William and Thomas Evans, eds., *The Friends' Library: Comprising Journals, Doctrinal Treatises, and Other Writings of Members of the Religious Society of Friends* (Philadelphia: Joseph Rakestraw, 1840) also proved useful. Also in the category of memoirs, broadly defined, is the testimony of various participants in the dispute contained in the two volumes of Jeremiah H. Foster, *An Authentic Report of the Testimony in a Cause at Issue in the Court of Chancery of the State of New Jersey, between Thomas L. Shotwell, Complainant, and Joseph Hendrickson and Stacy Decow, Defendants* (Philadelphia: J. Harding, 1831). Invaluable as they are, the student must use them with care and balance one against the other.

The pamphlet and polemical literature of the period is very extensive, most of it available in the collections at Haverford and Swarthmore. Swarthmore also has a useful collection of contemporary maps, without which I would have been unable to determine the membership of Ohio Friends. Its catalogue has also been printed, thus making its holdings familiar to a wider audience. Haverford holds the slowly expanding, multivolume typescript called the "Dictionary of Quaker Biography," which is, unfortunately, a bit thin on the Hicksite reformers, although its value should not be gainsaid.

Such "secular" sources as newspapers and magazines have often been overlooked by those writing the history of religious groups. For this study, at least, they proved very important, offering insights unavailable elsewhere. The *Saturday Evening Post* (Philadelphia) was especially useful, particularly when its pages carried a significant discussion between reformers and evangelicals. Others surveyed included the *Christian Repository* (Wilmington), the *Berean* (Wilmington), the *Reformer* (Philadelphia), the *Delaware Free Press* (Wilmington), the *Miscellaneous Repository* (Mount Pleasant, Ohio), the *Friend* (Philadelphia), the *Friend; or, Advocate of Truth* (Philadelphia), the *Philadelphia Recorder*, the *Quaker* (Philadelphia), the *Telescope* (New York), the *Christian Examiner* (Boston), and the *Spirit of the Pilgrims* (Boston).

Documentary collections played an important role, given the nature of the dispute: each side wanted to tie itself to past tradition and thus prove itself the true heirs of early Friends. From *Extracts from the Writings of Primitive Friends, concerning the Divinity of Our Lord and Saviour Jesus Christ* (Philadelphia: Solomon W. Conrad, 1823) through James Cockburn, *A Review of the General and Particular Causes Which Have Produced the Late Disorders and Divisions in the Yearly meeting of Friends, Held in Philadelphia* (Philadelphia: Philip Price, Jr., 1829) to the appendix of Foster, *An Authentic Report*, the relevant documents abound. Printed sermons and letters that should be consulted include, *Letters and Observations Relating to the Controversy Respecting the Doctrines of Elias Hicks* (Np: privately printed, 1824); Elias Hicks, *A Series of Extemporaneous Discourses, Delivered in the Several Meetings of the Society of Friends* (Philadelphia: Joseph & Edward Parker, 1825); L. H. Clarke and M.T.C. Gould, stenos, *Sermons Delivered by Elias Hicks and Edward Hicks in Friends Meetings, New York, in 5th Month, 1825* (New York: J.V. Seaman, 1825); Henry P. Hoag, steno, *Sermons by Elias Hicks, Ann Jones and Others of the Society of Friends* (New York: Privately printed, 1826); Marcus T. C. Gould, rpt, *Sermons by Thomas Wetherald and Elias Hicks* (Philadelphia: Marcus T.C. Gould, 1826); [Isaac T. Hopper, ed.,], *Letters of Elias Hicks* (New York: Isaac T. Hopper, 1834); and Emanuel Howitt, *Selections from Letters Written During a Tour through the United States, in the Summer and Autumn of 1819* (Nottingham: J. Dunn, [1820]).

Contemporary theological works not designed expressly for open polemical purposes include Henry Tuke, *The Principles of Religion, as Professed by the Society of Christians, usually called Quakers* (New York: Collins, Perkins, & Co., 1805); Elisha Bates, *The Doctrine of Friends: or the Principles of the Christian Religion, as held by the Society of Friends* (Mount Pleasant, OH: Elisha Bates, 1825); Elisha Bates, *An Examination of Certain Proceedings and Principles of the Society of Friends, called Quakers* (St. Clairsville, OH: Horton J. Howard, 1837); and Joseph J. Gurney, *A Letter to a Friend, on the Authority, Purposes, & Effects of Christianity, and Especially the Doctrine of Redemption* (Bradford: T. Inkersley, 1824; 15th ed.). Helpful theological insights that illuminate the disputes of the nineteenth century may be gleaned from two more recent works: Paul Tillich, *Perspectives on 19th and 20th Century Protestant Thought*, ed. Carl E. Braaten (New York: Harper & Row, 1967); and Langdon Gilkey, *Messages and Existence: An Introduction to Christian Theology* (New York: Seabury Press, 1980); see also Edward Grubb, *The Historic and Inward Christ: A Study in Quaker Thought* (London: Headley Brothers, 1914).

There are four historical journals, articles from the pages of which have informed this study. The two most obvious are *Quaker History* (and its predecessor, *Bulletin of the Friends Historical Association* [Philadelphia]) and *Journal of the Friends Historical Association* (London). The *Pennsylvania Magazine of History and Biography* and *Delaware History*, particularly the latter, also contain both primary and secondary source material that assisted me in filling in large gaps.

It is impossible to give complete listing to all the secondary works that have, in some ways directly, in others indirectly, influenced this study; those listed below are the more obvious and near the top of my consciousness. That the list is not exhaustive will become clear immediately to anyone who knows the field. A skilled analyst could probably read them and draw some cogent conclusions about the nature of my conscious and unconscious working assumptions — at the least, this listing should make that task a bit easier.

GENERAL WORKS

Sidney E. Ahlstrom, *A Religious History of the American People* (New Haven: Yale Univ. Press, 1972).

Leonard W. Bacon, *A History of American Christianity* (New York: Charles Scribner's Sons, 1925).

Lee Benson, *The Concept of Jacksonian Democracy: New York as a Test Case* (New York: Atheneum, 1964).
Peter Brock, *Pacifism in the United States, From the Colonial Era to the First World War* (Princeton: Princeton Univ. Press, 1968).
Henry S. Canby, *The Age of Confidence* (New York: Farrar & Rinehart. 1934).
David B. Davis, *The Problem of Slavery in the Age of Revolution, 1770-1823* (Ithaca: Cornell Univ. Press, 1975).
Ann Douglas, *The Feminization of American Culture* (New York: Avon Books, 1978).
Paul G. Faler, *Mechanics and Manufacturers in the Early Industrial Revolution: Lynn Massachusetts, 1780-1860* (Albany, N.Y.: State Univ. of New York Press, 1981).
Charles I. Foster, *An Errand of Mercy: The Evangelical Front, 1790-1837* (Chapel Hill: Univ. of North Carolina Press, 1960).
Lawrence J. Friedman, *Gregarious Saints: Self and Community in American Abolitionism, 1830-1870* (Cambridge: Cambridge Univ. Press, 1982).
Edwin S. Gaustad, ed., *Historical Atlas of Religion in America* (New York: Harper & Row, 1976).
Winthrop S. Hudson, *American Protestantism* (Chicago: Univ. of Chicago Press, 1961).
Kenneth S. Latourette, *A History of Christianity* (New York: Harper & Brothers, 1953).
T.J. Jackson Lears, *No Place of Grace: Antimodernism and the Transformation of American Culture: 1880-1920* (New York: Pantheon Books, 1981).
William G. McLoughlin, *The Meaning of Henry Ward Beecher: An Essay on the Shifting Values of Mid-Victorian America* (New York: Alfred A. Knopf, 1970).
Martin E. Marty, *Pilgrims in their Own Land: 500 Years of Religion in America* (Boston: Little, Brown and Co., 1984).
Marvin Meyers, *The Jacksonian Persuasion, Politics and Belief* (New York: Vintage Books, 1960).
Arthur M. Schlesinger, Jr., *The Age of Jackson* (Boston: Little, Brown and Co., 1950).
Timothy L. Smith, *Revivalism and Social Reform: American Protestantism on the Eve of the Civil War* (New York: Harper Torchbooks, 1965).
Willard L. Sperry, *Religion in America* (Boston: Beacon Press, 1963).
Alice F. Tyler, *Freedom's Ferment: Phases of American Social History from the Colonial Period to the Outbreak of the Civil War* (New York: Harper Torchbooks, 1962).
Anthony F.C. Wallace, *Rockdale* (New York: Alfred A. Knopf, 1978).
William A. Williams, *The Contours of American History* (New York: World Publishing Company, 1961).

Alan M. Zachary, "Social Thought in the Philadelphia Leadership community, 1800-1840," Ph.D. diss., Northwestern Univ., 1974.

WORKS ON QUAKERISM, NOT MENTIONED PREVIOUSLY:

E. Digby Baltzell, *Puritan Boston and Quaker Philadelphia* (Boston: Beacon Press, 1979).
William C. Braithwaite, *The Beginnings of Quakerism* (York, Eng.: William Sessions, Ltd., 1981; 2nd ed, rev. by Henry J. Cadbury), and *The Second Period of Quakerism* (York, Eng.: William Sessions, Ltd., 1979; 2nd ed, rev. by Henry J. Cadbury).
Richard Bauman, *For the Reputation of Truth: Politics, Religion, and Conflict among the Pennsylvania Quakers, 1750-1800* (Baltimore: Johns Hopkins Univ. Press, 1971).
David Bowen, "Quaker Orthodoxy and Jacksonian: Democracy: An Interpretation of the Hicksite Separation," M.A. Thesis, Swarthmore College, 1968.
Howard W. Brinton, *Friends for 300 Years* (New York: Harper & Brothers, 1952), and ed., *Byways in Quaker History* (Wallingford, Pa: Pendle Hill, 1944).
Henry J. Cadbury, *Friendly Heritage: Letters from the Quaker Past* (Norwalk, Conn: Silvermine Publishers, 1972).
Robert A. Davison, *Isaac Hicks: New York Merchant and Quaker, 1767-1820* (Cambridge: Harvard Univ. Press, 1964).
Errol T. Elliott, *Quakers on the American Frontier* (Richmond, Ind.: Friends United Press, 1969).
Bliss Forbush, *A History of Baltimore Yearly Meeting of Friends* (Silver Springs, Md.: Baltimore Yearly Meeting, 1972).
John Gest, *The Cause, Rise and Progress of the Late Unhappy Division of the Society of Friends Explained and the Mystery Unfolded* (Philadelphia: William K. Bodern, 1835).
Donald G, Good, "Elisha Bates: American Quaker Evangelical in the Early Nineteenth Century," Ph.D. diss., Univ. of Iowa, 1967.
Elizabeth Isichei, *Victorian Quakers* (Oxford: Oxford Univ. Press, 1970).
Sidney V. James, *A People Among Peoples: Quaker Benevolence in Eighteenth Century America* (Cambridge: Harvard Univ. Press, 1963).
Robert J. Leach, "Elisha Bates; 1817-1827: The Influence of an Early Ohio Publisher upon Quaker Reform," M.A. thesis, Ohio State Univ., 1939.
Jack D. Marietta, *The Reformation of American Quakerism, 1748-1783* (Philadelphia: Univ. of Pennsylvania Press, 1984).
Charles E. Nelson, "The Hicksite Separation in the Society of Friends," B.A. thesis, Harvard Univ., 1952.

Daisy Newman, *A Procession of Friends: Quakers in America* (New York: Doubleday & Co., 1972).

John Punshon, *Portrait in Grey: A Short History of Quakers* (London: Quaker Home Service, 1984).

Barry Reay, *The Quakers and the English Revolution* (London: Temple Smith, 1985).

John Sykes, *The Quakers, A New Look at Their Place in Society* (Philadelphia: Lippincott, 1959).

Frederick B. Tolles, *Meeting House and Counting House: The Quaker Merchants of Colonial Philadelphia* (Chapel Hill: Univ. of North Carolina Press, 1948), and *Quakers and the Atlantic Culture* (New York: Macmillan, 1960).

D. Elton Trueblood, *The People Called Quakers* (New York: Harper & Row, 1966).

John S. Turner, *The Quakers: A Study, Historical and Critical* (London: S. Sonnenschein and Co., 1889).

Henry W. Wilbur, *Job Scott: An Eighteenth Century Friend* (Philadelphia: Friends General Conference Advancement Committee, 1911).

Index

Abington Meeting, 208, 272n47
Abington Quarterly Meeting, 176, 177, 196, 197, 203, 209, 212f, 216–17, 221
Adams, John Quincy, 35
Allen, William, 87
Alsop, Othniel, 168
American Bible Society, 13, 25
American Sunday School Union, 13
Arch Street Meeting, 21, 51, 144, 151, 220f
Atlee, Edward A., 124, 157–58, 230, 280n48
Baltimore Yearly Meeting, 12, 68, 79, 105, 142f, 152, 222, 225, 243, 250; of 1825, 226; of 1827, 226–27; of 1828, 244–45; sketch of, 225–27
Baltimore Yearly Meeting (O), 245–46, 250
Barclay, Robert, 28, 120, 214
Barnard, Hannah Jenkins, 9–10, 12, 14, 75
Barrow, John, 232
Barton, Elizabeth, 21
Bates, Elisha, 142, 236, 256n55, 291n66; as evangelical leader, 29, 230–31, 234, 238, 241, 290n27; evangelical thought of, 28–29, 257n60, 257n61; sketch, 27

Bell, Isaiah, 108, 109, 112, 113, 272n47
Benezet, Anthony, 39, 89
Benson, Lewis, 249
Berean, 57, 58, 61, 131–33, 196, 215, 221, 229, 234, 254n1
Bettle, Edward, 198
Bettle, Samuel, 25, 29, 49, 63, 77, 84, 104, 105–6, 136f, 162, 164, 166, 212, 217, 236, 267n12; clerk of PYM, 122–25, 186ff; sketch, 22–23; view of controversy, 83, 167, 195.
Bonsall, Isaac, 171
Boustead, Joseph, 205, 207
Braithwaite, Anna, 63, 126, 130, 141, 142, 161, 163, 213, 226, 230, 237, 259n94, 275n21; conversation with Hicks, 127–29, 275n28; sketch, 33–34
Braithwaite, Isaac, 30–31, 33, 34, 141, 143, 161, 230, 275n21
Brobson, William, 45–46
Brown, Nicholas, 164, 232
Brownlee, William Craig, 254n1
Bucks Quarterly Meeting, 176, 177–78, 196, 197, 212f, 221
Bunyan, John, 99
Byberry Meeting, 48, 211, 282n26
Calvin, John, 89, 132, 153, 247

Carpenter's Hall Meeting, 212, 221
Celestial Magnet, 94-95, 106
Cherry Street Meeting (H), 212-13
Chesterfield Meeting, 221
Chopwell Meeting, 164
Christian Quakers, 4
Christian Repository, 58, 60, 98-102, 119, 270n7
Churchman, Joseph, 284n16
Clarke, Thomas C., 273n76
Cockburn, James, 139, 222-23, 276n60
Comfort, David, 209
Comfort, Ezra, 103, 108, 109, 112, 113-14, 115, 272n47, 284n9
Comfort, John, 124, 198
Comfort, Samuel, 198
Comly, John, 63, 68, 89, 93-94, 124, 163, 188, 212, 221f, 227, 266n53; and reformation cause, 111, 122, 172-76, 179, 185, 195-98, 208-9; candidate for PYM clerk, 187-90; efforts at 1827 PYM, 191-94; moderation of, 49, 102, 164-65, 172-177, 223, 283n10, 286n31; sketch 48-49, 186
Comly, Rebecca, 222
Concord Quarterly Meeting, 34, 61, 177, 208, 221, 282n26
Cope, Henry, 172, 203f, 213, 219
Cope, Thomas, 24, 192, 220, 227n63
Cornwall Quarter, 229
Cox, John, 106, 215; at 1827 PYM, 186, 187, 188, 190, 191, 197
Darby Meeting, 218-19
Davis, Isaac, 157-58, 277n63
Deism and deists, 10, 11, 19, 29, 95, 100, 101, 113, 144, 162, 235
Delaware Free Press, 61, 131
Docetism, 8
Doctrines of Friends, 27, 28-29
Eddy, Thomas, 29, 46, 107-8, 148,

Eddy, Thomas, (Cont.)
149, 228; sketch, 24-25
Edwards, Edward, 52
Erie Canal, 25, 46, 49, 107
evangelicalism, 247-48, 249-50; as viewed by reformers, 42, 79, 134-35, 201-2; rise of, 10ff, 68, 73-74, 78-79
evangelicals, xiii-xv, ch. 2, 61, 69; from England, 30ff, 63, 68, 154, 161, 184, 200, 275n21; social characteristics, 23-24, 31, 136; tactics of, 77-79, 103-12, 184, ch. 11 *passim; see also* individual names
Evans, Charles, 197-98
Evans family, 25, 208
Evans, Hannah, 19, 41, 77-78
Evans, Jonathan, 22, 29, 52f, 63, 77, 104, 107, 111, 118ff, 122, 125, 136, 147, 148f, 152, 159f, 186f, 197, 209, 218-19, 236, 238, 249, 277n63, 281n5; and use of products made with slave labor, 20, 84-86, 255n17; as clerk of Meeting for Sufferings, 18, 105-6, 165-67, 172, 214; as clerk of select yearly meeting of ministers and elders, 18, 184-85; anti-Hicks stance, 20, 84-85, 95, 105-6, 143f; distrust of innovations, 20-21, 71, 83, 164; sketch, 17-21; statement of faith, 170-71, 260n18
Evans, Thomas, 21, 107, 151, 198, 203, 206, 245
Evans, William, 22, 43, 48, 63, 68, 75-76, 77, 84, 107, 118, 136, 163, 188, 203, 207, 236, 239ff, 277n69, 283n10; gloom at Society's state, 123, 126, 130, 133, 142, 153-54, 160, 202, 205, 209, 211, 219; sketch, 21

INDEX   305

"Extracts from the Writings of
    Primitive Friends," 19–20, 119–20,
    122, 123–25
Ferris, Benjamin, 61, 63, 74, 79. 95,
    109, 112, 120, 164, 200, 229,
    264n98; as "Amicus," 98–102; as
    leader in separation, 196, 213,
    221–24; as pampleteer, 134–135;
    sketches, 58–60, 99–100; social at-
    titudes, 136, 178, 223–24;
    theology of, 59–60, 98–102, 134
First Day Society, 13
Fisher, Samuel, 85, 109, 116
Fisher, Thomas, 159, 172
Forster, William, 32–33, 63, 87, 96
    118, 1123, 126, 148
Foster, Thomas, 78
Fothergill, John, 29–30
Foulke, Joseph, 284n16
Fox, George, 3, 12, 42, 44, 69, 73,
    74, 75, 82, 88, 89, 92, 144, 152,
    221, 227, 231, 247
Free Quakers, 4
French, Israel, 237, 239, 241
Friend, 216, 231, 242
Friend: or, Advocate of Truth, 58
Gates, Theophilus R., 86
Gibbons, George, 207
Gibbons, William, 58, 63, 99,
    160–61, 200, 215; and case of
    Benjamin Webb, 60–61, 248–49,
    264n98; editor of *Berean,* 131–33,
    221, 234; role in separation, 196,
    213, 284n16; sketch, 57, 263n87
Gilbert, Eliphalet W. ("Paul")
    98–102
Gilkey, Langdon, 4
Gould, Marcus T.C., 151, 169, 172,
    193, 282n29
Green Street address (April 1827),
    199–200, 209ff, 226

Green Street epistle (June 1827), 213,
    217
Green Street Meeting, 24, 34, 51,
    52, 109–10, 112, 113, 119, 123, 218,
    282n26; conferences at, 195–96,
    199–200; 212–13; conflict within,
    135–36, 155–57; conflict with
    Philadelphia Quarter, 136–39,
    154–55, 165, 174–75, 192, 196,
    202ff, 276n61, 277n62
Grellet, Stephen (Etienne de Grellet
    du Mabillier), 63, 87, 122, 126,
    127, 148, 186, 202, 209; sketch,
    71–74
Griffitts, Samuel Powell, 106, 109
Griscom, John, 143, 148, 232f,
    261n30
Gurney, Joseph John, 11, 19, 20–21,
    33, 34, 73, 275n26; career of,
    31–32
Gurneynite movement, 249
Haines, Hinchman, 198
Haines, Noah, 242
Hester Street Meeting, 153, 259n107
Hicks, Edward, 36, 48, 63, 77, 79,
    110, 124, 152, 176, 178, 212, 217,
    255n28, 282n45; in 1823 yearly
    meeting, 125–26; sketch, 47
Hicks, Elias, 20, 24, 33, 38, 52ff,
    56, 63, 78, 81, 94f, 96, 99–100,
    126–27, 137, 141, 142, 145, 152,
    178, 179, 186, 194, 223f, 226,
    234, 247, 250, 259n94, 265n20,
    279n28, 282n26; at Indiana Year-
    ly Meeting (H), 244; at 1828
    Ohio Yearly Meeting, 236–39,
    241; attacks on evangelicalism, 17,
    41–45; attitudes toward modern
    world, 44–46, 107; combativeness,
    76–77, 84, 167, 227–228, 275n28;
    in NYYM, 227–28, 232–33;

Hicks, Elias (Cont.)
opponents' characterizations, 25–26, 30, 34f, 72, 75, 84, 86, 106–8, 113, 116, 119, 129, 133, 145–46, 151–52, 159, 185, 230, 267n17, 269n45, 289n26; personal traits, 39–41, 54, 127, 284n26; sketches, 39–46, 113, 127; symbol of reform, 22, 54, 115–16, 135, 147–48, 150, 157, 162; traditional Quaker position of, 41–45, 59–60, 71, 74–75, 81–83, ch. 5, 113–14, 127–28, 129, 140; travels in PYM, 40, 70–71, 77, 84–86, 108–16, 151, 161–71; views of reformation, 42–44, 70, 72, 74, 84, 89–90, 102, 168–71

Hicks, Jemima, 81

Hicksites, 21, 23, 24, 26, 29, 34, 49, 56, 60, 73, 112, 213, 222–24; disowning Orthodox, 286n31; approach to authority, 114; *see also* reformers

Hilles, David, 240, 241
Hilles, Eli, 112, 215
Hilles, Margaret, 160–61, 180, 215–216
Hilles, Samuel, 215
Hopper, Isaac T., 97, 105, 108
Howard, Luke, 134–35
Hubbard, Jeremiah, 230, 235
Hull, Henry, 68, 194, 237
Humphreys, Richard, 24, 237n85
Hunt, Nathan, 50
Hunt, Priscilla Coffin, 63, 68, 117–18; sketch, 50–51
Imlay, Maria, 158, 161–62, 281n27
Indiana Testimony, 231, 235f, 243, 290n27
Indiana Yearly Meeting, 225, 242–44; membership of, 242,

Indiana Yearly Meeting (Cont.) 292n72; of 1828, 244; sketch 229–31

Indiana Yearly Meeting (H), 244, 245

Informant, 235

Ireland Yearly Meeting, 10

Jackson, Halliday, 63, 77, 165–67, 176f, 177, 185, 186, 189, 200, 218, 223, 284n16; at 1828 Ohio Yearly Meeting, 237–41; sketch, 47–48

Jackson, William, 185, 186, 189, 214

Johnson, Phebe, 158, 280n50

Jones, Ann, 63, 72–73, 161–62, 185, 193, 197, 202, 203, 209, 230, 245, 258n91; sketch, 34–35

Jones, George, 63, 73, 161–62, 185, 187, 203, 204, 207, 209, 245; sketch, 34–35

Jordan, Richard, 79, 106, 163, 266n58; disputed memorial for, 178, 184, 195, 283n49

Judge, Hugh, 5, 7, 38–39, 43, 79, 230

Keith, George, 4

Kersey, Jesse, 63, 125, 171, 190, 208, 212, 284n16; sketch, 49–50, 262n49, 266n53

Kimber, Emmor, 168, 176; sketch, 50, 262n51, 266n53

Ladd, Benjamin, 236, 241

Lancaster, John, 52, 155–56, 285n7

Lewis, Evan, 99, 109, 111, 229, 231, 232; sketch, 58

Little Creek Meeting, 260n8

Lloyd, Isaac, 85, 103, 111, 165–66, 171

London Yearly Meeting, 10, 32, 34, 72, 74, 78, 104, 134, 154, 185

Longstreth, Morris, 207

Lower, Abraham, 53, 54, 63, 76, 77, 106, 109–110, 111, 138–39, 155–57, 162–63, 266n53, 267n14, 248n9;

INDEX 307

Lower, Abraham (Cont.)
  and separation activity, 172–76, 176–77, 202, 203–6, 209ff; as reformer, 87, 124f, 135–136, 137, ch. 10 *passim;* on Meeting for Sufferings, 103, 165; sketch, 51–52
Lower, Susan, 52
Lukens, Mary, 238
Lundy, Benjamin, 131
Luther, Martin, 82, 89, 132, 153, 247
Marcion, 8
Meeting for Sufferings (BYM), 226
Meeting for Sufferings (IYM), 243
Meeting for Sufferings (NEYM), 69
Meeting for Sufferings, (NYYM), 233
Meeting for Sufferings, (OYM), 234, 235
Meeting for Sufferings, (PYM), 16, 17–18, 19, 20, 21, 23f, 48f, 51, 66, 68f, 77, 96ff, 104, 108, 122–25, 136, 172, 177, 184, 190, 193, 214, 226; conflict with Southern Quarter, 165–67, 196; dealing with Hicks (1822), 105–6; reactions to "Paul" and "Amicus" debate, 103, 104, 119–20
Merion Meeting, 118
Miami Quarter, 243
Miscellaneous Repository, 29, 230, 231, 234, 236, 242
Moore, John Wilson, 165–66
Moore, Robert, 111, 112, 124, 178, 186, 197
Mosheim, Johann L., 265n20
Mott, John, 119
Mott, Richard, 69–70, 148, 149
Mott, Samuel, 232–33
McClintock, Thomas, 54, 63, 129, 144, 159, 172–6, 195, 217, 223; sketch, 53, 262n67

Nantucket Island, 246
Nayler, James, 12
Newbold, William, 198
"New Confession of Faith," 22
New England Yearly Meeting, 66, 69, 258n91
Newhall, Mary, 93
New Lights, 93–94, 97, 128, 158, 161
"New School" Presbyterian, 98
Newton, Isaac, 23, 124
New York Monthly Meeting, 161, 228–29
New York Yearly Meeting, 9, 12, 15, 68, 69, 79, 88, 106, 107, 142, 150, 177, 225, 250; of 1808; 71; of 1816, 78; of 1818, 83; of 1822, 105; of 1824, 129; of 1825, 46; of 1826, 133, 153–54; of 1827, 213, 228; of 1828, 231–34; sketch, 227–29
Nixon, Richard, 249
Noble, Samuel, 52, 63, 112, 136, 137, 155–57, 172–76, 177, 196, 204, 206, 212
North, John, 192
Northern District Meeting, 53, 139, 144, 168, 203, 210, 219f
Ohio Yearly Meeting, 27, 142, 225; membership of, 241, 291n70; of 1819, 84; of 1821, 96–97; of 1828, 237–42
Ohio Yearly Meeting (O), 241–42
Old Lights, 93
Orthodox, 48, 214; strategy after separation, 216–17, 219–20; *see also* evangelicals
Owen, Robert Dale, 61, 131
Paine, Thomas, 27, 61, 83, 131, 146
pamphlet warfare, 34, 128–29, 142–43, 144–51
Parrish, Joseph, 165, 211

Parson, Samuel, 143-49, 231
"Paul" and "Amicus" debate, 98-102, 270n7
peace testimony, 4, 9, 17
Peaslee, Amos, 237, 238, 239
Penn, William, 22, 59, 116, 144, 196, 214, 221
Philadelphia Quarterly Meeting, 52, 130, 173-75, 176, 177, 185, 190, 192, 209; conflict with Green Street Meeting, 135ff, 155-56, 165, 194, 196, 202ff, 210, 277n63
Philadelphia Yearly Meeting, 4, 5, 12, 49, 66, 67, 77, 96, 160, 177, 201, 218, 250; of 1817, 78, 268n53; of 1823, 122-26, 184, 274n9; of 1825, 19, 142; of 1826, 163; of 1827, ch. 10, 201; incidental mention, 8, 21, 70, 98, 131, 141, 179, 199
Philadelphia Yearly Meeting (H), 213-14, 217-18, 245, 250; first, 221-224
Philanthropist, 27
Pierce, Caleb, 103, 111, 136, 165-66
Pine Street Meeting, 18, 20, 42, 47, 53, 96, 104, 117f, 143, 159f, 164, 168, 171-72, 178, 210, 220; site of 1819 affront to Hicks, 84-85, 268n19
Plymouth Meeting, 108
Poole, William, 63, 95, 99, 111f, 115f, 130, 142, 144, 163, 166, 175f, 178f, 201-2, 205, 208, 216, 221, 224, 285n5; 288n63; sketch 56-57
Porter, Robert, 98, 207n7
Pryor, Thomas White, 141-42, 154, 163f, 179, 187, 195, 205, 220, 223
Purchase Quarterly Meeting, 37
Quaker ways, 65-68

Quakers, traditional. *See* reformers
Radnor Meeting, 221
Rakestraw, Joseph, 87, 108, 285n7
Randolph, Edmund, 219
Randolph, Mary, 53
ranterism, 12, 13, 93, 97, 105, 142, 161
reformation, as seen by evangelicals, 145; cause, 199, 248-49; end of, 223-24; need for, 9, 14, 42-45, 51, 70-71, 95, 132, 153; of 1790s, 5; pre-revolutionary, 4-5, 6-7; vision of, 9, 42-43, 59-60, 71, 82, 101-2, 130-31, 247
Reformation, sixteenth-century, 28, 59, 71, 82, 132, 247
reformation party, beginning, 112; rural segment, 46-47; urban element, 51-54, 174; Wilmington, Delaware, group, 55-61, 99, 131-33, 224, 249; tactics of, 87-88, 95, 122, 172-76, 229; Green Street address, 199-200
Reformer, 56, 86-88
reformers, traditional, xiii-xiv, 11-12, 13, 14, ch. 3; attitudes toward benevolent associations, 74-75, 86-87; attitudes toward education, 41, 70; attitudes toward reason, 44, 57, 118, 132; drift toward individualism, 59-61, 145, 248-50; theological positions, 88-91; *see also* Hicksites
representative committee (H), 222
Roberts, Charles, 162
Robson, Elizabeth, 63, 161, 163, 177, 185, 187, 192f, 202f, 208, 226, 259n94, 275n21, 282n45; sketch, 35
Rose Street Meeting, 152, 229
Ross, Cephas, 193

Ruggles, Micah, 94
Rules of Discipline, 66, 68, 78, 103, 137, 138, 139, 222, 288n63
Rush, Benjamin, 57
Salvation by Christ, 133
Sands, David, 12, 31
Saturday Evening Post, 116–17, 130, 135
Savery, William, 10
Scattergood, Ann, 136, 138, 155–57, 202, 207, 210, 285n7
Scattergood, Joseph, 24, 67, 76, 110, 123, 138
Scattergood, William, 207
Scott, Job, 13, 15, 42, 68ff, 77, 92, 133–35, 145; as a reformer, 7–9, 70–71
Seaman, David, 111
Seaman, Gideon, 143
Second Day Morning Meeting, 69, 104
Select Meeting of Ministers and Elders (PYM), 18, 184–85, 193–94
Servetus, Michael, 132
Shillitoe, Thomas, 63, 161, 221, 226–27, 228, 232f, 236f, 244, 248, 259n107; sketch, 35–37
Shoemaker, Nathan, 186, 190
Shotwell, Ann, 219
Shotwell, Edmund, 204, 205, 208
Slack, David B., 94–95, 269n56
slavery questions, Quaker attitudes toward, 5–6, 7, 20, 25, 26, 27, 40, 43, 44, 55, 76, 84–85, 86, 97, 125, 163, 194, 255n17, 286n23
Snowden, Jane, 136
Snowden, Joseph, 207
Snowden, Leonard, 24, 52, 110, 123, 136, 137f, 202, 285n7
Southern Quarterly Meeting, 48, 103–4, 108, 113, 165–67, 196f,

Southern Quarterly Meeting (Cont.) 212f, 221, 282n26
Stabler, Edward, 226, 245
Stephens, Stephen, 210
Stephenson, Isaac, 25, 161
Stewardson, Thomas, 24, 29, 33, 37, 63, 77, 111f, 136, 158, 173, 189, 197f, 236, 275n21
Stroud, Daniel, 188
Taylor, Jonathan, 230, 238, 240–41
Taylor, Mary, 136, 138, 155–57, 202, 285n7
Tillich, Paul, 44, 261n25
Thompson, Peter, 204
Tract Association of Friends (PYM), 77, 133
Tuke family, 73
Tuke, Henry, 73
Unitarians and unitarianism, 57, 67, 76, 78, 83, 92–93, 94, 107, 113, 116, 118, 132, 145, 152
Vaux, Roberts, 52, 173
Voltaire (François Marie Arouet de), 61, 71
Waln, Richard, 279n25
Walton, James, 111
Warder, John, 275n21
War of 1812, 45, 48, 55, 93
Warner, Joseph, 204
war taxes, 4
Washington, George, 22
Watson, John, 188
Webb, Benjamin, 60–61, 131, 248, 264n98
Wesley, Charles, 10
Wesley, John, 10–11, 36
Western Burial Ground, 219–20
Western District Meeting, 171, 178
Western Quarterly Meeting, 176, 212
Westtown School, 195
Wetherald, Thomas, 63, 153–54, 221,

Wetherald, Thomas (Cont.) 226–27, 233, 245, 259n94; sketch, 152
Wharton, William 40, 168, 172, 186, 196–97, 200, 210–11, 212; sketch, 53–54
Whitall, Joseph, 105–6, 109, 111, 113, 166, 215
Whitefield, George, 10
Whitman, Walt, 39–40
Willis, Phebe, 59, 81–83
Willis, Thomas, 81, 93, 94–95, 263n70, 281n24
Wilmington Meeting, 61, 215–16
Wilson, Marden, 188
Wistar, Bartholomew, 177
Wistar, Thomas, 35, 63, 111, 136, 166, 171, 189, 192, 203f
Withy, George, 32, 63, 123, 257n73
Wood, Samuel, 259n107
Wooley, George, 155
Woolman, John, 9, 13, 39, 85–86, 89, 92, 124, 145, 152; as a reformer, 6–7
Wright, Frances (Fanny), 61, 131
Wycliff, John, 132
Yarnall, Ellis, 23, 109, 110, 136, 245
Zollickoffer, Henry, 19